Enforcement Rights in Public and Private Law

Enforcement Rights in Public and Private Law

Paradigms, Exceptions and Hybrids

KIT BARKER
Professor, TC Beirne School of Law, The University of Queensland, Brisbane, Australia

OXFORD
UNIVERSITY PRESS

OXFORD
UNIVERSITY PRESS

Great Clarendon Street, Oxford, OX2 6DP,
United Kingdom

Oxford University Press is a department of the University of Oxford.
It furthers the University's objective of excellence in research, scholarship,
and education by publishing worldwide. Oxford is a registered trade mark of
Oxford University Press in the UK and in certain other countries.

Published in the United States of America by Oxford University Press
198 Madison Avenue, New York, NY 10016, United States of America.

British Library Cataloguing in Publication Data

Data available

Library of Congress Control Number: 2025950266

ISBN 9780192864499

DOI: 10.1093/9780191955006.001.0001

Printed and bound by
CPI Group (UK) Ltd., Croydon, CR0 4YY

The manufacturer's authorised representative in the EU for product safety is
Oxford University Press España S.A. of Parque Empresarial San Fernando de Henares,
Avenida de Castilla, 2 – 28830 Madrid (www.oup.es/en or product.safety@oup.com).
OUP España S.A. also acts as importer into Spain of products made by the manufacturer.

FSC www.fsc.org MIX Paper | Supporting responsible forestry FSC® C013604

'The truth is rarely pure, and never simple.'
Oscar Wilde

Foreword

This is a hugely ambitious work. It requires the reader to look across the whole of the law, both public and private. Even more importantly, it necessitates thinking about the law in a new way, through the lens of enforcement. Does the finished product match the ambition? The answer is a resounding 'yes'.

The consequence is that, within these pages, there is something of novel value for everyone interested in the law. Moreover, the scope of the enquiry is not confined to any one jurisdiction albeit that the primary concentration is on Anglo-Australian law (with significant references also to examples from the law in the United States and Europe). Professor Barker combines clarity of thought and expression with the insights gained from his deep and wide research (the footnotes are a treasure trove of references to articles and books many of which will be unfamiliar to most readers). While in many respects theoretical, this book is also a work of practical legal scholarship which primarily focuses on interpreting and understanding the rules and principles as they are rather than on what, arguably, they ought to be.

The essential thesis is that public law and private law are not enforced only by, respectively, public enforcement of public interests and private enforcement of private interests. That is the dominant paradigm. Hence the State through public agencies (such as the Crown Prosecution Service) prosecutes crimes, and individuals, whose rights have been infringed, can bring claims for breach of contract and torts. However, the true picture of the law is, and historically has been, much more complex. There can be private enforcement of public interests (for example, private prosecution of crimes or applications by those with sufficient standing for judicial review of executive action) and public enforcement of private interests (such as the Attorney-General's right to enforce charitable purpose trusts). There can also be parallel public and private enforcement (a rape is a crime that can be prosecuted by the State but is also a tort for which compensation can be sought by the victim) and merged or hybrid enforcement (as illustrated by compensation orders that may be made by a sentencing judge in favour of a victim against a convicted criminal).

The author seeks to make sense of all this complexity by presenting it as based on rational reasons of logic, morality, pragmatism, or as reflecting constitutional or political concerns. Those underpinning ideas are neatly pulled together and explained in the final chapter.

Part of the author's approach is a welcome commitment to conceptual reasoning and precision in language. As he explains, that enables the reader to have a clear view of what is going on, so that true disagreements between the reader and the author can be distinguished from false ones. For example, all of us have had to confront the distinction between public and private law, but I have rarely come across such a clear, succinct, and complete elucidation of the difference as that set out early in this book.

Perhaps not surprisingly in the light of the author's past publications, there is some reliance on the work of Hohfeld on rights. There will be readers who have an aversion to Hohfeldian analysis. I recall being at a private law conference where one of the participants commented how pleasantly surprised and relieved he was that we had almost reached the end of the conference and no one had yet mentioned Hohfeld. But in this book the merits of the Hohfeldian scheme can be appreciated without needing to understand or accept every aspect of it.

Clearly structured and beautifully written, thought-provoking and full of new insights, this is a book to which I will continually return. It provides a riveting and rewarding experience for the reader and deserves a place on the shelves of all lawyers, be they academics, judges, or practitioners.

Lord Burrows
Justice of the Supreme Court of the United Kingdom

Preface

This project started early and finished late. My interest in 'enforcement rights' was first piqued in 2017 by my former PhD student, Laura Guttoso, whose tragic death cut short what would surely have been a glowing career. Laura was interested in public and private enforcement techniques in competition law—not a field with which I was at all well acquainted at the time. The germ of interest she planted in me grew into a short contribution to the University of Queensland Law Review in 2018, published posthumously alongside a number of other articles celebrating her life and work. There I first set out the bare bones of the larger project contained in this book. The ambition in both cases has been to set about a clearer modelling of the way in which 'enforcement rights' are distributed between the State and private actors across the broad landscape of both public and private law. This has proven to be a highly ambitious task and it has taken me well outside my normal wheelhouse. Part of what drove the project from the start was the sense that my own assumptions concerning who it is that has the right to 'prosecute' our laws (in the broadest sense of the word) were seriously deficient. What appeared to me to be the paradigmatic way of thinking about public and private law as more or less airtight domains of public and private interest was wrong; as, clearly, was the associated assumption that it is the State that always exercises rights of action in public law and private parties that always exercise them in private law. The exceptions to the basic rules in each case were initially a source of hesitation and interest, then an irritant, and finally became an obsession calling for detailed explanation and justification.

This book is the product of that obsession. I certainly could not have written it on my own. I owe a great deal to all those whose work on this topic I cite, particularly to Ben Zipursky and John Goldberg, whose thinking about rights of action in the private law domain has been a wonderful spur on my own journey. They were kind enough to comment extensively on an early version of Chapter 3 of this book, which I presented to the Global Seminars in Private Law Theory Series in June 2021. I owe thanks to all who contributed to that seminar, as well as to members of the Australian Centre of Private Law at the University of Queensland, the Oxford Obligations Discussion Group, and members of the Cambridge Private Law Centre, all of whom have provided invaluable critical feedback on what now appears as Chapter 8. My thanks also to Charles Mitchell and Martin Fischer for organizing a terrific discussion at University College London in October 2024, where we were collectively able to reflect on these ideas as I shuffled toward the end of the project. Individuals who have generously commented on draft chapters include my former colleague and mentor Andrew Halpin (on the Hohfeldian analytics in Chapter 3), Mark Lunney and Warren Swain (on the early legal history in Chapter 4), Tim Liau (with whose wonderful work on standing in private law I have engaged in Chapter 8), Heather Douglas (private criminal prosecutions), Lionel Smith, Peter Cane, Donal Nolan, Ross Grantham, Rob Stevens, Charles Mitchell, Jessica Hudson, Rachel Leow, Rick Bigwood, John Murphy, Jason Neyers, Neil Foster, Rob Mullins, Alex Bruce, Sam Walpole, Tony Zhou, and Andrew Fell (in no special order). My thanks also to Dominic O'Sullivan for his encouragement, friendship and support. The deficiencies that undoubtedly remain in the text exist in spite of the help I have received and are, of course, my own.

I owe a debt of gratitude to those at Oxford University Press for their patience in waiting for the manuscript, which was delayed several times by personal factors, COVID and the additional workloads in Higher Education that have affected us all in recent years. My thanks to Jamie Berezin, the original commissioning editor, to Imogen Hill, Lisa Butts, and Rizwaan Ahmad for seeing me smoothly through the process.

Finally, my thanks to my wife, Kirstie, whose stoic patience, love, and support has sustained me in my madder moments.

Kit Barker
21 August 2025

Contents

Table of Cases

AUSTRALIA

CANADA

CARRIBEAN

EUROPEAN UNION

EUROPEAN COURT OF HUMAN RIGHTS

IRELAND

NEW ZEALAND

SINGAPORE

UNITED KINGDOM

UNITED STATES

Table of Legislation

ANCIENT LEGISLATION

AUSTRALIA

CANADA

EUROPEAN UNION

FRANCE

INTERNATIONAL TREATY

NEW ZEALAND

UNITED KINGDOM

UNITED STATES

PART I
PRELIMINARIES

This, first part of the book provides the basic tools required to understand contemporary debates about enforcement rights. It introduces the reader to the 'dominant law enforcement paradigm', 'exceptions' to that paradigm, 'parallel' enforcement systems, and 'hybrid' systems. To avoid confusion, it also defines some of the key terms used in the book and identifies four, different types of 'enforcement right' (of varying strength and significance) which feature in the debates which the book is concerned to address.

1
Introduction

1.1 The Dominant Enforcement Paradigm

This is a book about enforcement rights in both public and private law—about who gets to enforce our laws, how, and why.

When it comes to the enforcement of a law, there are essentially two choices, or so one might think—to place the initiative in the hands of some private party ('private enforcement'), or to assign the relevant rights to the State ('public enforcement'). That assumption, as we shall see in the following chapters, turns out to be too simplistic because there are now a great many cases in which the prosecutorial initiative of citizen and State are combined. Increasingly, both public and private enforcers can be—and are—involved in enforcing the same legal rules.

One might also assume—and one would be forgiven for doing so because this has been the dominant paradigm in common law jurisdictions since Blackstone[1]—that public law is 'public business' involving the protection of 'public interests', and is therefore always enforced publicly by the State, whilst private law is 'private business' involving 'private interests', and is accordingly enforced privately. The assumption, stated in that way, has an almost syllogistic ring to it and an attractive, symmetrical form in which all the 'privates' (private law, private interests, and private enforcement) line up on one side of the equation, and all the 'publics' line up on the other. Public law concerns public rights and wrongs and the protection of public interests and is prosecuted by public agents. Private law concerns private rights and wrongs, protects private interests, and is enforced by individuals and corporations. Everything is very neat. The model, which I shall from this point on call the 'dominant law enforcement paradigm', is presented in Figure 1.1.

There is no doubt that this vision of our law enforcement world is nowadays widely held, and for the most part it expresses the truth. In one's first years at law school, one is hence generally educated to accept that the criminal law is 'public' law, protecting the public interests of the whole community, and that the decision whether or not to prosecute a rapist therefore belongs not to the victim but to a Crown prosecutor. The victim has the right to complain and give evidence but is

[1] William Blackstone, *Commentaries on the Laws of England* (Robert Bell 1773) Books 3 and 4. Although Blackstone aligned public law with public interests and private law with the protection of private ones (on which see further Chapter 7, Section 7.3B) the paradigm was not fully complete in his time, since the enforcement of public law remained dependent on the initiative of private parties for another 150 years at least.

Enforcement Rights in Public and Private Law. Kit Barker, Oxford University Press. © Kit Barker 2026.
DOI: 10.1093/9780191955006.003.0002

Public Law Public Enforcement Public Interests	**Private Law** Private Enforcement Private Interests

Figure 1.1 The 'Dominant Law Enforcement Paradigm'

not generally involved in initiating or controlling the proceeding before a court of law, and technically has no legal power to prevent a prosecution going ahead. I remember finding this surprising. By contrast, in contract, tort, property law, the law of trusts, and unjust enrichment law, the power of enforcement lies squarely with individual litigators, and they have virtually complete control over decisions as to whether and when to bring, or terminate, a claim. The State provides the adjudicative machinery necessary to resolve the dispute and perhaps some financial assistance along the way (although this is now increasingly rare), but the matter is not one that concerns the broader community, so that the State itself has no need (or right) to be more actively involved. The difference in the configuration of enforcement rights as between public and private law is typically represented by the names that we find attached to the respective legal proceedings. Criminal proceedings hence bear the form '*R* (or *the State*) *v Jones*', signalling that it is the State that holds the prosecutorial power. Civil proceedings list the names of individual parties—plaintiff and defendant ('*Smith v Jones*').

1.2 Exceptions and Complications

The dominant enforcement paradigm is not without a basic moral and logical sense, but I hope to show in the course of this book that it cannot be fully trusted. It does not accurately represent the full range of law enforcement possibilities either historically or in the current day. As a matter of history, there was a time in our recent past when the familiar distinctions we now make between public and private law, public and private interests, and public and private enforcement, did not exist in the same way in formal legal thought. As long as we lacked fully fledged public enforcement machinery, private actors did almost all of the law enforcement work there was to be done in respect of both (what we now think of as) public and private law, and in doing it, they acted in protection of both their own interests and the broader interests of the community at one and the same time. The remedies courts awarded at the end of these private actions reflected the mixture of different legal interests and aims at stake in the proceeding, with declarations of rights, compensation, restitution of property, and both financial and physical penalties all being meted out simultaneously. For centuries, the prevailing paradigm of enforcement in respect of all law—both private *and* public—therefore depended overwhelmingly upon the initiative of private enforcers, and these enforcers were responsible for protecting interests other than their own. It is only more recently that there has been a transition toward a 'purer' conceptual separation of public and private law in the common law tradition, with public law fully assuming the role of 'public interest' law and being enforced by its own special vanguard of public agents.

As usual, history therefore provides a sobering corrective to our contemporary assumptions, reminding us, lest we forget, that the enforcement model we know today is a recent product. Even today, however, the paradigm remains subject to a good number of exceptions, which distort its otherwise perfect symmetry. This is true in respect of both public and (to a lesser degree) private law.[2]

On the public law side of the equation, private citizens hence retain the right in many jurisdictions to bring a criminal prosecution—a right that has undergone a startling renaissance in the United Kingdom for reasons to which we shall later come. The State's domestic human rights obligations—an increasingly important part of public law in many countries—are also overwhelmingly enforced by citizens. Modern competition, discrimination, and consumer protection laws can be enforced through the private actions of injured parties, as well as by public regulators and state prosecutors. Our laws of judicial review, which bind state actors to norms of legality and propriety in the use of public power, are enforced by 'interested' individuals, organizations, and groups. Exceptions to the basic public law enforcement pattern are especially evident in the United States, where 'private Attorneys-General'[3] have come to play a particularly prominent role in the enforcement of public laws in the late twentieth and twenty-first centuries for fascinating historical, social and political reasons. Some 90 per cent of all Federal regulatory provisions are now reported to be enforceable privately—an uplift since the 1960s of about 1000 per cent.[4] 'Citizen suit' provisions often enable individuals to enforce regulatory norms that might otherwise go neglected by executive agencies. Sometimes, citizens are even rewarded for prosecuting one another—a practice that went out of fashion in the United Kingdom a long time ago and which is startling and invidious to many European eyes. So important are private litigators to the enforcement of public laws in the United States, in fact, that private enforcement is now variously considered a key facet of a properly participatory constitutional

[2] For explanation of the respective categories of 'public' and 'private' law, see Chapter 2, Section 2.1.

[3] Since being coined by Jerome Frank in *Associated Industries of New York v Ickes* 134 F 2d 694, 704 (2d Cir 1943) (vacated as moot 320 US 707 (1943)), the use of this concept has exploded so dramatically that it is said that literally no day that goes by without it being used either judicially or academically in the US: W Rubenstein, 'On What a "Private Attorney General" Is—And Why it Matters' (2004) 57 Vanderbilt Law Review 2129, 2130.

[4] S Farhang, *The Litigation State: Public Regulation and Private Lawsuits in the US* (Princeton University Press 2010) 10–13.

democracy[5] (a form of social republicanism with a small 'r'), a means of citizen empowerment, a critical check on state overreach, a component of debates about public choice, a primary form of (ex-post) behavioural regulation, and even sometimes simply the most efficient way of getting the law enforcement job done when one considers the question pragmatically.

These American debates about the potential advantages of enforcing public laws privately have spiralled outward to a wide range of different policy spheres in which the case for using private enforcers is being pressed with increasing frequency, both within the United States and elsewhere.[6] These spheres include environmental protection, financial regulation,[7] public fraud, gun control, consumer protection, the regulation of anticompetitive practices, the prosecution of domestic violence, and even, most recently, the enforcement of British higher education institutions' obligations to protect freedom of speech.[8] The results are not always pretty and some cases in which they are being used in the United States cast very dark shadows indeed, with citizens reportedly being encouraged to use their enforcement powers to attack the civil rights of transgender persons, the rights of public schools to teach critical race theory,[9] and even—infamously in Texas—the liberty of women safely to seek an abortion,[10] a right that was until recently subject to strong, constitutional protection.

On the private law side, exceptions to the normal private enforcement paradigm are less common, but there are nonetheless clear instances in which the State gets involved. State guardianship *parens patriae* is a good example, with public agents sometimes stepping in to enforce the private law rights of those who cannot enforce them for themselves. Other examples include the Attorney-General's historic right to enforce charitable purpose trusts, and the Official Receiver's right to enforce and settle the rights of personal bankrupts and insolvent corporations in some cases. An increasing number of public agencies now have the right to enforce the rights of consumers and corporations—ordinarily (but not always) with their consent, as an extension of the State's modern welfare role.

We shall explore each of these exceptions in due course. The point at this stage is not exhaustively to articulate all of the cases in which the dominant enforcement

5 See eg S Lawrence, 'Justice, Democracy, Litigation, and Political Participation' (1991) 72 Social Science Quarterly 464, 466–72.

6 On recent European developments in the transnational economic law space, see H Micklitz and A Wechsler (eds), *The Transformation of Enforcement in Europe* (Hart 2016).

7 See eg B Thomson Jr, 'The Continuing Innovation of Citizen Enforcement' [2000] University of Illinois Law Review 185; P Bucy, 'Private Justice' (2002) 76 Southern California Law Review 1, 76–77 (advocating the extension of reward-based *qui tam* actions to the environmental and financial regulatory spheres).

8 Higher Education and Research Act 2017 (UK) s A7 (inserted by the Higher Education (Freedom of Speech) Act 2023 s 4).

9 L Norris 'The Promise and Perils of Private Enforcement' (2022) 108 Virginia Law Review 1483; R Beck, 'Popular Enforcement of Controversial Legislation' (2022) 57 Wake Forest Law Review 553.

10 See Chapter 7, Section 7.2B(i).

paradigm breaks down, or even necessarily to approve or disapprove of the various departures from it, but simply to point out that the perfect alignment which it suggests between public law, public enforcement, and public interests, on the one hand, and private law, private enforcement, and private interests on the other, is misleading as a matter of both past and current practice. There are very clear exceptions to the rule that public law is enforced publicly and private law enforced privately, which need to be fully articulated, explained, and justified. Private enforcers sometimes have powers to enforce public laws, protecting public interests, and public enforcers are sometimes involved in the enforcement of private laws, protecting private ones.

A. Parallel Public and Private Enforcement

To add to the complexity of this dynamic, it is increasingly common these days for a wrongdoer's actions to constitute a breach of both public and private laws—and an interference with both public and private interests—at one and the same time. This is, at least in part, a consequence of the growing reach (and therefore overlap) of the two fields of law. A rape is hence not *just* a crime that harms public interests, actionable by the State in criminal courts, but also, concurrently, a tortious interference with a person's private right to bodily autonomy, actionable separately by that person in a civil court. A breach of the anti-cartel provisions of competition law is both a public law wrong against the State, harmful to society's collective interest in the operation of a free market, that is actionable by central state prosecutors and public agencies, and potentially a tortious conspiracy or breach of statutory duty actionable by individuals and corporations in private law. There are, furthermore, some instances in which a single public law protects *both* public and private interests at the same time, such that the breach of a statutory rule can give rise both to public enforcement action by a regulator and to separate claims for compensation by those affected. An Australian company that imposes excessive payment surcharges on its customers contrary to section 55B of the Compensation and Consumer Act 2010 (Cth) may, for example, be pursued both by the regulator for a civil penalty and, separately, by customers for damages for loss they have been caused by the public wrong.[11]

Wherever parallel public and private enforcement processes exist in this way, there is potential for their aims and procedures to chafe. The basic objectives of the two actions—typically punishment or deterrence (in public law) and corrective justice (in private law)—or their procedures (rules of disclosure, evidence, time

[11] Compensation and Consumer Act 2010 (Cth) s 82(1). The number of such instances is large. For a survey in the US (and defence of the system of overlapping claims that it produces), see Z Clopton, 'Redundant Enforcement' (2016) 69 Vanderbilt Law Review 285.

limits, and so on) can get in one another's way. If a successful state prosecution of a cartel is to be feasible, for example, it may be necessary to offer leniency in respect of the public penalty imposed in order to encourage wrongdoers to confess and disclose their part in the wrong. But they may be reluctant to do so, if this in turn exposes them to further financial liabilities in private follow-on actions brought by competitors or consumers. Working out how to coordinate the two actions and their various rules in such cases, so as to achieve a coherent overall enforcement system in which every aim is met, is a complicated contemporary challenge akin to the search for the Holy Grail.

B. Hybrid Enforcement Procedures

A final complicating feature of the modern enforcement landscape is that, in some areas of law, the two, separate, public and parallel enforcement processes that are available in respect of a single wrong are merged into one, '*hybrid*' procedure that allows for the integrated protection of both public and private interests simultaneously. In many jurisdictions, criminal proceedings initiated by the State can hence result in an offender being sentenced both to serve a term of imprisonment and to compensate those whose private interests have been harmed by the crime. Similar (albeit distinct) mechanisms exist in France and other European continental systems for victims to add private law claims for damages on to the State's criminal proceeding.[12] Private applicants for judicial review may add private law claims for damages or restitution to the application in order to avoid the need for parallel proceedings.[13] Some modern, regulatory agencies may seek (or themselves dispense) both civil penalties and compensatory remedies for public law violations in one go. Hybrid enforcement systems of this kind have recently been scaled up in the domestic consumer protection context,[14] which begs the important contemporary question whether similar processes could, or should, be introduced in other public law fields.[15] It also connects to a persistent debate in private law about the propriety of allowing private litigants to recover not just compensatory but punitive or exemplary damages in their civil proceedings in order to promote broader social ends. Such hybrid systems seem to offer a more fully integrated and

[12] JA Jolowicz, *Civil Procedure* (CUP 2000) 15–16. In such cases, the public and private law claims are heard together, whereas under the English compensation order system, the compensation order is a public law remedy. See further Chapter 5, Section 5.5A.

[13] Currently, there must be a separate civil cause of action, since no compensation is available in respect of the public illegality per se.

[14] See Chapter 5, Section 5.5B.

[15] Assessing this question in the context of European competition law (and concluding that it is difficult) see K Voss, 'Facilitating Follow-on Actions? Public and Private Enforcement of EU Competition Law after Directive 2014/104' in M Strand, V Venegas, and M Iacovides (eds), *EU Competition Litigation: Transposition and First Experiences of the New Regime* (Hart 2019) Ch 7, 114–19.

efficient regime in some instances—a 'one-stop shop' in which a single enforcement process (either public or private) addresses the violation of both public and private law rights, and the protection of public and private interests, at one and the same time.

We shall discuss much (if not all)[16] of this in this book. The basic upshot for now is that the enforcement of public and private law is a far more complex and nuanced affair in the modern age than the blunt, conventional paradigm suggests. Whilst it is important to seek simplicity in things, we must therefore also distrust it.[17] The dominant enforcement paradigm is just too neat to be true. In fact, the chapters that follow suggest that a more accurate representation of current patterns of enforcement in public and private law looks more like that set out in Figure 1.2.

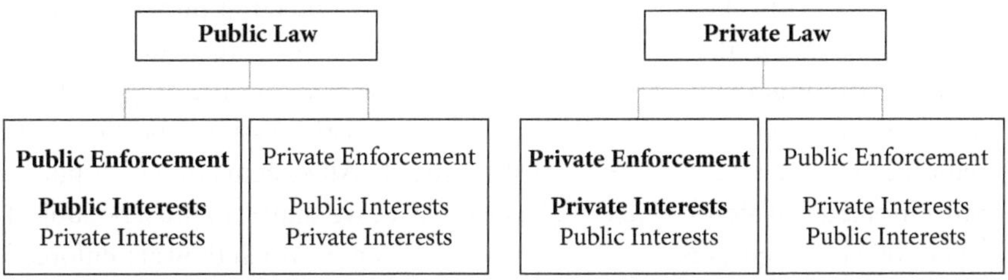

Figure 1.2 A More Accurate Representation of Modern Enforcement Paths and the Interests they Protect

The adjusted picture suggests that whilst there is indeed a very strong relationship between public law, public interests, and public enforcement, on the one hand, and private law, private interests, and private enforcement on the other (depicted in each case by the bold font in Figure 1.2), these relationships are neither exclusive nor immutable. They change in response to a variety of complex factors—moral, pragmatic, and constitutional. Not only can both public and private law be enforced both publicly and privately but public and private law both protect, to a greater or lesser extent, *both* public and private interests, such that interests of each type are represented and protected to some degree in both public and private enforcement proceedings.

Why does all this matter? At one level, it is simply a matter of descriptive accuracy—of more precisely representing the truth of our law enforcement world. But the reasons for being picky about enforcement rights and thinking them through clearly go beyond this. Decisions about who holds the right(s) of action

[16] The debate about the coordination of parallel public and private enforcement processes is sadly too involved and too extensive to be covered in this book. It requires one of its own.

[17] A Whitehead, *The Concept of Nature: The Tarner Lectures* (Trinity College, Cambridge, November 1919) 163.

when a law is breached—the State, its citizens, or both—materially affect the distribution of legal power in our community, the autonomy of its citizens, and the constitutional legitimacy of the State itself. A State that reserved to itself all the powers to enforce all of its rules would lack the basic guarantees of accountability required by the rule of law, and citizens themselves would have little capacity to flex the rights (either public or private) that they have. It would also, quite frankly, be attempting the impossible, since state resources will never be equal to enforcing all the legal rights that it (and its citizens) now possess. On the other hand, a society that provided no public mechanisms of enforcement at all would be a pale shadow of a State—one wholly reliant on private initiative for the protection of both personal welfare and the public good. Not only would this be a serious lapse in the State's responsibility to its people and a reversal of centuries of social progress but it would be an inefficient and unpredictable way of protecting public interests, and it would entail significant moral risk. Unconstrained private action too often results in corruption, collusion, private oppression, unjust profiteering, and unfounded litigation that strains the capacities of our justice system and brings its reputation into disrepute. A balance must be struck. All systems in which public laws are enforced privately (which can be justified, as we shall see) must be subject to keen public oversight, just as the systems according to which they are enforced publicly must be subject to individual scrutiny, private supplementation, and challenge by private citizens.

Whilst the content and distribution of primary rights—both public and private—are hence key markers of the constitutional health of a modern liberal state, so too is the distribution of powers to access and enforce the guarantees which these primary rights provide. Indeed, if it is true to say that there are no meaningful rights for citizens without remedies (secondary rights),[18] then it is equally true to say that there is *neither* a meaningful legal right, *nor* a meaningful remedy without there first being a right of action.[19] Modelling the distribution of such rights between public and private enforcers correctly is no mere technicality or pilgrimage to descriptive accuracy but fundamentally important to the balance of power between citizen and state, and the welfare of us all. Rights of action are fundamental markers of liberty and power in respect of our primary and secondary rights—important constituents of an autonomous life for the individuals who enjoy those rights, as well as of the effective operation of legal systems and of the commitment of liberal states to the advancement of our personal and collective goods.

[18] An idea classically encapsulated in the Latin maxim '*ubi ius, ibi remedium*'.

[19] This is, I think, what John Gardner was getting at when he said that 'there is no law of torts (or private law either)' without rights of action: J Gardner, 'Torts and Other Wrongs' (2011) 39 Florida State University Law Review 43, 44–45.

1.3 The Aims and Scheme of the Book

The most basic aim of this book is to provide a more complete description of the enforcement possibilities that currently exist across public and private law. It provides an account of the main enforcement models operating in the two fields and of some of the exceptions to them. In the process, it draws selectively upon examples from a range of different jurisdictions, but it is not a serious comparative work; nor does it attempt to be comprehensive. The modest objective is more fully to inform future enforcement choices by assembling and charting just some of our current enforcement practices and interrogating their historical origins, logic, and wisdom.

In the pages that follow, I shall examine what it means for someone to have an 'enforcement right' and the reasons why such rights are important. I shall also ask whether the exceptions to the dominant enforcement paradigm mentioned above are simply historical anomalies that are overdue for elimination—leftovers in the law's evolutionary development, as it were—or whether they disclose a convincing, modern rationale of their own that offers insight into the paradigm's limitations and suggests further possibilities. Is there anything that necessarily *requires* public enforcement to be married to public law, and private enforcement to private law, or is greater variation possible? Are enforcement techniques naturally monogamous, like beavers and swans, or polygamous, like baboons and the Bengal tiger? What pressures—moral, political, or otherwise—explain current enforcement arrangements and, equally importantly, what factors *ought* to govern choices as to whether we use public agents or private parties in the enforcement of our laws? Does it make sense to have distinct, parallel public and private enforcement systems dealing with wrongdoers who have harmed both public and private interests? Should systems be more extensively hybridized, so as to incorporate the aims of both private and public law within a singular enforcement process on more occasions, to save on wasteful doubling-up? If this is so, the irony will be that the law's evolution will be working, if not exactly in reverse, then in more than one direction at the same time. For in those instances in which we do choose to embrace hybrid enforcement procedures, we will be reverting to patterns of a more ancient configuration, albeit (one would hope) in a rather more conscious and considered way than we defaulted to them in the past.

Part 1 of the book ('**Preliminaries**'), of which this introduction forms the opening gambit, deals with essential prefatory matters. As an important part of the set-up, Chapter 2 provides a primer to the key concepts used throughout its pages and which I have already thrown at the reader without much, if any, explanation. Here, I explain more carefully what I mean by public and private law, public and private interests, and public and private enforcement. Readers probably already have their own sense of what these ideas mean, but a reason for being very precise about the terminology is to ensure that statements I make later in the book are not misconstrued. The complex nature of the investigation and the notoriously protean nature of the language of 'public and private' makes this a serious risk. My hope is that by drawing three clear, preliminary distinctions between public and private laws, public and private interests, and public and private enforcement, it will be possible at least to maintain a clear view of what is going on, so that true disagreements between the reader and the author can be distinguished from false ones. I also seek to bring clarity to the enforcement debate by differentiating between several different types of 'enforcement right' that may be in play in a legal proceeding—an enforcer's right of complaint, a right of action, a right of joinder or intervention, and the right of a party to terminate or settle a proceeding. Of these rights, it is rights of action and termination that are the main focus of the book, but there will also be some allusion to the other types of rights, which form an important part of modern law enforcement frameworks.

Part 2 ('Analytics and Legal History') engages in some important analytical and historical groundwork. Chapter 3 ('Analytics') has had a previous airing.[20] It asks what is meant and implied by the idea that an enforcer has a legal 'right of action'. Much excellent work on this question has already been done in the private law context by civil recourse theorists, but I extend their analysis here to take account of rights of action in public law too, and the understanding that results is slightly different. The conclusion I reach is that rights of action are composite 'aggregates' of both legal liberties and powers in the Hohfeldian sense, which enable persons to trigger courts' jurisdiction to hear their claims and impose public liabilities and duties on others to respond to them. They are distinct from both primary and remedial rights and should be treated as such in legal discourse in both public and private law. Sometimes rights of action are reinforced by giving an enforcer additional rights against others in order to make their exercise possible. They are also, however, accompanied by important public duties that restrict the way in which they can be used, and they can sometimes be suspended, or taken away. This backdrop is important because it means that the use of both public and private rights of action is subject to a series of supports, checks, and balances that distribute the power that they represent, rather than concentrating it in a single set of hands. Another important conclusion reached in this chapter is that from an *analytical* perspective, there is nothing to suggest that public law need be attended *only* by public rights of action, or private law *only* by private rights of action. These are choices we may choose to make, but they are not dictated by any essential structural relationship between different types of rights. The door is therefore open to variation and innovation.

Chapter 4 ('Primordia') provides historical context for the enforcement debates considered later in the book, charting the way in which enforcement processes

[20] K Barker, 'Rights of Action in Public and Private Law: the Analytics of Enforcement' (June 2021) SSRN: http://dx.doi.org/10.2139/ssrn.3883088 accessed 1 December 2025.

tend to develop over time. It focuses on the evolution of such processes in ancient Rome and medieval England by way of illustration. We find that private parties used to play a more central role in the enforcement of all law (both public and private) than they now do. We also see that enforcement evolution is complex and rarely follows a strictly linear pattern of progression. The comparison is important because, for some, the recent transition to public enforcement modes in public law, whilst both constitutionally and practically desirable, has distanced citizens from processes of justice in ways that require their re-inclusion, or it still leaves gaps which only private enforcers can fill as modern regulation burgeons. There is therefore an important resonance between society's historic reliance on private enforcement techniques, detailed in this chapter, and contemporary policy debates which suggest the need to make greater use of them in the modern world. We shall also see that the ancient practices often (necessarily) entailed a high degree of hybridity in enforcement process, providing early precedents for the hybrid enforcement systems that exist in the modern day.

Part 3 of the book ('**Modelling**') is its heartland. It sets about modelling the enforcement processes that exist in the modern era, by examining in turn the four, main enforcement models currently in operation across public and private law. These represent the four, logical combinations of law and enforcer types, models (1) and (3) of which make up the dominant paradigm:

(1) The public enforcement of public law (Chapter 5);
(2) The private enforcement of public law (Chapters 6 and 7);
(3) The private enforcement of private law (Chapter 8); and
(4) The public enforcement of private law (Chapter 9).

We hence move from public law to private law as we progress through the book.

Chapter 5 starts off with the public law model with which we are most familiar, where laws are predominantly enforced by public prosecutors and agencies, using examples mainly from the criminal law and from European and Australian competition and consumer law. It notes the dramatic rise in public regulation and the corresponding burgeoning of public agencies in the twentieth and twenty-first centuries. It sets out the traditional justifications for the public enforcement model and two of the most common problems that it faces—resource scarcity and enforcement capture. It also identifies some of the hybrid enforcement processes currently existing in public law, through which public agents are empowered to protect both public and private interests simultaneously, imposing penalties and obtaining compensation or restitution for victims within the same legal proceeding. These processes, we shall see, involve some efficiencies but also have their practical limitations.

Chapters 6 and 7 then examine two categories of exceptional case in which private enforcers enforce public laws. Chapter 6 details cases in which citizens enforce the public duties and liabilities of the State. It covers actions for State violations of human rights, private claims for the tort of misfeasance in public office, and applications for judicial review, examining in each case the legal norms enforced, the regime attaching to their enforcement, the interests protected, and (in lesser detail) the remedies available to a private enforcer. Chapter 7 examines a second, more controversial category of case, in which private parties enforce the duties of their fellow citizens, either altruistically or for reward. We consider cases of public nuisance, private criminal prosecution, and a series of actions known in the United States as '*qui tam*' actions and 'citizen suits', in which private persons act in the protection of public interests. Although they have numerous historical precedents, these cases raise more serious challenges for traditional constitutional conceptions of the State's own law enforcement prerogative; and they carry significant ethical risks which require careful thinking if they are to be adequately moderated.

Chapters 8 and 9 then switch the focus to private law. Chapter 8 sets out the standard private enforcement paradigm according to which rights of action in this domain belong to those who hold the relevant primary or secondary private law 'rights'. A point I make here is that although we tend to think of rights of action as enforcing a person's primary claim rights, it is apparent that they also protect his or her legal powers, liberties, and immunities as well—the whole range of his or her Hohfeldian rights. This is most visible in the law relating to declaratory relief. I spend some time examining the justifications for the basic 'right-holder' enforcement model and for a range of exceptions to it, in which third parties are accorded rights to enforce another person's rights, sometimes without the need for their consent. Here, I engage with Tim Liau's important recent work on standing in private law.[21] I also examine 'hybrid' private law actions in which private parties seek 'punitive' damages as well as compensation, and I make some suggestions concerning the way in which the remedy should be structured, if it is retained, that will better protect public interests and prevent private enforcers being left with improper 'windfall' advantages.

Chapter 9 examines a small range of exceptional cases in which private law rights and duties are enforced by public agents. Such cases are frequently associated with the State's status as '*parens patriae*' (parent of the people) and therefore with its welfare role, which is both ancient and modern. They include cases in which it steps in to enforce the rights of incapable persons on their behalf as a guardian or litigation guardian, disputes about charitable trusts, cases of personal or corporate insolvency, and some instances in which it acts in protection of the private law rights of consumers. Many of these cases again involve hybrid enforcement processes, in so far as the state protects both private and public interests in the same proceeding.

[21] T Liau, *Standing in Private Law: Powers of Enforcement in the Law of Obligations and Trusts* (OUP 2023).

Chapter 10 ('Rationalizing Enforcement Choices') draws together the modelling exercise conducted in the previous chapters. Here, I look for patterns of explanation and justification for the various enforcement choices detailed in both public and private law. The particular goal here is to determine whether there are any detectable, common factors affecting the choice between public and private enforcement techniques that might be generalizable. A variety of arguments are considered, including forms of deontic logic (arguments about the relationship between rights of action and primary rights, or the interests which such primary rights are designed to protect), moral reasoning, pragmatic arguments, and constitutional and political factors. The reach and limits of each type of argument are tested in terms of its explanatory power and normative force. Although some lines of reasoning have strong explanatory fit and are highly persuasive, no single rationale can ultimately explain or justify all enforcement choices across all the areas of law we have examined. The normative account of enforcement rights presented in this book is hence ultimately a determinedly pluralist one. Given the size of the field examined, this is scarcely surprising. In both fields of law, rights of action show significant fidelity to the logic of right-holding, such that they operate to protect the primary rights of right-holders (whether this is the State or a private individual), but in both fields there are important departures from this pattern. Rights of action are not limited to protecting one's own rights in either domain. Sometimes they are granted in both instances to persons who are not themselves right-holders, but who are instead persons whose interests the right-holder's right was designed to protect, or whose interests are closely aligned with the interests of the right-holder. Sometimes, again in both fields, rights of action are granted to third parties, so that they can protect the interests of *others*—the State sometimes acts to protect to protect private rights and interests, and private citizens sometimes act to protect public rights and interests. In private law, moral arguments about the importance of rights of action for a person's sovereignty and autonomy play a greater role in justifying and explaining enforcement patterns than they do in public law. In public law, the justifications for enforcer choice tend to be more constitutional, pragmatic, and political, but the key message is that there are no hard and fast divisions between the sorts of reasons that count toward enforcer choices in either public or private law. No single reason, or set of reasons, is siloed within either legal category as I have constructed it. Although private law shows greater stability than public law in its enforcement patterns, there is also no assurance that the reasons for choosing between public and private enforcement are static. They vary in their application as between different contexts and time frames as legislative priorities change with economic and social conditions. This lesson is salutary, since the challenges facing modern regulation suggest that the public enforcement of public law will most likely always need to be supplemented by private enforcers, just as our modern welfare commitments suggest that the powers of private enforcers to enforce their private rights will always need to be backed by public enforcement guarantees in a significant range of cases. The range of cases in which this form of supplementation will be required will inevitably vary from time to time, depending on the size of the gap that exists between regulatory ambition and either public or private enforcement capacity.

2
Enforcement Primer: Concepts, Terms, and Definitions

To present a clear picture of the role and rationale of public and private enforcement in public and private law, it is crucial to provide a stable definition of three key sets of terms. First, we must be clear what we mean by *public and private laws.* Second, one must distinguish between the *public and private interests* that these laws protect. Finally, we must explain what we mean by *public and private enforcement.* Readers may already have a sense of what I intend by each of these terms, given the way I have used them in the last chapter. Nonetheless, each is subject to a range of different possible interpretations. Indeed, the distinction between 'public and private' can be cast in so many ways that it is sometimes considered unhelpful, or it is thought to have disintegrated so completely in modern conditions as to lack much utility.[1] My own view is that the distinction is useful, provided only that one is clear exactly what one means by it.[2]

2.1 Public and Private Law

In this book, I take *public law* to be the set of laws governing legal relationships[3] between one State agency and another, or between the State (acting *qua* State) and private persons, as opposed to the law governing relationships between one private person and another ('private law').[4] This is a common way of thinking.

[1] See eg C Harlow, '"Public" and "Private" Law": Definition without Distinction' (1980) 43 Modern Law Review 241; 'Public and Private Law: A Redundant Divide' in J Varuhas and S Stark (eds), *The Frontiers of Public Law* (Hart 2020) Ch 14; D Kennedy, 'The Stages of the Decline of the Public/Private Distinction' (1982) 130 University of Pennsylvania Law Review 1349. cf P Cane, 'Public Law and Private Law: A Study of the Analysis and Use of a Legal Concept' in J Eekalaar and J Bell (eds), *Oxford Essays in Jurisprudence* (Clarendon 1987) 64.

[2] K Barker, 'Private Law: Key Encounters with Public Law' in K Barker and D Jensen (eds), *Private Law Key Encounters with Public Law* (CUP 2013) Ch 1, 19–22 (pointing to multiple binary distinctions). On the protean nature of the distinction and the blurred lines that this can cause, see further D Feldman, 'The Distinctiveness of Public Law' in M Elliott and D Feldman (eds), *The Cambridge Companion to Public Law* (CUP 2015) Ch 1.

[3] This means the full set of Hohfeldian claim rights, powers, immunities, liberties, duties, and so on, referenced in Chapter 3, Section 3.2.

[4] This approach assumes that 'the State' is a separate entity capable of having legal relationships. On one view, Britain has no abstract legal conception of the State even today, but that, to my mind, remains very contentious. For a brief discussion and references to the relevant literature, see Chapter 3, Section 3.2A n 11.

Enforcement Rights in Public and Private Law. Kit Barker, Oxford University Press. © Kit Barker 2026.
DOI: 10.1093/9780191955006.003.0003

Figure 2.1 Public and Private Law

All that counts in these definitions, note, is the identity of the parties at each end of the relevant legal relationship—whether these are purely private persons, or include the State acting in its public capacity—not whether the law in question takes a statutory form. A manufacturer's duty under the Consumer Protection Act 1987 (UK) not to injure consumers by producing defective products[5] is hence still part of private law, even though it came into being via a 'public' (parliamentary, democratic) process. Equally, the common law duty of a public officer not to commit the tort of misfeasance in his or her office is part of public law because it is a duty owed to private citizens in the exercise of the officer's state functions, not one that can be owed by one private citizen to another.

'Public law' on this approach includes both laws operating horizontally between one state and another (as in public international law) and those operating between one organ or agent of domestic government and another (as in constitutional and administrative law).[6] It also includes laws governing 'vertical' relationships between the State (or State agents) and private persons. Some such vertical relationships impose duties on the citizen toward the State (as in the criminal law), and some place duties and liabilities on the State towards its citizens (as in social security law, for example). Private law, by contrast, comprises only 'horizontal' legal relationships between private persons (see Figure 2.1).

A 'private person' in this scheme includes some non-natural persons, such as corporations, and 'the State' includes all three branches of government—legislative, executive, and judicial—as well as agents (both public and private) to whom it has delegated the exercise of its public functions. The need to include some 'private agents' within the definition of the State stems from well-known changes in the way that modern States nowadays carry out their functions for reasons of efficiency or political ideology,[7] and from the necessity in such circumstances to look to the substance of the function performed, not purely to the

[5] Consumer Protection Act 1987 (UK) s 2.

[6] Depending on the way in which these areas of law are defined, which varies, both also govern the relationship between organs of government or public agents and private citizens. Either way, they are public laws.

[7] I Harden, *The Contracting State* (Open University Press 1992); P Vincent-Jones, *The New Public Contracting* (OUP 2006).

agent's form. The special laws governing the obligations of prisons to their prisoners deriving from the prison's correctional functions are therefore public laws, even where the prison is owned and operated by a private corporation that aims to make a profit.

An important consequence of defining public and private law in this way is that many statutes and many 'contextual' legal categories, such as 'health and safety law', 'consumer law', 'intellectual property law', 'medical law', or 'competition' law, are neither simply 'public law' nor simply 'private law' but rather comprise a mixture of many, distinct public *and* private laws. A health and safety statute which imposes both a duty on an employer to the State to abide by its provisions on pain of financial penalty and a duty to its employees to protect them from injury, therefore contains both public and private law norms in one and the same public document.[8] This is increasingly common and a significant proportion of modern regulatory statutes are therefore public–private law hybrids.

2.2 Public and Private Interests

Public law typically protects public interests and private law, private interests. *Public interests* are the interests we share in consequence of our membership of a political community, whereas private interests are those we have as individuals, independently of the community to which we belong.[9] The two types of interest regularly coalesce in the same person or persons but always remain conceptually distinct. I hence have a private interest in not being hit by you, or in you keeping your contracts with me, but I also have a broader public interest, in common with all other members of society, in living in a community that is peaceful and in which commercial transactions are reasonably reliable.

Public interests are easily confused with the collected, private interests of large groups of individuals, but the two must be distinguished. Being a community interest, a public interest cannot be reduced to constituent, individual parts, but

[8] It is unfortunately not always easy to tell from a statute's text whether it creates *only* a duty owed to the State, or *both* duties to the State *and* separate duties to private persons individually to avoid the type of conduct in question, which can cause classification problems. For ambiguities in respect of some of the primary rights and duties created by domestic competition and consumer law statutes, see Chapter 5.

[9] In the context of discussing what it is that is 'publicly' wrong about a rape, such that it should qualify as a crime, Marshall and Duff encapsulate the idea perfectly in the proposition that a rape is not simply a private wrong to 'her' (which I infer to mean an interference with the victim's private interests) but a wrong to 'us', by virtue of the way we identify with the victim as a member of our community, 'genuinely sharing' the same values and interests: S Marshall and R Duff, 'Criminalization and Sharing Wrongs' (1998) 11 Canadian Journal of Law and Jurisprudence 7, 19–20. For further development of the idea of a public wrong, see R Duff and S Marshall, 'Public and Private Wrongs' in J Chalmers, F Leverick, and L Farmer (eds), *Essays in Criminal Law in Honour of Sir Gerald Gordon* (Edinburgh University Press 2010) 70–71. Group interests are interests that are shared with particular social groups, rather than with the whole body politic.

exists only by virtue of the existence of the community itself. Where a person reveals state secrets to a foreign power, he hence prejudices a public interest in our national security flowing from our common association as a single political community, and which would not exist without it. Where, by contrast, a pharmaceutical company produces a drug that injures thousands of people, the fact that multiple victims join in a class action against it does not (on this approach) make their litigation 'public interest' litigation. Of course, it may be that the action *indirectly advances* public interests. There is no doubt, for example, that the assertion of the private interests of thousands of Prozac victims in collective proceedings in the United States advanced the shared public interest of Americans in having a safer pharmaceutical industry, but it was not public interests that lay at the heart of that litigation—it was a banded coalition of separate, private ones. By contrast, it was ironically States' assertion of the public interest in the Medicaid system itself that ultimately brought some accountability home to the tobacco industry in the United States, not the assertion of the private interests of those injured or killed by its products.[10] Only incidentally or indirectly (if indeed at all) were the private health interests of individual victims protected by the relevant public settlement. Whilst private and public interests are hence often *aligned* and the protection of one may *indirectly serve* to protect the other, they remain fundamentally distinct.

Although the dominant paradigm suggests that public law exists primarily to protect public interests, it also protects private ones. This is now an accepted viewpoint amongst many public lawyers[11] and is demonstrated in detail in later chapters of this book. Criminal compensation orders, for example, aim to compensate victims of crime for personal injury and property damage,[12] as do awards of damages to victims of the State's violation of its public duties under the Human Rights Act 1998 (UK). In the same way, although private law sets out predominantly to protect private interests, it often takes public interest arguments into account in determining the scope and content of the rights it provides,[13] and some of the remedies it supplies—exemplary damages for torts and accounts (or constructive trusts) of profits for breaches of fiduciary duty being notable examples—have

[10] Although multiple private interest claims were brought against the tobacco industry in the early days, none was successful until 46 States themselves weighed in as litigants, claiming that public interests in the Medicaid healthcare system had been prejudiced by the harm caused to victims. Multiple State actions resulted in a 1998 Master Settlement Agreement requiring the four largest tobacco companies to pay some US$250 billion over twenty-five years to the states. See R Ieyoub and T Eisenberg, 'State Attorney General Actions, the Tobacco Litigation, and the Doctrine of Parens Patriae' (2000) 74 Tulane Law Review 1859; V Engstrom and R Rabin, 'Pursuing Public Health Through Litigation: Lessons from Tobacco and Opioids' (2021) 73 Stanford Law Review 285.

[11] See eg Duff and Marshall (n 9); J Varuhas, *Damages and Human Rights* (Hart 2016) Ch 4.

[12] See Chapter 5, Section 5.5A.

[13] This can be seen, for example, in private law defences, such as the defence of illegality to contract, tort, and unjust enrichment claims, or the public interest defence to claims for breach of confidence or defamation.

prophylactic or deterrent aims that advance public ends. Charitable purpose trusts, whilst disposing of private property in accordance with a settlor's intentions, are valid only to the extent that they also benefit the public. Both public and private law therefore (on occasion) either directly or indirectly protect both public and private interests.

2.3 Public and Private Enforcement—Enforcement Rights

The final step is to define public and private enforcement. By '*public enforcement*', I mean to refer to any enforcement process initiated and controlled by the State, or a public agency, as opposed to a private individual, corporation, or group of individuals ('*private enforcement*'). Criminal law enforcement is hence predominantly public because it is the State that prosecutes an offender, not a victim of the crime. In tort law, enforcement is usually private, because in the vast majority of cases it is a private person[14] that exercises the power of suit and settlement.

'Private enforcers' can be individuals, corporations, or associations, whether operating singly or in the sort of class action proceeding used in the Prozac litigation mentioned above. 'Public enforcers' include central State prosecutors and regulatory agencies to whom state functions have been delegated or assigned. Some enforcers that I place within the 'public' category, such as statutory human rights commissions, are awkward in the sense that they are supposed to be 'independent' of the executive and unbiased in their enforcement decisions, but are nonetheless publicly funded, report to, and are sometimes even appointed by government.[15] The independence of a public agency from executive government is therefore always a matter of degree.

The core concept of 'enforcement' can mean different things to different people. My own use of the term in this book is quite narrow, perhaps even rather eclectic. I am not, for example, concerned with policing in the sense of the day-to-day detection of offences and detention of offenders. Nor am I concerned with the informal processes increasingly used by regulatory agencies to educate or persuade corporate actors to comply with the law, or with the procedures used at the end of legal proceedings to execute court orders or judgments against defaulting judgment debtors, such as the seizure of a debtor's personal property by court bailiffs (rights of execution). These phenomena are all clearly important and can perfectly legitimately be regarded as involving enforcement of one sort or another, but each would require a book of its own. My focus here is on a particular and narrower set of rights that public and private parties respectively have to instigate and control

[14] Sometimes it may be the State, if acting in its private capacity.

[15] This creates tensions. See D Isaac, 'Reflections on the EHRC' (2020) 6 European Human Rights Law Review 578, 579 (pressing for greater Equality and Human Rights Commission independence).

legal proceedings. These rights, which I collectively call 'enforcement rights' exist on a graduated scale.

A. Rights of Complaint and Information

The weakest type of enforcement right to which reference is made in this book is a 'right of complaint', or 'information right'. Such rights are not unimportant, but they are small-calibre ammunition—they are bare liberties and powers[16] to bring a legal infraction to the attention of someone else (usually a public agent) who has the right to bring legal proceedings. The exercise of a 'right of complaint' may trigger new duties and responsibilities in the agency to whom the complaint is made (for example, a duty owed to the complainant to properly consider and investigate it), but it does not itself enliven the powers of a court of law. I may hence complain to the police about an assault, to a consumer watchdog about offensive advertisements on my television, or to the public services ombudsman about official misconduct. Doing so undoubtedly gets me something—consideration, respect (one hopes), the opportunity for my information to influence decisions about the enforcement of public standards, perhaps a certain degree of catharsis and personal satisfaction in knowing that I am acting in conscientious defence of rights. But this does not make me an 'enforcer' of the law in any very powerful sense. If my complaint is ignored, I am at best limited to bringing legal action against the relevant agency for not enforcing properly, which may, or may not, prove effective in addressing my original concern.

The use of rights of complaint is sometimes incentivized by giving informers the right to claim a reward, should the information they provide to a prosecuting authority result in a successful conviction. Such devices have a long history[17] and are still in use today as an encouragement to whistleblowers to provide information to relevant authorities, especially in cases involving secretive corporate misconduct that is otherwise hard for the latter to detect.[18] They are combinations of liberties and conditional claim rights in a Hohfeldian sense that I shall explain properly in the next chapter. They are nonetheless still weak because they do not give the informant any control over legal proceedings and the provision of the relevant

[16] For a fuller definition of these terms, see Chapter 3 Section 3.2.

[17] For an early example (where the reward was discretionary), see the Sunday Observance Act 1677 29 Car II, c 7.

[18] See eg the system under the Dodd–Frank Wall Street Reform and Consumer Protection Act, Pub L No 111-203, 124 Stat 1376 (2010) (financial securities—whistleblower right to claim between 10 per cent and 30 per cent of penalties collected). On the set-up and its implications, see A Rose, 'Better Bounty-Hunting: How the SEC's New Whistleblower Program Changes the Securities Class Act Debate' (2014) 108 North Western University Law Review 1235, esp 1260–87; F Lipman, *Whistleblowers: Incentives, Disincentives, and Protection Strategies* (Wiley 2012) esp Chs 1 and 11.

information may not even place its receiving agency under any obligation to put it to use.

B. Rights of Action

Of far greater strength—and central to this book—are 'rights of action'. These, as we shall see,[19] are liberties and powers for an enforcer to initiate legal proceedings against another party. They are the hallmark of a strong system of rights protection because they enable an enforcer not just to enliven the powers (jurisdiction) and duties of courts of law to do justice but also potentially to affect the legal rights and duties that an offending party then owes to the court. Before legal systems matured, 'action rights' took a cruder and rather more risky form—they consisted in the liberty for individuals literally to 'act' directly against their offenders on their own initiative (subject to certain restraining conditions and social conventions that we unpick further in Chapter 4). Nowadays, however, the liberty to act in this way has wisely been exchanged for the power to enlist the coercive force of the State against the offender instead, in the form of rights to initiate a legal process against him.[20] Rights of action are a third type of right recognized in the law alongside primary rights and secondary (remedial) rights. They are conceptually distinct from both. Like information rights, their exercise is sometimes incentivized by the offer of a bounty, but this is not common practice in most jurisdictions on account of the tension it creates between an enforcer's self-interest and the broader public interest.[21]

C. Rights of Joinder and Intervention

A third type of 'enforcement right' is a right of 'joinder'—the power to make oneself a party to another's legal proceeding. Private enforcers can choose to be added in this way to another's civil suit where their own private rights have been affected (or stand to be affected) by a defendant's actions in a manner that is sufficiently similar to the way in which the main party's rights are affected, and which raises common issues.[22] They then stand in the same position as the originator of the action.

[19] Chapter 3.

[20] Parties still retain some liberties of self-help in respect of their own rights, examples being the power of self-defence in the criminal law, or the power in the civil law to abate a nuisance, eject a trespasser, make recaption of chattels, or rescind a contract at law.

[21] On modern rewards, their risks, and the devices used to moderate them, see Chapter 7, Section 7.2B.

[22] In Australia, the conditions are usually that the cause of action (i) arises out of the same transaction or event, or series of transactions or events, and (ii) raises common questions of fact or law. In many jurisdictions, the leave of the court is also required. See generally B Cairns, *Australian Civil*

'Intervention rights'[23] are similar, consisting in liberties and (sometimes) powers for persons to add themselves to another's action in order to protect additional interests. Intervenors again become full parties to the action and typically have the same powers to tender evidence, appeal, and participate in the proceeding as the original parties. The difference is that no legal *right* of theirs is generally at issue in the proceeding, they merely have an *interest* in its outcome.[24] Rights of intervention are rare in private law, since the normal rule is that personal litigation is private business and should not be subject to third party interference. The Attorney-General nonetheless has a power to intervene in *any* litigation in which Crown prerogatives are implicated,[25] and in the United Kingdom the Crown may intervene under section 5(2) of the Human Rights Act 1998 (UK) if the compatibility of any legislation with the European Convention on Human Rights is being contested by the parties to a dispute. State, Territory, and Commonwealth governments in Australia have similar powers to intervene in any matter before the High Court that involves interpreting the Australian Constitution.[26]

Joinder and intervention rights create efficiencies by allowing all rights and interests affected by a wrongdoer's conduct to be considered at one time and in the same place before a decision that implicates them is made. They also promote natural justice by preventing persons whose rights and interests might be prejudiced by a proceeding being bound without first being given the opportunity to participate in it.

D. Rights of Termination, Settlement, and Discontinuance

A final form of 'enforcement' right (although this sounds a little odd, since the right is a right 'not to enforce') is the legal power to settle, terminate, or discontinue a proceeding. Such rights are also important, because they allow an enforcer to kill a proceeding off, thereby releasing others from legal duties and liabilities in the process. In private law, claims may be settled right up until the hour of judgment.[27]

Procedure (12th edn, Thomson Reuters 2019) Ch 9, esp 366–68. A person may also 'be joined' by an existing party to the action, or by the court, rather than exercising his or her own joinder power.

[23] The language of intervention is slippery and is sometime used more broadly to include what I refer to further below as 'court assistance' rights. See G Williams, 'The Amicus Curiae and Intervener in the High Court of Australia: A Comparative Analysis' (2000) 28 Federal Law Review 365, 366.

[24] ibid 368 (but see the discussion of the mixed Australian jurisprudence at 379–84); S Kenny, 'Interveners and Amici Curiae in the High Court' (1998) 20 Adelaide Law Review 159, 160.

[25] The power exists at common law and, in some jurisdictions, under statute.

[26] Judiciary Act 1903 (Cth) s 78A, 78AA.

[27] Some settlements of private law claims require judicial approval, as in where they relate to representative or class action proceedings, or where one of the parties involved is a minor or otherwise lacks legal capacity.

In the criminal law, public prosecutors can similarly drop claims that they have initiated at any time, although they now have a duty to review their decision at a victim's request, and that decision may itself be subject to judicial review.[28] They also have powers to terminate private criminal prosecutions. In the United States, public prosecutors can take over '*qui tam*' penal actions brought by citizens in respect of frauds against government where it is in the public interest for the State to pursue them instead.[29] And all courts of law have extensive powers to terminate proceedings initiated by private parties on a case-by-case basis where these are considered vexatious or improperly motivated.

This is not a full list of the types of right attending law enforcement processes. It leaves out 'amicus' or 'court assistance rights', which are rights for persons with special knowledge or expertise, such as human rights commissions and public interest advocacy groups, to make representations and present arguments to a court in respect of a matter that is being heard. Such rights are liberties and (sometimes) powers to furnish the court with expertise and information that might not otherwise be available to it. Like joinder and intervention rights, they ensure wider interest representation, but an amicus is never made a formal party to the action and consequently does not have the same powers or liabilities.[30] The use of such rights is reportedly on the rise in England and Wales[31] and their more extensive use by expert advocacy groups before the European Court of Human Rights is said to have made a real and positive difference in some cases, resulting, for example, in significantly increased success rates before that court in claims involving violence against women.[32]

In this book, my main focus is on rights of action and termination, for these are the powers of life and death over a legal proceeding. They express most fundamentally what it means for an enforcer to have power to prosecute rights and interests. We shall nonetheless encounter other types of enforcement right from time to time when charting the broader landscape. For example, personal rights of complaint to commissions and public agencies now form a very important part of many modern regulatory frameworks, providing a cheaper and quicker way for individuals to bring wrongdoing to light and giving them some degree of involvement in their resolution.

[28] Courts intervene 'very rarely': *R (Bermingham) v Director of the Serious Fraud Office* [2006] EWHC 200 (Admin) [63] (Laws LJ).

[29] See Chapter 7 Section 7.2B(ii).

[30] An amicus has no power of appeal, or necessarily any liberty to present argument in oral opposed to written form. An amicus is also not liable in costs: Williams (n 23) 366–69.

[31] S Shah, T Poole, and M Blackwell, 'Rights, Interveners and the Law Lords' (2014) 34 Oxford Journal of Legal Studies 295.

[32] R Cichowski, 'The European Court of Human Rights, Amicus Curiae, and Violence against Women' (2016) 50 Law & Society Review 890.

PART II

ANALYTICS AND EARLY LEGAL HISTORY

This Part analyses the nature of rights of action in both public and private law from a Hohfeldian perspective. It identifies them as aggregates of legal liberties and powers that are also often accompanied by claim-rights, dutiers and liabilities which protect and strengthen their use (on the one hand) and constrain their operation (on the other). The picture presented here of rights of action differs from that provided by civil recourse theorists in denying that rights of action give litigators the power to place other citizens under remedial duties to pay damages. Such powers, the analysis suggests, always lie in the hands of courts. Given the significance of rights of action for the powers of courts and the liabilities of others, a key theme of this chapters is that it is important that all such rights be subject to checks and balances which ensure a distribution of power between public and private actors.

3
Enforcement Analytics

At the end of the last chapter, I identified four, basic types of 'enforcement right'—rights for a party to complain to prosecutors about a legal infraction, rights to initiate legal proceedings before a court of law in respect of it ('rights of action'), rights to join or intervene in another's legal action, and rights to terminate or settle it. This chapter engages in more detailed analysis of what is meant (and who is implicated) by the idea that someone has a right of the second type—a 'right of action'. Much important work has previously been done on this question in the private law context by John Goldberg and Ben Zipursky.[1] I gratefully build upon their work here, but I am concerned not just with what they call a person's 'rights of civil recourse' in respect of torts and other private law wrongs but with rights of action more generally in both private and public law. The broader focus of the inquiry yields a slightly different understanding of what rights of action are—and of their implications for the legal duties and liabilities of others.

3.1 Preview

The most important conclusion of this chapter, which is an extended homage to the insights of Goldberg, Zipursky, Stephen Smith,[2] and others, is that rights of action

[1] B Zipursky, 'Rights, Wrongs and Recourse in the Law of Torts' (1998) 51 Vanderbilt Law Review 1; B Zipursky, 'Civil Recourse, Not Corrective Justice' (2002–2003) 91 Georgia Law Journal 695; B Zipursky, 'Substantive Standing, Civil Recourse, and Corrective Justice' (2011) 39 Florida State University Law Review 299; B Zipursky, 'The Philosophy of Private Law' in J Coleman, K Himma, and S Shapiro (eds), *The Oxford Handbook of Jurisprudence and Philosophy of Law* (OUP 2015) Ch 16; J Goldberg, 'The Constitutional Status of Tort Law: Due Process and the Right to a Law for the Redress of Wrongs' (2005) 115 Yale Law Journal 524; J Goldberg and B Zipursky, 'Torts as Wrongs' (2009–2010) 88 Texas Law Review 917; J Goldberg and B Zipursky, 'Civil Recourse Revisited' (2011) 39 Florida State University Law Review 341; B Zipursky, 'Rights and Responsibility in the Law of Torts' in D Nolan and A Robertson (eds), *Rights and Private Law* (Hart 2011) Ch 9; J Goldberg and B Zipursky, 'Civil Recourse Defended: A Reply to Posner, Calabresi, Rustad, Chamallas, and Robinette' (2013) 88 Indiana Law Journal 569; J Goldberg and B Zipursky, *Recognizing Wrongs* (Harvard University Press 2020) esp Ch 3.

[2] Note, however, that Smith's concept of an 'action right' entails much more than a mere liberty and power to initiate proceedings. It is a Hohfeldian claim right that a person has against a court *to a legal order* (remedy) that arises once she has established a legal cause of action. See S Smith, *Rights, Wrongs and Injustices: The Structure of Remedial Law* (OUP 2019) 58. A *cause of action* comprises the full set of conditions that is necessary and sufficient (a 'cause') to give rise to a right to obtain a remedy from the court: *Letang v Cooper* [1965] 1 QB 232, 242–43 (Diplock LJ), although the concept can also be defined either more broadly, or narrowly: S Harris, 'What Is a Cause of Action?' (1928) 16 California Law Review 459.

Enforcement Rights in Public and Private Law. Kit Barker, Oxford University Press. © Kit Barker 2026.
DOI: 10.1093/9780191955006.003.0005

in both public and private law can usefully be understood as particular groups of Hohfeldian[3] rights that exist between enforcers, defendants (here meaning all those who violate either public or private law norms), and the State. They are important legal liberties, as well as powers. Sometimes, such rights are backed by further claim rights that serve to reinforce them. At the same time, however, they are neither unconditional nor absolute. Their exercise may be contingent on preconditions being met or permission being obtained, and all enforcers are subject to an important range of duties not to abuse their powers. Rights of action may also be suspended or removed from a private enforcer on public interest grounds, and public enforcers may have their decisions about whether or not to exercise a right of action reviewed, appealed, or set aside at the initiative of private citizens. In this way, those holding rights of action in both public and private law are almost always subject to what Hohfeld calls 'liabilities'—they are susceptible to having their legal rights changed by someone else possessing a distinct legal power of their own. The precise set of preconditions, duties, and liabilities attaching to those with rights of action is complex and varies significantly between the public and private enforcement processes.

Since the analytical framework used here is Hohfeld's, Section 3.2 provides a brief overview of the essentials of his scheme for those who may be less familiar with it. Section 3.3 explains its particular value in understanding rights of action. Section 3.4 then considers some of the main conditions and constraints (Hohfeldian duties and liabilities) attending the exercise of such rights. Section 3.5 concludes with an analysis of the relationship between rights of action and the 'primary' (substantive) and secondary (remedial) rights that they serve to enforce. The point made here is that although there are good reasons to give primary right-holders rights of action, there is no necessary *analytical* connection between a right of action and either a primary or secondary (remedial) right. The existence and location of any such right of action is not dictated *a priori* by the location of the right it serves to enforce. This is important for the rest of the book since it means that there is no necessary reason why private law rights should always, or only, be enforceable by the private parties that hold them, or why, on the other hand, the State's public law rights should only ever be enforceable by State agents. We always have a choice.[4]

[3] WN Hohfeld, *Fundamental Conceptions as Applied in Judicial Reasoning* (ed W Cook, Yale University Press 1919); J Goldberg and B Zipursky, 'Hohfeldian Analysis and the Separation of Rights and Powers' in S Balganesh, T Sichelman, and H Smith (eds), *Wesley Hohfeld A Century Later* (CUP 2022) Ch 12.

[4] On the various configurations, see K Barker, 'Modelling Public and Private Enforcement: The Rationality of Hybridity' (2018) 37 University of Queensland Law Journal 9.

3.2 The Hohfeldian 'Rights' Framework

This is no place to provide a full account of Hohfeld's work,[5] but a brief outline of his scheme will be helpful in explaining the sense in which it is true to say that rights of action are liberties and powers that are sometimes supported by claim rights and subject to liabilities and duties. It is important to remember that it was not Hohfeld's ambition to tell us what rights we should or should not have, but simply to ensure that we are clear what we mean when we talk about them; and clear also, therefore, about the implications of saying that somebody has one. Being clear about what we mean by rights is an essential precondition to our making appropriate normative choices about whether or not to grant them.[6] This is as true in respect of 'rights of action', I suggest, as it is of any other type of right.

Hohfeld's scheme distinguishes between four 'fundamental' conceptions of legal 'right' that a person (A) might have: claim rights, privileges (which I shall call 'liberties'), powers, and immunities. So far, I have used the word 'rights' indiscriminately to refer to all four of these conceptions. This is not true to Hohfeld, but it is helpful nonetheless, I believe, to have a collective term for the total set and I use the term 'rights' in this generic sense throughout the book. Each right that A might have in the scheme has a jural 'correlative' from the point of view of another party, B, and it also has an 'opposite'.[7] Crucially, each form of right that A holds therefore predicates a different type of legal relationship to someone else, B.

A. Claim Rights

If A has a claim right against B, this means that B has a correlative *duty* to A. The opposite of A having a claim right is simply that he has '*no claim right*' against B. Here are two examples of my own drawn from private and public law respectively:

Example 1: Claim right: A has a contractual claim right that B deliver a car. Correlative: B owes A a contractual duty to deliver the car. Opposite: A has no claim right that B deliver the car.

[5] For centennial reviews containing references to much of the literature, see K Barker, 'Private Law, Analytical Philosophy and the Modern Value of Wesley Newcomb Hohfeld: A Centennial Appraisal' (2018) 38 Oxford Journal of Legal Studies 585; Balganesh, Sicherman, and Smith (eds) (n 3).

[6] Hohfeld, *Fundamental Conceptions* (n 3) 64.

[7] The opposition is mutual and can work either way. On the fuller nature of the 'opposition' see A Halpin, 'The Value of Hohfeldian Neutrality When Theorising about Legal Rights' in M McBride (ed), *New Essays on the Nature of Rights* (Hart 2017) Ch 1, 6–7.

> *Example 2:*
> Claim right: The State (A) has a claim right that I do not commit treason.
> Correlative: I owe the State (A) a duty not to commit treason.
> Opposite: The State (A) has no claim right that I not commit treason.

There is some controversy, which I personally consider needless, as to whether Hohfeld envisaged his scheme as being applicable in public law.[8] It is true that he was not a public lawyer and some still claim that only individuals can hold Hohfeldian claim rights, not groups or the State. Sedley J once suggested, unfortunately and misleadingly I think (if his statement is taken to imply a general rule), that 'public law is not at base about rights' but rather that it is 'about wrongs—that is to say misuses of public power'.[9] Hohfeld nonetheless clearly accepted that states can make contracts[10] and he never presented a full theory of agency. So it makes sense, I think, to say that the State, acting as the constitutional representative of its citizen community, can hold claim rights, just as it can owe duties, exercise powers, and enjoy immunities. In other words, once one recognizes the State as a legal agent,[11] then it can logically hold all of the relevant kinds of Hohfeldian right on its citizens' behalf, claim rights included. Where the claim right is held against a large, indefinite class of citizens (as in *Example 2*), Hohfeld would refer to it as a 'multital' one, to contrast it with the case in which the right is held against one, or a small, definite number of persons (*Example 1*), where it would be described as 'paucital'.[12] On this view, the criminal law comprises multital substantive claim

[8] For the controversy and reference to the weight of literature suggesting that it can be, see Barker (n 5) 595–96, 599–600.

[9] *R v Somerset CC ex parte Dixon* (1997) Crown Office Digest 323, 331. The idea that public law is not about the primary claim rights of individuals is true of much of the law of judicial review—the area of law Sedley J was addressing—but is not true of public law more generally, where citizens often hold claim rights against the State, and the State holds claim rights against citizens. Even in the law of judicial review, there are arguably some cases in which review is triggered by the breach of a duty to consult that a decision-maker owes to a particular individual (see Chapter 6). Moreover, individuals have multital primary legal powers to set aside unlawful public decisions, which are rights in the broader sense referred to in the text.

[10] WN Hohfeld, 'The Individual Liability of Stockholders and the Conflict of Laws' (1909) 9 Columbia Law Review 492, 495–96.

[11] Depending on what one means by statehood, it is obviously possible to debate the existence of a legal 'State' entity in some constitutions. Civilian jurisdictions have been happier to accept that abstraction historically than common law ones and it is often pointed out that in Britain, public agency has been identified with individual agents, not with the State as an abstract entity. See eg C Turpin and A Tomkins, *British Government and the Constitution* (7th edn, CUP 2011) 10–11. But this is probably just a different idea of statehood: J McLean, *Searching for the State in British Legal Thought* (CUP 2012). For a refined examination of the concept and its importance to modern understandings of public law, see M Loughlin, *Foundations of Public Law* (OUP 2010) Chs 7–9.

[12] Hohfeld, *Fundamental Conceptions* (n 3) 72. The distinction between multital and paucital rights is ambiguously presented as relating both to the size and the definiteness of the class bearing the correlative disadvantage. It is probably the latter that is key: M Radin, 'A Restatement of Hohfeld' (1938) 51 Harvard Law Review 1141, 1155–56.

rights that are held by the State against its citizens (and others) on behalf of society as a whole,[13] whereas the law of torts usually comprises multital claim rights held by private individuals against one another.

B. Liberties

The second type of right that A may enjoy is a *liberty* (privilege). Where such a right is held against B, B has (correlatively) *no claim right* against A. The opposite of A having a liberty is that A has a *duty* to B. The following two examples are again drawn from both private and public law.

Example 3:
Liberty: A has a liberty as against B to walk upon his own land.
Correlative: B has no right that A not walk upon the land.
Opposite: A has a duty to B not to walk on the land.

Example 4:
Liberty: A has a liberty as against the State (B) to speak.
Correlative: The State (B) has no-right that A not speak.
Opposite: A has a duty to the State (B) not to speak.

Liberties are sometimes said to be the weakest type of Hohfeldian right,[14] but in so far as they describe for A a range of conduct in respect of which A owes no obligation to B, they clearly promote his autonomy in a negative sense. A's liberties to walk upon his land, or to speak freely, are important for A in expanding his range of choices in pursuit of an autonomous life. This is not the same as saying that A has a claim right as against B that he (A) be able to walk upon the land, or speak out in the press, for if this were so then actions of B that prevented A from walking or speaking would be actionable wrongs and could themselves be restrained or sanctioned. This would obviously further enhance A's autonomy in so far as it would give A additional choices in the event that his liberty were obstructed by B. But liberties are nonetheless of great importance to human welfare. Indeed, this is why

[13] A contrasting view is that public law cannot be fitted within the Hohfeldian scheme and that citizens owe public duties that have no associated claim rights. See eg R Stevens, 'Private Rights and Public Wrongs' in A Dyson (ed), *Unravelling Tort and Crime* (CUP 2014) Ch 5, 113–14; L Smith, *The Law of Loyalty* (OUP 2023) 337–38.

[14] FKH Maher, 'The Kinds of Legal Rights' (1965) 5 Melbourne University Law Review 47, 72 (a liberty is a 'nothing' in law).

freedom of speech is regarded as a fundamental 'human' right,[15] as well an instrument for the promotion of broader social goods such as truth, or democracy.

C. Powers

A third type of right in the Hohfeldian scheme, that is key to our analysis, is a *power*. To say that A has a power is to say that A is able, of his or her own volition, to change the legal relationship between himself and B, or indeed between B and another party (C). In such a case, B (or both B and C) is (are) *liable* to have their legal relations changed by A and they therefore have a correlative *liability* (or *liabilities*). The opposite of a power is a 'disability'. Here are two more examples, again drawn from both private and public law.

Example 5:
Power: A has the power to enter into a contract with B.
Correlative: B is liable to obtain new contractual rights vis à vis A.
Opposite: A has a disability to enter a contract with B.

Example 6:
Power: A, a local authority, has the power to terminate B's liquor licence.
Correlative: B has a liability to have his license terminated by A.
Opposite: A has a disability to terminate B's license.

The implication of having a legal power is hence that its holder can bring into being, alter, or extinguish any or all of the other types of rights in the scheme. This can make the position of others either better (as in *Example 5*) or worse (as in *Example 6*). In public law, governments commonly have powers to create not just claim rights and duties in citizens (perhaps the commonest examples) but also new immunities and powers for themselves. This makes them apex agents for good or evil in the world and illustrates why it is important that the exercise of *all* legal powers is subject to close scrutiny and attended by stringent conditions, constraints, checks, and balances that safeguard vigilantly against corruption and abuse. We return to this theme in Section 3.4 because rights of action, involving as

[15] For a thicker, more powerful ('normatively rich') understanding of liberties which aggregates the absence of a duty on the part of A and duties on the part of B not to obstruct its enjoyment, see A Halpin, 'No Rights and Its Correlative' (2020) 65 American Journal of Jurisprudence 147, 163–65. This aggregate conception is closer to what people often mean when they talk of liberties in the context of 'fundamental' human rights, since in this context Hohfeldian liberties are often combined with obligations on the part of others not to interfere with them and sometimes to act positively to secure them.

they do legal powers, carry with them precisely this risk of abuse and consequently need to be set about by constraining legal norms.

D. Immunities

The final type of right in Hohfeld's scheme is an *immunity*. A has such an immunity as against B when A is not liable to have his or her legal relations changed by B. B then has a correlative *disability* (no legal power) to change A's legal relations. The opposite of A having a legal immunity is that A has a *liability* to some change in his or her legal relations by B.

Example 7:
Immunity: A, a judge, has an immunity as against B to legal proceedings for negligence in court.
Correlative: B has no power to take proceedings in respect of the negligence of A.
Opposite: A has a liability to legal proceedings by B for negligence.

Blanket immunities against both either private or public law proceedings are now rare, although they do still exist. Technically, in the United States, federal immunity against civil actions persists even to this day, save in so far as it has been abandoned under statute. Public prosecutors also retain an absolute immunity against civil action in that jurisdiction, even in cases in which they have been involved in the most scandalous forms of wrongdoing.[16] Certain individuals (commonly heads of State, or presidents) retain immunities in respect of even public criminal proceedings whilst they remain in office. In so far as such immunities effectively disable others from pursuing rights of action, they eliminate the relevant prosecutorial power and eradicate protections for the underlying substantive rights.

Importantly for our purposes, the above four Hohfeldian rights are not mutually exclusive and can coalesce in the same legal person. For example, A's liberty as against B to walk around on his own property (*Example 3*) is usually accompanied by a multital claim right protecting that liberty—others are under a duty not to prevent him walking there. A also has a power, because he can alienate both his liberty to walk on the land and his right that others not prevent him doing so, simply by selling the land to someone else. In doing so, A changes the legal rights and duties of others in relation to both himself and the purchaser. The combination in one legal agent of different types of Hohfeldian 'right' is very common in practice, so common, in fact, that it is sometimes suggested that special terms may

[16] *Imbler v Pachtman* 424 US 409 (1976); *Taylor v Kavanagh* 640 F 2d 450 (2d Cir 1981).

be helpful in designating particular 'rights groupings'.[17] 'Rights of action' are, I suggest, effectively one such grouping of different types of Hohfeldian rights in one and the same person.

3.3 Rights of Action as Aggregate Clusters of Rights

Those holding rights of action—whether they are public or private enforcers—hold more than one type of Hohfeldian right, with the consequence that rights of action are best understood as composite *clusters* or *aggregates* of rights,[18] the precise composition of which can vary. The most stable 'rights components' of rights of action in both public and private law are liberties and powers, but the exercise of these liberties and powers is also protected to some degree by claim rights.

A. Liberties

First, then, rights of action are multital liberties in so far as an enforcer is under no legal duty to *anyone* not to commence a legal proceeding. As I intimated above, however, a bare liberty to make a legal claim is weak on its own because it entails no obligation on the part of anyone else. It does not connote any duty on the part of the State to support a private claim, for example. Nor does it imply any duty on the part of an offender or anyone else not to obstruct an enforcer from exercising the right of action. If rights of action were mere liberties to sue, they would therefore be worth something, but not very much.

B. Powers

Secondly, rights of action are also Hohfeldian powers because their holders have the ability, by choosing to file a civil claim, or initiate a public prosecution, both to

[17] T Sichelman, 'Very Tight "Bundles of Sticks": Hohfeld's Complex Legal Relations' in Balganesh, Sichelman, and Smith (eds) (n 3). For a reaffirmation of the importance of aggregates of this type in Hohfeld's work, see A Halpin, 'Hohfeld and Rules' in Balganesh, Sichelman, and Smith (eds) (n 3) Ch 3.

[18] Hohfeld used the term 'aggregates' rather than 'bundles', but the modern conception of property rights as bundles of different types of right is nonetheless regularly attributed to him. It is not always popular. For the full story see J Penner, 'The "Bundle of Rights" Picture of Property' (1996) 43 University of California Los Angeles Law Review 711. In Goldberg and Zipursky's understanding, rights of action in private law are combinations of: (i) claim rights against the State that the State make available an avenue of civil recourse to plaintiffs (which are 'political', 'natural', and sometimes also 'legal' rights); (ii) liberties that the plaintiff holds against the State and against wrongdoers to bring an action; and (iii) powers that the plaintiff has *against a defendant* to alter the defendant's legal obligations through courts. See Zipursky, 'Civil Recourse' (n 1) 739; Zipursky, 'Philosophy of Private Law' (n 1) 633–36, 639–40, 643–44; Goldberg and Zipursky, 'Rights and Responsibility'(n 1) 268–69; 'Tort Law and Responsibility' (n 1) 27–28; Goldberg and Zipursky, *Recognizing Wrongs* (n 1) 98.

enliven a court's jurisdiction (liberty and power) to hear the claim and to change a defendant's legal relationship to the court. He is able, for example, to place a defendant under public liabilities or duties to the court to respond to the claim. He is also able, by issuing proceedings, to trigger procedural duties such as the duties that all parties to legal proceedings owe to courts in respect of process and evidence.

In the private law context of tort law, Goldberg and Zipursky have gone further in suggesting that rights of action also empower plaintiffs to change the *remedial* duties that defendants owe *to plaintiffs themselves.*[19] This view is hard to sustain in public law for reasons to which we shall shortly come, but in tort law their claim is nonetheless that a plaintiff's right of action gives him the power to impose secondary duties on a defendant *to him (the plaintiff)* to remedy a wrong done. Rights of action are in fact central to Goldberg and Zipursky's account of tort law for precisely this reason—it is because they give plaintiffs powers to oblige defendants to remedy the personal wrongs that they have done that they instantiate tort law as a manifestation of the principle of civil recourse. By empowering a victim to require remedial action from a wrongdoer, rights of action put the wrongdoer's fate 'in the victim's hands'.[20]

In my view, this additional claim goes too far, even in private law. Its accuracy rather depends on what one means by a legal power and this highlights an important ambiguity at the heart of the idea. Although Hohfeld made no determined attempt to flesh out the concept, a power in his lexicon appears to be simply the ability to bring about a change in someone else's legal position through one's own volitional action—the ability to *choose intentionally to act* in a way that will lead to that consequence.[21] Goldberg and Zipursky's view that rights of action entail powers to impose remedial obligations on defendants is true to this conception because a voluntary act on the part of a plaintiff in initiating an action can indeed lead to an obligation on the part of a defendant to remedy his or her wrong. One would surely hope so. Nonetheless, the idea that I have the power to bring about X simply if I can *choose to act in a way that will result in* X seems questionable. On this approach, it could be said that I have the legal power to imprison myself (to remove my own legal liberty) by choosing to commit murder and then surrendering myself to the police. Citing a testing example similar to this, Andrew Halpin has hence suggested that it would really only make sense to say that I have the power to impose a remedial obligation on a defendant if it were I that *decided* (determined)

[19] Above n 18. It is this that makes rights of action powers that a plaintiff has 'against a defendant' entailing corresponding liabilities in the defendant.

[20] Goldberg and Zipurksy, 'Civil Recourse Defended' (n 1) 572.

[21] Hohfeld's definition was stated to be 'only as an approximate explanation, sufficient for all practical purposes'. 'Volitional control' over changes in legal relations nonetheless seems to be the key. Where more than one person has volitional control, it is the person whose control is 'paramount' that has the power: Hohfeld, *Fundamental Conceptions* (n 3) 50–51. No explanation of 'paramountcy' is given.

the obligation.[22] And there are good reasons to think that it is courts that *decide* the remedial obligations that tortfeasors owe, not plaintiffs, even if courts themselves are bound to decide those obligations (and bound in the way that they do so) by guidelines and rules of public law.[23]

I think that this point is tacitly acknowledged by Zipursky when he says that the powers of those who hold private rights of action to impose remedial obligations on defendants are 'mediated', not 'direct'—they are powers exercised '*through*' courts.[24] Writing with John Goldberg, he has also suggested (this is a different way of recognizing the same point, I think) that it is probably inappropriate to think of a plaintiff exercising a 'right' of action, or a 'right' to recourse, in cases in which an equitable remedy is granted at a court's discretion, because in such instances the plaintiff really only has the ability to ask ('petition') the court to give a remedy and has no power himself to bring about any particular remedial consequence.[25] Since the distinction between legal and equitable remedies is, as Goldberg and Zipursky themselves admit, far from being watertight when it comes to determining the presence of discretion in a court's award of a remedy[26]—and also because equitable injunctive remedies are widely available for a range of common law torts—it seems possible that their view that rights of action in tort always entail *remedial powers* as against defendants is undergoing some refinement and revision.

Working outward from these points in the private law context, it is, I suggest, impossible to think of public law rights of action as giving State prosecutors the power to impose a sentence on an offender in the criminal law,[27] or as giving private applicants for judicial review the legal 'power' to quash a public decision, or to mandate a public agent to act in accordance with his or her public duty. These

[22] A Halpin, 'The Concept of a Legal Power' (1996) 16 Oxford Journal of Legal Studies 129, 140–47, 151–52. See further A Halpin, 'Some Central Puzzles Regarding the Relationships between Competence (Power), Permission (Liberty), Decision and Choice' (29th IVR World Congress, Lucerne, Switzerland, July 2019) (distinguishing a power to X from the voluntary satisfaction of a condition precedent to another person's exercise of power to X). Note that it seems possible (probable?) that Hohfeld himself would have balked at the suggestion that I have a power to imprison myself in the example cited. This could well be one of the cases he mentions in which both I and the court have some degree of 'volitional control' over the legal result, but where he would think that the court's control is 'paramount': ibid.

[23] The fact that a court is under a duty (even to the plaintiff) to grant a remedy of a particular sort does not necessarily mean that the relevant remedial power lies with the plaintiff, because, as Halpin suggests, '[l]egal power may exist without choice': ibid 151. In other words, there can be duties to exercise powers in particular ways.

[24] Zipursky, *Philosophy of Private Law* (n 1) 633–34. See also Goldberg and Zipursky, *Recognizing Wrongs* (n 1) 98 (the power 'requires for its exercise the acts of others'), and Goldberg and Zipursky, 'Rights and Responsibility' (n 1) 266 ('the power . . . is always asserted provisionally or conditionally, subject to authoritative determination by a court as to the validity of the assertion').

[25] J Goldberg and B Zipursky, 'From Riggs v Palmer to Shelley v Kramer: The Continuing Significance of the Law–Equity Distinction' in D Klimchuk, I Sarnet, and H Smith (eds), *Philosophical Foundations of the Law of Equity* (OUP 2018) Ch 14, 291, 296, 312.

[26] ibid 296.

[27] See, hinting at this point in the context of private rights of action in respect of the breach of public laws concerned with consumer protection, J Goldberg, A Sebok, and B Zipursky, 'The Place of Reliance in Fraud' (2006) 48 Arizona Law Review 1001, 1015–16.

penalties and remedies again lie at the discretion and decision of the court, even though the way in which that discretion is exercised is guided and constrained by public law rules. Rights of action in public law—whether held by state agents or private individuals—do not then involve *remedial* (or 'sanctioning') powers in any meaningful sense.

To some readers, this may seem like angels dancing on the head of a pin. What approach is one to take? There are two possibilities. The first is to keep faith with the Hohfeldian definition of a power, ignore these doubts, and say that rights of action empower enforcers 'indirectly' to impose new secondary (remedial) duties and sanctions on others, making the sorts of concessions and adjustments that Goldberg and Zipursky suggest. The idea would then be that wherever a court is bound by a common law precedent or statutory rule to provide a particular remedy or sanction on a set of facts presented by an enforcer's claim, then the power to change the defendant's remedial duties lies with the enforcer, in the same way that it can be said that it is a couple that has the power to marry, even if they need an official formally to conclude the arrangement.[28] But one then has to vary one's conclusion as to whether an enforcer has that power as between cases in which a remedy or penalty issues automatically on his or her application to a court or is awarded only on a discretionary basis, and one runs into insuperable difficulties in concluding that rights of action can be understood in this way in public law.

The alternative, which I prefer, is to tinker slightly with the Hohfeldian scheme by defining the concept of a power more narrowly in the way that Halpin suggests as a capacity to *decide* (determine) changes in one's own or others' legal rights. In this case, the proper conclusion is that rights of action almost never include powers to impose remedial duties or sanctions on offenders, in either public or private law. This is because, even accepting that a court awarding common law damages in a tort case is granting an enforcer a remedy that is available 'as of right', it is still the court's decision to grant them, not the decision of the enforcer. The court may have a public duty to the State, or to the enforcer, to grant the remedy, but it is nonetheless still the court that makes the decision and holds the legal power to alter a defendant's remedial duties. The enforcer's power in respect of the remedy or sanction lies in his or her ability to appeal the court's decision if it is denied,[29] rather than in the ability unilaterally to change a defendant's remedial obligations for himself in the first place.

[28] Goldberg and Zipursky, *Recognizing Wrongs* (n 1) 98, fn 25. As indicated above (nn 21, 22), it unclear whether Hohfeld himself would himself have seen the remedial power in this case as being the plaintiff's—this would depend on whose volitional control over the award of a remedy was 'paramount'. For a sceptical critique of the Goldman and Zipursky view, see O Herstein, 'How Tort law Empowers' (2015) 65 University of Toronto Law Journal 99.

[29] Whilst P has no power to strike the first instance decision down, he or she has the power to enliven the jurisdiction and power of an appellate court to do so, and to trigger procedural duties on D's part to respond to the appeal.

Taking Halpin's view, my own conclusion is therefore that a right of action is something much more limited that Goldberg and Zipursky suggest it to be. It is a unilateral liberty and power for an enforcer to enliven a court's jurisdiction and to change a defendant's relationship to the court by imposing new public law duties or liabilities or duties upon him or her,[30] but it is not a power for the enforcer himself to impose remedial obligations or sanctions upon the defendant. On this view, a right of action is still a powerful and important legal tool, but its implications for others' legal duties and liabilities are less extensive than is suggested by the idea of a 'right of recourse'. Indeed, on the view that I take here, the idea of a right of recourse improperly elides a right-holder's right of action with his or her secondary right to claim a remedy, which is an analytically distinct question customarily lying within the decisional power of a judge. Goldberg and Zipurksy are not alone in running rights of action and remedial rights together in this way since, as we shall see in Chapter 6, courts considering applications for judicial review sometimes still treat the preconditions that a person must satisfy to establish a right of action (their 'standing' to make the application) and the conditions attaching to their entitlement to claim a particular type of public law remedy as effectively one and the same, when they are in fact logically distinct and should therefore technically be considered apart.

C. Claim Rights

Rights of action are therefore aggregate clusters of legal liberties and powers. Sometimes, however—this is a third point—they are accompanied by claim rights that reinforce their holder's legal position. All public bodies in the United Kingdom—including courts—hence owe citizens public law duties under the Human Rights Act 1998 (UK) to ensure their access to a court so that they may air their claims.[31] Citizens almost certainly enjoy such claim rights even outside this

[30] There is still a question, I acknowledge, whether it is always the enforcer that *decides* to impose any procedural duties (owed to the court) that attach to a defendant when a claim is lodged. In most civil cases, the procedural duties flowing from the issue of proceedings are so automatic that this analysis may be feasible. Such cases are close to Goldberg and Zipursky's wedding example, cited above at n 28, in so far as no other person's agency or judgement is meaningfully placed between the enforcer's action and the resulting change in the defendant's legal position. The case is much weaker in the criminal law, since the issue of a summons on the filing of a charge by a prosecutor is still ultimately subject to the discretion of the issuing judge. In such instances, it is more realistic to say that the enforcer imposes a liability on the defendant to the court that the court exercise its powers to impose public duties on the defendant. The exact rights bundle comprising an enforcer's right of action may therefore be different in different cases.

[31] Human Rights Act 1998 (UK) s 6; *Golder v United Kingdom* [1975] ECHR 1 [28]–[36]; *Naït-Liman v Switzerland* [2016] ECHR 574: ECHR 21 Jun 2016 [112]–[113] (art 6). See further Council of Europe/European Court of Human Rights, *Guide on Article 6 of the European Convention on Human Rights, Right to A Fair Trial (civil limb)* (31 August 2019) 22–30.

statutory framework[32] as an aspect of the rule of law.[33] As Goldberg and Zipursky point out, it is therefore not just that citizens hold *political* claim rights against the State to have access to justice[34] but that these rights have concrete manifestations[35] in a wide variety of legal norms—constitutional,[36] statutory, and common law. To the extent that all persons owe public duties not to interfere with civil actions or public prosecutions by intimidating the parties[37] or otherwise perverting the course of justice, the exercise of an enforcer's right of action is also indirectly protected by public law claim rights that courts hold against all those who threaten to bring the judicial process into contempt,[38] as well as by analogous provisions of the substantive criminal law.[39]

None of this, remember, means that the liberties and powers that instantiate rights of action *correlate* to duties in others in the Hohfeldian sense, but it does mean that in practice those who hold such rights are accorded significant additional protections in the form of both positive and negative legal duties owed by the State and other citizens. The extent to which private litigants enjoy positive claim rights against the State to support them in the exercise of their rights of action varies greatly across jurisdictions.[40] The more support a State provides, the more seriously it takes rights of action and, by extension, the substantive rights that those rights enforce. The general trend through the neoliberal era and beyond has been to reduce State duties of support across the board. This manifests itself not just in reductions in financial legal aid to private litigants and recent cuts in the United Kingdom to public prosecution budgets but in the broader shift toward de-formalized, 'privatized' forms of justice in which claims are diverted away from courts of law and settled in private claims markets. Although this reduces costs and increases access to dispute resolution services, every reduction in judicial resources, every criminal plea bargain, and every compulsory diversion of claims to arbitration or mediation is a detraction from the duties of the State to support rights of action and a weakening of its commitment to the 'enforcement' of law in the core, conventional sense examined here.

[32] See eg S Rares, 'Is Access to Justice a Right or a Service?' [2015] Federal Judicial Scholarship 11 [38].

[33] *R (Unison) v Lord Chancellor)* [2017] UKSC 51 [66] (Lord Reed, Lords Neuberger, Mance, Kerr, Wilson, and Hughes agreeing) (obligation to provide access to employment tribunal system free of charge).

[34] Goldberg and Zipursky, *Recognizing Wrongs* (n 1) 113.

[35] ibid 113 ('the principle of civil recourse is part of our positive law').

[36] For an argument that the US Constitution imposes legal duties on the State to provide redress, see Goldberg, 'The Constitutional Status of Tort Law' (n 1); Goldberg and Zipursky, *Recognizing Wrongs* (n 1) 30–43.

[37] *Harkianakis v Skalkos* (1997) 42 NSWLR 22, 28.

[38] See generally CJ Miller, *Contempt of Court* (OUP 2000).

[39] There is significant overlap between the law of contempt and the substantive criminal law in this regard. See generally, ALRC Rep No 35, *Contempt* (1987).

[40] For a comparative review as between the US and other jurisdictions (albeit now a bit out of date) see E Johnson, Jnr, 'Equal Access to Justice: Comparing Access to Justice in America and Other Industrial Democracies (2000) 24 Fordham International Law Review 83.

3.4 Enforcement Conditions and Constraints

It is because rights of action include liberties and powers to affect the rights, duties, and liberties of others that they are attended by risk. Their exercise burdens other parties to the proceeding and implicates judicial resources and broader public interests. Giving free rein to a law enforcer can result in collusion, corruption, oppression, extortion, and intimidation,[41] and it can undermine the public interest in fair and accountable systems of justice. For this reason, the exercise of all rights of action is subject to constraints and checks. These take three, main forms: (A) the setting of preconditions to the exercise of a right of action; (B) the imposition of duties on enforcers that bind their conduct; and (C) the subjection of the latter to liabilities to having their powers suspended or removed, or decisions regarding their exercise reviewed and set aside.

A. Preconditions and Permissions

Although it is now rare, some classes of person (prisoners, for example) may be temporarily or permanently barred from exercising rights of action altogether, thereby being subjected to a legal disability.[42] More often, a private party wanting to exercise a right of action to enforce a public law must either obtain prior State permission, or notify the State so that the latter has the opportunity to pursue the action on its own account if it wishes. Even free Roman citizens had to obtain State *fiat* to prosecute a crime in some cases in the times of the Empire,[43] and that remains the case in most modern jurisdictions that allow for private prosecutions today, in some[44] or all[45] instances. Those seeking to wield prosecutorial rights in ways that are prejudicial to the public interest are thereby halted in their tracks before a proceeding even begins. Relator actions, which are commenced by private parties to enforce public rights on the State's behalf, require the Attorney-General's

[41] On the risks, see Chapter 4 and Chapter 5 Section 5.3B.

[42] Insolvent persons, minors, and incompetents fall into this category, as do some prisoners and vexatious litigants. Under Roman law, the class included slaves and domestics (save in cases of treason or counterfeiting) and (save where they were prosecuting injuria to themselves) women. See *The Theodosian Code and Novels and the Sirmondian Constitutions* (Trans Pharr, Lawbook Exchange Ltd 2001) Book 9, [9.1.3], [9.6.2], [9.6.3], [9.21.2]. Stephen also mentions minors, soldiers, and those convicted of crime: Sir James Stephen, *A History of the Criminal Law in England* (Macmillan 1883) 45.

[43] Stephen (n 42) 45. Permission of the praetor was required in order to proceed before one of the permanent courts (quaestiones perpetuate). It is unclear how often permission was denied: A Riggsby, *Roman Law and the Legal World of the Romans* (CUP 2010) 197.

[44] In the UK, the power was historically unconstrained, but an increasing number of exceptions have been admitted since the middle of the C19th: J Ll J Edwards, *The Law Officers of the Crown* (Sweet and Maxwell 1968) 237–46. A modern example relates to proceedings for assisting suicide. See further Chapter 7.

[45] This is the case in South Africa: J Mujuzi, 'The Right to Institute a Private Prosecution A Comparative Analysis' (2015) 4 International Human Rights Law Review 222, 234–35.

prior consent, and the latter's decision is currently not subject to judicial review.[46] In the United States, where the private prosecution of criminal offences is exceptionally rare, private relators seeking civil penalties for public fraud under the False Claims Act 1863 are barred from proceeding if they have themselves been convicted of criminal misconduct in connection with a violation, and the action may go ahead only if the State has first been accorded the opportunity to investigate the offence and has decided not to pursue the prosecution itself.[47] Once upon a time in America, the application of a prisoner to a court for the writ of habeas corpus had first to be approved by prison officials, but those regulations were mercifully struck down by the Supreme Court in 1941 for what now appear to us to be glaringly obvious reasons.[48]

The extent to which the exercise of private powers to bring a public law action should be contingent on prior *executive* permission remains contentious, especially where citizens are seeking to enforce the public duties and liabilities of State agents, such as the police, administrative officials, or agencies. Prior restraints upon actions against the State, the keys to which are held by the State itself, are unacceptable threats to the rule of law. From this point of view, it is appropriate that the standing of private parties to challenge administrative actions by way of judicial review, to initiate public law proceedings against public bodies under the Human Rights Act 1998, or to sue officials for the tort of misfeasance in public office is *never* contingent on prior executive consent.[49] There is also good sense in the view expressed by the Law Commission of England and Wales in 1998 that private criminal prosecutions should only require prior executive approval in a small range of exceptional cases,[50] if at all. The logic is that executive permission requirements undermine the role of private prosecution as a constitutional safeguard against State bias and inertia. As in other areas of the law where civil liberties are at stake, the law must strike a careful balance between prior restraint upon the exercise of the liberty, on the one hand, and the regulation of its exercise through the imposition of precautionary duties and liabilities on those choosing to wield it, on the other.

[46] *London County Council v Attorney General* [1902] AC 165 (HL); *Gouriet v Union of Post Office Workers* [1978] AC 435 (HL). This is a doubtful position, because the Attorney-General is a minister of government and (in the UK) a member of Cabinet and could therefore be open to party political influence: C McCormick, 'Reviewing the Reviewability of the Attorney General for Northern Ireland' [2018] Public Law 22; P Radan, 'Law, Politics, and the Attorney-General: the Context and Impact of Gouriet v Union of Post Office Workers' (2016) 16 Macquarie Law Journal 105; B Hough, 'Judicial Review where the Attorney General Refuses to Act: Time for a Change' (1988) Legal Studies 189. Being quasi-judicial, not political in nature, decisions should probably be subject to judicial review.

[47] False Claims Act 31 USC § 3730(b), (c), (d)(3). See Chapter 7 Section 7.2B(iii).

[48] *Ex parte Hull* 312 US 546 (1941) 548–49.

[49] Where judicial review is sought, the prior permission of a court is required to insure against vexatious or ill-motivated litigation, but the independence of the decision alleviates the rule of law concern.

[50] Law Com No 255, *Consents to Prosecution* (HMSO 1998). This is a reversal of the earlier recommendation of the *Royal Commission Report on Criminal Procedure* (Cmnd 8092, 1981) [7.50]–[7.51] that exercise of the power always require the leave of a Crown prosecutor or magistrate.

In general, the presumption should be *against* prior restraint. If a private right of action is (exceptionally) granted in public law, it is safer from a constitutional point of view that courts operate as guardians of the integrity of the enforcement process and/or that the State have powers to review and discontinue the action *ex post* on publicly stated and reviewable public interest grounds, than that the launch of a proceeding itself be dependent upon prior State *fiat*. Where that *fiat* is still required, as in relator actions, for example,[51] the decision whether to grant or deny it should always be subject to independent review. It is very rarely suggested, by contrast, that public enforcers should have to obtain the permission of private persons before exercising their rights to enforce public laws, although we shall encounter some interesting recommendations to that effect later in this book in respect of minor crimes against the person.[52] Criminal prosecutors are nonetheless under duties, considered further in the next section, to consult with victims and take account of their views when exercising their discretion whether or not to proceed.

By contrast with public law, in private law, all those who are legally competent are generally free to exercise their rights of action in furtherance of their private interests unilaterally and without prior State consent, although in doing so, they are subject to the public duties and liabilities identified below. This reflects the conventional logic that private law protects private interests and is therefore the business of private parties themselves, so that, subject to public interest concerns about vexatious litigation or abuse of process that can be weeded out by judges at early stages of the proceeding, there is no reason for the State itself to police or control the launch of a private action.

B. Enforcer Duties

There is no carte blanche in the use of either liberty or power. All those exercising rights of action, whether in respect of public or private laws, are hence subject to important duties. The duty not to make false accusations was taken particularly seriously in the times of the late Roman Republic, with false accusers standing to suffer both infamy and branding on the forehead.[53] In modern days, the consequences are less severe, but enforcers still owe primary duties in tort law not to abuse the legal process[54] or to prosecute a legal claim maliciously,[55] and they are subject to criminal law duties not to perjure themselves or otherwise

[51] Above n 46.

[52] See Chapter 7 Section 7.3B, n 225 and text.

[53] Such were the penalties under the Lex Remmia: H Jolowicz and B Nicholas, *Historical Introduction to the Study of Roman Law* (3rd edn, CUP 1972) 318. See further Chapter 4 Section 4.3B(ii) nn 67, 68.

[54] *Burton v Office of the Director of Public Prosecutions* [2019] NSWCA 245; E Hynard and A Lynch, 'The Tort of Collateral Abuse of Process' (2021) 44 University of New South Wales Law Journal 714.

[55] The claim may be either criminal or civil. There was some hesitancy historically about the latter, but see now *Willers v Joyce and Anor* [2015] UKSC 43.

pervert the course of justice, the breach of which can result in serious sentences of imprisonment.

Public prosecutors deciding whether or not to lay a criminal charge against an alleged offender must have regard to the strength of the evidence and the public interest,[56] and if deciding to discontinue a proceeding against him, they must respect the victim's human rights.[57] In many jurisdictions, they must now also provide victims with information during the decision-making process, and conduct a review of any decision not to prosecute an offender, if the victim requests it.[58] These duties reflect the modern perception of restorative justice theorists that public prosecution processes otherwise leave victims too far outside the circle of influence. Whilst victims have no claim right to be joined as parties to a public prosecution (and do not usually want such rights),[59] they are hence owed basic informational and consultative duties by public prosecutors.

Additional to these are the public law duties that all parties to civil and criminal proceedings owe to the court to abide by detailed rules of evidence and process, and not to commit acts of contempt. Such duties are designed in part to preserve the integrity and dignity of the court, but they also protect party interests, and can vary widely in their strictness. Collectively, the range of duties attaching to those exercising rights of action therefore spans both public and private law and requires standards of conduct ranging from mere honesty at one end of the scale (in instituting proceedings) to absolute precaution (eg strict disclosure duties in relation to evidence within a proceeding) at the other. Unsurprisingly, the duties attaching to those engaged in criminal prosecutions are more exacting than those applying in a civil action, since the potential consequences of the process for the accused are much more serious.

C. Enforcer Liabilities

A final form of constraint upon the exercise of rights of action is that they may sometimes be suspended or removed at another's motion. In such cases, the enforcer is subject to an important Hohfeldian liability. Such liabilities are a less extreme form of check upon enforcer power than the prior restraint technique

[56] See, in the UK, Crown Prosecution Service, *The Code for Crown Prosecutors* (8th edn, Crown Prosecution Service, October 2018).

[57] *R (B) v Director of Public Prosecutions* [2009] EWHC 106 (Admin).

[58] *R v Killick* [2011] EWCA Crim 1608 [49]. These developments flow in Europe from Directive 2012/29/EU (25 October 2012) establishing minimum standards on the rights, support, and protection of victims of crime. See now Ministry of Justice, *Code of Practice for Victims of Crime in England and Wales* (2020). For similar developments in the US (albeit with slightly different rights) see the Crime Victims' Rights Act, 18 USC § 377.

[59] J Doak, *Victims' Rights, Human Rights and Criminal Justice: Reconceiving the Role of Third Parties* (Hart 2008) 116–17.

examined above, but they allow measures to be taken to address the misuse of that power after a civil claim or criminal prosecution has already been initiated.

In the criminal law context, private prosecutors are hence liable to have their action taken over and discontinued at any stage by the State.[60] In England, this can be done simply by a Crown prosecutor making an appearance in court and offering no evidence in the case. Their action may also be terminated by the Attorney-General entering a plea of *nolle prosequi*[61] or (early on in proceedings) by a magistrate refusing to issue an originating summons on the ground that the prosecution is malicious or obviously unfounded. In certain instances (this is admittedly rare) the Attorney-General has the power to apply to the High Court for an order declaring a person to be a vexatious litigant, which has the effect of disabling that person from continuing both current and future actions without first obtaining court permission.[62] Until such permission is obtained, courts and relevant potential parties to the action effectively have an immunity against the normal legal consequences of the issuance of a proceeding by that person.

Public prosecutors are also subject to important liabilities in respect of their decisions whether or not to exercise a right of action in a criminal case. This is so whether their decision is made in the first instance or only after they have taken over a prosecution from a private individual. Such liabilities are imposed by the internal public review procedures, mentioned in the previous section, which permit victims of crime in the United Kingdom to seek a review of a prosecutor's decision not to proceed with a case.[63] Victims therefore have powers to have a decision reconsidered, and this can result in alterations in the rights and duties of both the initial decision-maker and all those affected by his or her decision. If a review is deficient, anyone with a sufficient interest may seek judicial review of its outcome,[64] which can spark a further, fresh set of public law consequences for the decision-maker and those affected by the original determination.

This is far from being a complete account of the liabilities attaching to those exercising rights of action, but it is sufficient to illustrate the way in which such rights can be changed at the initiative of others so as to regulate their use. In the criminal law context, both the State and private citizens have some power to control the

[60] This is happening with increasing regularity in the UK, probably in response to the burgeoning of recent private prosecutions: C Baksi, 'CPS drops more than half its private prosecutions' Law Society Gazette (20 March 2021).

[61] Edwards (n 44) 227–37.

[62] See eg *Attorney General v Hunter* [2002] WASC 189 and Chapter 5 Section 5.3F.

[63] See generally Crown Prosecution Service, *Victims Right to Review—Policy and Guidance 2020*; T Kirchengast, 'Victims Rights and Right to Review' in H Berents and J Scott (eds), *Crime Justice and Social Democracy* (Proceedings of the 3rd International Conference, 2015) Vol 1, 54; T Kirchengast, 'Victims' Rights and the Right to Review: A Corollary of the Victim's Pre-Trial Rights to Justice' (2016) 5 International Journal for Crime Justice and Social Democracy 103. On the position in civil jurisdictions, see J Göehler, 'Victim Rights in Civil Jurisdictions' in D Brown, J Turner, and B Weisser (eds), *The Oxford Handbook of Criminal Process* (OUP 2019) 267.

[64] *R v Director of Public Prosecutions ex parte C* [1995] 1 Cr App 136; *Killick* (n 58) [49]; *R (on app of Gujra) v Crown Prosecution Service* [2012] UKSC 52.

other in respect of the way in which in rights of action are exercised. The State's powers to control private prosecutions in public law are more far-reaching than those of citizens to control public ones, but in each case, a balance is struck. The rights of citizens to seek review of public prosecution decisions operates as a safeguard against public failure and assists in the protection of both the private interests of victims and the broader public good. Likewise, the power of the State to intervene to terminate private prosecutions prevents the harm which misjudged or ill-motivated private actions can sometimes do to both to public welfare and the private interests of an accused. This pattern of public checks on private rights of action and private checks on the use of public ones characterises many (if not quite all)[65] of the enforcement processes explored in this book and is essential to overall system design, distributing power as it does between citizen and State, rather than leaving it in any single set of hands.

3.5 Rights of Action and Primary and Secondary Rights

The final task of this chapter is to clarify the analytical relationship between rights of action as I have described them and the primary rights that they serve to enforce. Primary rights are the basic, substantive rights that define the legal relationships between parties (both public and private) and which exist prior to—and independently of—any order that a court makes in the course of a particular legal proceeding. They comprise not just claim rights but also the substantive legal powers, liberties, and immunities between public and private parties. They are sometimes contrasted in private law with the 'secondary' ('remedial') rights that arise when a primary right is violated and which are described in court orders. Rights of action, I have said, are a third type of 'right', analytically distinct from both primary and secondary rights.

What, then, is the relationship between a right of action and the underlying primary right that it serves to protect? In particular, does it follow from the fact that a particular party, A, holds a primary private or public law right: (i) that A *always* holds a right of action to enforce that right, and/or (ii) that *only* A holds a right of action in respect of it? For example, in private law, if you trespass upon my land and thereby wrong me, does it follow from the fact that I am the person wronged *that I* and *only I* have the right to sue you in vindication of my right? Could my mother choose to sue you instead? Conversely, if a person betrays state secrets, rapes another citizen, defrauds public finances, or otherwise threatens to breach the criminal law in a way that will violate the State's primary rights, does it follow that the State (and only the State) has the right to initiate a criminal prosecution?

[65] For a particularly controversial example where state intervention rights in respect of private actions are absent, see the radical abortion law known as the Texas Heartbeat Law discussed in Chapter 7 Section 7.2B(i) n 82.

Neither proposition (i) or (ii) holds true, at least not in the Hohfedlian analytical scheme. Although it is common for Hohfeldian rights of different types to coalesce in the same person, it is not a feature of the scheme that any one type of right is *necessarily entailed* by any other. To take a basic example, it cannot be inferred from the fact that A holds a liberty against B to speak that A also holds a claim right as against B that B not prevent him from speaking, even if one might consider this to be desirable in some cases. This is because the presence of a liberty in A does not correlate in the Hohfeldian scheme to any duty in B, so as to be entailed by it. In the same way, it cannot be deduced from the fact that A holds a *primary* claim right against B, that A necessarily has a *secondary* claim right to any remedy when B infringes that primary right, even though we might consider the lack of such a secondary right to be frankly outrageous and to make the enjoyment of the primary right practically nugatory.[66]

Following the same pattern, it does not follow analytically from the fact that B has breached a primary claim right of A's that A *necessarily* has a right of action in respect of B's breach; or that C *necessarily lacks* such a right of action.[67] The existence of A's primary right does not *entail* an accompanying right of action for A in the Hohfeldian scheme, or exclude a right of action for C. This is the case, even if the lack of such a right in A would make his primary right effectively worthless, or, conversely, even if the presence of such a right in C might be undesirable because it gives her a power to intermeddle in A's affairs. The Hohfeldian framework, being a purely formal analytical device, exists merely to express and explain the network of legal rights—primary rights, secondary rights and rights (liberties and powers) of action. It expresses no conclusion about the way in which rights of the various different types should be configured or associated with one another. Hohfeld would probably say that the precise configuration and association (aggregation) of those rights is a matter for us to decide, once we have properly considered all of the relevant normative implications.

The reason why this conclusion is so important is because if things were otherwise, none of the departures from the basic enforcement paradigm to which we alluded to in Chapter 1 and which we explore further in later chapters of this book would even be theoretically possible. This would be very odd indeed. All of the exceptions to the paradigm in which private enforcers are able to enforce public rights belonging to the State, or where public enforcers are able to enforce the private rights of individuals, would be not just open to criticism but would be frankly

[66] The maxim *ubi ius, ibi remedium* (where there is a right, there is a remedy) therefore expresses a normative aspiration, not a necessary analytical truth. See, similarly, J Gardner, *From Personal Life to Private Law* (OUP 2018) 204 ('That is a norm . . . not a conceptual truth').

[67] See similarly Gardner ibid 205 and Chapter 7. For the same insight in understanding third party rights ('standing') to enforce a contract, see T Liau, 'Privity: Rights, Standing and the Road Not Taken' (2021) 41 Oxford Journal of Legal Studies 803 and more recently T Liau, *Standing in Private Law* (OUP 2023) 34–40. See also Goldberg and Zipursky 'Hohfeldian Analysis' (n 3) 366, 371–72, 384–85.

paradoxical. In fact, as we shall see, they are clearly practically possible (otherwise we would have no examples) and analytically, they entail no contradiction. It is only their wisdom, not their possibility that can be contested.

These conclusions, I must stress again, are purely analytical. We shall later in the book examine a number of powerful arguments concerning the *normative* relationship between rights of action and primary rights which suggest that that there is indeed both moral and pragmatic sense in connecting them closely. Those individuals who have primary rights should generally, I agree, have the power to enforce them because the power to hold others accountable (or to forgive them) for infringing one's rights is, as Joel Feinberg once observed, part of what makes those rights morally valuable.[68] It promotes one's autonomy. From the pragmatic point of view, it also places the enforcement incentive in the hands of the party with the strongest motive to act and (usually) the best information about the infringement, which can be more efficient. It is therefore generally true to say, as Arthur Ripstein does in the private law context, that primary claim rights and powers to enforce them 'come as a package'.[69] But they do so, I suggest, because putting them together usually makes moral and/or pragmatic sense, not because substantive rights and rights of action are mutually *constitutive* of one another in any formal sense.[70] Indeed, it is significant that Ripstein himself accepts that it is perfectly possible to chop up and allocate different Hohfeldian rights into different packages, albeit that he counsels us strongly against doing so in the private law context.[71] My suggestion, conversely, is that realizing that it is possible to divide and allocate rights of different types into different bundles forces us to consider openly the reasons why we have the bundles we currently have and why we might (or might not) wish to create new ones. This, in my view, is one of Hohfeld's most powerful, valuable, and enduring legacies and it is an insight that we can valuably build into our understanding and development of the modern enforcement landscape. The clarity that Hohfeld offers about enforcement possibilities is simultaneously an invitation to rationality and innovation.

[68] J Feinberg, 'The Nature and Value of Rights' in J Feinberg, *Rights, Justice, and the Bounds of Liberty: Essays in Social Philosophy* (Princeton University Press 1980) 143, 151, 156–57; J Feinberg, 'Duties, Rights and Claims' in Feinberg, ibid, 130, 141–42 (the ability to claim and the liberty to waive one's rights elicits respect, self-respect and magnanimity and explains the value of those rights).

[69] A Ripstein, *Private Wrongs* (Harvard University Press 2016) 12. See similarly H Steiner, 'Working Rights' in M Kramer, N Simmonds, and H Steiner (eds), *A Debate Over Rights* (OUP 1998) 233, 239–47 (as a will theorist, rights of action appear for Steiner to be constitutive of primary rights).

[70] Zipursky's understanding of the justification for rights of action is complex but appears to be distinct from that of both instrumentalists and corrective justice theorists. In answer to critics, he has recently sought to cast off the implication that such rights are justified (or required) politically as a trade-off for the confiscation by the State of private liberties of reprisal or revenge. Instead, he suggests a 'constructive' social justification for such rights, according to which they give expression to our social understanding of what it means to have primary relational duties to others. See Zipursky, 'Substantive Standing' (n 1) 310–12, 326, 328–29 and Chapter 8 below.

[71] Ripstein (n 69) 10–12 and 271–72. This is because the justifications for primary rights and enforcement powers are one and the same and the bond should not be broken for purely pragmatic reasons. For further discussion, see Chapter 8.

3.6 Summation

The most important point to take forward from this chapter is that rights of action in modern public and private law are not one, single right but aggregates of Hohfeldian liberties and powers that are also accompanied by a variable group of legal claim rights serving to reinforce them. At root, they constitute important liberties to enliven the public powers and duties of courts to see that justice is done, and to subject defendants to those judicial powers.[72] They are in this way a very important source of autonomy for individuals who exercise them and an essential feature of the efficacy and legitimacy of any system of law. At the same time, however, their potentially powerful effects upon the interests of other parties, both private and public, means that their exercise is necessarily channelled and constrained by precautionary devices in the form of preconditions, duties, and liabilities, which distribute power in respect of their use in different ways as between public and private law and public and private agents. This creates an important jural network of cross-checks and balances upon their abuse, or neglect. Those designing this network should, I have suggested, lean strongly away from mechanisms of prior executive restraint upon private rights of action, especially (but not only) where the duties being enforced are state duties.

Finally, I have suggested that whilst rights of action are clearly of great normative importance in making the possession of primary rights meaningful and in enabling right-holders to enforce their rights, there is no analytical reason why the holder of a primary right should *always* hold the power to enforce it, or indeed why the holder of that right should be the *only one* to be accorded that power. This means that in both public and private law, it cannot be taken for granted that only those holding the primary claim right should be accorded rights of action when it is violated, nor indeed that they should universally be granted that right of action. These conclusions are born out in large measure by the experience of legal history and early law enforcement systems, which form the subject of the next chapter. They will also blossom into practical illustration as we dive into the substantive modern examples set out in Chapters 5 to 9.

[72] The High Court of Australia appears recently to have come very close to endorsing this this position in explaining the concept of standing in public law, accepting that standing may be regarded as empowering courts to hear claim by giving them jurisdiction, empowering plaintiffs to invoke that jurisdiction and providing plaintiffs with a 'liberty' of access to the court: *Forestry Corporation of New South Wales v South East Forest Rescue Inc* [2025] HCA 15 [9] (Gageler CJ, Edelman, Steward, Jagot, and Beech-Jones JJ).

4
Primordia

'Some things that today are seen as anomalies have roots that go deep, too deep for them to be easily uprooted.'[1]

Having spent time in the last chapter examining the legal anatomy of enforcement rights from a particular analytical perspective, this chapter takes a step back into the past. In doing so, it peels away the paradigms that are now second nature to us in the twenty-first century and examines those that prevailed in earlier legal systems. The point of this exercise is both to provide historical context and to highlight some constant themes and patterns that recur through the time frames, and which therefore connect importantly to modern enforcement debates.

4.1 Preview

Necessarily, the historical exercise in a work of this sort is limited. I only look, in rudimentary detail, at enforcement patterns in Roman law and the law of medieval England. Even then, I shall examine only patterns in respect of what we now know as crimes and torts. This short treatment will nonetheless suffice to illustrate the far greater role that private citizens used to play in *all* law enforcement. It will also show that the distinctions that we now make between public and private law (taxonomically, functionally, and procedurally) were far more fluid in antiquity than in the current day. Private plaintiffs regularly sued for wrongs that we would nowadays consider to be crimes against the State, and they were allowed to keep the relevant penalties, as well as to receive compensation for their own injury. Conversely, some public enforcement actions brought in respect of public crimes resulted in reparative payments to victims. In this primordial state, public and private law and public and private interests (and ends) existed as an undifferentiated mass, enforced and protected predominately, although not exclusively, at the initiative of private parties. The disaggregation of public law and public interests from private law and private interests, and their respective assignment to separate public

[1] *Uren v John Fairfax & Sons Pty Ltd* (1966) 117 CLR 118 (HCA) 149-50 (Windeyer J).

Enforcement Rights in Public and Private Law. Kit Barker, Oxford University Press. © Kit Barker 2026.
DOI: 10.1093/9780191955006.003.0006

and private enforcement processes was a gradual, non-linear process. This process of disaggregation is still incomplete, and the question this raises is whether the remaining exceptions to the predominant law enforcement paradigm that we encounter today are effectively anomalies awaiting final eradication, or legitimate, rational exceptions to the general rules of the law enforcement game.

4.2 Phases of Enforcement Evolution

Generally speaking, history chronicles four, distinct phases in the development of enforcement processes in respect of wrongs. In the first phase, the wrong is sanctioned and redressed through acts of private accounting, retaliation, or vengeance exacted upon the wrongdoer by victims of the wrong, their families, and peer groups. This is the age of self-help, feud, and private emendation,[2] when the State (if it exists at all) exercises no jurisdiction of its own over the events in question, or their consequences for an offender or his victim. The retaliation responds to an injury to a victim's private interests, but the private enforcer can also be seen to be acting in protection of public interests, in so far as the community is concerned by the wrong and supports the action taken against the wrongdoer. Colourful examples appear throughout E Adamson Hoebel's fascinating comparative study of what he refers to as 'primitive' legal systems.[3] The Eskimo way of handling recidivist homicide, he informs us, is for the killer to be despatched by a public-spirited private individual after the latter has consulted with, and obtained the consent of all adult members of the community.[4] Private practices of blood feud were especially unswerving in Iceland, it seems, right up to the time of the Norman Conquest, with attempts at private composition or arbitration regularly coming to nought.[5]

The second phase is characterized by the intervention of the nascent State to regulate and limit the consequences that private parties are permitted to bring to bear upon wrongdoers, curbing retaliatory excess, regulating the terms of private emendation, and preventing social violence. The distinction between Phase 1 and

[2] See generally W Miller, *Bloodtaking and Peacemaking: Feud, Law, and Society in Saga Iceland* (University of Chicago Press 1990) esp Chs 7, 8; *An Eye for an Eye* (CUP 2005); P Hyams, *Rancor and Reconciliation in Medieval England* (Cornell University Press 2003); R Fletcher, *Bloodfeud Murder and Revenge in Anglo-Saxon England* (OUP 2003); W Miller, S Throop and P Hyams (eds), *Vengeance in the Middle Ages* (Ashgate 2010).

[3] EA Hoebel, *The Law of Primitive Man A Study in Comparative Legal Dynamics* (Harvard University Press 1967). Note that Hoebel would say that this phase of private initiative is still an example of a legal system at work—just one without the modern conception of the State—the community acts as the 'court'. He also insists that, in any primitive society, any private party prosecuting a private injury in this way is 'implicitly' a public official because the support of the community for his action makes him a representative of that community: ibid 27.

[4] ibid 25–26.

[5] F Pollock and FW Maitland, *The History of English Law Before the Time of Edward 1* (2nd edn, CUP 1898) 47.

Phase 2 is not defined by the presence of a restraining influence, because even in early societies, private retaliation was constrained by important and sometimes quite complex social norms. These are present in the Eskimo example provided by Hoebel and by the well-known biblical exhortation to take no more than 'an eye for an eye'.[6] What characterizes the transition to Phase 2 is instead the fact that 'the State' (usually a king, initially) gets involved for the first time in restraining acts of personal accounting, as in the Hammurabi Code of early Babylonian times.[7] It is the stage at which public power begins to wax, the liberty of private avengers is officially curbed, and private feud is put into 'legal harness'.[8]

In the third phase, the developing State typically goes a step further, removing the liberty of private parties and their kin to act directly against their offenders altogether and substituting rights of action that enable them to initiate a legal process instead. This is a critical move, marked by the development of a system of public courts and the interposition of public authority between citizens, acting as an impartial agent of both retributive and corrective justice. Hoebel suggests that it is here that we leave 'primitive' society behind and transition into the modern legal realm. The key difference, he suggested in 1967, is that in 'primitive' societies, private enforcers have multitital, Hohfeldian liberties and immunities to act against wrongdoers themselves, whereas in more complex legal systems, these are removed by a central authority and replaced by claim rights (which he called 'demand-rights') that individuals have against courts and public law enforcement agents that those agents dispense the justice that is required.[9]

In Phase 4, a separate, public enforcement system is developed in which State prosecutors and agencies are given rights of action in respect of offences that are perceived to be matters of State concern. This final phase is marked by the development of significant public enforcement machinery, supplementing and/or displacing private rights of action in respect of what are understood to be public wrongs. Private parties are left to control legal actions in respect of their own interests and infringements of their own private rights. Public interests and public wrongs are prosecuted by the community through State actors and gradually

[6] Exodus 21:23–25; Leviticus 24:19–21. In early manifestations, norms demanded a higher ratio of penalty to offence than one of mere equality, but the ratio moderated over time.

[7] Code of Hammurabi (*c* 1772 BC) (trans LW King) (Avalon Project, Yale Law School). For an excellent account of the measures under both this and the later Hittite Code (*c* 1650–1500 BC), see HF Jolowicz, 'The Assessment of Penalties in Primitive Law' in HF Jolowicz, *Cambridge Legal Essays Written in Honour of and Presented to Doctor Bond, Professor Buckland and Professor Kenny* (Heffer & Sons Ltd 1926) 203.

[8] Pollock and Maitland (n 5) 32.

[9] Hoebel (n 3) 50: 'The outstanding difference, then, is this: in our [modern] system, a failure to meet a demand-right by one party engenders a series of further demand-rights by the aggrieved on the courts and law-enforcing agents that they compel performance, exact damages or impose penalties; in primitive systems . . . a failure to meet a demand-right by one party engenders a privilege-right in the aggrieved party and his kinsmen to compel performance, exact damages, or impose penalties, in a regularized manner.' See also 329.

removed from private control. The motivations for the assumption of public control over public wrongs is often ideological—for example, the political sense that such wrongs are the rightful domain of the State alone, as representative of the common good. But they can also be pragmatic, such as the desire to avoid private abuses, or even simply to garner more lucre to State coffers. It has hence been said that the expansion of the criminal laws of the Ashanti Kingdom in Western Africa by the King and his chieftains was so cynically encouraged for the latter purpose that justice 'became a royal prostitute'.[10] Similarly, whilst the primary motivation of the centralizing reforms of Henry II, to which we shall come, appears to have been to restore order after the English Civil War of 1139–1149, Professor Baker is unable to resist the wry observation that they probably also bore 'golden fruit' for the king in terms of fines and property forfeitures.[11] The final shift toward this model of State control is hence not just a matter of political morality, but also, frankly, a matter of raw financial interest.

Historians, anthropologists, and sociologists would be most surprised if I were to suggest that these phases of development occurred in a strict linear progression, or in the same way in different societies. I make no such claim. It is clear, for example, that in both English law[12] and the Roman law of the Republic, there were examples of the public prosecution of some crimes (that is, Phase 4), at the same time as private individuals continued to make use of self-help (Phases 1 and 2) and took the prosecutorial initiative in legal actions in respect of others (Phase 3). Recourse to systems of self-help remains a feature of even modern societies in which state enforcement systems are fully established,[13] and its permissibility in a variety of different instances in private law was noted in modern times by Blackstone.[14] Social and legal systems rarely evolve in a linear way, any more than biological ones. The main point is nonetheless that a systematic public enforcement apparatus tends, for practical reasons as much as any other, to evolve later in the day and that, up until this point, private actors in practice remain the primary enforcers of both public and private laws. Likewise, it should not be thought that all systems progress through all four stages, or all stages completely, or that there cannot be a fifth or sixth developmental phase that again reconfigures the respective roles of public and private agents within the system. We will see in Chapters 6 and 7 that the growth of the State's regulatory responsibilities and a proportional decline in

[10] ibid 233.

[11] JH Baker, *An Introduction to English Legal History* (5th edn, OUP 2019) 18.

[12] For a helpful summative account of the modern histories of the medieval English law which reject evolutionary linearity, see J Taliadoros, 'The Roots of Punitive Damages at Common Law: A Longer History' (2016) 64 Cleveland State Law Rev 251, 289–95.

[13] In the criminal context, see L Buckle and S Thomas-Buckle, 'Doing unto Others: Disputes and Dispute Processing in an Urban American Neighborhood' in R Tomasic and M Feeley (eds), *Neighbourhood Justice: An Assessment of an Emerging Idea* (Longman 1982) 78.

[14] William Blackstone, *Commentaries on the Laws of England* (Robert Bell 1773) Book 3, Ch 1. For a contemporary Australian account, see K Barnett and S Harder, *Remedies in Australian Private Law* (3rd edn, CUP 2024) Ch 14.

the resources available to support public enforcement has in recent years led to a reversion in some instances to former patterns of private initiative, or to systems in which public and private enforcement processes are combined. These four phases nonetheless capture in very broad outline, I suggest, the development of enforcement practices in early legal systems such as that of Rome and medieval England, and probably many others too.

4.3 Rome

A. Public and Private Law in Rome

Before we can understand the Roman law enforcement process, we must first note the way in which the Romans understood the distinction between what we now call public and private law, and between crime and tort in particular. The way they conceived of the former distinction will have a familiar feel to modern thinkers and followers of Blackstone, but it is not the same as the one that I proffered in Chapter 2 of this book. Ulpian defined public law (*ius publicum*) as the law concerning the State of the Roman Commonwealth ('*quod ad statum rei romanae spectat*') which is 'useful to the public' ('*publice utilia*'), and private law (*ius privatum*) as that which concerns the interests of private individuals and which is of benefit to them.[15] This approach defines public law as the law which protects public interests and private law as that which protects private ones, whereas my own taxonomic distinction is based solely on whether the State (or only private individuals) is (are) party to the legal relationship created by the relevant law, thereby leaving open the logical possibility that both public and private laws could be used to protect both public and private interests. In any event, the passage from Ulpian attests to the fact that the distinction between public and private interests was well known and very important to the Romans, as indeed it was to the ancient Greeks and many other early societies. In a different part of the world, Hoebel tells us that it was familiar to the Ashanti tribe of Western Africa well before 1875, criminal acts being those that were 'hated by the tribe' because they were prejudicial to its whole well-being, and other matters being regarded simply as personal business suitable for individual mediation and settlement.[16]

When it comes to the modern distinction we now draw between crime and tort, the position in Roman law is more complicated, because there was no exact

[15] D.1.1.4 '*Huius studii duae sunt positiones, publicum et privatum. Publicum ius est quod ad statum rei romanae spectat, privatum quod ad singulorum utilitatem: sunt enim quaedam publice utilia, quaedam privatim.*' The English translation in this instance is drawn from AJB Sirks, 'Public Law' in D Johnston (ed), *The Cambridge Companion to Roman Law* (CUP 2015) Ch 16, 332.

[16] Hoebel (n 3) 232.

equivalent.[17] Crimes (*crimena*) were generally considered wrongs concerning the public, and delicts (*delicta*) as private wrongs. In this respect, the Romans were on much the same page as Blackstone. *Crimena* were thus part of the *ius publicum* and included acts such as treason, sedition, electoral corruption, forgery, and homicide. The penalties in such cases were often physical and severe but could also entail confiscation of property to the State. Delicts, by contrast, were part of the *ius privatum*, as are most torts[18] in our modern law. But the category of delicts itself covered many wrongs that we today would consider to be crimes—theft (*furtum*), robbery (*rapina*), assault (a form of *injuria*), and the later Praetorian delict of fraud (*dolus*) being notable examples. As is evident from the remnants of what is commonly labelled the eighth of the twelve Tables[19] (*c* 455 BC), delictal actions often resulted not simply in the payment of compensation for an affected individual's loss,[20] as our modern torts do, but also the payment to him of a fine—either set at a fixed sum,[21] or calculated as two,[22] three,[23] or even (later) four times[24] the damage suffered. In the case of theft, these delictal penalties were in addition to the separate private action that an owner might have for the recovery of the goods themselves (*vindicatio*) or their value (*condictio*).[25] Delicts could also lead to much more serious consequences for a wrongdoer, such as scourging,[26] slavery,[27] outlawing, or even, in some extreme cases, death.[28] Of the thirty or so 'private' delicts that were

[17] On the complex relationship between delict and crime in the Roman system, see B Nicholas, *An Introduction to Roman Law* (rev'd edn, OUP 2008) 207–10; C Cascione, 'Roman Delicts and Criminal Law' in T McQuinn (ed), *Obligations in Roman Law: Past Present and Future* (University of Michigan Press 2013) 267; M Frydek, 'Terminology of Roman Criminal Law—Crimen et Delictum' (2010) 1 Journal on European History of Law 69; A Riggsby, 'Public and Private Criminal Law' in P du Plessis, C Ando, and K Tuori (eds), *The Oxford Handbook of Roman Law and Society* (OUP 2016) 310. Although the terms are normally opposed, Riggsby points out that the term '*crimena*' is also sometimes used in the Digest to refer more generically to 'bad behaviour', so as to include *delicta*: ibid 314.

[18] Exceptions, on my definitions, are the torts of misfeasance in public office and public nuisance: see Chapters 6 and 7.

[19] A Johnson, P Coleman-Norton, and F Bourne, *Ancient Roman Statutes: A Translation with Introduction, Commentary, Glossary, and Index. The Corpus of Roman Law*, Vol 2 (University of Texas Press 1961) 11–12.

[20] Most examples in Table 8 concern accidental harm: 8.5 (accidental damage to property- repair); 8.6 (damage caused by a quadruped-repair or forfeiture of the animal); 8.10 (accidental burning of a house or stack of corn—damages).

[21] Table 8.3 (300 asses for breaking the bone or tooth of a free man); 8.4 (25 asses for insult—which included the idea of minor injury to the person).

[22] Table 8.16 (non-manifest theft); 8.19 (breach of trust in respect of a deposit); 8.20 (acquisition of a ward's property by a guardian).

[23] Table 8.15 (thief discovered in possession of stolen property, or hiding the property in a third party's house).

[24] D 4.1.5 (manifest theft). The change came about by later Praetorian edict, in substitution for the harsher penalty of flogging and slavery under the twelve Tables: AJB Sirks, 'Delicts' Ch 13 in Johnston (ed) (n 15) 248; P Birks and E Descheemaeker, *The Roman Law of Obligations* (OUP 2014) 182–83.

[25] D 4.1.19; Nicholas (n 17) 208, 210.

[26] Table 8.14 (manifest theft).

[27] Table 8.14 (free men guilty of manifest theft made bondsmen to the victim, in addition to being scourged).

[28] Table 8.1b (libels or insulting songs); 8.9 (nocturnal destruction of crops by an adult); 8.10 (intentional burning of a house or stack of grain); 8.12 (nocturnal theft); 8.23 (speaking false witness).

in existence at the time of the Principate, we are reliably informed that compensation was payable in respect of only five, with fines applicable to the rest.[29]

The 'private' law of delicts thus always had a public, 'punitive character'[30] which our modern torts generally lack. This was evident not just in the penalties imposed but also in the fact that the action lay against multiple wrongdoers responsible for the same wrong, each being obliged to pay the full penalty amount—something that would make no sense if the object of the action were simply to redress damage to private interests.[31] In the time of the Empire, many delicts came also to be crimes—the rise of public disorder at the end of the Republican period seeing a marked shift toward the development of the criminal law and the use of mechanisms of inquisitorial prosecution to which we refer further below. The private delict of theft was hence largely overtaken by the equivalent public crime by the time Ulpian was writing at the end of the second century AD,[32] not least because the system of monetary penalties available in delict proved pretty useless against impecunious thieves.[33] Indeed, one must seriously doubt whether the delict of theft was ever of much use to victims in protecting their private property interests. In late antiquity and Justinian's times, private delictal actions were still very much in evidence and the latter's Digest (551 AD) itself explicitly points to their functions as being sometimes purely penal and sometimes mixing punishment and private reparation,[34] but the expansion of the criminal law had by this time resulted in the punitive role of the delictal action shrinking. Growth in the arm of the public law and a new procedure for its enforcement (*cognitio*)[35] hence led to a gradual shift in the functions of the law of delict, with it tending to focus more on the protection of private interests.

B. Enforcement Process

What, then, of enforcement process? Of the early, regal years (753–509 BC) we know very little, since written records only really begin in the middle of the fifth century BC. Commentators credibly attest to an initial phase of private revenge and composition in respect of what we now regard as both public and private wrongs (Phase 1), as in other early societies.[36] It is also clear that there were concerted

29 Sirks, 'Delicts' (n 24) 247.
30 Nicholas (n 17) 208.
31 ibid 210.
32 D 47.2.93.
33 Sir James Stephen, *A History of the Criminal Law of England* Vol I (Macmillan and Co 1883) 29–30. For this reason, it has been suggested that victims often simply did not bother to bring the action: F de Zuleta, *The Institutes of Gaius*, Vol 2 (Clarendon Press 1953) 199.
34 D 4.6.16.
35 See Section 4.3B(ii).
36 A Lintott, 'Crime and Punishment' in Johnston (ed) (n 15) 301, 303; R Bauman, *Crime and Punishment in Ancient Rome* (Routledge 1996) 1; H Wolff, *Roman Law An Historical Introduction* (University of Oklahoma Press 1976) 53.

attempts during the Republic in the Twelve Tables (*c* 455 BC) to limit private retribution through the introduction of a *lex talionis* (Phase 2). This restricted the available sanction in some cases of physical injury in accordance with the 'eye for an eye' philosophy of the Old Testament and earlier Babylonian traditions,[37] and fixed composition amounts in others.[38] Similar restrictions on the use of self-help were evident in both Republican and later Augustan laws (the *Lex Iulia de Adulteriis*) which limited the power of fathers and husbands to exact revenge upon their wives, daughters, and their respective lovers.[39] Self-help by victims and the populace may have diminished as a mechanism of enforcement by the middle of the Republic, but vestiges clearly remained in the Empire—most visibly in the form of the occasional popular lynching.[40]

Once we get past the raw dynamics of Phases 1 and 2 and start to reach the phase in which Roman laws were enforced through more developed legal processes, enforcement paths split. Below, I detail the process in respect of *delicta* and *crimena* in turn. In almost all instances, private parties took the initiative in the sense of being the first source of information or complaint, but in a high proportion of what we would now think of as criminal cases they also held rights of action and termination in respect of the proceeding in the sense explained in Chapter 2. Moreover, although there was, toward the end, greater movement toward state control of the prosecution process in respect of more crimes, the progression was far from being linear, or complete, as I suggested above tends to be the case.

(i) *Delicta*

Delictal actions, which formed the bulk of what we would now think of as ordinary criminal actions, were always initiated and 'prosecuted' by private parties.[41] Although not a great deal is known of the precise process, it seems that the responsibility for issuing a summons ('*in ius vocatio*') to a wrongdoer was entirely that of the private plaintiff and that such summonses were, in the early years of the Republic, only weakly supported by the State. It was therefore down to the plaintiff physically to bring the wrongdoer before a magistrate and he enjoyed a bare liberty as against others to do so.[42] Later Praetorian measures backed the liberty with a duty on the part of the wrongdoer to appear, or provide someone else to stand in

[37] For example Table 8.2 (breaking of another's limb).

[38] For example Table 8.3 (breaking a free man's bone—300 asses); 8.4 (causing outrage to another—25 asses).

[39] Lintott (n 36) 317.

[40] W Nippel, *Public Order in Ancient Rome* (CUP 1995) 35 (manifest theft), 42–46 (lynching as popular justice).

[41] For an overview of the civil process and references to the very extensive secondary literature, see E Metzger, 'An Outline of Roman Civil Procedure' (2013) 9 Roman Legal Tradition 1; *Litigation in Roman Law* (OUP 2005) Ch 1. See also, on the strange, penal category of 'quasi-delicts' that were also enforced privately through the '*actio popularis*' and which allowed the private enforcer to keep the relevant penalty, Chapter 7 Section 7.2A.

[42] Metzger (n 41) 19.

his or her place (a '*vindex*'), but the penal action for the enforcement of this duty also had to be prosecuted by the plaintiff in order for it to be effective.[43] The entire weight of responsibility for gathering and presenting evidence and prosecuting a case therefore lay, as it does today in respect of private law wrongs, with the private actor. Furthermore, despite the fact that these actions had a significant punitive component and therefore overtly served the protection of public as well as private interests, private litigants always had the power to terminate the suit by compromise. The long list of more savage punishments for delict that existed at the time of the Twelve Tables could thus be avoided if the offender had the means and the nous to buy his victim off. To the extent that delictal actions were concerned with public interests, they therefore always questionably allowed the public interest aspect of the action to be captured by the private prosecutor for his own benefit—either by keeping the relevant penalty (when it should rightly inure to the benefit of the public as a whole), or by compromising the public ends of the action in exchange for a cash settlement with the offender. As we shall see in Chapters 7 and 8, the same hazards and asymmetries remain a focus of concern in modern debates about private prosecutions in the criminal law and exemplary damages in the modern law of torts. The puzzle of how to achieve the benefits of public interest deterrence through private actions without the system simultaneously becoming a means for the personal enrichment of private prosecutors continues to trouble us today, although there are some interesting and inventive solutions now on the table involving the splitting of proceeds between private prosecutors and the State that may offer promise in particular instances. We explore these further at the end of Chapter 8.

(ii) *Crimena*

By contrast, crimes in the technical Roman sense were prosecuted in several different ways. Rome, it is critical to remember, never had a professional public prosecution service or civil police force, although the army certainly played an important role in keeping the public peace. Legal actions would therefore almost invariably rely upon a private individual's initiative for their genesis in so far as it was up to citizens to detect and report crime. But the role of private actors in the ensuing proceeding then varied significantly according to the mode of trial. In some instances, they enjoyed little more than a liberty to make the initial accusation to an investigator. In others, however, they had fuller prosecutorial control, holding both rights of action and termination in respect of the proceeding.

[43] ibid 22. Later still, as the course of proceedings shifted from the formulary to the cognitio procedure in the early empire, magistrates themselves issued summonses by way of letters (*litterae*) or public notice (*edictum*) and a special contempt proceeding (*contumacia*) was developed to punish defendants for non-appearance: ibid 27–28. On private prosecution and enforcement more generally, see D Friedman, 'Private Prosecution and Enforcement in Roman Law' Ch 21 in G Dari-Mattiacci and D Kehoe (eds) *Roman Law and Economics: Volume II Exchange, Ownership, and Disputes* (OUP 2020).

Sadly, much less is known of Roman criminal law and process than of its civil law, since the field only attracted the attention of jurists in the first two centuries of the Empire.[44] Even less is known of public criminal prosecutions than private ones. Stephen suggests that, although the former were probably the 'ordinary course' by the time of the Empire, they attracted little attention by comparison to Cicero's accounts of the private trials of the later republic, and 'left no monuments behind'.[45] There is therefore inevitably some speculation involved in that which follows. Nonetheless, the work of modern commentators[46] has enabled us to glean a reasonably clear picture of the basic features of the enforcement process in respect of public *crimena*.

Three main criminal law enforcement systems were in place at the time of the Republic. In the first, there was no trial at all, just executive punishment, with State officials imposing direct penalties on offenders. Depending on their level of seniority, magistrates could hence use powers of *imperium* or *coercitio* to exact sanctions for a wide variety of reported offences without recourse to a trial in the early years.[47] This caused much public disquiet and, in the wake of a period of significant class unrest that need not detain us here, prompted the introduction of a system of appeals (*provocatio*).[48] Public censors also had what will seem to us in the modern day to be highly controversial powers to punish moral wrongdoing either on the accusation of a private party, or on their own initiative, up until the latter part of the first century BC, although these powers were exercised only infrequently, generally only directed at the political classes, and led to lesser types of penalty.[49]

The second mode—trial by the people (*iudicium populi*) was at its peak up until around the second century BC.[50] To accuse (*accusare*) and investigate (*anquirere*) in this mode of trial were the jobs of a public magistrate (normally but not always a tribune, or aedile) who would issue the summons, present the accused, and propose a discretionary penalty for the crime that would then be voted upon by one of

[44] Writers included Gaius Aetius Capito, *On Public Trials* (*De Iudiciis Publicis*) (written in the early Principate) and later works toward the end of the second century on penalties (*De Poenis*) by Saturninus, Modestinus, and Paul, and public criminal inquires (*De Cognitionibus*) by Callistratus. See Lintott (n 36) 302 and, for the full story, Bauman (n 36) Ch 10.

[45] J Stephen (n 33) 43.

[46] See generally J Stephen (n 33) Ch 2; H Jolowicz and B Nicholas, *A Historical Introduction to the Study of Roman Law* (3rd edn, CUP 1972) Ch 18; AHM Jones, *The Criminal Courts of the Roman Republic and Principate* (Blackwell 1972); OF Robinson, *The Criminal Law of Ancient Rome* (John Hopkins University Press 1995) Ch 1; A Riggsby, *Roman Law and the Legal World of the Romans* (CUP 2012) Ch 19; Lintott (n 36); Nippel (n 40); Bauman (n 36) esp Chs 2, 3, 5.

[47] Nippel (n 40) 5–12.

[48] The first source of the *provocatio* seems to have been the Lex Valeria of 509 BC: Jolowicz and Nicholas (n 46) 305–06. There is however some uncertainty: Lintott (n 36) 305.

[49] Nippel (n 40) 8–9; Cascione (n 17) 284–85. Some of the immoralities tackled clearly overlapped with our modern conceptions of crime including, for example, cases of theft, perjury, abuse of public duties, bearing false witness, avoiding conscription, and overdoing the exercise of the powers of the paterfamilias.

[50] Bauman (n 36) 4 and see generally Ch 2. The extent to which it was linked the development of *provocatio* is hotly contested (ibid 7–8) but need not trouble us here.

the popular assemblies (*comitia*). Almost all trials prosecuted by tribunes related to political offences committed by public officials accused of breaching their public duties,[51] but the aediles sometimes also pursued cases involving more ordinary offences, such as adultery and breaches of rules relating to moneylending.[52] The system fizzled out in the first century BC,[53] largely, one suspects, because it was cumbersome and time-consuming, but also perhaps because its dependence on the popular vote made it unappealing to the ruling class. Although a private party clearly made the initial accusation to the relevant magistrate, he seems to have had no formal control over the proceeding itself, which adopted an inquisitorial style, and the State—through the magistrate—had the power to terminate the prosecution at any stage.[54] So far, then, prosecutorial 'rights of action' in respect of *crimena*, as we have conceptualized them, lay with public magistrates, at the information of private parties. But this picture is about to change.

The third mode—trial by jury (*iudicium publicum*) came into being as a consequence of the establishment of a series of permanent courts (*quaestones perpetuae*) to deal with particular crimes under statute, such as treason, adultery, homicide, parricide, forgery, and electoral corruption.[55] The first example was a court set up in 149 BC to deal with the consequences of official extortion by Roman officials in the new provinces.[56] It rode on the back of an earlier cluster of ad hoc, special commissions that had been introduced to supplement and sidestep the cumbersome *iudicium populi* from the second century BC onwards.[57] The system was consolidated and remodelled during the dictatorship of Sulla (82–81 BC) and then survived patchily until the 220s AD.[58] Its key feature from our point of view is that prosecution was an entirely private process, albeit one in which the State sometimes granted assistance to the prosecutor (in the form of a patronus[59] to help with case organization) and in which it added its weight by compelling witnesses.[60] By 103 BC, it was not necessary for the prosecutor to be a victim of the crime, or to have

[51] Jones (n 46) 5–6 cites only two cases in the life of Cicero involving what might be called 'ordinary crimes'—one involving murder and the other adultery.

[52] ibid 15–16.

[53] ibid 16. Robinson (n 46) 2 speculates that the final example was probably the trial of Milo by Clodius in 56 BC.

[54] Jones (n 46) 13.

[55] For a list of the various statutes, see J Stephen (n 33) 13–24; Bauman (n 36) 18. See also generally Bauman (n 36) Ch 3.

[56] The Lex Calpurnia de Repetundis (149 BC); Bauman (n 36) 17; Jones (n 46) 48.

[57] These special commissions were similar in many ways to the later forms of public prosecution under the cognitio procedure introduced in the Principate. They were established either by statute or by decrees of the Senate. The role of private parties was confined to making complaint and penalties were payable to the State. An example is the commission of 186 BC into Bacchanalian crimes, which resulted in many thousands of prosecutions: Lintott (n 36) 307.

[58] Bauman (n 36) 39. Robinson (n 46) 7 speculates that many of the courts dealing with political offences probably disappeared early on in the Principate, and that it was the courts dealing with more ordinary criminal offences like adultery, murder, and forgery that survived longer.

[59] Lintott (n 36) 309.

[60] Jones (n 46) 46; Robinson (n 46) 5.

suffered any harm to his private interests—any male citizen of good repute could raise the prosecution,[61] subject to obtaining the consent of the relevant magistrate (praetor).[62] In some instances (cases of official extortion being notorious in this regard), significant public incentives to private prosecution were offered.[63] Women and minors might prosecute if their personal interests were affected, but not otherwise. Certain groups were barred—for example, convicts, false accusers, gladiators, and actors (who had a curiously bad rap in Rome, perhaps because they tended to be outspoken).[64] The fact that the action was in the public interest made it important that there be a state screening process to ensure the legitimacy of the prosecuting party's qualifications and motives. Since only one prosecutor was allowed, in cases in which more than one person stepped up to the plate, a hearing (*divinatio*) was held to determine who should be allowed to proceed.[65] In such instances, actual victims were often preferred, but without detraction from the general principle that anyone might assume the role.[66]

Disincentives to overzealous or corrupt private enforcement practices in the context of this procedure took the form of harsh penalties for false accusation, such as *infamia* (which involved the stripping of a host of civil and legal rights),[67] branding on the forehead for calumny,[68] and liability to retaliation in the event that the prosecution failed, although it has been suggested that the last of these penalties was probably commuted during the Empire to a discretionary monetary fine, since it would otherwise have deterred private prosecutions altogether.[69] Prosecutors were also 'bound over to prosecute' once they had made their accusation and could be penalized if they subsequently failed to appear, as well as being required to pay an accused's costs and travel expenses.[70] Attempts were therefore made to prevent the concoction of private prosecutions that could lead to the damnation of the innocent, on the one hand, or collusions between private prosecutors and offenders designed to protect the guilty and occlude the veins of public justice, on the other. There is no evidence as to how successful these measures were, but they are important early testaments to the hazards of private prosecution that have recently made headlines in England and which we address later in the book.[71] The

[61] Bauman (n 36) 18.

[62] J Stephen (n 33) 45; Robinson (n 46) 4. On the procedure for obtaining permission (*postulatio*) see Jones (n 46) 63.

[63] See further text to nn 76, 77 below.

[64] Jones (n 46) 61–62.

[65] Robinson (n 46) 5; Jones (n 46) 117. In practice, others could (and frequently were) added as supporting speakers (*subscriptiones*), but only one person could make the formal accusation and control the trial: Jones (n 46) 63.

[66] Jones (n 46) 47.

[67] A Greenidge, *Infamia Its Place in Roman Public and Private Law* (Kessinger Publishing 2005).

[68] Jolowicz and Nicholas (n 46) 318 (citing the Lex Remmia of not later than 80 BC).

[69] J Stephen (n 33) 45–46.

[70] ibid 46. See also Jones (n 46) 118. On the 'bond' of inscription, see Codex Theodosianus 9.1.11.

[71] See Chapter 7.

following passage from Jones attests to the wide range of motives that drove private criminal prosecutors:

> The motives of accusers were . . . various. In the courts of murder and forgery it was no doubt usually an injured party that who brought the accusation, and the same must also have been true for ambitus [electoral bribery] and sodalicia [electoral conspiracy] . . . Young men sought to make themselves a name in the political world by the successful prosecution of one of their elders. Political enemies tried to break each other's careers by securing their condemnation in the courts. There were also accusers whose motive was the reward offered by law for a condemnation . . . Accusers such as this were commonly called quadruplatores [informers for gain] and held in low esteem by politicians. Others again made accusations with the object of cutting out serious accusers and procuring an acquittal by deliberately bungling the case: the most famous instance is Caecilius, Verres' quaestor. Finally, there were doubtless some who acted out of genuine public spirit.[72]

As Jones hints, a notable feature of prosecutions before the extortion courts was that they could result both in compensation for harm to affected private interests (or restitution of monies or property extorted), and in statutory penalties payable to the private prosecutor—double damages under the *Lex Acilia* of 123–122 BC and possibly more (two and a half times damage) under the *Lex Cornelia* (81 BC).[73] This gave the system a 'curious blend of public and private legal procedure'[74]—the same sort of curiosity that we noted in the previous section in relation to private actions in delict. The action was initiated and prosecuted privately by way of indictment and denunciation (*nominis delatio*), but it gave rise to both punitive and compensatory measures. According to one account (which has admittedly been doubted),[75] the multiple damages penalties payable under the *Lex Acilia* did not inure entirely to the benefit of the private prosecutor but could be split with the State. Extortion courts were not the only ones before which the private prosecutor could keep the relevant penalty.[76] In addition, as the above extract from Jones indicates, a good number of the relevant statutes offered prosecutors rewards for their efforts in the form of citizenship, or exemptions from military service and other

72 Jones (n 46) 62.

73 M Alexander, 'Compensation in A Roman Criminal Law' (1984) 3 University of Illinois Law Review 521, 528. Alexander indicates at 523 that some of the earliest extortion statutes (of which there were seven in total) were designed primarily with restitution in mind, so that the protection of private interests was their dominant feature. See further AN Sherwin-White, 'The Lex Repetundarum and the Political Ideas of Gaius Gracchus' (1982) 72 Journal of Roman Studies 18.

74 Jones (n 46) 50.

75 Alexander (n 73) 535 doubts this view in the case of the Lex Acilia itself but cites other the criminal statutes (eg the Lex Municipii Tarentini (89–62 BC)) under which such a division did take place.

76 Lintott (n 36) 301, citing Sulla's statute on injuries (*de iniuriis*).

unpopular public duties.[77] In these incentives to private prosecution, we see precursors of some of the notorious English practices to which we refer in the next section, and of some contemporary private enforcement systems that exist in the United States, examined in Chapter 7.

A fourth and final mode of trial—the *cognitio extraordinaria*—was introduced by Augustus in the early days of the Principate, from 27 BC. This process eventually took over from the *quaestones perpetuae*[78] and had a much more public style. It continued the basic laws enforced by the permanent courts but allowed for their variation so as to create a more flexible system of discretionary penalties. It also permitted the investigation of matters which did not fall neatly within the rubric of the various permanent court statutes. Offences were investigated by the emperor himself, his delegates (prefects and other officials) acting with advisory panels, or by the senate acting through its consuls. The system of prefects' courts which formed the backbone of this new and ultimately dominant approach was still dependent on private parties to make denunciations, but the latter did not hold the same prosecutorial powers as they did before the *quaestones perpetuae*,[79] and the right to conduct and terminate proceedings lay with the investigating prefect.[80] In Nero's time, a private prosecutor was punished for initiating and then deliberately flunking a prosecution under the older jury trial system as a way of avoiding the offender being prosecuted under the new *cognitio* procedure,[81] which points to the tension between the old (private) and new (more public) enforcement processes and the priority increasingly accorded to the latter over the former. There is also some evidence during the Empire that minor crimes involving breaches of the peace were investigated by a lower magistrate (*eirenarcha*) (roughly comparable to a modern justice of the peace) who acted 'to some extent as a public prosecutor' in forwarding a report to the investigating judges (*praeses*) and who remained accountable to the latter for the propriety of the process used to obtain it.[82] This shift in the ethos of enforcement away from the use of private prosecutors to a public inquisitorial process, in which both the rights and the burdens of prosecution lay more squarely in the hands of public actors appears to have been clear by the time of the Dominate,

77 ibid 310; Alexander (n 73) 526.

78 Exactly when and how quickly is hard to establish and, although it seems likely that this had occurred by the end of the third century AD. Lintott (n 36) 322–23 and Jones (n 46) 96 both prefer to leave the exact timelines open. Bauman (n 36) 39 suggests that the 220s AD were the final point.

79 Lintott (n 36) 322 observes that for this reason the process of denunciation required less action and commitment than that of accusation before a permanent court and was likely to have been more attractive to those lacking suitable patrons.

80 Pliny hence apparently took the same approach to the control of the trial under the cognitio procedure, whether the case came to him by virtue of a denunciation or an accuser—in either case, he controlled the trial: Jones (n 46) 114.

81 Lintott (n 36) 322; Robinson (n 46) 96.

82 J Stephen (n 33) 44. The evidence stems from an account of Marcian of an edict of Antoninus Pius in the first century AD: D 48.3.6.

although Robinson suggests that even at this time, private victims of crime retained the important right of accusation.[83]

(iii) Observations

Drawing all of this together, there is much that proves informative. For a very long period of time from the early Republic all the way through until the second century AD and beyond, private individuals were the ones holding rights of action and termination in respect of a wide variety of wrongs that we, today, would classify as crimes, including some carrying capital penalties.[84] Vengeance was regarded as a perfectly legitimate motivation for such private action[85] and the participation of the victims of crime in the process leading to the punishment of their offenders as entirely uncontroversial. Private actions protected both private and public interests—in delict, the public interest component may have shrunk gradually as the criminal law grew, but it never completely disappeared. In the criminal law, which was in theory defined as public interest law, private individuals were empowered and harnessed to the public good in the absence of (or in substitution for unsatisfactory) public prosecutorial mechanisms, which only began to develop later in the day. They were strongly incentivized to act in the public interest in some instances, particularly against official corruption. The private prosecution system undoubtedly gave rise to some abuses, and measures were accordingly taken to try to snuff these out. Public, criminal laws could sometimes give rise to restitution and compensation for victims, as well as to penalties payable both to the State and to private prosecutors. And there were some interesting, reported examples of cases in which those financial penalties were split between private prosecutors and the State in a way that prefigures some of the modern solutions we shall encounter in respect of punitive damages later in this book.

Even beyond the payment of penalties to private prosecutors, reward mechanisms were quite commonly available in the Roman system for informers providing information in respect of the breach of a good range of criminal laws, both major and minor, for example: treason, official corruption, conspiracy, breach of marriage laws and rules concerning interference with public water supply, official misconduct in the distribution of grain, and the breach of regulations concerning building and the proper conduct of funerals.[86] Such rewards could be high—as much as 100,000 sesterces in two conspiracy cases documented by Livy.[87] The reasons for giving such rewards lay in a mix of political and public interest factors, but also sometimes stemmed from the raw financial interest of the State in collecting more penalties.[88] Some crimes were of such a secretive nature (conspiracy,

[83] Robinson (n 46) 13.
[84] Wolff (n 36) 53.
[85] M Cicero, *De Officiis* (trans W Miller) (Heinemann Ltd 1913) 2.50.
[86] Nippel (n 40) 19–21, 28.
[87] Livy 32:26.14, 39:19.4.
[88] Nippel (n 40) 21 (citing the Augustan marriage laws as a particularly notorious example).

for example) that inducements for the provision of private information were regarded as a natural course. The Roman system was therefore generally unabashed about using the energy and intelligence of private citizens by giving them active informational roles and responsibilities in respect of the enforcement of public laws, even when they were not accorded full prosecutorial rights of action as such. Whilst Tacitus therefore spoke of informers in the time of Tiberius in excoriating terms—as men contriving the destruction of themselves and others[89]—their risks were clearly regarded from time to time as being pragmatically outweighed by their public utility. From the risk point of view, the offering of limited financial rewards for information about crime is clearly also a much less dangerous game than handing over to private individuals the rights of action and the power of settlement.

4.4 Medieval England

A. Public and Private Law in England: A World of Undifferentiated Wrongs

It seems probable that the above system of thinking was known in Roman Britain (at least to Roman citizens) but, if this is so, the collapse of the Empire in the West in the fifth century AD took all traces of the learning with it.[90] The result is that the Roman distinctions between public and private law and between *crimen* and *delictum* that we examined above were almost completely lost (the word *crimen* often being used simply to denote 'sin') and—with some exceptions amongst learned ecclesiasts—really only reappeared in the revived academic law schools as they spread from Italy in the late eleventh century.[91] In the early days of English law, there was therefore no clear-cut scheme of crime and tort, or even *crimena* and *delicta* in the Roman sense, only an undifferentiated notion of 'wrongdoing,' 'offending', 'trespassing', or 'transgressing' that did not discriminate clearly between the public and private aspects of wrongdoing in the sense of wrongs to individuals and wrongs to the public as a whole.

This is not to say that the difference between a wrong to the community and a wrong to an individual in the Roman sense was not at some visceral or practical level understood. In Anglo-Saxon times, wrongs could result both in penalties payable to the king in his royal capacity (*wite*) and separate redress to victims and

[89] See WW Flint, 'The Delatores in the Reign of Tiberius, As Described by Tacitus' (1912) 8 The Classical Journal 37, 38.

[90] Baker, *An Introduction to English Legal History* (n 11) 4.

[91] P Hyams, 'Does it Matter When the English Began to Distinguish Between Crime and Tort?' Ch 6 in R Kaeuper (ed), *Violence in Medieval Society* (Boydell Press 2000) 108, 109–10 and 115. For the beginnings in Pavia and Bologna, see Pollock and Maitland (n 5) 21–22.

their kin (*wergeld* and *bot*),[92] as well as acts of private retaliation. The different destination of the payments a wrongdoer had to make in such cases must have signalled something to him and to others about who it was that he had wronged. The idea that one might wrong one's community would also have been clearly understood by subjects on account of the real threat of being 'outlawed' from it.[93] But the distinction between public and private wrongs had no formal manifestation as such in legal doctrine. Beyond acts of private retaliation, legal actions in respect of wrongs were largely initiated and prosecuted by private individuals or their peer groups in a way that conglomerated public and private ends—vengeance, punishment, deterrence, and corrective justice—in a singular process.

The modern categories of crime and tort were very slow to emerge in England. Paul Hyams suggests that Glanvill[94] (1187–1189) was 'first witness' to the common law's acceptance of the modern distinction in the late 1100s,[95] but the distinction which the author of that treatise himself drew between 'civil' and 'criminal' pleas bore little resemblance to modern categories, or to the Roman categories of *crimen* and *delictum*. His 'criminal' pleas comprised a fairly short list of major offences falling within the king's jurisdiction[96]—a subset of pleas of the Crown.[97] The taxonomic distinction between 'civil' and 'criminal' wrongs in Glanvill was hence drawn up using different criteria to those used by Ulpian—it depended on procedure and jurisdiction, not on the distinction between wronging individuals and wronging the public as a whole.

Historians differ in the extent to which they attribute the eventual development of the modern categories of crime and tort in English law to the earlier Roman learning.[98] They nonetheless all agree that the Assize of Clarendon in 1166 was a key catalyst for the process, marking as it did an important attempt by Henry II to assume greater royal control over the punishment of serious wrongs in a

[92] *Wergeld* was payable in cases of homicide, *Bot* for other forms of non-fatal personal injury and other personal harms, including harm to the King's private interests.

[93] Pollock and Maitland (n 5) 47.

[94] GDG Hall (ed), *The Treatise on the Laws and Customs of the Realm of England Commonly Known as Glanvill* (OUP 1965).

[95] Hyams, 'Does it Matter When the English Began to Distinguish Between Crime and Tort?' (n 91) 110.

[96] Treason, concealment of treasure, breach of the King's peace, homicide, arson, rape, forgery, and other crimes punishable by death. For an accessible, basic account of the scheme in Glanvill, see J Hudson, *The Oxford History of the Laws of England Vol II 871–1216* (OUP 2012) 710–16.

[97] This was itself a category comprising matters both civil and criminal (in the modern sense) of special interest to the king.

[98] C Donahue, 'The Emergence of the Crime Tort Distinction in England' in W Brown and P Górecki (eds), *Conflict in Medieval Europe: Changing Perspectives on Society and Culture* (Routledge 2003) in Ch 11 accords less significance to this than does Hyams, 'Does it Matter When the English Began to Distinguish Between Crime and Tort?' (n 91) and L Pike, *A History of Crime in England* (Smith Elder & Co 1873) 133. Hyams has since moderated his emphasis a little: Hyams, *Rancor and Reconciliation in Medieval England* (n 2) 221. On the historical development of the distinction (but eschewing any definitive response to the 'imponderable' question of when exactly it occurred) see further Taliadoros (n 12) 295–99.

time of social disarray, and laying the foundations of the modern system of trial by jury.[99] That move signalled—in a way that Anglo-Saxon kings had sometimes also done (by demanding *wite* for an offence) but in a rather more determined way—a range of especially serious wrongs that were thought to concern the King personally, which should be singled out for his own courts. Such wrongs were now seen to 'belong' to the early 'State', or as Bracton put it in the mid-1220s, to violate the 'King's peace' so as to concern the 'common welfare'.[100] Henry's reforms appear to have been largely unsuccessful as a power grab[101] and to have been surprisingly unpopular not just with his own barons (who resented the attempt to wrest seigniorial control over justice from their own hands) but also with the public in general, for whom the new courts appeared to be just one more source of official interference and financial extortion.[102] The intrusion of the central 'State' into law enforcement was therefore a source of significant political tension, as well as popular resistance. In any event, the list of offences deemed eligible to be tried in this novel way before the King's courts, with super-additions over time, came to represent an embryonic category of wrongs belonging to 'the public as a whole', which Blackstone would later identify as the domain of 'crime'. The initial jurisdictional and procedural shifts set in motion by Henry contributed in this way to the development of the later substantive categories of public and private wrongdoing that we now accept as standard.

The precise process via which 'public' actions for wrongs to the King, society, or State, came to separate out from private actions for wrongs to individuals is complicated. Hyams suggests[103] that the critical phase was the development in the thirteenth century of private trespass actions for compensation in the new royal courts, on the one hand (the early forebear of our actions in tort), and, on the other hand, felony appeals and then jury presentments on indictment, giving rise to serious punishments (the forebears of crime).[104] He identifies the key moment as being the point at which trespass was finally recognized as a distinct form of writ action

[99] Hyams, 'Does it Matter When the English Began to Distinguish Between Crime and Tort?' (n 91) 123; 'Nastiness and Wrong, Rancor and Reconciliation' Ch 10 in Brown and Górecki (eds) (n 98).

[100] S Thorne (trans), *Bracton on the Laws and Customs of England* (Belknap Press 1968) 283: 'by criminal proceedings, I seek not only what is due to me but to every person, because of the king's peace and the common welfare'.

[101] Hyams, 'Does it Matter When the English Began to Distinguish Between Crime and Tort?' (n 91) 123; Pike (n 98) 134–36. Pike indicates that by the end of Henry's reign, the King's justices could be expected to make an appearance in most parts of the country only one year in three. By the reign of Henry III, this had dwindled to one in seven. A significant problem for the King was that presenting juries remained under strong local baronial influence, so that using them to pick out crimes for diversion to his own courts was fraught with practical difficulty.

[102] Pike (n 98) 134.

[103] Hyams, *Rancor and Reconciliation in Medieval England* (n 2) Ch 7.

[104] For other helpful expositions, see D Seipp, 'The Distinction Between Crime and Tort in the Early Common Law' (1996) 76 Boston University Law Review 59; Pollock and Maitland (n 5) 510–11; A Harding, 'The Roll of the Shropshire Eyre of 1256' Selden Society, Vol 96 for 1980 (Selden Society) xxxii–lviii.

in the period after 1258.[105] He describes this point metaphorically as entailing the delicate separation of two Siamese twins[106]—each twin previously feeding from a single bloodline and then, the cut being made, beginning its own autonomous life.

It is important to note that even after these threads had begun to disentangle, the functions of the different actions and the forms of justice they instantiated remained for a long while mixed. The private writ of trespass in the King's courts could give rise not just to compensation of the injured party for harm to his private interests, but also to punishment of the wrongdoer, either corporal, or in the form of fines payable to the King, for the breach of his peace.[107] Holdsworth accordingly describes the action for trespass in the reign of Edward I as being a 'quasi-criminal' proceeding,[108] and as being an important expedient to make good failings in criminal process.[109] It was only as the scope of the writ was gradually extended so as to include claims not alleging violence against this peace (*'vi et armis'*, *'contra pacem regis'*) that this punitive component began to shrink.[110] Under a number of statutes, private actions in respect of certain trespassory offences could give rise to punitive awards in the form of double or triple damages. Many of the wrongs singled out in this way by Edward I[111] (1272–1307) were committed by public officials, which interestingly presages a pattern of punitive damages awards in modern tort cases examined later in this book, but they were not confined to such abuses of state power. A later statute of Henry VI in 1429, for example, provided for treble awards in cases of forced entry,[112] which might of course be committed by official

[105] Hyams, *Rancor and Reconciliation in Medieval England* (n 2) 233.

[106] ibid 171–72.

[107] Seipp (n 104) 70; Baker, *An Introduction to English Legal History* (n 11) 67. It has been suggested that criminal sanctions for trespass were available as late at 1694, via the writ of capias in withernam (a form of 'reprisal' against a distrainor for refusing to return wrongly distrained goods, which allowed for execution against the distrainor's own goods): Note, 'Exemplary Damages in the Law of Torts' (1957) 70 Harvard Law Review 517, 523.

[108] WS Holdsworth, *A History of English Law* Vol 2 (3rd edn, Methuen and Co 1923) 364.

[109] ibid 453.

[110] It was violence breaching the king's peace that initially gave the action its public, punitive component and justified recourse to the king's court, but the allegations of force and violence became more and more fictional, and in the later thirteenth century were no longer required: SFC Milsom, 'Reason in the Development of the Common Law' (1965) 81 Law Quarterly Review 496, 502–03; 'Trespass from Henry III to Edward III' (1958) 74 Law Quarterly Review 195. On the transition and the development of trespass on the case, see further D Ibbetson, *A Historical Introduction to the Law of Obligations* (OUP 1999) 39–56.

[111] Stat West I (3 Edw 1) cc 1 (1275) (acts of trespass against the goods of clerics—double damages plus punishment determined by king's court), 15 (unlawful detention—double and placed in mercy of the king), 17 (unlawful distraint on goods within a fort or castle—double damages), 19 (official corruption in refusing to discharge debts received—triple damages plus fine to the king), 24 (wrongful seizure of land by public officials—double damages, plus fine to the king), 26 (official extortion by king's officers—double damages plus punishment at king's pleasure), 27 (extortion by clerks—triple damages plus loss of service for a year), 30 (extortion by officers of a justice—triple damages plus grievous punishment at king's pleasure); 32 (taking horses or carts for the king's carriage—triple plus 40 days imprisonment) 35 (arrest in absence of authority—double plus high fine to the king). See further Taliadoros (n 12) 273–78.

[112] Forcible Entry Act 8 Hen 6 c 9 (1429).

actors, but need not be. Rather in the same way that we saw the delictal action in Roman law maintaining a punitive edge even into its later phases, so too, therefore, the private action in trespass continued to generate both corrective and retributive legal responses protecting both private and public interests. Conversely, whilst the felonies that we would now classify as crimes normally resulted in serious physical punishments and forfeiture of an offender's land and goods to the Crown, there are documented cases in the fourteenth century involving larceny, robbery, and mahem (maiming) in which courts also granted restitution or compensation to victims bringing their case by way of private appeal.[113] One and the same wrongful action could also clearly give rise to both to a private writ action for the victim in trespass and an appeal of felony, the victim choosing which course to take according to whether retribution or personal redress was his immediate priority, and according to the extent to which he was willing to risk the dangerous consequences of the appeal process.[114]

English medieval law was therefore conceptually messier than Roman law. The latter at least appeared to have a reasonably modern-looking distinction between crime and delict, albeit that these categories had different content to our own modern categories of crime and tort and mixed the pursuit of public and private ends between them in a way that our own modern categories generally do not. By contrast, early medieval English law lacked anything like those conceptual categories altogether and survived for centuries with a largely undifferentiated conception of wrongdoing in which actions initiated by private individuals resulted in a mix of penalties and compensation being payable to victims and early manifestations of the State. Sometimes the penalties for a wrong were payable to the King or local lord, but there were also occasions in Anglo-Saxon times when a penalty (*wite*) payable to the king for a wrong such as theft, was accompanied by an obligation to pay multiples of compensation (*bot*) to the victim.[115] Although the distinctions we now make may in practice have been felt, they were not explicit in the law. Furthermore, even after the Norman Conquest, the obsession of the developing common law with procedures and forms of action from the late medieval period right up until the nineteenth century prevented any more expeditious development of the modern distinction between public, criminal law and the private law of torts that ultimately attracted Blackstone. Indeed, although the word 'tort' crops up repeatedly in its undifferentiated meaning ('wrong') in the yearbooks and early reports, the evidence is that it only started to be used by commentators

[113] Seipp (n 104) 67–68; JH Baker, *The Oxford History of the Laws of England* Vol VI 1483–1558 (OUP 2003) 513. The availability of damages in felony appeals at any earlier stage is contested, it being suggested that no such remedy was needed because the victim could compromise the action: G Woodbine, 'The Origins of the Action for Trespass' (1925) 33 Yale Law Journal 799, 802–03.

[114] The appellor might be required to put his own body to the proof through battle or, if losing the action, himself be punished: Seipp (n 104) 65–66. See further below.

[115] See eg Aethelbirht 9 (theft from a freeman).

in England in anything like the modern sense toward the end of the seventeenth century.[116]

B. Enforcement Process

If this all seems to have been rather involved, the point to take home is that it is impossible to state the way in which public and private law was enforced in medieval England without being aware of the general lack of anything akin to the modern categories, and of the later, procedural orientation of the developing common law. Of the first and second phases of enforcement, we know more than we do of the equivalents in ancient Rome. Practices of private vengeance, feud, and social composition were common in Anglo-Saxon times and are relatively well documented.[117] There is evidence that they persisted well into the century after the Norman Conquest and beyond.[118] Some of the best of this evidence lies in in the persistent provision of sanctuary for criminals fleeing the vengeance of their victims.[119] Although private retaliation was never a claim right in Germanic law,[120] it was therefore a liberty that was long assumed and tolerated and which continued to be enjoyed long after courts and legal recourse became a rudimentary reality. In defiance of the apparently linear logic of evolutionary development set out at the beginning of this chapter, ideas of feud and private vengeance therefore continued to inform social practice well beyond the point at which public institutions of justice were first made available.

The secondary phase of bringing private retaliation and practices of feud under 'State'[121] legal control was a very gradual business in England but started pretty early. The Dooms (Laws) of King Ine (688–725) contain a clear mandate (which was probably practically unenforceable) for subjects to seek justice before exacting

[116] Milsom (n 110) 504–05.

[117] P Hyams, 'Feud and the State in Late Anglo-Saxon England' (2001) 40 Journal of British Studies 1 and the works cited at n 2 above. Note, however, that, depending on exactly what one means by a 'feud', it has sometimes been suggested that the Anglo-Saxons engaged in something else: J Niles, 'The Myth of the Feud in Anglo-Saxon England' (2015) 114 The Journal of English and Germanic Philology 163 (feud in the sense of 'long-lasting hostility between rival individuals or groups' was lacking in Anglo-Saxon times).

[118] Hyams, *Rancor and Reconciliation in Medieval England* (n 2) Ch 4, 127–28 cites the *Leges Henrici* and accounts of the Benedictine monk Orderic Vitalis for many a 'rattling good yarn' of blood and vengeance in the twelfth century. He also traces aspects of feud culture well into the thirteenth: ibid Ch 8.

[119] Hudson (n 96) 396–97.

[120] Pollock and Maitland (n 5) 46 (although the reference to Hohfeld is obviously not used).

[121] I make no attempt here to define the point at which one can claim a 'state' to exist (a vexed point, to say the least) and refer in what follows also to early assertions of regal authority. At one level, of course, I confess that this is unsatisfactory, but it takes me well beyond the ground I need to cover. I accept that, for many, the conception of a state is tied to a much later period in Western political thought: see eg W Ullmann, 'Juristic Obstacles to the Emergence of the Concept of the State in the Middle Ages' (1969) 13 Annali di Storia del Diritto 43, cited in G Samuel, 'Governmental Liability in Tort and the Public and Private Law Division' (1988) 8 Legal Studies 277, 281.

revenge.[122] The exhortation is repeated by Alfred (871–901) in his later laws.[123] The laws of many of the Anglo-Saxon Kings, Ine included, contained tallies of *bot* and *wergeld* payable for private injury that were designed to limit retaliation and promote and regulate private composition. The system grew to be far more sophisticated than anything the Twelve Tables had to offer, with very specific sums payable for injuries ranging from something as serious as rape to finely graduated types of ear injury.[124] The liberty of private individuals to take matters summarily into their own hands by killing manifest (red-handed) thieves (infangthief) was gradually hedged about by conditions and made a franchise of local lords.[125] A person seeking to seize a thief who was not actually caught in the act had first to raise the 'hue and cry'.[126] Some wrongs were also made 'botless'—meaning that that they could no longer be dealt with by private composition without the King's assent.[127] Alfred, Edmund (940–946) and Cnut (1017–1035) all legislated to regulate particular aspects of the practice of feud toward the end of the Anglo-Saxon era, for example by setting cooling-off periods of delay that had to be observed before direct action against an offender's person could take place.[128] All of these measures signal a gradual transition toward greater State regulation of private enforcement initiatives and increasing claims to royal control, although it is hard to be sure of the extent to which they were truly successful.[129] Baker suggests that the practice of feud did not become illegal until the twelfth century[130] and there is good evidence, as I intimated above, that some aspects of feud culture persisted well into the thirteenth. It was only really at this stage, Hyams credibly suggests, that the nascent common law came to offer anything like a viable practical alternative to the older ways in the consciousness of most English subjects.[131]

[122] Ine 9.

[123] Alfred 42.

[124] The laws of Aethelbirht I of Kent (560–616 AD) and Alfred were particularly detailed in this regard. For the ear injury examples, see Aethelbirht 39–42 (severing, deafness, piercing and mutilation). The system disappeared after the Norman Conquest, although Hudson (n 96) 409–12 suggests that payments of compensation probably continued to be made until actions in trespass took over.

[125] J Stephen (n 33) 61–64 suggests that the franchise was commonly exercised in the reign of Edward I and only disappeared towards the end of the reign of Edward III. An exception, the 'Halifax gibbet law' remained in place from the thirteenth to the middle of seventeenth century: Baker, *An Introduction to English Legal History* (n 11) 543; Holdsworth, *A History of English Law* (n 108) 102.

[126] Hudson (n 96) 171, 395–96, 723.

[127] See eg 8 Aethelred 1.1 (homicide within church walls); 2 Cnut 64 (housebreaking). The concept resurfaces in the idea of unamendable 'felonies' in Norman times, which led to confiscation of land, and life by the King: Baker, *An Introduction to English Legal History* (n 11) 542.

[128] Alfred 42; Edmund 7; 1 Cnut 5.

[129] The debate about the extent to which the Anglo-Saxon Kings succeeded in establishing royal control in something akin to a modern state is disputed. Their laws clearly made important claims to such control, but they are themselves weak evidence of it as a social fact and 'maximal' claims about statehood in the period are probably exaggerated: Hyams, *Rancor and Reconciliation in Medieval England* (n 2) Ch 3.

[130] Baker, *An Introduction to English Legal History* (n 11) 6. See also 541

[131] Hyams, *Rancor and Reconciliation in Medieval England* (n 2) 264–65 and generally Ch 8. There is some understandable variation around the estimated dates which is probably attributable to different understandings of what is meant by a feud. Hudson (n 96) 395 suggests that evidence of 'extended

So much for extra-legal private action and royal attempts to moderate and control it. What of the legal enforcement processes that were on offer to subjects? Virtually all of what we would nowadays consider to be private law was throughout the period enforced by private enforcers.[132] As regards 'criminal' wrongs, they were again very much at the forefront of enforcement activity, owing to the absence of anything akin to a developed sense of 'public' wrongdoing, or public prosecution process. Under the Anglo-Saxon kings, some legal accusations were undoubtedly brought by public officials and committees representing local townships and tithings—either the local reeve and four men,[133] or (under Aethelred's third code), the twelve leading thanes in a district.[134] These were the early predecessors of the presentment jury (below) and the nearest thing that the Anglo-Saxons had to a mechanism for the 'public' prosecution of crime.[135] However, the vast majority of cases in Anglo-Saxon times were initiated and prosecuted by private victims and their families, each accuser taking an oath as to the propriety of his purpose and the genuineness of his belief in the accusation,[136] and himself issuing the summons.[137] The private action could always be settled and discontinued by the victim.[138] Occasionally, as in Roman law, private actions were incentivized. An early example from the seventh century is a provision of King Wihtraed of Kent (*c* 690–724) that allowed anyone supplying information concerning the breach of the rule against Sunday working to receive half the allotted penalty, together with the benefit of the labour done.[139]

(i) Criminal Appeals and Approvers

In Norman times, two distinct, main modes of criminal process then developed. The first, the appeal,[140] was again based on private accusation. In many ways, it

feuds' is scarce after 1066, which is not inconsistent with Hyams' account. See further J Hudson, 'Feud, Vengeance and Violence in England from the Tenth to the Twelfth Centuries' in B Tuten and T Billado (eds), *Feud, Violence and Practice: Essays in Medieval Studies in Honour of Stephen D White* (Farnham 2010) 29. Pollock and Maitland (n 5) 221 interestingly cite a request made in the thirteenth century by inhabitants of Hereford to the King's Justices that they be allowed to observe practices of feudal composition in respect of homicide, rather than the King's own justice, which tends to support the Hyams position. They also suggest that the culture died out much later in Wales and Ireland than England.

[132] For exceptions in which the King acted *parens patriae*, see Chapter 8.

[133] J Stephen (n 33) 69.

[134] 3 Aethelred 3.1. See Patrick Wormald, 'Frederick William Maitland and the Earliest English Law' (1998) 16 Law and History Review 1, 11–12.

[135] See N Hurnard, 'The Jury of Presentment and the Assize of Clarendon,' (1941) 56 English Historical Review 374. The actual lineal connection between the twelve thanes and the later jury of presentment is doubted by both Hudson (n 96) 735 and RC Van Caenegem, *Legal History, A European Perspective* (Hambledon Press 1991) Ch 1, esp 4–10.

[136] J Stephen (n 33) 70; T Plucknett, *A Concise History of the Common Law* (Liberty Fund 2010) 427.

[137] Holdsworth, *A History of English Law* (n 108) 103–05. Failure to appear would result in a fine, distraint, or worse: ibid.

[138] Save in exceptional cases where the crime was 'botless' or unamendable. See the text to n 127 above.

[139] Wihtraed 11 (695 AD).

[140] See generally Hudson (n 96) 721–35.

replicated the patterns of private reprisal embedded in old customs of feud, offering the accuser at it did (in the early days at least) a mechanism of trial by ordeal, or combat,[141] together with the power of compromise. The rights of action lay either with the victim,[142] or with 'approvers'—persons themselves accused of treason or felony, who were permitted to save their own necks by prosecuting (and fighting) their accomplices in a form of judicialized duel.[143] Appeals were most common in the twelfth and thirteenth centuries and were used in respect of a wide variety of serious felonies including homicide, rape, arson, robbery, larceny, and assault,[144] but declined in popularity thereafter owing to the rise of jury presentments (below) and the availability of private trespass actions for those victims whose main desire was simply to obtain compensation for their injury. The risks of the appeal process—which included being killed in battle or fined or imprisoned if the appeal was withdrawn or unsuccessful—made it a pretty unattractive option to anyone whose only real interest in a suit was to obtain financial redress. Once the trespass writ was up and running, the appeal tended to attract only those intent on exacting revenge, or who (more often, perhaps) wished to pressure a generous settlement. Stephen suggests that by the end of the fifteenth century, appeals only really featured in cases of murder.[145] According to Baker, they tended in later years to be used either to press a case in which grand juries refused to indict (or where the indictment failed satisfactorily to produce a conviction), or as a dubious mechanism for leveraging settlements, there never being any real intention of pressing the suit at all.[146] Appeals were finally abolished, at the third attempt, in 1819,[147] but this was not the end of private prosecution, as we shall see later in Chapter 7 of this book, because the power to mount a private prosecution remains intact in England even today as a final palladium of civil rights.

The controversy of allowing private victims the power to settle disputes as serious as homicide on their own terms was not lost on judges even as early as the

[141] Trial by ordeal was abolished in 1215. Trial by battle was more or less obsolete by the middle of the thirteenth century (save in cases involving approvers, on which see below), being replaced by a mode of jury trial—Baker, *An Introduction to English Legal History* (n 11) 544. In the royal courts, the appeal procedure was confined to the most serious cases (felonies) carrying sentences of death or maiming and the confiscation of his entire property: ibid 542.

[142] Or, in homicide cases, the widow, or heir.

[143] The practice of using approvers developed from the time of Henry I and is reported to have been common in the time of Henry II. The upside for the approver (who fought on behalf of—and was armed and sometimes trained by—the King) was the chance of keeping his life. The downside was that trial was always by combat and, if the approver lost, he was hanged. Where he accused a large number of accomplices, he had to beat them all to survive. See F Hamil, 'The King's Approvers: A Chapter in the History of English Criminal Law' (1936) 11 Speculum 238.

[144] For a list, see T Kirchengast, *The Victim in Criminal Law and Justice* (Palgrave MacMillan 2006) 31; and for a breakdown of the statistics between 1194 and 1294, D Klerman, 'Settlement and the Decline of Private Prosecution in Thirteenth-Century England' (2001) 19 Law & History Review 1, 8.

[145] J Stephen (n 33) 248.

[146] Baker, *An Introduction to English Legal History* (n 11) 544–45.

[147] J Stephen (n 33) 249.

thirteenth century. There was always a risk that accusers might drop actions in the public interest in return for bribes or exorbitant settlements. The consequence was that judges became more reluctant at this time to discontinue appeals that a private party had dropped and more willing to allow them to be taken over by the Crown.[148] The power of private accusation in such cases could also give rise to the malicious, long-term imprisonment of an accused pending trial without bail,[149] with the consequence that it became necessary to protect accused persons against this mischief by introducing a writ action allowing them to allege hatred and ill-will ('*odio et atia*') on the part of their accusers.[150]

The granting of rights of action to 'approvers' was a feature of this system that was especially replete with moral peril. It enlisted serious criminals as private attorneys-general and potential executioners—something which not even the Romans had allowed. It gave rise to instances of extortion by corrupt gaolers and sheriffs, who tortured prisoners to make them turn approvers and then used them as a threat to extort money from innocent parties.[151] The phenomenon of the approver thereby arguably ended up filling the pockets of one criminal constituency as fast as it emptied those of another. Some approvers were nothing less than the King's hitmen, armed and trained at his expense in the art of battle and moved tactically around the country in order to target wrongdoers. Various attempts to ameliorate some of these hazards were undertaken by Edward II and Edward III in the fourteenth century,[152] but the antidotes were probably never quite equal to the bane. The practice appears to have died out by the end of the fifteenth century,[153] although it was never formally abolished. From that point onward, criminal accomplices could turn King's evidence and throw themselves on the mercy of a court, or might even be granted immunity against suit, but they would never again be granted the right of prosecution as such.

(ii) Jury Presentment and Trial on Indictment

The second criminal prosecution process—jury presentment and trial on indictment[154]—developed out of the post-Assize of Clarendon reforms of the twelfth century mentioned in the previous section. Here, it was local jury

148 Hudson (n 96) 733 suggests that about 10 per cent of cases were continued by justices in this fashion. On the ups and downs of settlement and trends in judicial attitudes towards it, see further Klerman (n 144) (suggesting that the increased readiness of judges to continue actions despite private settlement was another reason for the appeal's decline); Kirchengast (n 144) 44–46.

149 This was apparently raised as an issue in a large number of cases: Hudson (n 96) 729.

150 ibid 725, 729–30; S Jenks, 'The Writ and the Exception de Odio et Atia' (2002) 23 Journal of Legal History 1.

151 Hamil (n 143) 248–49. There were also instances in which the approver himself participated in blackmail: ibid 251.

152 ibid 250–51.

153 ibid 257.

154 Hudson (n 96) 735–40; Baker, *An Introduction to English Legal History* (n 11) 545–46;

committees (predecessors of the later grand juries) that were responsible for reporting the names of offenders and crimes to the King's justices. The power of formal accusation and control over indictment was hence held not by private victims, as in the appeal process, but by representatives of local communities. The process was therefore public in the sense of being 'communal',[155] even though it yet lacked anything akin to a 'public prosecutor' in the modern sense. Once the indictment was issued, an action was initiated between the King and the accused. The use of this system of 'presenting juries' to accuse a wrongdoer is sometimes said to signal the real dawn of the public prosecution in England[156] and one can see why. In the early days, such juries not only made the formal accusation, but conducted the relevant investigation and therefore had a proactive information-gathering role, stating their opinion and conclusions to the judge on behalf of the community and the 'public interest', rather in the way that a modern prosecutor might make a case.[157] It was also upon their motion that the King's action was formally initiated. On the other hand, they were still technically groups of private individuals, not 'state officials'. Furthermore, from the fourteenth century onwards, the role of the presenting jury appears to have become much more neutral and the practical initiative of prosecution on indictment seems to have passed back to individual accusers.[158] From the 1360s, 'accusations' were rarely made by the jury itself (now the 'grand jury' with a slightly different composition), but were made in written form by private individuals (bills of indictment), the jury effectively simply screening the sworn document and deciding whether or not to give it the go-ahead.[159]

It is therefore only later in the medieval and Tudor periods that the system of private accusation was supplemented in any very meaningful way by agents of the King or 'State' with their own, independent powers to investigate and lay accusations. Hudson suggests that there was some sporadic prosecutorial activity by royal officials in the King's name in the Anglo-Norman period preceding the reign of Henry II (1154–1189),[160] and the King himself was clearly able to lay information directly before his own court in the reign of Edward I (1272–1307).[161] Justices of

[155] Plucknett (n 136) 428.

[156] See eg Kirchengast (n 144) 41 (characterizing the shift as one of transfer of power from the victim to the Crown).

[157] Hudson (n 96) 737–38. Note, however that juries did not gather fact evidence as such—they just sounded views.

[158] Klerman (n 144) 7. No one really understands the process by which this transformation to passivity occurred, but Langbein credibly speculates that the system of self-informing investigating juries could never have survived the dramatic increases in social mobility that have since occurred: J Langbein, 'The Origins of Public Prosecution at Common Law' (1973) 17 American Journal of Legal History 313, 314–15.

[159] Baker, *An Introduction to English Legal History* (n 11) 546; Kirchengast (n 144) 40.

[160] Hudson (n 96) 735; Van Caenegem (n 135) 11–21, 29-35. The latter references local justices and their subordinate officials, suggesting that these acted ex officio in cases in which no private appellor came forward, even before the system of jury presentment was put in place by Henry II.

[161] Holdsworth, *A History of English Law* (n 108) 303; H Stephen, *New Commentaries on the Laws of England* Vol 4 (5th edn, Butterworths 1863) 460–61 (indicating that this power is as 'ancient as the common law itself'). The power was initially available in respect of felonies but was restricted to serious

the Peace (JPs) (possibly as early as the fourteenth century, but increasingly from the mid-sixteenth),[162] the Attorney-General (from the fifteenth century),[163] his deputy the Solicitor-General (appearing at the same time but officially so named from 1515), police constables (in respect of misdemeanours from the 1790s or so),[164] and eventually the Director of Public Prosecutions[165] (1879) would gradually begin to assume some of these functions of formal accusation and prosecution, but the process would only be truly systematic with the establishment of the central Crown Prosecution Service in the late twentieth century. Up until that time, private accusation by victims remained a standard component of the jury trial and they retained a high degree of control over it. Douglas Hay's research suggests that 80 per cent of prosecutions for indictable offences in the latter part of the eighteenth century were initiated and controlled by the victim or his agent,[166] which gives one a breathtaking sense of the dominance of private over state initiative in England until a very late stage in the day.

(iii) Observations

Much detail has been left out of this account, but the key points to draw from it are similar to those emanating from our analysis of the Roman law. There is a shift toward the end of the period, sluggish but accelerating from the thirteenth century, toward greater differentiation between public and private law in the strictly Roman and Blackstonian sense, and toward greater use of 'public' enforcement procedures

misdemeanours with the introduction of jury presentment. See further Blackstone (n 14) Book 4, Ch 23, Section III.

162 Plucknett (n 136) 429 places the point at which Justices were first able to take indictments as the reign of Edward II (1307–1327). Baker, *The Oxford History of the Laws of England* (n 113) 270, 515 suggests that the development of an investigative role was still new in the later fifteenth century. Langbein (who provides perhaps the most detailed account) suggests that although JPs were clearly involved in basic policing from an early stage in the fourteenth century, their prosecutorial role took off in earnest as a supplement to private prosecution as a result of the Marian statutes of 1554–1555: Langbein (n 158) 318. Although JPs were clearly more actively involved in prosecution process from this time, it has been suggested that they still preferred to leave prosecution at trial to the victim: J Barth, 'Criminal Prosecution in American History: Private or Public? (2022) 67 South Dakota Law Review 119, 122 (citing Pound). See further CA Beard, *The Office of the Justice of the Peace in England in its Origin and Development* (Macmillan 1904).

163 The time the title was first used was 1461, but the King clearly had, and used, his own attorneys to prosecute his business in the courts long before this time, from the mid-thirteenth century: J Ll J Edwards, *The Law Officers of the Crown* (Sweet and Maxwell 1964) Ch 1, esp 2–3.

164 B Smith, 'The Emergence of Public Prosecution in London 1790–1850' (2006) 18 Yale Journal of Law and the Humanities 29, 32 suggests that constables in police offices may have been routinely responsible for prosecutions in London's lower criminal courts from this time onwards. Note, however, that there is evidence that both petty and high constables were involved in making direct presentments from a much earlier period: H Simpson, 'The Office of Constable' (1895) 10 The English Historical Review 625, 628–29; M Davies, The Enforcement of English Apprenticeship 1563–1642 (Harvard University Press 1956) 197–98.

165 On the evolution of the office see Edwards (n 163) Ch 16.

166 D Hay, 'Controlling the English Prosecutor' (1983) 21 Osgoode Hall Law Journal 165, 167. See also D Friedmann, 'Making Sense of English Law Enforcement in the 18th Century' (1995) 2 University of Chicago Law School Roundtable 475.

in respect of public wrongdoing over time. A 'king's' (public) law of wrongs starts to emerge from the shadows as he asserts a broader jurisdiction, and a distinct form of action for trespass takes shape, but the protection of public and private interests is still not distributed cleanly across the weakly emergent categories. The developing trespass action, whilst protecting private interests, simultaneously retains significant punitive, public interest components. At the same time, some private appeals in respect of serious criminal felonies give rise to restitution or compensation for victims, not just punishment of the wrongdoer. Moreover, despite the increase in public court machinery, the extent to which the State (King and his officials) exercises enforcement rights in respect of the emerging category of public law is very limited well up to the end of the medieval period and beyond. Private parties retain high degrees of control over the initiation, conduct and settlement of most actions in respect of both civil and 'criminal' cases in the more modern sense. Some private parties who are not even victims of a crime, but who have insider information about it on account of their own involvement, are, for a while, given powers to prosecute on official 'approval'. Others ('common informers') are granted the power to lay information about a wide range of non-felonious offences directly before a court without having to get the case past a jury of public representatives, so as to speed up the process of bringing offenders to book and the efficient flow of penalties to the king.[167] In some instances, such private prosecutions are incentivized by allowing the common informer a share of the spoils in actions '*qui tam*'. This started at least as early as the seventh century with King Wihtraed, as we saw, but revived and flared up again in the fourteenth.[168] A fifteenth century example is a provision in a statute of Henry VI[169] granting informers the right to claim a third of the penalty imposed for official embezzlement on a successful private prosecution *qui tam*. Another statute in the following century allowed common informers to prosecute a town or village for tolerating vagrants, and split the resulting penalty with the Crown.[170] The enthusiasm for such provisions died back for a while on account of the serious abuses to which they gave rise and resulted in

[167] Baker, *An Introduction to English Legal History* (n 11) 546–47. Holdsworth, *A History of English Law* (n 108) 307 reports that Henry VII made particular use of this device as a means of getting speedy justice done, granting justices of the peace the power to prosecute all statutory non-capital offences on private information in 1495, but this apparently gave rise to such serious abuses in the form of extortion that the measure was repealed by Henry VIII in 1509. See further H Stephen (n 161) 461 (referring to the mechanism as a 'tyrannical mode of prosecution' that led to continual harassment of subjects and the 'shameful enrichment' of the Crown). Since the information was filed in the Crown's name and its approval by the King's Crown Office Master was subject to no oversight, they carried little to no risk in terms of costs for a private party lodging them. This was later changed. For a full history of the criminal information (which could be used either by private parties, or lodged at the suit of the King, see WS Holdsworth, 'The History of the Criminal Information' (1923) 1 Canadian Bar Review 300.

[168] J Beck, 'The False Claims Act and the English Eradication of Qui Tam Legislation' (2000) 78 North Carolina Law Review 539, 567–73; J Beck 'The History and Development of Qui Tam' (1972) Washington University Law Quarterly 81.

[169] Customs Act 3 Henry 6 c 3 (1425).

[170] Vagabonds Act 1547 1 Edw 6 c 3 (1547).

curbing legislation in the sixteenth and early seventeenth centuries,[171] but it re-ignited again dramatically in the late seventeenth and eighteenth centuries in the face of a perception of exploding crime rates and the continuing absence of an effective police force.[172] At this time, the practice was certainly neither isolated nor sporadic, but 'formed part of the deliberate and consistent policy of the legislature' and 'pervaded the entire body of the criminal law'.[173] Corrupt 'thieftakers', such as the infamous Jonathan Wild,[174] often made serious livings off the fruits of the *qui tam* system, before it once again faced serious popular opposition, was gradually downgraded during the eighteenth and nineteenth centuries and then finally abolished in England in 1951.[175] The renewed interest in using common informers to convict felons under William and Mary's statute of 1692[176] was noted by Gummow J recently in the High Court of Australia in the context of modern debates about the constitutional permissibility of consumer protection laws allowing for private enforcement by 'any person' at the turn of the twenty-first century.[177] Such incentive devices also existed in Scotland from an early stage through 'popular actions'.[178] They were used to fill a significant gap in regulatory enforcement, as well, in later years, in attempts to inspire a spirit of competition and prompt greater vigilance and prosecutorial initiative from the police.[179] As we shall see in Chapter 7, they are not extinct and are raising their heads again in the United States under laws designed to combat frauds upon the State and violations of controversial abortion legislation known as the 'Texas Heartbeat law', to name but two of the most visible instances.

Throughout the medieval period and beyond, private enforcement clearly carried tangible risks that are no less real today in terms of permitting oppression, collusion, and settlement in terms that were contrary to the public interest. We come to think more carefully about these risks and the measures taken to deal with them in the modern law later in this book. For now, we leave the primordial era

[171] 7 Co Rep 36. One example is a statute of 1624 effectively limiting the ability of a common informer to prosecute any offence committed outside his own county: Common Informers Act 21 Jas 1 c 4 (1623). See further Beck, 'History and Development' (n 168) 89–90; M Beresford, 'The Common Informer, the Penal Statutes and Economic Regulation' (1957) 10 The Economic History Review 221, esp 234–37.

[172] See L Radnizowicz, *A History of the English Criminal Law and Its Administration from 1750* Vol 2 (Stevens and Sons 1956) 138–55. Some *qui tam* provisions, analogously to Roman equivalents, allowed for part of the penalty to be payable to the private prosecutor/informer and part to be distributed to public causes: see further Blackstone (n 14) 160 and Chapter 7 Section 7.2B(i).

[173] Radnizowicz (n 172) 146.

[174] G Howson (ed), *Thief-Taker General: Jonathan Wild and the Emergence of Crime and Corruption as a Way of Life in Eighteenth-Century England* (Routledge 1985). Wild was hanged in 1725.

[175] Common Informers Act 14 & 15 Geo 6 c 39 (1951) (Eng).

[176] Apprehension of Highwaymen Act 4 Will & Mary c 8 (1692).

[177] *Truth About Motorways Pty Limited v Macquarie Infrastructure Investment Management Ltd* [2000] HCA 11 [72].

[178] J Pender, 'Standing to Sue: Lessons from Scotland's Actio Popularis' (2017) 66 Duke Law Journal 1493, 1527. The provision of bounties declined in Scotland, as it did in England: ibid 1533.

[179] Radnizowicz (n 172) 146.

with a keen sense of the early, radical hybridity of enforcement processes and the high degree of historical reliance on private individuals for the enforcement of laws both public and private. We also leave it in the knowledge that some aspects of this hybridity and reliance remain with us today. Indeed, recent proposals to increase the role of private enforcers in the enforcement of public law and the protection of public interests—and to increase the extent to which private and public interests can be protected within the same enforcement process—seem, in the light of this review, to be modern reverberations of more ancient patterns of the past.

PART III
MODELLING

This part of the book describes current law enforcement patterns, identifying four main enforcement models: (1) the public enforcement of public law, (2) the private enforcement of public law, (3) the private enforcememt of private law, and (4) the public enforcement of private law. The first and third of these models together make up the dominant 'Blackstonian' paradigm described in the first chapter of the book. The text provides substantive examples of each enforcement model in turn, drawing on particular public and private law examples across a wide range of legal fields. In each case, it identifies the most likely explanations and justifications for the way in which enforcement rights are configured in respect of the laws in question, and the type (or types) of interest (public, private, or both) protected within the enforcement process. It also suggests adjustments to the models in particular cases. The concluding chapter draws the material in this part together, asking whether there are generalisable reasons for choosing between public and private enforcement techniques that may assist lawyers and policymakers in making future enforcement choices.

5
Public Law, Public Enforcement

The last chapter traced the gradual emergence of the modern category of public law in England from the primordial mass, and a steady progression toward the now dominant enforcement paradigm in which public laws are enforced by agents of the State. This part of the book brings us up to date and engages in its core descriptive work, modelling the main configurations of enforcement rights that exist in public and private law in the modern day. There are four, core models currently in operation, each one expressing one of the four possible logical combinations of laws and enforcer types: (1) the public enforcement of public laws; (2) the private enforcement of public laws; (3) the private enforcement of private laws; and (4) the public enforcement of private laws. The first and third of these models in combination constitute the dominant enforcement paradigm.

5.1 Preview

This chapter engages with the first model in which public laws are enforced by public agents. It examines the model's traditional justifications and two recurring challenges that it faces, which in turn help to explain the continuing use of private enforcement techniques in some areas of public law documented in the following two chapters. The final section examines a residual interest hybridity that exists within the model, which flows from the ability of public enforcers sometimes to seek both penal and compensatory measures in one and the same proceeding. This part demonstrates the way in which the hybridity of past law enforcement arrangements continues—indeed is being determinedly reinvigorated in some areas of public law—in the modern day.

To make the task manageable, I have chosen to focus on the law of jurisdictions in which the public enforcement paradigm is strongest, and even then, I have been very selective. The following account draws mainly on the laws of England and Wales, the European Union, and Australia, concentrating upon the criminal law and laws that concern themselves with economic competition and consumer protection. These laws are just one small part of the wider public law constellation, but my hope is that they nonetheless provide a representative sample from which to draw accurate observations and conclusions for the purposes of the limited modelling exercise that I have in mind.

Enforcement Rights in Public and Private Law. Kit Barker, Oxford University Press. © Kit Barker 2026.
DOI: 10.1093/9780191955006.003.0008

5.2 The Public Enforcement Model

Although there has been a recent resurgence in England of the ancient tradition of private prosecution,[1] the great majority of crimes are now prosecuted by the Crown Prosecution Service, the Attorney-General, or one of a number of specialized public agencies, which include the Civil Aviation Authority, Serious Fraud Office (SFO), Health and Safety Executive (HSE), Environment Agency, and local public authorities. Delegation of the enforcement role to such agencies is thought to concentrate decisions in the hands of those with specialized experience and expertise in the field in question and to encourage a more consistent and potentially more efficient approach to the implementation of prosecution policy. It also, quite frankly, spreads the now very heavy workload that would otherwise rest upon the shoulders of the central service.[2]

The public enforcement paradigm that applies in the criminal law is largely replicated in England, Europe, and Australia in the modern field of competition law. Serious cartel offences committed by individuals under Section 188 of the Enterprise Act 2002 (UK) (which are crimes) are hence prosecuted by the Competition and Markets Authority (CMA), or SFO. The CMA also has the right to make its own investigations, issue directions, extract commitments, and impose civil penalties in respect of anticompetitive practices and abuses of market position under the Competition Act 1998 (UK), and has associated rights of action to ensure that such penalties and other measures are judicially enforced.[3] Penalties for breach of the equivalent provisions of the European Treaty[4] are enforced by a specialized directorate of the European Commission, or one of the National Competition Authorities responsible for their implementation in the national courts of Member States.[5] In Australia, cartel offences fall within the prosecutorial remit of the Commonwealth Director of Public Prosecutions, and civil penalties for other types of anticompetitive conduct are recovered at the suit of the Australian Competition and Consumer Commission (ACCC).[6]

[1] See Chapter 7.

[2] T Hetherington, *Prosecution and the Public Interest* (Waterlow Publishers 1989) 113–14. See further Chapter 7, Part IIIA(i).

[3] Competition Act 1998 (UK) (CA) s 2 (anticompetitive practices such as price fixing), s 18 (abuses of dominant market position), s 36(1), 36(2). For a penalty to issue in respect of the violation of these sections, the infringement must be either negligent or intentional: s 36(3). If the infringer fails to comply with a commitment, direction, or penalty, the CMA has the right to seek a court order (s 31E, s 34) or issue civil proceedings to recover the penalty as a civil debt (s 37).

[4] Consolidated Version of the Treaty on the Functioning of the European Union 2016 OJ C202/1, arts 101, 102. These provisions provide the basis of the UK ones and are virtually identical. Since Brexit, they are no longer enforceable directly in UK courts, save as a breach of foreign law applicable for the purposes of domestic litigation.

[5] Council Reg 1/2003, arts 4, 5. See generally R Whish and D Bailey, *Competition Law* (11th edn, OUP 2024) Ch 7; C Kerse and N Khan, *EU Antitrust Procedure* (6th edn, Sweet and Maxwell 2012).

[6] Competition and Consumer Act 2010 (Cth) (CCA) s 45AF, s 45AG (cartel offences), s 76, s 77 (civil penalties). The Commission also has right to institute civil proceedings to seek injunctive relief

The same basic enforcement pattern is repeated in respect of breaches of the public law provisions of modern consumer protection,[7] workplace health and safety,[8] and financial services legislation.[9] Long-overdue upgrades to the CMA's enforcement powers in the consumer protection space took effect in the UK from April 2025 so as to bring them more into line with those that it enjoys in respect of domestic competition law.[10] Environmental laws are also overwhelmingly prosecuted in England and Australia at the suit of local authorities and environment agencies.[11]

The enforcement rights of public agents in all these instances stand alongside the concurrent rights of private parties to exercise rights of action of their own. These are of two main types. The first is the right of any person to bring an action for the violation of his or her private law rights. A party suffering economic loss as the result of an anticompetitive practice contrary to the Competition Act 1998 (UK) may hence sue independently for damages for breach of statutory duty, conspiracy, or any other economic tort the elements of which can be made out.[12] The second is the right of a private individual or corporation to bring an action

(s 80) or a declaration (s 163A). See further A Duke, *Corones' Competition Law in Australia* (Thomson Reuters 2018) Ch 17.

[7] In the UK, the principal public consumer protection agency is again the CMA (see n 10 below and text thereto). In Australia, the Commonwealth powers are held by the Australian Competition and Consumer Commission (ACCC), as in competition matters: Competition and Consumer Act 2010 (Cth) sch 2 (the Australian Consumer Law) (ACL) s 224, s 225, s 228 (penalties), ss 232–35 (injunctive relief), s 237 (compensation orders, with the consent of one or more private victims), s 239 (redress orders), s 243B (orders prospectively preventing inclusion of unfair terms in future contracts); D Mayall, 'Civil Penalties and Other Civil Remedies in the Consumer Law Context' in D Kayis, E Gluer, and S Walpole (eds), *The Law of Civil Penalties* (Federation Press 2023) Ch 11. Any private party may also seek injunctive relief: ACL s 232(2).

[8] The main enforcers in the UK are the Health and Safety Executive (UK) (HSE) (Health and Safety at Work Act 1974 (UK) ss 10–14, s 18), local authorities, and other public agencies such as the Office of Road and Rail and the Office for Nuclear Regulation: *HSE Enforcement Policy Statement* (2015). HSE Inspectors have powers to initiate prosecutions for violations of the Act: s 38, s 39. In Australia, separate regulators operate in the Commonwealth, States, and Territories to enforce uniform Work Health Safety Laws (with the exception of Victoria, where the regulator enforces similar duties under the Occupational Health and Safety Act 2004 (Vic)). The Commonwealth regulator is Comcare.

[9] The primary regulator in the UK is the Financial Conduct Authority (UK) (FCA) (acting under the Financial Services and Markets Act 2000 (UK) (FSMA), and, in Australia, the Australian Securities and Investments Commission (ASIC). Both have rights of action in respect of both criminal and civil penalty provisions.

[10] Digital Markets, Competition and Consumers Act 2024 (UK), Part 3, Chapter 4 and sch 16. The Act gives the CMA the power directly to enforce certain consumer protection laws and to impose and enforce penalties, following the domestic competition model for the first time: see further CMA, *Direct Consumer Enforcement Guidance* (31 July 2024).

[11] Agencies in both jurisdictions have powers to take enforcement action, including the power to prosecute major offences and to impose financial penalties at their own motion in respect of lesser ones (and to seek their enforcement through courts, if need be). See, in the UK, Environment Agency, *Environment Agency Enforcement and Sanctions Policy* (12 December 2024).

[12] See eg CA s 47A. The cause of action giving rise to a private action for damages under this section is not identified, but courts have interpreted it broadly so as to include breach of statutory duty in respect of violations of the CA s 2 and s 18, conspiracy and potentially any other legal cause: *WH Newson Holding Ltd & Ors v IMI Plc & Ors* [2013] EWCA Civ 1377 [20]–[25].

to claim full or partial compensation for harm that he, she (or it) has been caused by the offender's breach of one of the public law duties contained in the relevant statute[13] or Treaty.[14] In cases of this type, the plaintiff's compensatory remedy flows from the violation of a primary *public* law right held by the State, not—as in the previous example—a primary private law right held by the individual or corporation concerned, although it is easy to miss that fact if one blinks.[15] Historically, both rights of action may have helped indirectly to incentivize observance of the relevant public laws and to police economic markets (rather in the same way that we observed in Chapter 2 that private Prozac litigation has helped to clean up the pharmaceutical industry)[16] but they have so far played only a minor role in Europe and Australia.[17]

The number and variety of public agencies enforcing public law increased dramatically in the latter part of the twentieth century.[18] Such agencies are children of the regulatory State, the emergence of which in England is usually placed in the nineteenth century, but which can be traced much further back, depending on one's meaning.[19] The earliest 'agents' involved in enforcing statutory economic or

[13] See eg CCA s 82 (damages), s 87(1A)(a) (other orders for compensation of loss and damage).

[14] Case C-453/99 [2001] ECR I-6297 *Courage Ltd v Crehan*; Directive 2014/104/EU. On private damages claims for breaches of the various competition provisions under UK and EU law, see B Rodger 'Private Enforcement of Competition Law: The Hidden Story 2000–2005' (2008) 29 European Competition Law Review 96 (noting the high proportion of claims that get settled).

[15] This is often left unclear, since the exact location of the relevant primary right is virtually never discussed. It is significant nonetheless that damages payable under s 82 and compensation orders payable under s 87 of the CCA respond to a variety of different offences under the statute and are not calculated in exactly the same as they would be if the breach were a tort or an equitable wrong to a particular person: *Marks v GIO Australia Holdings Ltd* (1998) 196 CLR 494, 510 (McHugh, Hayne, and Callinan JJ).

[16] Chapter 2 Section 2.2.

[17] The pattern in the United States is very different, with some 90 per cent of anti-trust proceedings reportedly being initiated by private litigants enforcing their private law rights: C Beaton-Wells and K Tomasic, 'Private Enforcement of Competition Law: Time for an Australian Debate' (2012) 35 University of New South Wales Law Journal 648, 651. It should be noted that greater emphasis is now being given to private actions in Europe, with new procedures in domestic competition law allowing private claims to follow on from public ones, and providing for the possibility of opt-out as well as opt-in class action procedures (but significantly not providing for the recovery of triple damages, which, alongside greater rights to disclosure, is one of the keys to the greater use of private enforcement in US proceedings): CA s 47B, s 47C (introduced by the Consumer Rights Act 2015 (UK) sch 8); Directive 2020/1828/EU; A Stephan, 'Does the EU's Drive for Private Enforcement of Competition Law Have a Coherent Purpose' (2018) 37 University of Queensland Law Journal 153; W Moeschel, 'Should Private Enforcement of Competition Law be Strengthened ?' (2013) 6 Global Competition Litigation Review 1; D Baker, 'Private and Public Enforcement: Complements, Substitutes and Conflicts—a Global Perspective' in A Ezrachi (ed), *Research Handbook on International Competition Law* (Edward Elgar 2012) Ch 10. For a global examination of private enforcement techniques, see P Caro de Sousa, *The Private Enforcement of Competition Law* (OUP 2024).

[18] A study of forty-five countries suggests that the sharpest increase has occurred since the 1980s: M Maggetti, F Di Mascio, and A Natalini (eds), *Handbook of Regulatory Authorities* (Edward Elgar 2022) Ch 1, 1–3. See further E Windholz, *Governing Through Regulation: Public Policy, Regulation and the Law* (Taylor and Francis 2017) Ch 2.

[19] The instincts toward 'regulation' in the sense of centralized state direction and control of social and economic interests were present in the even the earliest Crown aspirations (Chapter 4 this

social 'regulation' were not public officers at all, or even necessarily directed, overseen, or funded by government—they were the common informers we encountered in the previous chapter:[20] (later) private prosecution associations, or (later still) specialized statutory inspectorates or commissions that were independent of the executive and/or unanswerable to Parliament[21] and which therefore enjoyed a 'problematic' legal status.[22] Regulatory bodies of this sort were vaguely analogous to the nineteenth-century police constable, who may have worn a uniform and had a public interest job to do, but whose formal connection to the State was loose and variable.[23] In the modern day, eclectic variations in the exact relationship of public agencies to government (funding mechanisms, reporting, control, and so on) persist, a fact which is important when it comes to understanding some of the problems they face in doing their jobs. Too loose a relationship between a public agency and central government institutions can weaken its accountability, but if the relationship with the executive is too strong, this can prejudice its political independence.[24]

We explore these difficulties further below. For now, I take it as read that the State's power to enforce public laws—whether centrally or through designated public agencies—is so firmly accepted in the modern day as to be uncontroversially paradigmatic.

book), but strengthened in the Tudor and Stuart Periods, softened and they then re-emerged as a result of complex social and political factors in the nineteenth century. For useful overviews, see A Ogus, *Regulation: Legal Form and Economic Theory* (Hart 1994) Ch 1 esp 6–12; O MacDonagh, 'The Nineteenth Century Revolution in Government: A Reappraisal' (1958) 1 The Historical Journal 52, esp 57–61.

[20] M Beresford, 'The Common Informer, the Penal Statute and Economic Regulation' (1957–1958) 10 Economic History Review 221; A Ogus, 'Regulatory Law: Some Lessons from the Past' (1992) 12 Legal Studies 1, 17.

[21] H Arthurs, *Without the Law: Administrative Justice and Legal Pluralism in the Nineteenth Century* (University of Toronto Press 1985) Ch 4, esp 103–31. The earliest regulatory inspectorate in England (which comprised only four men) sprung from the need for more effective enforcement of the Factories Act 1833 3 & 4 Wm IV c 103. Independent regulatory boards and commissions existed from the sixteenth century (the first being the sewers commission) but rose to prominence in the Victorian era in respect of enclosures, poor laws, public health, and railways. Although they variously had powers to enforce penalties or directives before courts, prosecution was never the preferred method of securing compliance and met with limited success: ibid 123–24.

[22] ibid 113–14; Ogus, *Regulation* (n 19) 8.

[23] L Radzinowicz, *A History of the Criminal Law and its Administration from 1750* (Stevens & Sons 1956) Vol 2, Chs 7, 8.

[24] For explorations of this delicate balance and the devices used to preserve agency accountability, see Ogus, *Regulation* (n 19) Ch 6; A Bianculli, X Fernández-i-Marín, and J Jordana (eds), *Accountability and Regulatory Governance: Audiences, Controls and Responsibilities in the Politics of Regulation* (Palgrave Macmillan 2015).

5.3 Rationale

A. Constitutional Prerogative

It is unlikely that there is any single reason for this, but the foremost is almost certainly constitutional. From the earliest days, as we saw in the last chapter, the King's interest in the public peace formed the basis for him claiming personal jurisdiction in more serious criminal matters. The birth of the felony was in this way wedded to the emergent view that public laws were designed for the protection of public interests and therefore laws in respect of which the State itself, as the people's representative, had the right of initiative. By the time Blackstone came to write about crime at the end of the eighteenth century, this thought had settled into a firm position:

> [W]e are now therefore, lastly, to proceed to the consideration of public wrongs, or crimes and misdemeanors; with the means of their prevention and punishment....
>
> First, as to the general nature of crimes and their punishment: the discussion and admeasurement of which forms in every country the code of criminal law; or, as it is more usually denominated with us in England, the doctrine of the pleas of the crown: so called, because the king, in whom centers the majesty of the whole community, is supposed by the law to be the person injured by every infraction of the public right belonging to that community, and is therefore in all cases the proper prosecutor for every public offense.[25]

The view was extant much earlier. The following opinion was hence expressed by the judges of England in a letter of 1604, the purport of which was to criticize Elizabeth I's grant of enforcement rights to common informers:

> [W]hen a statute is made by Parliament for the good of the commonwealth, the King cannot give the penalty, benefit, and dispensation of such Act to any subject; or give power to any subject to dispense with it... : for when a statute is made *pro bono publico,* and the King (as the head of the commonwealth, and the fountain of justice and mercy) is by the whole realm trusted with it; this confidence and trust is so inseparably joined and annexed to the Royal person of the King in so high a point of sovereignty, that he cannot transfer it to the disposition or power of any private person, or to any private use: for it was committed to the King by all his subjects for the good of the commonwealth.[26]

[25] William Blackstone, *Commentaries on the Laws of England* (Robert Bell 1773) Book 4, Ch 1.
[26] 7 Co Rep 36.

The point being made here was not just that the monarch had a right to enforce Parliament's public laws but that it was inappropriate for him or her to devolve the right to anyone else. Constitutional arguments of this type—now understandably stripped of the language of royal prerogative—remain very active in the United States, where critics claim that the wide array of modern Federal provisions giving citizens the power to prosecute public laws violate constitutional safeguards concerning the separation of powers,[27] executive control over the enforcement process,[28] or the jurisdiction of courts to entertain claims by those with proper standing.[29] The main advantage of public enforcement from the modern constitutional perspective is that public enforcers are democratically accountable to those on whose behalf they enforce in a way that private parties are not.

Arguments of this type are now second nature but nonetheless remain jurisdiction-sensitive. A polity that was strongly committed to a more minimal ideal of the State,[30] or persuaded of the populist ideal of a sovereign citizenry,[31] might well set less store by the idea of *exclusive* State rights of action in respect of public laws, even if these were still the basic norm. It might provide for a more diverse set of enforcement arrangements in which citizens enjoyed greater liberty and power to play a role in the detection and prosecution of public wrongs. Constitutional arguments can also cut in different ways because constitutions comprise a set of values, not just one, and, whilst giving enforcement rights to the executive in accordance with the logic just stated, they also generally require States to be legally accountable to their citizens as an aspect of the rule of law.[32] A clear normative implication of the accountability principle is that citizens themselves have legal rights to hold the State to the duties that it owes to them, and to challenge its excesses of power through independent courts of law. When the rule of law is brought into the frame, it is therefore readily apparent that rights of action in respect of public laws cannot be confined to the State itself.

[27] US Const art II, § 1, cl 1. See further S Hamer, 'Lincoln's Law: Constitutional and Policy Issues Posed by the Qui Tam Provisions of the False Claims Act' (1996) 6 Kansas Journal of Law and Public Policy 89; Chapter 7 Sections 7.2B(iii), 7.2C(ii).

[28] US Const Art II, § 2, cl 2 (the appointments clause)

[29] US Const Art III.

[30] The concept of the 'minimal state' is most often associated with the work of R Nozick, *Anarchy, State and Utopia* (Blackwell 1974) but I have no intention to reference that idea here. Interestingly, Nozick recognized good arguments as to why the State has some 'special legitimacy' to enforce criminal laws—as the agent of many people who themselves have a right to punish, it has more enforcement rights than any one of them. He nonetheless appears to have denied that either the State—or anyone else—is especially 'entitled to be the dominant agency' to whom enforcement falls: 139–40.

[31] J Weir, 'Sovereign Citizens: A Reasoned Response to the Madness' (2015) 19 Lewis and Clark Law Review 829; C Kalinowski IV, 'A Legal Response to the Sovereign Citizen Movement' (2019) 80 Montana Law Review 153; H Hobbs and G Williams, *Micronations and the Search for Sovereignty* (CUP 2022).

[32] AV Dicey, *Introduction to the Study of the Law of the Constitution* 7th edn (Macmillan 1908) Ch 4.

B. The Ethical Risks of Private Initiative

A second, pragmatic justification for Blackstone's public enforcement vision could lie in the abuse and corruption to which private enforcement had given rise in the centuries that preceded it.[33] We certainly saw plenty of evidence of this in the last chapter, private prosecutorial powers having been used by informers for the purpose of blackmail, personal advancement, or spite; to settle claims in ways prejudicial to the public interest; or even to collude with offenders to defraud the public purse.[34] Radzinowicz's seminal account of eighteenth-century England is replete with appalling abuses of these kinds and the intense public resentment they generated.[35] Attempts were made to quell them. Barring criminal accomplices from prosecuting their co-conspirators was a good start. So was criminalizing the 'compounding' (gainful settlement) of claims,[36] but such laws had themselves to be enforced, and if this were again left purely to private persons, it seems reasonable to speculate that they too might have become the objects of further corruption or compromise so that the intervention of a State agent was inevitably required at some stage to break the cycle of self-interest and moral abuse. Other measures, such as granting enforcement monopolies to just a few, trusted persons (common practice in the reigns of Elizabeth I and James I) failed spectacularly,[37] it being found that private monopolies simply increase the risk of corruption.[38] Abandoning the system of rewards for private prosecutors was probably the most effective step taken to tackle moral risk, but this occurred in England only late in the day (1951) and did not entirely eliminate the ethical problem, as scandals canvassed later in the book will show.[39]

The moral risks associated with private action might therefore point to the wisdom of locating prosecutorial power in respect of public laws in the hands of

[33] Royal Commission on the Criminal Law, *Eighth Report* PP 1845 XIV 161 (leaving prosecutions to private persons leaves a 'wide door to bribery, collusion and illegal compromises') cited in Hetherington (n 2) 5; N Garoupa and D Klerman, 'Corruption and Private Law Enforcement: Theory and History' (2010) 6 Review of Law and Economics 75.

[34] An example cited by Radzinowicz (n 23) 308 is that of persons being persuaded to commit acts of vagrancy in violation of a statute of George II (17 Geo 2 c 5) in order to share in the common informer's reward. Collusion of this sort is only likely where the public reward offered to the prosecutor is greater than the penalty the offender must pay. By contrast, where the reward is less than the penalty, extortion on the part of the prosecutor, or bribery on the part of the offender are more likely.

[35] ibid Ch 6, esp 138–61. Similar abuses were common in the Roman system: W Nippel *Public Order in Ancient Rome* (CUP 1995) 20–21.

[36] Radzinowicz (n 23) 313. On further measures, see Chapter 7 Section 7.2B(i), n 95 and text thereto.

[37] Beresford (n 20) 232 (noting the imprisonment of Sir Stephen Proctor, one such grantee of a monopoly, in the Tower of London, at the insistence of the Commons). Other measures designed to quell the abuse included stays of proceedings, a register of compositions, official pardons for those falsely accused, and eventually the devolution of prosecutions to local courts, such that the threat of having to incur travel expense to defend a claim was no longer available to informer as a lever for extortion: ibid 234–37.

[38] N Garpoupa and D Klerman, 'Corruption and Private Law Enforcement: Theory and History'(2010) 6 Review of Law and Economics 75, 89.

[39] Chapter 7 Section 7.3 (Post Office scandal).

salaried public servants, who are more easily held accountable, and perhaps less susceptible to illicit temptation by virtue of their regular remuneration and public service culture. It is unlikely, however, that the ethical risks associated with prosecutorial power themselves explain the modern preference for using public agents to enforce public laws. Private corruption exists to some degree in private law claims too (albeit that the consequences are less serious), and it is certainly not just private enforcers that have engaged historically in oppression, improper compromise, and collusion.[40] Indeed, the corruption that can be engendered by the concentrated power of public offices provided the core motivation of many early private Roman actions and measures for their incentivization, as we saw in the last chapter.[41] Whether enforcement is public or private, measures to safeguard the integrity of the process are needed and are now more or less standard.[42] Moral risk therefore seems unlikely to provide a full explanation for choosing the public enforcement pattern in public law, however large that risk sometimes seems to loom.

C. No Private Incentive to Suit

Another justification for public enforcement is the practical reality that leaving the prosecution of public offences to private citizens will be ineffective because the latter lack any incentive to enforce laws protecting State interests.[43] The problem is that the costs of prosecuting almost always exceed the personal benefits of altruism. Historically, the incentive to sue was increased from time to time by refunding a prosecutor's costs even where the prosecution was unsuccessful,[44] but this proved insufficient. Reimbursement does not compensate for the opportunity cost of a person's involvement in a protracted legal proceeding, nor for the stress, or (in earlier times) the risks of violent personal reprisal. The public spirit of a private enforcer must therefore be exceptionally strong if she is to be moved to enforce a law that protects *only* the public interest, unless she has also been caused personal harm by the wrong. Even then, she must be prepared to invest significant resources of her own, unless public restitution for her time and effort is provided, or some form of positive reward by way of a share of the financial penalty,[45] at which latter point, however, we tend to re-enter the zone of ethical risk that we sought in the previous section to escape.

40 Radzinowicz (n 23) Chs 10, 11.
41 Chapter 4 Section 4.3B nn 56, 63, and text thereto.
42 Chapter 3 Sections 3.4B and C.
43 J Bentham, *An Introduction to the Principles of Morals and Legislation* (Clarendon 1907) 307.
44 Hetherington (n 2) 5.
45 For a radical model, advocating the complete competitive privatization of public law enforcement, with any private person or firm having standing to enforce and taking all the spoils (or sharing them with victims), see G Becker and GJ Stigler, 'Law Enforcement, Malfeasance, and Compensation of Enforcers' (1974) 3 Journal of Legal Studies 1.

The argument about a private person's general lack of personal interest in enforcing a public law is clearly sound but does not conclusively rule out private action: it is a reason why private enforcement of public laws is not normally a good idea, not a reason why public enforcement is always better. A private enforcer might club together with others to share costs and distribute risk, or cost orders could impose those risks upon offenders, assuming the latter are solvent.[46] An enforcer might be well resourced and her sense of public right might be stronger than her self-interest, or stronger than the interest of an overworked and jaded bureaucrat. The public law in question might also be designed fully, or in part, to protect private interests of hers that have been harmed (her liberty, for example, or her life), or those of a group to which she belongs (perhaps the dignity of her race), as well as the interests of society as a whole, so that she has a sufficient personal stake in the proceeding to be motivated to act.[47] There is also no guarantee that if an enforcement decision is placed in public hands, a public agency will prosecute every suitable case.[48] It may lack the resources to proceed, or its motivation to sue could be distorted by other operational priorities, capture, or incompetence—issues we explore further below. The most one can say is that it generally makes sense to place a right of action in public hands where a public law protects purely public interests, without necessarily precluding a private enforcer from having such a right in particular cases if she has sufficient capacity and motivation, and provided there are appropriate controls in place to deal with the moral risks. The argument for public enforcement from the point of view of enforcer incentives is therefore also general and contingent, not absolute.

D. Efficiency

The literature considering the question whether it is more economically efficient for public or private enforcers to enforce public law provides no clear-cut answer.[49]

[46] Traditionally, the problem in the US has been that parties bear their own costs, but this has been varied in respect of many private enforcement provisions. See further Chapter 7.

[47] Bentham (n 43) 302–07 notes that private enforcers will have incentives to sue in respect of private offences and 'semi-public' offences which protect the interest of a group to which the enforcer belongs, as well as in some cases of purely public wrongdoing (against State or societal interests) where she has herself been harmed. Where private interests are at the heart of the relevant public law, incentives can also clearly be increased by offering full compensatory remedies for personal harm. The increase in remedial incentives opened the door to the dramatic rise of private actions for discrimination under Title VII of the Civil Rights 1964, from 1991: on which see S Farhang, *The Litigation State: Public Regulation and Private Lawsuits in the US* (Princeton University Press 2010) 182–90.

[48] N Cohen and P Rubin, 'Private Enforcement of Public Policy' (1985) 3 Yale Journal on Regulation 167 (public agencies do not have the correct incentives to enforce many areas of regulatory policy such as automobile safety and environmental offset policies; private agencies should be used instead).

[49] See seminally Becker and Stigler (n 45) (advocating free-market private enforcement); W Landes and R Posner, 'The Private Enforcement of Law' (1975) 4 Journal of Legal Studies 1 (responding critically on the basis that private enforcement of fines will tend to yield over-enforcement); R Posner, *Economic Analysis of Law* (Wolters Kluwer 2014) Ch 24; A Polinski, 'Private Versus Public

If the aim is not to ensure that the law is enforced *fully*, but (only) to the extent that this achieves the greatest overall social benefit, complex calculations are required as to which type of enforcer is most likely to enforce in a way that achieves 'optimal' deterrence of wrongdoing, and under what conditions. A guarded, general view expressed by Landes and Posner in 1975 was that public enforcement is more likely to be efficient than private enforcement because (putting it crudely) for a private enforcer to be motivated to act, one has to offer her a cut of a financial penalty that has been greatly inflated in its deterrence value so as to offset the statistical probability of other offences going undetected, but that this in turn tends to send a false signal to other enforcers, who will be lured by the size of the reward to over-invest in enforcement. In short, if you want to deter wrongdoers by using private actions you must impose a large penalty on those you sometimes catch and offer a large corresponding bounty to the enforcer, but that is then likely to cause an unhealthy popular rush to litigation, the costs of which exceed the social benefits. Public agents, by contrast, are free of the same incentive distortion because they lack profit motive and are hence more likely to prosecute only when it is socially efficient to do so.[50]

Enforcement of Fines' (1980) 9 Journal of Legal Studies 105 (making further adjustments and concluding that whatever the costs of private enforcement under either competitive or monopolistic conditions, public enforcement yields *more* enforcement); Cohen and Rubin (n 48). For representative studies in different public law contexts, see R Van den Bergh, 'Enforcement of Consumer Law by Consumer Associations' in M Faure and F Stephen (eds), *Essays in the Law and Economic of Regulation* (Intersentia 2008) Ch 15, 300 (both private and public enforcement can be suboptimal: coexistence of the two is the 'only policy option'); M Faure, A Ogus, and N Philipsen, 'Curbing Consumer Financial Losses: The Economics of Regulatory Enforcement' (2009) 31 Law and Policy 161, 182–83 (no final conclusion as to whether allowing private enforcement of public law is to be allowed, but favouring allowing private law claims to be added into the public law process); M Faure and L Tilindyte, 'Toward an Effective Enforcement of Occupational Health and Safety Regulation' in Faure and Stephen (eds), *Essays in the Law and Economic of Regulation* (Intersentia 2008) Ch 17, 328–30 (public enforcement is most likely to be optimal in the workplace health and safety context). In the competition (antitrust) law context, the debate in the US as to whether private or public enforcement offers greater deterrence value is especially vexed: R Lande and J Davis, 'Benefits From Private Antitrust Enforcement: An Analysis of Forty Cases' (2008) 42 University of San Francisco Law Review 879 (nearly half of all antitrust violations in the study were uncovered by private parties and private action is likely to have higher deterrence value than public enforcement); R Lande and J Davis, 'Comparative Deterrence from Private Enforcement and Criminal Enforcement of the US Antitrust Laws' (2011) Brigham Young University Law Review 315; R Lande, 'Introduction: Benefits of Private Enforcement' in A Foer and R Stutz (eds), *Private Enforcement of Antitrust Law in the United States: A Handbook* (Edward Elgar 2012) Ch 1, 7–9 (estimating private enforcement deterrence value at three times that of public enforcement); G Werden, S Hammond, and B Barnett, 'Deterrence and Detection of Cartels: Using All the Tools and Sanctions' (2011) 56 Antitrust Bulletin 207; R Lande and J Davis, 'The Extraordinary Deterrence of Private Antitrust Enforcement: A Reply to Werden, Hammond, and Barnett' (2013) 58 Antitrust Bulletin 173; G Werden, 'Cartel Deterrence through Criminal Enforcement; A Rejoinder to Lande and Davis' (2013) 58 Antitrust Bulletin 191.

[50] Landes and Posner (n 49) 15; Posner, *Economic Analysis of Law* (n 49) 859–62. The claim that overenforcement is likely in respect of US antitrust laws has been questioned on the basis that the recoverable penalty is in practice not as high as the 'triple damages' advertised, in fact being closer to 'single' damages: R Lande, *Five Myths about Antitrust Damages* (2006) 40 University of San Francisco Law Review 651, 655–57. For further subtleties, see AM Polinsky, 'Private Versus Public Enforcement of Fines' (1980) 9 Journal of Legal Studies 105.

The point that private parties are generally inefficient enforcers of public laws is very likely to be true. Steven Shavell points out that they will in fact tend to *both over-* and *under*-enforce penalties because even assuming that they are fully rational economic actors (often questionable), they will be unable accurately to determine the social costs and benefits of their litigation and feed the numbers into their calculations about whether, when, and whom to prosecute.[51] Private persons also generally have no easy way of ascertaining that an offence against the State, or other citizens, has been committed, and even if they are themselves the victim of a wrong, they still may not know who did it.[52] The costs (both financial and social) of giving them the technical means to find out would likely be so high as to be economically self-defeating. Imagine the cost and social consequences, for example, of enabling you or I to detect and prosecute breaches of national security, or acts of treason, even if we could be persuaded that it was financially worth our while to do so. It makes more sense for the costs of expensive detection tools to be borne only once, and by a central agency. Furthermore, even if a private prosecutor already has all the information she needs about an offence, unless she is granted an enforcement monopoly and thereby placed in control of all prosecution decisions (which is itself ethically risky for reasons mentioned above and which cuts out the normal advantages of competition), she will be unable to benefit from economies of scale, and other private citizens may end up wastefully duplicating her efforts. A final problem is that if she enforces a public law benefitting the community as a whole, others will tend to 'free-ride' on her enforcement investment.[53] Whilst she may not care about this personally, and at one level it seems laudably generous and public-spirited of her and therefore something one might wish to encourage, free-riding is a problem for economists because it represents a form of market failure.

These factors suggest that the basic public enforcement pattern makes sense on at least some scales of efficiency and in most common circumstances and contexts—especially where the damage caused by an offence is widespread and/or hard for a private individual to discover, where the laws in question are so complicated or

[51] S Shavell, 'The Fundamental Divergence Between the Private and the Social Motive to Use the Legal System' (1997) 26 Journal of Legal Studies 575, 579. Public agents, by contrast, *may* have more access to information about social effects, but the truth is that the social costs and benefits of enforcing or not enforcing are very hard to assess accurately even for a public agency, and gathering that empirical information will itself be very costly. On the serious problems of cost–benefit calculation, see A Ogus, *Costs and Cautionary Tales* (Hart 2006) 283–87.

[52] AM Polinski and S Shavell, 'Economic Theory of Public Enforcement of Law' (2000) 38 Journal of Economic Literature 45, 46; S Shavell, 'The Optimal Structure of Law Enforcement' (1993) 36 Journal of Law and Economics 255, 268–70, 278–79, 282. The problem is not just that the facts about wider social harms may be unknown but also that private persons may not know that behaviour breaches the relevant rule, where the rule itself is complex and its application to the facts unclear.

[53] Van den Bergh (n 49) 282–83, 287–88. The free-riding problem in respect of collective goods is not just of interest to economists but also to political scientists, philosophers, social psychologists, and game theorists. For perhaps the seminal exploration by an economist and political scientist, see M Olson, *The Logic of Collective Action: Public Goods and the Theory of Groups* (Harvard University Press 1965).

arcane that it is difficult for a private person to determine whether or not they have been breached, or where there are (as tends to be the case in the employee health and safety context, for example)[54] especially strong disincentives for an ordinary individual to sue, such as risks of reprisal. Public enforcers' motivations also tend to align with the (public) interests of the community that the laws are generally intended to protect, avoiding the distortion caused by private self-interest;[55] they can channel and coordinate action for breaches of the law affecting large societal groups through a single conduit, avoiding duplication and achieving efficiencies of scale by virtue of their enforcement monopoly, and—since they are funded by the entire body of taxpayers—no one gets to free-ride on their enforcement efforts.[56]

There are, however, no absolutes in the law and economics game. Everything depends on relative information and enforcement costs; on the size of the harm caused by an offence; on the nature and extent of the private incentives to suit; and on the extent to which a monopoly in enforcement is permitted. Collective private enforcement processes can tackle some information problems, reduce the private disincentives to suit, and allay concerns over the multiplicity of actions. Sometimes—secretive offences such as public fraud or cartel collusion seem to provide examples—private individuals may even be in a better position to know about a wrong than the State, even with the latter's increasingly powerful technologies. Equally, public enforcement incentives can themselves be blunted by incompetence, resource constraint, or capture, as we consider further below.

The safest general conclusion is that public enforcement usually makes economic sense in public law in a way that it does not in private law, but that there are probably some cases where it does not, or where it may at least make sense to supplement the public system with private enforcers. From this point of view, the economic arguments both support the basic public enforcement paradigm and potentially justify exceptional departures from it.

E. Consistency and Transparency

A further reason to favour public enforcement is that this promotes consistency and transparency in enforcement policy, which is important to citizens from the point of view of their equal treatment before the law and their ability to choose how to act in its shadow. Both values are important constitutionally, but they have independent moral valence of their own. Although public enforcement is itself not monolithic and comprises a host of individual decisions taken by different

[54] Faure and Tilindyte (n 49) 330.
[55] This kind of problem is known in the economic literature as the 'principal–agent problem': Van den Bergh (n 49) 288–95.
[56] ibid 300.

enforcement officers (often quite widely spread geographically), policy can be co-ordinated by assigning decisions in particular fields to specialized agencies (see above), and by issuing binding and widely publicized guidance to individual officers and members of the public. Private prosecutions, by contrast, are dispersed, atomistic, and guided by an undisclosed logic. This could be changed if private prosecutors were required by law to join private prosecution associations, the membership of which was bound to follow official public guidance. But to ensure the values of consistency and transparency were adhered to, the State would inevitably have to get involved so as to guarantee proper coordination and auditing of the dispersed decisions of disparate private actors, which itself entails significant cost.

F. The Vexatious Private Litigant

A final concern is that allowing private actions in public law invites 'vexatious' litigation. This is an old chestnut and is hard to crack. The vexatious private litigant is not necessarily morally corrupt in the sense considered above. He or she is simply a nuisance—a busybody who 'habitually and persistently institutes legal proceedings without reasonable grounds'.[57] Such characters (mostly male, according to the limited research) are a mysterious and heterogeneous group, ranging from the aggressive, entitled, or disingenuous to those who are most likely suffering some form of psychiatric condition, including schizophrenia.[58] They are a source of concern both because they waste court time and money and because they harass their fellow citizens and public institutions.

At first blush, one might imagine that vexatious suits would be more common in respect of public laws than private ones, since public rules are likely (owing both to their broader reach and publicity) to excite the interest of a greater number of busybodies. Following that logic, it would be no coincidence that the first Australian legislation enacted to deal with vexatious litigants responded to a rash of querulous proceedings against public authorities and agents,[59] or that the concern is regularly cited in the context of judicial review proceedings and misfeasance in public office, where a single public decision can excite large sections of the population and therefore potentially spawn many baseless challenges.[60] There is something

[57] Vexatious Actions Act 1896 (UK) s 1. Definitions vary markedly between jurisdictions and statutes.

[58] G Lester, 'The Vexatious Litigant' (2005) 17 Judicial Officers' Bulletin 17, 18; G Lester and S Smith, 'Inventor, Entrepreneur, Rascal, Crank or Querulent? Australia's Vexatious Litigant Sanction 75 Years On' (2006) 13 Psychiatry, Psychology and Law 1.

[59] Supreme Court (Vexatious Actions) Amendment Act 1927 (Vic); N Kirby, 'When Rights Cause Injustice: A Critique of the Vexatious Proceedings Act 2008 (NSW)' (2009) 31 Sydney Law Review 163, 174. For a recent example in which a vexatious litigant's targets were primarily public entities and their agents, see *Storry v Parkyn (Vexatious Proceedings Order)* [2024] FCAFC 100.

[60] In the judicial review context see eg *Jones v Skyring* [1992] HCA 39; *Jones v Cusack* [1992] HCA 40 (challenges to the validity of legal tender). It is in part to deal with such issues that applications

about bureaucratic State power that undoubtedly inflames citizen reaction. In fact, however, such (scanty) evidence as there is about the vexatious litigant tends to suggest that there is no consistent pattern, with litigation spanning a wide variety of disputes involving not just public authorities but family proceedings and property matters, and litigants reaching randomly for whatever laws they feel may avail them in their personal sense of grievance.[61]

It is therefore unlikely that the risk of private vexation provides the reason—or a good reason—for the systematic choice in favour of public enforcement. As far as we know, although the phenomenon is real,[62] the number of litigants is small,[63] they exist in private law proceedings as well as public law ones, and they can, if push comes to shove, be barred from further vexation without having first to obtain court permission[64]—an extreme measure, perhaps, but one that stops the most persistent offenders in their tracks. Like corruption, the risk is a wrinkle in the fabric of justice, to be ironed out through proper procedural safeguards, not a basic determinant of enforcement system design. In the same way, I shall later suggest, concerns about vexatious litigation provide a questionable basis for restricting a private party's *standing*—his or her entitlement to a *right of action*—in either public or private law.[65]

5.4 Two Recurrent Problems

Although there are good reasons for the public enforcement paradigm, it runs into difficulties. There are two common issues of recurrent concern and particular contemporary importance that echo through the chapters on private enforcement that follow and which therefore require special prefatory mention as a foreword to much that is to come.

for judicial review require judicial leave: see Chapter 6 Section 6.4. On misfeasance see Chapter 6 Section 6.3.

[61] Victoria Law Reform Committee (VLRC), *Inquiry into Vexatious Litigants* No 162 (2008) 38–40.

[62] There were twenty-three registered in Queensland in 2015: Justice Debra Mullins, 'Vexatious Litigation: Dealing with Vexatious Litigants' (September 2015): https://archive.sclqld.org.au/judgepub/2015/mullins010915.pdf accessed 4 December 2025. On the phenomenon in family proceedings (which is the field in Australia in which such proceedings are perhaps most common) see E Fitch and P Easteal, 'Vexatious Litigation in Family Law and Coercive Control: Ways to Improve Legal Remedies and Better Protect the Victims' (2017) 7 Family Law Review 103.

[63] Kirby (n 59) 174–75; VLRC Report No 162 (n 61) 29–32 (305 vexatious litigant orders in all Australian jurisdictions since the 1930s). Broad-ranging empirical assessments are hard to find and the figures available represent only those against whom orders have been issued: ibid 33–34. One of the biggest and best studies of 105 litigants is by S Hedley, 'Vexatious Litigants in England and Wales 1990–Present' (Paper presented at the 'Access to Justice: How Much is Too Much?' Conference, Prato, Italy, 30 June–1 July 2006, available on request from the author).

[64] Supreme Court Act 1981 (UK) s 42; Vexatious Proceedings Act 2008 s 8 (NSW).

[65] See Chapter 6 Sections 6.2A, 6.3A n 60, and text thereto; Chapter 7 Section 7.1A(ii) n 54 and text thereto, Section 7.3A(ii) n 196, Section 7.4.

A. Capture

The first is the concern that a public enforcer may not do its job (that is, promote the interests that the relevant public laws are intended to protect)[66] because it is 'captured' either by a political agenda ('political capture') or by the interests of the group of offenders that it is supposed to be regulating ('offender capture').[67]

'Political capture' can occur where a law enforcement officer is also a member of executive government (as is the Attorney-General in some jurisdictions), or—more topically perhaps—if he or she has been appointed to direct an 'independent' agency in order implement the party-political aims of the government of the day. A notorious example was Donald Trump's appointment of Scott Pruitt, a well-known climate change sceptic and industry ally, to head the US Environmental Protection Agency in furtherance of the deregulatory agenda of his first presidential term, and there is alarming evidence of the same disruptive strategy being repeated in his second term. Another notorious example was the appointment by Ronald Reagan of William Bradford Reynolds, an outspoken critic of race-conscious civil rights policy, to head up the Justice Department's Civil Rights Division during the 1980s.[68] We might call this practice of agency disablement 'neutering from the top'. It is hard to prevent where agency staff are appointed and funded by—and report directly to—Ministers, rather than to Parliament or Congress as a whole.

'Offender capture' occurs, by contrast, where an enforcer identifies too closely with the interests of the party against whom it is charged to enforce a law. This is not so much a matter of corruption (bribery, for example), which is a conceptually different problem, but stems from an enforcer becoming unconsciously so integrated into the culture of the offender group as to be influenced by the latter's values and aims. Think of this as the institutional equivalent of Lima syndrome (the flipside of the better-known Stockholm syndrome).[69] Long-term relationships often develop between public regulators and the private industries they regulate because regulation is a graduated process in which legal proceedings are always a

[66] These are usually public interests but can also include a mix of public and private interests, as in the case of laws against rape, anticompetitive practices, or the violation of human rights.

[67] The two can be—and often are—integrally related where government itself is captured by industry interests through lobbying. Most work focuses on offender capture. For useful overviews of the now vast literature, see J Rex, 'Agency Capture' Ch 24 in Maggetti, Di Mascio, and Natalini (eds) (n 18); J Laffont and J Tirole, 'The Politics of Government Decision-Making: A Theory of Regulatory Capture' (1991) 106 Quarterly Journal of Economics 1089; E Dale Bó, 'Regulatory Capture: A Review' (2006) 22 Oxford Review of Economic Policy 203; R Posner, 'The Concept of Regulatory Capture: A Short, Inglorious History' in D Carpenter and D Moss (eds), *Preventing Regulatory Capture Special Interest Influence and How to Limit It* (CUP 2014) Ch 2. For a seminal general treatment, see G Stigler, 'The Theory of Economic Regulation' (1971) 3 Bell Journal of Economics and Management Sciences 3.

[68] Farhang (n 47) 173–74. See further on the phenomenon in the civil rights context, S Burbank, S Farhang, and H Kritzer, 'Private Enforcement' (2013) 17 Lewis and Clark Law Review 637, 692–93.

[69] In Lima syndrome (so called after the 1996 Japanese embassy hostage crisis in Lima, Peru) the empowered hostage-taker becomes sympathetic to the plight of his victims—the opposite dynamic to that found in Stockholm syndrome.

measure of last resort, being initiated only after softer compliance measures such as education, persuasion, and warning have been tried over an extended period of time.[70] Agencies may also have to rely upon the offending industry to supply the very information that is needed if they are to discover and prosecute infractions, and they often draw their staff from the industry itself, in order to benefit from its specialized knowledge and expertise—a problem known in the literature as the 'revolving door' problem. All of this tacit cooperation can lead to witting or unwitting alignment—in varying degrees and over different timescales—of a public enforcer's motives with those of an offender group, even if the latter has no provable intention to manipulate. The risk is especially great where an agency is responsible in the long term for overseeing a single industry, and at its most acute where that industry enjoys a monopoly, such that its power is highly concentrated.[71]

Capture of either type is problematic from both the constitutional and economic points of view. From the constitutional perspective, the object of public law enforcement is to advance the interests protected by the various public laws, which are (usually) public interests—it is not a commodity to be used for the advancement of private individuals[72] such as politicians obsessed with their own re-election, or commercial corporations whose driving motivation is their share price. Even the *perception* of capture breaks the bond of trust between citizen and government upon which the entrustment of enforcement power to the latter is based and is therefore a source of serious constitutional concern. From the economic standpoint, any divorce between the motivations of a public enforcer and the interests that a public law is intended to protect distorts the enforcement incentive and yields suboptimal outcomes in terms of social deterrence.

The evidence that enforcement capture of either kind actually exists in practice is contested, and the case is difficult to prove beyond doubt.[73] To show that enforcers are actually deviating from the public interest in favour of particular political

[70] See seminally I Ayres and J Braithwaite, *Responsive Regulation: Transcending the Deregulation Debate* (OUP 1992). For a useful review of the subsequent literature, adjustments and remaining challenges, see M Rorie, 'Responsive Regulation' in *Oxford Handbooks Online* (OUP 2015).

[71] Rex (n 67) 365.

[72] Save, of course, where a public law is specifically designed to protect the private interests of that group.

[73] Firm empirical evidence is lacking and hard to obtain. Posner, 'The Concept of Regulatory Capture' (n 67) 54–56 bluntly denies its likelihood in respect of new-model agencies in the United States (such as environment and consumer protection agencies) that are non-industry-specific, on the basis that it is hard for disparate regulated industries to organize intense and focused influence. One early, empirical study of the nursing home sector found no evidence of capture resulting from 'revolving doors' (staff swaps) between the regulator and the regulated industry, whilst accepting that capture is likely to be institution- and context-specific: T Makkai and J Braithwaite, 'In and out of the Revolving Door: Making Sense of Regulatory Capture' (1992) 12 Journal of Public Policy 61. The phenomenon is nonetheless considered by many to be a credible risk, particularly in the financial services and environmental regulation sectors: Rex (n 67) 364, 366. For a call for more empirical research and a new approach to the topic, see D Carpenter and D Moss, 'Introduction' in Carpenter and Moss (eds) (n 67) Ch 1.

or private interests, one must first define the public interest[74] and then prove causation in respect of government or offender influence.[75] It may also be difficult to distinguish between capture, on the one hand, and legitimate agency receptiveness to private or political concerns, the consideration of which might improve the chances of achieving overall public good, on the other. There are nonetheless grounds for thinking that capture is a real *risk* that exists in a variety of public law domains, in particular (and topically) those of financial regulation[76] and environmental protection,[77] where enforcers face up to some of the most powerful and influential industry opponents. Where such risk exists, it is both reasonable and appropriate for the law to respond in a precautionary fashion—much as it responds to cases of 'presumed undue influence' in private law—by adjusting its approach to causal judgments and evidential standards.[78] To say that influence is not provable beyond doubt, or even on the balance of probabilities, and that its possibility should therefore be disregarded, misses the point about the importance of constitutional *precaution*, the point being that *risk itself* can require robust intervention and sometimes even the adjustment of law enforcement processes. Concern about capture is historically partly responsible for federal agency enforcement powers being supplemented in the United States by rights for citizens to enforce a wide variety of environmental laws, as we shall see.[79] It has also prompted the introduction of extraordinary recent legislation in that jurisdiction that is designed to reduce the influence of concentrated economic interests on Federal agencies.[80] Furthermore, the possibility that a public official might be captured in such a way as to be disinclined to prosecute a colleague for misconduct in public office is an obviously good reason not to rely exclusively on public rights of action, as we shall see in the next chapter. It is a reason to supplement them with private ones where the enforcement of the State's own public duties and liabilities is concerned.

[74] This could variously be constructed in economic or social welfare terms: E Windholz, *Governing Through Regulation: Public Policy, Regulation and the Law* (Taylor & Francis 2017) 35–43.

[75] It seems reasonable to presume capture if an agency consistency adopts a policy favoured by regulated entities: S Shapiro, 'The Complexity of Regulatory Capture: Diagnosis, Causality, and Remediation' (2012) 17 Roger Williams University Law Review 101, 105.

[76] L Baxter, 'Capture' in Financial Regulation: Can we Channel it toward the Common Good?'(2011) 21 Cornell Journal of Law and Public Policy 175; 'Understanding Regulatory Capture: An Academic Perspective from the United States' in S Pagliari (ed), *The Making Good of Financial Regulation* (Grosvenor House Publishing 2012) Ch 2.

[77] See eg J MacLean, 'Striking at the Root Problem of Canadian Environmental Law: Identifying and Escaping Regulatory Capture' (2016) 29 Journal of Environmental Law and Practice 111; M Briody and T Prenzler, 'The Enforcement of Environmental Protection Laws in Queensland: A Case of Regulatory Capture?' (1998) 15 Environmental and Planning Law Journal 55; L Dillon, C Sellers, and V Underhill, 'The Environmental Protection Agency in the Early Trump Administration: Prelude to Regulatory Capture' (2018) 108 American Journal of Public Health 92.

[78] The doctrine of presumed undue influence in private law focusses on the risk for decision-making generated by personal relations of trust and confidence. Once such a relationship is established between the parties, the law responds to the risk by raising an evidential presumption that any subsequent decision was affected by the relationship, unless the opposite is shown: *Thorne v Kennedy* [2017] HCA 49 [34]; *Royal Bank of Scotland plc v Etridge (No 2)* [2002] 2 AC (HL) 773.

[79] Chapter 7 Section7.2C.

[80] Section 1338 Regulatory Capture Prevention Act 2011.

Capture is therefore a credible risk that attends public law enforcement and which potentially calls for a diverse enforcement strategy, as well as for constant scrutiny of the relationship between public agency enforcers, industry, and government.

B. Resource—When Regulatory Ambition Outstrips Capacity

A second, increasingly pressing problem concerns resource. An obvious reason why public enforcement was deficient in the medieval period was that there was no—or very little—public enforcement machinery. Nowadays, we have the machinery but face a different challenge in so far as the enforcement job itself has grown exponentially. The State's regulatory ambitions are at risk of so exceeding its enforcement capacity as to once again leave serious enforcement gaps. As and when this occurs (it probably already has, and probably always will), there are a limited number of logical choices open to us: (1) to regulate less[81] (although unwinding existing legislative commitments is notoriously difficult);[82] (2) to enforce less (which is counterintuitive, *if* one is still committed to the relevant regulatory aims); (3) to spend more on enforcement by diverting resources from elsewhere, or raising taxes (neither of which is politically popular); (4) to find new efficiencies, so as to do more enforcement with less resource (which has clear limits); or (5) to enlist private enforcers to assist in the enforcement task. Some of these paths are rockier than others, but all of them are theoretically possible and selection between them is ultimately a matter for democratic debate.

Without preconceiving which path should be taken, public enforcement systems are currently very obviously feeling the squeeze. In the United Kingdom, in the period 2010–2020, the operating budget of the Health and Safety Executive was slashed by 43 per cent, and staff cut by more than a third;[83] that of the CPS by 33 per cent in real terms;[84] that of the Environment Agency by more than 50 per cent;[85] and that of the English Equality and Human Rights Commission (ECHR)—the watchdog responsible for enforcing the government's own obligations to protect

[81] Better Regulation Task Force, 'Regulation—Less is More: Reducing Burdens, Improving Outcomes', Report to the Prime Minister (March 2005). See also (suggesting that we have already moved to a 'post-interventionist' or 'post-regulatory' phase in which, if there is to be State regulation, it is 'meta regulation'—'regulation of self-regulation') C Scott, 'Self-Regulation and the Meta-regulatory State' in F Cafaggi (ed), *Reframing Self-Regulation in European Private Law* (Kluwer 2006) Ch 4.

[82] F McChesney, 'Of Stranded Costs and Stranded Hopes: The Difficulties of Deregulation' (1999) 3 The Independent Review 485, 506 (once adopted, regulation is a series of 'ratchets upward'). For a sceptical analysis of the extent which this proved possible even during the first Trump administration, see C Coglianese, N Sarin, and S Shapiro, 'The Deregulation Deception' (21 June 2021) University of Pennsylvania Law School, Public Law Research Paper No 20-44, <http://dx.doi.org/10.2139/ssrn.3723915> accessed 4 December 2025.

[83] https://www.britsafe.org/safety-management/2023/a-perfect-storm-why-funding-cuts-are-affecting-hse-s-ability-to-regulate> accessed 4 December 2025.

[84] Rt Hon Geofrey Cox QC AG, evidence to the House of Commons Justice Committee HC 1887 (23 January 2019).

[85] Hansard, Vol 722, Col 810, 17 November 2022.

equality rights—by a whopping 70 per cent.[86] Some of these cuts to enforcer budgets may have been attributable to measures introduced across the board to deal with recent economic downturn, but the data suggest that this is not always the case. An independent study commissioned by the Bar Council of England and Wales found, for example, that the reduction in the CPS's budget was out of step with reductions to other government services and took place against a backdrop of positive growth in the economy and a real-term increase in government expenditure of about 13 per cent.[87] Similarly, the ECHR's commissioner of the time has stated openly that the reduction in his budget had little to do with economic shortfall, but was politically motivated.[88] Although it is hard to prove the accusation, clipping the Commission's wings through budgetary cuts would be consistent with the Conservative government's aim during the same time period of reducing its own exposure to challenge in judicial review proceedings.[89] It would also be consistent with observed strategies in the United States, where agencies have from time to time purposely been starved of resources to give effect to presidential distaste for the regulatory projects with which they have been charged by Congress.[90] It is easy to see at this point how the constraints of resource and political capture connect—public resource being always partly a matter of political will.

Choices will always have to be made between resourcing law enforcement and other social priorities, but the idea that public enforcement agents might be hamstrung deliberately in order to protect the State itself against challenge, or to frustrate the aims of legislation that Parliament has approved, is deeply troubling. The effect of the CPS cuts was a serious drop in charging rates and a corresponding increase in the number of private prosecutions, some of which have proven highly contentious.[91] The British Safety Council and the Royal Society for the Prevention of Accidents both present a similarly bleak view of the impact of budgetary restrictions upon health and safety in the workplace, reporting a drop in HSE inspections of nearly 40 per cent since 2010,[92] and a halving of the rate at which fatal accidents are being reduced, relative to the two decades prior to 2009. Environment Agency prosecutions reportedly declined between 2012 and 2021 by 76 per cent,[93] 93 per cent

[86] D Isaac, 'Reflections on the EHRC' (2020) 6 European Human Rights Law Review 578, 580.

[87] M Chalkley, *Funding for Justice* (1 November 2018): <https://www.barcouncil.org.uk/resource/funding-for-justice-2008-2018.html> accessed 4 December 2025.

[88] Isaac (n 86) 580.

[89] See Chapter 6 Section 6.4 n 74 and text thereto.

[90] A classic example is again the Environmental Protection Agency, which suffered particularly serious budget cuts during the Reagan administration in 1984 of some 44 per cent in real terms relative to 1980 levels. Similar swingeing measures (a 31 per cent cut in 2017 and 26 per cent cut in 2021) were proposed during the first Trump administration but ultimately rejected by Congress.

[91] See Chapter 7 Section 7.3.

[92] <http://www.britsafe.org/safety-management/2023/a-perfect-storm-why-funding-cuts-are-affecting-hse-s-ability-to-regulate> accessed 4 December 2025.

[93] T Colle, '76% drop in Environment Agency prosecutions in last decade, ENDS analysis shows' ENDS Report (31 October 2022) < http://www.endsreport.com/article/1803690/76-drop-environment-agency-prosecutions-last-decade-ends-analysis-shows#:~:text=Analysis%20of%20two%20decades%20worth,carried%20out%20by%20the%20regulator.> accessed 6 December 2025.

of prosecutions for serious pollution were downgraded between 2016 and 2020,[94] and morale has been at an all-time low, with experienced staff leaving the agency in droves.[95]

The point here is not to list all the resource constraints that public enforcement faces—these are part and parcel of political life and they tend to come and go—but to highlight the temptation that they provide to governments in the modern administrative State, or in a community of such States, to revert (or turn for the first time) to private enforcers to advance regulatory objectives. This is less controversial for fiscal conservatives than cutting other services or raising taxes to meet enforcement targets. If governments remain committed to their regulatory aims (or unable to deregulate without losing face, or public office) then embracing a mixed public–private enforcement pattern begins to look very attractive in comparison to the more visible and potentially unpopular political alternatives.[96]

None of this is to say that the public enforcement paradigm is unsound, merely that its capacity is increasingly limited in a way that requires creative thinking. The resourcing arguments suggest that although public enforcement is a good constitutional paradigm, unless we are prepared to change our regulatory priorities or pay more in tax, in the current economic environment there are increasingly likely to be gaps in its coverage, and that in consequence agencies and governments will be tempted to lever private resources once again to make up the deficit.

5.5 Private Interest Protection

Whilst public law and public enforcement very often protect public interests, they are not confined to this role. There are, in fact, an increasing number of modern examples in which public prosecutors not only seek the imposition of public penalties but obtain remedies that protect the private interests of particular persons or groups impacted by a public wrong that they are prosecuting. This relief again supplements the rights that victims themselves may have to seek compensation for their injury under distinct social welfare legislation, such as a criminal injuries compensation scheme, or in private law proceedings. These cases present a fascinating, mirror image of the historical examples we observed in the previous chapter, in which *private* enforcers sometimes sought—and were granted—both private restoration and the imposition of a penalty upon an offender in one and

[94] A Laville and R Salvidge 'Environment Agency Downgrading 93% of Prosecutions for Serious Pollution' *Guardian* (2 March 2022).

[95] H O'Brien, 'Dirty Waters: How the Environment Agency Lost its Way' *Guardian* (13 June 2024).

[96] See the Panel remarks of Sarah Cardell, CEO of the CMA, Competition Appeal Tribunal 20th Anniversary Conference (4 May 2023), which emphasize the 'complementary' operation of public and private enforcement as parts of a single regime, and the need for coordination between the various actions: <http://www.gov.uk/government/speeches/private-actions-and-public-enforcement> accessed 4 December 2025.

the same judicial proceeding. I sketch two examples below. The first relates to the powers of criminal courts to make compensation orders against an offender as part of the sentencing process. The second relates to powers that modern regulatory consumer protection agencies are increasingly given to apply to a court (or even sometimes to seek at their own motion) redress from a wrongdoer in respect of a regulatory infringement. In both instances, the public enforcement proceeding is a hybrid, wrapping the protection of both public and private interests into one and the same procedural sleeve.

A. Criminal Compensation Orders

Criminal courts in both England[97] and Australia[98] may order an offender to pay compensation to anyone suffering personal injury, loss, or damage as a result of his crime. Orders are available for crimes of any type and, whilst normally being granted to the immediate victim, can inure to the benefit of anyone suffering relevant harm.[99] In England, they are made once an offender has been convicted as a formal part of the sentencing process, alongside fines and other punitive, rehabilitative, or restorative measures. They cover a wide range of injuries to property, person, and mind, and are not subject to any formal cap:[100] whilst courts are guided by a tariff system as a starting point in personal injury cases, the governing principle is that they award such compensation as they consider to be appropriate for the loss or damage suffered.[101]

Orders of this kind have been available in England on a limited basis since 1948,[102] but governments have recently given them much higher priority. This is both a reaction to calls for the better protection of crime victims, and, it is fair to say, a way of trying to take pressure off the State-funded Criminal Injuries Compensation Scheme (CICS),[103] which has shrunk from its original ambitions and is facing new financial restrictions of its own.[104] Responding to public resource

[97] Sentencing Act 2020 (UK) (SAUK) Part 7, Ch 2. See generally D Miers, *Criminal Injuries Compensation State and Offender Compensation for Violent Crime* (OUP 2018) Part 2.

[98] See eg Sentencing Act 1991 (Vic) s 85B, s 86; Penalties and Sentences Act 1992 (Qld) s 35; Crimes Act 1914 (Cth) s 21B; Criminal Law (Sentencing) Act 1988 (SA) s 53; CCA s 45AI, s 87 (cartel offences).

[99] See eg SAUK s 133 (b) (ii), s 138; Sentencing Act 1991 (Vic) s 85B(1); Penalties and Sentences Act 1992 (Qld) s 35(1)(c).

[100] In the UK, this rule applies provided the offender is 18 or over. Orders imposed upon those under eighteen years in Magistrates' Courts are currently limited to £5,000: SAUK s 139. Note also special exclusions concerning criminal road accidents: s 136.

[101] SAUK s 135 (2). The tariff figures are guidelines only and do no displace the Court's overall discretion: Miers, *Criminal Injuries Compensation State and Offender Compensation for Violent Crime* (n 97) [8.22]–[8.23].

[102] Criminal Justice Act 1948 s 11(2) (cases of conditional discharge or probation).

[103] Criminal Injuries Compensation Act 1995 (UK).

[104] For the history and context, see Ministry of Justice, *Getting it Right for Victims and Witnesses, the Government Response* Cm 8397 (2012); *Restorative Justice Action Plan for the Criminal Justice System* (2012); Miers, *Criminal Injuries Compensation State and Offender Compensation for Violent*

constraints and simultaneously making a popular statement about the importance of bringing responsibility home to criminals, the policy has been to shift the private costs of crime away from taxpayers and back to offenders themselves wherever possible.

The increased importance now given to protecting private interests within the sentencing process is visible in several features of the modern English scheme. First, courts *must* now *consider* making a compensation order whenever harm has resulted from an offence and give reasons if they choose not to do so.[105] Public prosecutors are expected to draw attention to their obligations. Second, orders must be made *wherever possible* and without regard to other sources of relief that might be available to a victim, such as damages in subsequent civil proceedings or a potential award under the CICS.[106] The intention is therefore to give a victim quick access to a payout from the offender as a first port of call, and if she later obtains further compensation elsewhere, the amount of the payout is simply deducted from the relief subsequently received. Third, if a court is forced to choose between requiring an offender to compensate his victim, on the one hand, and fining him (or confiscating any proceeds of his crime) on the other, it is the compensatory aim that now takes precedence.[107] Choices of this type have often to be made because so many offenders are in practice impecunious. The policy setting is then that the public interest that could be served by confiscating an offender's assets, or punishing him financially, must take a back seat to the more important aim of protecting the victim's private interests.

Although the system was designed to avoid the need for victims to launch separate civil proceedings, it is crucial to realize that it does not simply join the equivalent of a civil claim onto the State's criminal action.[108] Orders are not contingent on a victim having a civil cause of action—her entitlement to relief is based purely on her having been harmed by the offender's breach of his duty to the public as a whole not to commit the crime. The system thus provides a distinct, compensatory remedy for harm to an individual's private interests that has been caused by a public law wrong against the State or community as a whole. Furthermore, the

Crime (n 97) Ch 1. The original 1964 CICS was one of executive discretion, demand-led, and it closely parallelled the approach taken to judicial damages awards. It became unworkable, prompting statutory intervention, downscaling, simplification and more recent reduction in scope in the 2012 iteration to focus on the most serious cases. Post-2012, the number of applications to the scheme is reported to have halved: Miers, *Criminal Injuries Compensation State and Offender Compensation for Violent Crime* (n 97) [1.13], [1.22]–[1.25].

[105] SAUK s 55, Sentencing Council, Magistrates' Court Sentencing Guidelines (SCG), Compensation [1].

[106] SCG (n 105) [4].

[107] SAUK ss 135(4), (6); Proceeds of Crime Act 2002 (UK) s 13(4),(6).

[108] *R v Chappell* (1985) 80 Cr App R 31; *Jawad v R* [2013] EWCA Crim 644 [16] (Hughes LJ); M Wasik, 'Compensation Orders and Civil Liability' (1985) 48 Modern Law Review 707. The system is in this way distinct from those, common in Europe, which allow a victim to be added as a 'civil party' to a criminal proceeding.

victim's right to compensation is moderated in the light of the other aims of the criminal sentencing process—a fact most clearly instantiated in a court's obligation, when making the award, to take account of the offender's ability to pay it.[109] This moderation principle contrasts dramatically with the governing norm in tort cases, where courts routinely disregard a defendant's means in accordance with the principles of corrective justice. In the corrective justice conception of tort law, it does not matter whether a rich person injures a poor one, or vice versa—the amount payable in each case is the same, this being the sum required to set right the wrong the between them.[110] When it comes to public law compensation orders, however, it *does* matter. Criminal sentences that are designed variously to exact retribution upon the offender, rehabilitate him, and/or achieve effective deterrence must take account of the size of his wallet and the impact of any compensatory award upon it, if they are to achieve their other, desired ends. The compensation principle at stake in public law hence softens its commitment to corrective justice in the light of the mixed public objectives of the criminal sentencing system as a whole. In the view of some leading commentators, it is not just that compensation orders operate against a *background* of other public interest aims that must be juggled when determining their scope, but that they themselves *serve* public interest functions distinct from those of private law damages awards, their purpose being not just to protect a victim's private interests, as in tort claims, but publicly to recognize the wrong done, morally re-educate the offender, and contribute to the reduction of future offending.[111]

The difference between the public law award and any separate private law right to compensation is evident in several other features of the system. First, compensation orders are discretionary, whereas tort damages are available as of right. Second, the victim is never formally a party to the criminal action and consequently has no power to settle the claim.[112] Third, in the English system, the victim makes no formal application for the order.[113] It is the public prosecutor that raises

[109] SAUK s 135(3); Sentencing Act 1991 (Vic) s 85H; SCG (n 105) [9]; Miers, *Criminal Injuries Compensation State and Offender Compensation for Violent Crime* (n 97) [8.35]–[8.61].

[110] For the principle of moral equality in corrective justice, see Aristotle, *Nichomachean Ethics* (trans R Crisp, CUP 2000) Book V Ch 4, 1132a; E Weinrib, *The Idea of Private Law* (Harvard University Press 1995); E Weinrib, *Corrective Justice* (OUP 2012).

[111] D Miers, 'Offender and State Compensation for Victims of Crime: Two Decades of Development and Change' (2014) 20 International Review of Criminology 145, 160; A Ashworth, 'Punishment and Compensation: Victims, Offenders and the State' (1986) 6 Oxford Journal of Legal Studies 86, 111–12. The same claims are sometimes made in respect of some types of extra-compensatory damages awards in private law, including both punitive awards and 'vindicatory damages' (on which, see K Barker, 'Private and Public: The Meaning of Vindication in Torts and Private Law' in S Pitel, J Neyers, and E Chamberlain (eds), *Tort Law: Challenging Orthodoxy* (Hart 2013) Ch 3.

[112] In Victoria (where orders are ancillary only), negotiation by the parties is permitted prior to the making of an order, but settlement by private agreement is barred once it has been made: Sentencing Advisory Council (Vic), *Restitution and Compensation Orders Issues and Options* (March 2018) [2.26].

[113] Miers, *Criminal Injuries Compensation State and Offender Compensation for Violent Crime* (n 97) [7.34]–[7.37] (pointing to some lack of clarity around the issue). In Victoria, an application can be made either by the public prosecutor, or by the victim herself: SAC *Issues and Options* (n 112) [2.16]–[2.28].

the court's duty to consider making an award and who collects information about the victim's injury.[114] Courts can also technically make orders at their own motion,[115] without a formal application for an award being made by *anyone*, which rather makes the same point. Although victims are *included* in the process of compensation and their views about the desirability of an award must formally be respected,[116] they do not themselves *drive* or *control* the process in the way they would if they were exercising their own right of action in private law.

Realistically, the extent to which compensation orders achieve any serious protection for victims' private interests in the criminal system is very doubtful.[117] The process is notoriously unable to handle complex cases, which are routinely left by courts for individuals to litigate through the tort system in the usual way.[118] The informational constraints of the sentencing process make it impractical for it to accommodate disputes about the aetiology, prognosis, or long-term costs of complex personal injuries, and prosecutors typically have only a very short time within which to prepare a brief of evidence.[119] If one were to obtain all of the information required to make assessment possible in such cases, sentencing would be greatly delayed, which is not something that either offenders or victims are likely to want. In practice, the system therefore focuses on straightforward instances of property damage, minor personal injury, and psychological harm, and awards are modest. Orders were made in only 18 per cent of cases in the first decade of this century,[120] and the mean value of awards across both Magistrates' courts and the Crown Court in 2010 was just £306.[121]

Although informational constraints are partly responsible for the scheme's limitations, the real fly in the ointment is simply that offenders are an unreliable source of money. Even where they are solvent, execution can be a problem. This is particularly so in jurisdictions such as the State of Victoria, where relief is only ever ancillary and the victim is therefore obliged to pursue his or her debt through the normal civil process.[122] But the uncollectable debt problem is present even in the

[114] CPS Guidance on Sentencing—Ancillary Orders (24 August 2024). This evidence can be garnered from the police, the relevant victim- or witness-care officer, or can be provided to the court by the victim herself in the form of a personal impact statement prior to a sentence being delivered.

[115] See also (and explicitly) Sentencing Act 1991 (Vic) s 86(1A)(b).

[116] SCG (n 105) [8].

[117] This was the view of the Advisory Council on the Penal System in its report, *Reparation by the Offender* (1970) [24], but remains an equally fair assessment today: Miers, *Criminal Injuries Compensation State and Offender Compensation for Violent Crime* (n 97) [7.01].

[118] *R v Donovan* (1981) 3 Cr App R (S) 192.

[119] SAC *Issues and Options* (n 112) [2.22] fn 67. On the evidential issues, see Miers, *Criminal Injuries Compensation State and Offender Compensation for Violent Crime* (n 97) [8.02]–[8.12].

[120] Miers, 'Offender and State Compensation for Victims of Crime' (n 111) 150–51.

[121] Miers, *Criminal Injuries Compensation State and Offender Compensation for Violent Crime* (n 97) [8.27]. The statistics in the Australian State of Victoria present a similar picture: SAC *Issues and Options* (n 112) [2.52]–[2.53] (median awards in the years 2006–2017 ranged between AUS$400 and AUS$550 in the Magistrates' courts, although they were significantly higher in superior courts).

[122] A review of this approach was recommended in 2016 by the Victoria Law Reform Commission in *The Role of Victims in the Criminal Trial Process* (August 2016), but the Victoria Sentencing Council instead proposed waiving fees for private proceedings and allowing the Department of Justice to enforce

English system, where orders form part of the sentence imposed and are therefore backed by the full array of State enforcement powers, including the imprisonment of an offender for contempt.

Although the government rhetoric is that compensation orders will play an increasingly important part in protecting the private interests of victims of crime, the truth is therefore rather different. Such claims can even seem disingenuous when in practice they yield so little.[123] Orders do nonetheless offer advantages in some cases. They can be useful where the harm suffered falls below the threshold at which the State-sponsored criminal injuries compensation scheme kicks in (currently £1,000), or where an offence is not a 'crime of violence' and so falls outside the CISC's current scope.[124] They also cover some types of injury not covered by the tort system, such as the pure terror or mental distress that a criminal encounter can engender.[125] Where the offender is reasonably pecunious and cooperative, the harm straightforward, and the required evidence readily available, they can therefore play a limited role in supplementing the private interest protection available to victims under other systems. Perhaps most interestingly and importantly from our point of view, by permitting the State to press a compensatory claim on the latter's behalf, they relieve individuals of the costs and concerns associated with pursuing the offender themselves in private litigation, and they create efficiency in the enforcement process by consolidating the protection of public and private legal interests into a single enforcement brief. If those paying out were a more solvent constituency—big corporations, for example—the basic hybrid enforcement model might offer considerable advantages.

B. Public Law Compensation and Redress

The procedural merits of this hybrid public enforcement system have not gone unnoticed and have prompted exactly the suggestion that the model be expanded beyond the criminal courts to public agencies more generally so that regulators are

orders civilly on a victim's behalf: *Restitution and Compensation Orders Report* (Oct 2018) Recs 1, 6, 7. The reasons given for not making orders a formal part of the sentence included the fact that some victims don't want them and may be at risk of domestic violence if they are made, as well as the potentially disproportionate impact of State enforcement measures on disadvantaged groups, including women and indigenous persons: [3.76]–[3.77].

[123] K Warner and Gawlik, 'Mandatory Compensation Orders for Crime Victims and the Rhetoric of Restorative Justice' (2003) 36 Australian & New Zealand Journal of Criminology 60 (critiquing Tasmania's introduction of compulsory compensation orders in respect of certain offences as a token gesture and political stunt).

[124] For full coverage of this question, see Miers, *Criminal Injuries Compensation State and Offender Compensation for Violent Crime* (n 97) Ch 2 esp [2.03]–[2.98].

[125] *Bond v The Chief Constable of Kent* [1983] QB 34; SGC (n 105) [8].

able simultaneously to impose penalties for a regulatory breach and obtain 'public law compensation' for its victims.[126]

This proposal is being taken up with enthusiasm in some quarters because there is an increasing number of mechanisms in modern public law empowering public agencies both to impose penalties for regulatory breaches and to either seek through courts—or themselves order—public law redress for individuals, or broader groups harmed by the breach.[127] This is especially common in the financial services, competition law, and consumer protection fields. The prospects of finding solvent defendants are in these contexts much better than in cases of criminal assault or property damage.

The structure of arrangements varies. Sometimes an agency has rights of action that allow it to apply for a court order that compensation or restitution be paid to it for distribution to the victims of the regulatory breach,[128] or that redress be made directly to those victims to eliminate or reduce their losses.[129] In other instances, the agency has its own legal powers to order offenders to pay compensation to individual victims,[130] or to make rules (or accept voluntary undertakings or arrangements) requiring the offender to set up a redress scheme in favour of broad groups of persons adversely affected by its conduct. Powers of this bolder cast, which extend beyond rights of action in the sense that we have defined them, are now more

[126] See eg A Ezrachi and M Ioannidou, 'Public Compensation as a Complementary Mechanism to Damages Actions: From Policy Justifications to Formal Implementation' (2012) 3 Journal of European Competition Law & Practice 536; B Lisse, 'Redress Facilitation Orders as a Sanction against Corporations' (2018) 37 University of Queensland Law Journal 85.

[127] C Hodges, 'From Class Actions to Collective Redress: A Revolution in Approach to Compensation' (2009) 28 Civil Justice Quarterly 41 esp 60–66; C Hodges and N Creutzfeldt, 'Transformations in Public and Private Enforcement' in H-W Micklitz and A Wechsler (eds), *The Transformation of Enforcement: European Economic Law in Global Perspective* (Hart 2016) Ch 6, 115, 118–24; C Riefa and C Willett, 'Enforcement and Effectiveness of Consumer Law in the UK' in H Micklitz and G Saumier (eds), *Enforcement and Effectiveness of Consumer Law, Ius Comparatum—Global Studies in Comparative Law* (Springer, 2018) 27. In the US, State Attorney-Generals have similar powers to obtain compensation for injuries caused to citizens by the breach of public competition laws '*parens patriae*' under 15 USC § 15(c)–(e). The sums recovered may be either paid to the State or distributed as the court thinks fit amongst victims.

[128] See eg FSMA s 382, s 383 ('restitution' orders—which can provide both compensation to those suffering loss, and transfer profits obtained by an offender to those at whose expense they were wrongly made).

[129] In Australia, see eg the powers of the ACCC to seek judicial orders for compensation and redress under the CCA s 51ADB, s 51ADC (orders to redress loss or damage suffered by non-parties in respect of violations of Part IVB of the ACL, which can include making refunds or returning property, but not orders to pay damages); s 87(1A)(b) (compensation for one or more persons suffering loss or damage as a result of anticompetitive conduct, with their consent); s 87 (1A)(baa) (compensation for a class of persons in respect of consumer data right violations, no consent needed); sch 2 (ACL) s 237 (compensation orders with private party consent); s 239 (orders to redress non-party loss or damage); s 243A (orders to redress loss or damage caused to parties to contracts containing unfair terms, with their consent), s 243B (orders on regulator application to redress loss or damage caused to persons containing unfair contract terms). See also the powers of ASIC under the Corporations Act 2001 (Cth) s 994P (orders to redress non-party loss or damage).

[130] See eg FSMA s 384 (FCA power to require 'restitution' where losses have been caused, or profits wrongfully made).

common. They are potentially extremely useful, since no prior court approval is required for a private remedy, and they enable some sort of relief for wide-ranging harm to private interests to be dispensed at a fraction of the cost of judicial proceedings. They also bypass the need for groups to commence class action proceedings, which may now be more effective than they once were, but which may also require the use of private litigation funders, who take a significant slice of the compensation pie.

Agency powers of this type are reportedly common in the United States,[131] but are also now enjoyed in the United Kingdom by the Financial Conduct Authority,[132] the Environment Agency,[133] the CMA,[134] and the Gas and Electricity Markets Authority (operating through OfGem). In OfGem's case, the regulator is able not just to issue its own orders requiring an offender to make good loss, damage, and inconvenience suffered by affected energy users[135] but can approve voluntary schemes that benefit *all* such consumers (eg by undertaking to provide general sector advisory services) or particularly vulnerable persons.[136] The proportion of redress payments relative to fines collected by the agency has grown perpetually since 2010[137] and virtually all the recoveries obtained are now used to grant redress of one sort or another. Between 2018 and 2020, some £19 million was paid out in grants to 120 charitable projects under energy sector redress

[131] C Scott, 'Enforcing Consumer Protection Laws' in G Howells, I Ramsay, and T Wilhelmsson, *Handbook of Research on International Consumer Law* (Edward Elgar 2010) Ch 18, 545, 549 (citing powers of the Federal Trade Commission and Consumer Product Safety Commission).

[132] FSMA s 404, s 404A (as enacted by the Financial Services Act 2010 (UK), s 14) (consumer redress schemes). The power can be used against single or multiple firms, where the FCA is satisfied that there have been widespread failures and that consumers have suffered loss or damage in respect of which, if they brought legal proceedings, relief would be available. A consumer making a complaint to the Financial Services Ombudsman about any matter covered by the scheme may in turn be awarded monetary relief by the Ombudsman: s 404B.

[133] The Agency may require an undertaking by an offender to restore environmental damage and private harm caused by an offence under the Environmental Civil Sanctions (England) Order 2010/1157, sch 4 (enforcement undertakings). Actions (including monetary payments) may be agreed that will benefit persons affected by the offence, or, if restoration is not possible, that will equivalently benefit the environment more generally.

[134] In relation to competition infringements, see CA 1998 s 49C–E (the CMA has power to approve a voluntary redress scheme on the application of an offender, the breach of which scheme is actionable civilly by anyone suffering loss or damage, or by the CMA itself to obtain any appropriate relief or remedy: s 49E. In respect of consumer law breaches, the CMA now has similar powers to accept undertakings that include 'enhanced measures' for the payment of compensation, or provision of other redress, to adversely affected consumers: Digital Markets, Competition and Consumers Act 2024 (UK) ss 163–65. For detailed draft guidance on the new consumer enforcement regime, see CMA, *Consumer Protection: Enforcement Guidance* CMA58ii Draft (11 December 2024) and *Direct Consumer Enforcement Guidance CMA200con* (31 July 2024).

[135] Gas Act 1986 (UK) ss 30G, 30H; and Electricity Act 1989, s 27G (inserted by the Energy Act 2013 (UK) sch 14, para 1(2), s 144.

[136] These schemes operate either by way of settlement of an investigation, or as a form of 'alternative' action to taking further investigative action by way of agreement with the company: Ofgem, *Consultation to Review the Energy Industry Voluntary Redress Scheme* (11 Feb 2021) [1.1]–[1.2].

[137] Ofgem, *Allocation of Voluntary Redress Payments in the Context of Enforcement Cases* (June 2016) [3.5].

schemes.[138] This shift in regulator enforcement policy from penalty collection to an offender's provision of private redress again reflects the increased influence upon public law of restorative justice ideology in recent decades and the higher priority devoted in public law to protecting private interests.

Not all redress schemes have proven as apparently successful as those operated by OfGem. For example, not a single voluntary scheme had been agreed in the UK competition law field in 2020, cartels apparently seeing no reason to pay out a negotiated settlement when they can force affected private interests to rely on their own rights of action and fight their way through the courts using class action procedures.[139] To bring offenders to the table, something more like the UK financial services model of regulatory redress is likely to be needed, where the regulator's power compulsorily to impose a redress scheme provides a stronger incentive for offenders to take such interests seriously.

Before we leave public law compensation, it is important again to note the differences between the types of private redress that can be obtained by a regulator and that which a private party can obtain in private law litigation of her own. Although regulators do sometimes enforce the *private law* rights of consumers and corporations,[140] that is not what is going on in the cases discussed in this section. As with criminal compensation orders, the underlying norms are public law ones owed by an offender to the State. Agencies themselves have no power to grant damages awards. Many payments are made as agreed settlements or undertakings between the offender and the regulator as a pragmatic alternative to undergoing further investigation or prosecution, and the offender itself can be placed in charge of quantifying the losses it has caused, when it comes to designing a redress scheme of acceptable size and scope.[141] Even in the simplest case, where an agency such as the Financial Conduct Authority exercises a right of action to obtain a court order for an offender to compensate one or more investors,[142] it need only take reasonable steps to identify the latter's losses and it does not require precise evidence in order to be able to distribute the final award. The process is 'rough and ready' given the limited information available to the authority, and distribution amongst affected investors is made in the simplest way possible consistent with fairness—for example, on a per capita, or pro rata basis.[143] The payment criteria are therefore those of distributive, not corrective justice in the strict sense. That fact is most obvious in

[138] Seventy per cent of funds are used for these purposes. For examples of the way they are used see Energy Saving Trust, *Energy Industry Voluntary Redress Scheme—Impact Report 2020*.

[139] B Hollway and C Mansfield, 'Five Years of the CRA: a Lot Done, More to Do' (2020) 13 Global Competition Litigation Review 124, 129.

[140] See eg Australian Securities and Investments Commission Act 2001 (Cth) s 50; National Consumer Credit Protection Act 2009 (Cth) s 275 and Chapter 9 this book. In case of corporations, no consent is required.

[141] See eg FSMA s 404(6), (7).

[142] FSMA s 382, s 383.

[143] *Financial Conduct Authority v Exall* [2023] EWHC 1130 (Ch) [15].

voluntary redress schemes agreed with OfGem, where offenders pay a lump sum that is then predominantly distributed to charities for the benefit of persons who may never have been harmed by the infraction in question. The philosophy of such schemes is not to rectify harm to private interests on the 'tort' model but to provide benefits to the broader consumer community that are roughly commensurate with the harm that an offender is thought to have done. The extent of a redress obligation can also take account of an offender's post-breach behaviour; and is considered in determining the extent of any penalty applied.[144]

5.6 Summation

The public enforcement paradigm in public law has very deep roots in most jurisdictions. There are nonetheless some surprises.

The first point to note is that while there are good reasons for the paradigm, there is more contingency in these reasons than we might at first have assumed. None of them necessarily precludes the use of private enforcers in all cases and conditions. The most influential constitutional arguments in favour of public enforcement are jurisdiction-specific and whilst they tend to support the use of accountable public agents wherever these laws are designed for the protection of public interests, there can be significant variations in the public construction of the State's role vis-à-vis its citizens that can result in its status as a monopoly protector of the public interest being questioned. A particularly important constitutional principle, which is generally accepted and which plays out strongly in favour of some level of exceptionalism in virtually all systems, is the principle that the State must itself be equally accountable before the law to its people, such that citizens themselves have powers to enforce its obligations in courts of law. This theme is central to most of the exceptions examined in the next chapter. To the extent that pragmatic arguments about adequate enforcer incentive and efficiency support the public enforcement paradigm (which again they seem to, in the main) they are also subject to possible exceptions. The other arguments we identified (moral risk, vexatious litigation, and the importance of consistency and transparency in enforcement policy) again press with varying degrees of strength in favour of public enforcers, but their steer is again inconclusive.

The second point is that, however justified from a constitutional perspective, public enforcement is itself subject to some serious deficiencies and risks that inevitably fuel the appetite for alternative, private enforcement arrangements. Enforcement capture is one such threat that is greater or lesser according to constitutional arrangements concerning agency independence and culture, but the most

[144] FCA *Decision Procedure and Penalties (DEPP) Manual* (Financial Conduct Authority), DEPP 6.2.1G(2)(d).

significant problem currently spanning all of the jurisdictions we have examined is the fact that public resource is currently unable to keep pace with regulatory appetite. Although private enforcement should not be used simply because governments lack the money (or the political courage) to fund public enforcement measures properly, there is much evidence to suggest that modern regulatory agencies are increasingly being forced to turn to private initiative in order to make good on their targets and responsibilities, and that governments see the additional private enforcement resource as a salve for their budgetary problems. Although the challenges of resource wax and wane over time, they are a universal constant, and whenever pressure on the system increases, governments are at least as likely to think about public–private 'partnerships' as they are about rolling back expressed regulatory commitments or stripping the required resource from health care or social security budgets.

The third point is that the dominant conception of public enforcement as being concerned exclusively with public interest protection is false, if anyone ever really believed in it. Public enforcers are increasingly tasked with protecting the interests of individuals and groups that have been personally harmed by public wrongdoers in criminal and regulatory proceedings at the same time as they seek to advance public interests by punishing and deterring wrongdoers. Sometimes, the new focus on remediating private harm is viewed simply as a way of providing additional behavioural incentives for offenders to obey the law—and therefore as promoting public deterrence ends. This is a particular habit in the United States in the competition law context, where private actions are still predominantly viewed as additional disincentives to public harm that should be modelled accordingly and therefore play second fiddle to public aims. But it is increasingly also viewed as important in its own right. The readiness of public law and the public enforcement process to embrace the protection of private interests as well as other public aims can create efficiencies. It also perpetuates and accelerates the use of hybrid enforcement systems that we saw in the context of private enforcement in medieval times. The perpetuation of these hybrid enforcement patterns cannot therefore be written off as simply a hangover of history but reflects a deeper and more resilient rationality that continues to make itself felt in the modern day. Indeed, we shall witness the further perpetuation of these patterns in private law in the context of exemplary and punitive damages awards in Chapter 8.

6

Public Law, Private Enforcement: State Duties and Liabilities

6.1 The Persistence of Private Rights of Action

The last chapter described the dominant paradigm of public enforcement in public law. The historical rise of this model seems to have been attributable to at least two associated factors: an explicit identification of certain areas of the law such as the criminal law with the public interest, such that its enforcement came to be seen as the prerogative of the State, and the gradual but accelerating expansion of the latter's enforcement resources, which permitted that vision to be put into practical operation. The movement toward public enforcement was no doubt also judiciously oiled by awareness of some of the inadequacies and moral risks associated with private enforcement. Whatever the precise mix of reasons, the result was that the enforcement of public laws came increasingly to be regarded as the exclusive preserve of the Attorney-General as representative of the Crown and sole guardian of the public good, or one of his delegates. Although the Attorney-General might (and still may) consent to individuals bringing actions on his or her behalf ('by relation') to restrain a public wrong, such permission can be refused or withdrawn at any time and the decision is final because it is not, on the current law, subject to judicial review.[1] So settled was this public enforcement paradigm by the time of the *Gouriet* case in 1977 that Lord Wilberforce declared it to be 'a fundamental principle of English law . . . that public rights can only be asserted by the Attorney-General'.[2] This he regarded as no technical or procedural happenstance but a constitutional tenet.[3]

Nonetheless, if this is now the accepted position in England, there have always been exceptions to it. One is the ancient common law right of any person to seek the public law writ of habeas corpus in defence of another's liberty.[4] Another (now obsolete) was the right of any 'stranger' to lay information before the King's Court

[1] See further Chapter 7 Section 7.1A(i).

[2] *Gouriet v Union of Post Office Workers* [1978] AC 435, 477E-F.

[3] ibid 481.

[4] *Somerset v Stewart* (1772) Lofft 1, 98 ER 499; *Ex Parte West* (1861) 2 Legge 1475. Other examples are provided by the other prerogative writs: see below, Section 6.3.

Enforcement Rights in Public and Private Law. Kit Barker, Oxford University Press. © Kit Barker 2026.
DOI: 10.1093/9780191955006.003.0009

quo warranto to challenge the unlawful usurpation of a public office,[5] or, possibly, to seek any of the ancient prerogative writs. The right to launch a private criminal prosecution survives, as we shall see, in many jurisdictions. In 1902, in *Boyce v Paddington Borough Council*, Buckley J identified two further exceptions of established pedigree and general application that are also still broadly accepted: cases in which an interference with public rights simultaneously violates an individual's own (private law) rights (some examples of which we noted in the previous chapter in the consumer protection context), and those in which it has resulted in 'special damage' to him or her.[6]

To these common law exceptions, we must add all those cases in which private enforcement of public laws has from time to time been authorized by statute. I noted some ancient Roman and medieval English examples in Chapter 4,[7] but there are still a good number of active statutory provisions, and the figure is on the rise. The examples include statutes targeting discrimination and civil rights abuses, anticompetitive practices, frauds upon the State, the violation of environmental or consumer protection laws,[8] and—most controversially in Texas—abortion laws, which are enforceable by any United States citizen for reward.[9] A similar (if less emotive) example in Australia that was the subject of a High Court appeal in 2018[10] describes the right of any private citizen to prosecute any member of the Commonwealth Parliament who sits when disqualified and to keep the relevant penalty—an exceptional, modern example of the common informer's action *qui tam* that has long been abandoned in England. This right is not simply a child of statute but an express provision in the Australian Constitution.[11]

[5] *R v Speyer* [1916] 1 KB 595, 609. See now in England, Senior Courts Act 1981(UK) s 30.

[6] [1903] Ch 109, 114 (applied in *Gouriet* (n 2)). Australian courts have significantly liberalized the second of these exceptions, requiring only that the plaintiff have a 'special', 'real', or 'sufficiently material' interest: *Australian Conservation Foundation Inc v Commonwealth* (1980) 146 CLR 493; *Bateman's Bay Local Aboriginal Land Council v Aboriginal Community Benefit Fund Pty Ltd* (1998) 194 CLR 247, 281; *Truth About Motorways Pty Ltd v Macquarie Infrastructure Investment Management Ltd* (2000) 200 CLR 591; *Hobart International Airport Pty Ltd v Clarence City Council* [2022] HCA 5 [62]–[65] ('sufficiently material interest') (Kiefel CJ, Keane and Gordon JJ); [90]–[95]; (specially or sufficiently affected, or having a special interest) (Edelman and Steward JJ); *Unions NSW v New South Wales* [2023] HCA 4 [22] ('an interest other than that which any other ordinary member of the public has in upholding the law generally . . . sufficiently interested' . . . standing to obtain 'some benefit or advantage' from the litigation) (Kiefel CJ, Gageler, Gordon, Gleeson, and Jagot JJ); *Forestry Corporation of NSW v South East Forest Rescue Inc* [2025] HCA 15 [8] ('special, sufficient, or real interest') (Gageler CJ, Edelman, Steward, Jagot, and Beech-Jones JJ).

[7] Chapter 4 Section 4.3B(ii) n 55 (*quaestones perpetuae* dealing with particular statutory crimes), text to nn 167–72 (common informer statutes).

[8] For a list of examples in Australia, see *Truth about Motorways* (n 6) 640–42, [131]–[133] (Kirby J). A key provision in consumer protection (the constitutionality of which was affirmed ibid) now appears as s 232(2) of the Competition and Consumer Act 2010 (Cth) Sch 2 (the Australian Consumer Law), which allows 'any person' to apply for injunctive relief in respect of violations of Chapters 2–4 of the Act.

[9] See Chapter 7 Section 7.2B(i).

[10] *Alley v Gillespie* [2018] HCA 11.

[11] Australian Constitution, s 46. The Commonwealth Parliament has since limited the penalty payable and barred direct use of s 46 in favour of a statutory action under the Common Informers

In these cases, the precise identity of those granted private rights of action—and the conditions that they must satisfy to exercise them—vary according to the precise wording and purposes of the provision in question. In the United States, they are also affected by constitutional norms bearing upon court jurisdiction, even when the statute appears on its face to leave enforcement open to 'any person'.[12] This is because a citizen's right to invoke a court's power to enforce public laws is thought fundamentally to challenge the respective constitutional roles of the judiciary and executive government and the latter's monopoly on public law enforcement. There is no doubt that private enforcement rights do change the balance of power between citizens, courts, and the executive and for some they are desirable for precisely this reason. In any event, it means that the scope of such rights is always affected by constitutional, as well as deontic considerations; and that they vary greatly from State to State. It is quite clear, for example, that the High Court of Australia does not share the absolutist position that the enforcement of public laws is the exclusive constitutional preserve of the Attorney-General. Indeed, the Court has recently jealously safeguarded the common law right of interested persons to enforce public laws against being excluded by statute save in cases in which Parliament's intention to do so is unmistakeably clear.[13]

I consider these and other examples of the private enforcement of public laws in this and the next chapter. I split the examples into two groups. This chapter considers cases in which private persons have rights to enforce the State's public duties and liabilities to its citizens. The next addresses the rights of private parties to enforce the duties which their fellow citizens owe to the State.

In canvassing each example, I proceed by first setting out some basic details of the relevant public norm(s) being enforced and the conditions governing private rights of action in respect of them. I then consider the interests which the private enforcement process protects and, in lesser detail, the remedies available to private enforcers through that process. Finally, I identify some of the potential justifications for the private enforcement regime—its 'rationale'. These justifications will be revisited at the end of the book in Chapter 10, where I consider their influence on enforcement patterns more generally.

(Parliamentary Disqualifications) Act 1975 (Cth), s 3(1), s 4 (AUS$200 per day for every day of sitting whilst disqualified).

[12] Concerns about Federal Court jurisdiction in the US have hence restricted the standing of private plaintiffs in both citizen suits and qui tam actions (discussed in Chapter 7 this book) to cases in which they can show 'injury in fact', although this concept has sometimes been diluted as to encompass injury to even quite trivial interests: H Monaghan, 'Constitutional Adjudication: The Who and When' (1973) 82 Yale Law Journal 1363, 1382.

[13] *Bateman's Bay* (n 6) [35]–[38]; *Truth About Motorways* (n 6); *Hobart* (n 6) [68] (Gageler and Gleeson JJ); *Forestry Corporation* (n 6) (any statute must have a clear and unmistakeable intention to exclude the common law right of action).

6.2 Duties to Protect Human Rights

Modern human rights law,[14] both international and domestic, is public law, because it describes duties[15] that States owe one to another under international treaties, or which they owe domestically to their citizens under the terms of their constitutions, or statutory bills of rights.[16] I focus here on just one human rights statute—the Human Rights Act 1998 (UK) (HRA)[17]—as an example of a domestic human rights regime in which private enforcement currently plays an especially prominent role.

The HRA imposes a number of duties on public authorities, but arguably the most important is their strict duty under Section 6 to act in accordance with European Convention on Human Rights when exercising their public functions. The duty is expressed in the form of a statement that it is 'unlawful' for an authority to act incompatibly with those rights, rather than that it owes a duty to act compatibly with them, but the difference in this instance is formal. The unlawfulness of acting incompatibly with the rights (which is a ground for judicial review, as we shall see in the next section of this chapter) also describes a duty to protect them,[18] the breach of which can give rise to secondary legal remedies, including damages. A public authority therefore has an obligation to protect psychiatric patients within its care against suicide risk and may be liable in damages if it fails to prevent his or her death.[19] The duty is potentially exacting because, as the example shows, it requires authorities to take positive measures to protect the various rights protected under the Convention—a feature which contrasts with the normal position

[14] Definitions of the field vary. Here I take it to comprise laws protecting fundamental or basic rights at international level, in the express or implied terms of State constitutions, or under domestic bills of rights or statutes bearing the human rights 'label'. This leaves out much standard domestic legislation such as antidiscrimination legislation, as well as all the ancient common law protections in the criminal law and the law of torts, which safeguard many of the same sorts of interest.

[15] Not all the legal relationships created by human rights instruments take the form of Hohfeldian duty–claim right relationships. They also create liberties (privileges), immunities, and powers for citizens that correlate correspondingly to no rights, disabilities, and liabilities in the State.

[16] In some jurisdictions, the laws bind private parties too, and in such instances, the norms form part of both public and private law: see eg the constitutional human rights norms in Ireland, the Netherlands, Switzerland, Estonia, and Slovenia, and human rights codes in the Canadian Provinces and under the Federal Canadian Human Rights Act (RSC 1985, c H-6) (discrimination). See E Bagińska (ed), *Damages for Violations of Human Rights—A Comparative Study of Domestic Legal Systems* (Springer 2016) esp Ch 20; K Gledhill, *Human Rights Acts—The Mechanisms Compared* (Hart 2015).

[17] The future of the Act was at one stage threatened by a proposal (Bill 117 2022-23 of 22 June 2022) to replace it with a British Bill of Rights. After strong criticism from the Joint Committee on Human Rights, the proposal was finally dropped on 27 June 2023. See further J Wright, *Tort Law and Human Rights* (2nd edn, Hart 2017) Ch 1.

[18] Whether the duty is a multital Hohfeldian one that public authorities owe to each citizen individually or one that they owe to the public 'as a whole' (but the breach of which can give rise to statutory remedies for affected victims) is unclear. The latter construction seems more probable, given the discretionary nature of compensation awards, discussed below. For the contrary view, see J Varuhas, *Damages and Human Rights* (Hart 2016) 205–07. If Varuhas is correct (I would actually prefer him to be) then damages should be available as of right. See further the references at n 36 below.

[19] *Rabone v Pennine Care NHS Foundation Trust* [2012] UKSC 2.

at common law and which sometimes raises eyebrows for exactly this reason, but which is justified by the importance of the rights in question, by the State's agreement to act positively under international law, and by its undertaking to its citizens to render that international commitment meaningful domestically.

A. Enforcement Regime—'The Focus on Victims'

The rights of action in respect of breaches of the State's duty under section 6 currently lie overwhelmingly with 'victims' of the breach.[20] Whilst the English Equality and Human Rights Commission (EHRC) also has some rights of action, these are limited to the protection of equality norms, not the full range of human rights.[21] The Northern Ireland Human Rights Commission (NIHRC) has rights of action in respect of the entire gamut,[22] but only where there is (or will be) a private victim of their breach, which gives it a more significant enforcement role but nevertheless still leaves it powerless to challenge the compatibility of legislation (or other proposed government action) with human rights in the abstract.[23] Weakest of all is the Scottish Human Rights Commission, which has no rights of action at all, merely a conditional liberty to intervene in proceedings commenced by victims, with the permission, or at the invitation of a court.[24]

Even within its own, narrow sphere of operation, the EHRC's record of success has been limited. As noted in the last chapter, its funding was controversially cut by 70 per cent between 2010 and 2020.[25] For an agency that is supposed to be policing the State's observation of its duties, the Commission is also highly dependent for its effectiveness upon government: it reports to government, not to Parliament, its officers are government appointed (subject to Parliamentary oversight, admittedly), and it has constantly to petition government for money, in the same way that government departments do. The lack of confidence in the EHRC as a human rights enforcer was reflected in the recommendations of the 10th Report of the Joint House of Commons Committee on Human Rights in 2018, which pressed for

[20] HRA s 7(1) (a).

[21] Equality Act 2006 (UK) (EA), s 24, s 30. The Commission may rely on s 7(1)(b) of the HRA in judicial review proceedings instituted in respect of its functions under the EA, but only if there are actual or potential victims of the relevant violation. It also cannot recover damages: s 30(3)(d).

[22] Northern Ireland Act 1998 (NIA) s 69(5)(b), s 71(2B)(c).

[23] *In the matter of an application by the Northern Ireland Human Rights Commission for Judicial Review (Northern Ireland) Reference by the Court of Appeal in Northern Ireland pursuant to Paragraph 33 of Schedule 10 to the Northern Ireland Act 1998 (Abortion)* [2018] UKSC 27. For criticism, see J Rooney, 'Standing and the Northern Ireland Human Rights Commission' (2019) 82 Modern Law Review 525.

[24] Scottish Human Rights Commission Act 2006, s 14. By contrast, under the HRA s 5, the Crown has the power to join any action implicating human rights as a party.

[25] D Isaac, 'Reflections on the EHRC' (2020) 6 European Human Rights Law Review 578, 580 (the Commission now has less resource than just one of the three predecessor entities whose briefs it now combines).

its rights of action to be extended to cover the full range of human rights guaranteed by the Convention, and for its funding to be put on a securer footing.[26]

In the meantime, private 'victims' are the main enforcers of the State's duty. The definition of a 'victim' is drawn from the jurisprudence of the European Court of Human Rights[27] and refers to a person whose private interests are directly or indirectly affected—or stand to be affected—by a breach. Whether it is direct or indirect, a victim must therefore have some '*personal* interest'[28] in the proceeding—a claim simply to be interested as a public citizen is not enough. Provided this can be proven, however, a victim needs no State permission to launch an action.

The limitation of private enforcers to those with affected private interests mirrors the European regime that the Act imported domestically, but is arguably too restrictive.[29] It might make administrative sense for the European Court of Human Rights, given the latter's limited resources and the vast size of the jurisdiction that it services, but workload stress is less acute in the domestic context, given that all courts are in theory empowered to hear claims. Moreover, if the reason for 'bringing human rights home' to the United Kingdom was to make it easier for British citizens to enforce them, then it is somewhat counterintuitive that domestic standing rules are the same as they are in Strasbourg. The walk to court may be shorter, but the number of citizens able to enter it is no greater than before.

The victim rule clearly effectively precludes private enforcement where the norms violated by the State—and the only injury suffered in consequence of their violation—concern purely *public* interests, such as the shared interest we have in free elections.[30] It also produces some bizarre anomalies. Those wishing to challenge a governmental decision in judicial review proceedings on human rights grounds must prove some private interest, when the very same decision can be

[26] Joint House of Commons Committee on Human Rights, 10th Report—Enforcing Human Rights (2018) [121]–[132], Recs 14, 15.

[27] HRA s 7(7). The victim focus is not confined to European jurisdictions. See eg Human Rights Act 2004 (ACT) s 40C(1)(b).

[28] European Court of Human Rights, *Practical Guide on Admissibility Criteria* (Council of Europe 2025) [25] and generally [24]–[51]. An interest may be affected even when not immediately threatened. See eg *Dudgeon v UK* (1982) 4 EHRR 149. For further discussion, see *Daniel v St George's Healthcare NHS Trust* [2016] EWHC 23 [149]–[175]. An indirect victim of a breach of the State's obligation to protect life must hence suffer grave emotional distress as a result of the death, and have a significant family tie or legal relationship to the deceased: *Daniel* ibid [153].

[29] ECHR art 34; D Nicol and J Marriott, 'The Human Rights Act, Representative Standing and the Victim Culture' [1998] European Human Rights Law Review 730; J Miles, 'Standing Under the Human Rights Act 1998: Theories of Rights Enforcement & the Nature of Public Law Adjudication' (2000) 59 Cambridge Law Journal 133, esp 142–47; J Varuhas, 'A Tort-Based Approach to Damages under the Human Rights Act 1998' (2009) 72 Modern Law Review 750, 753–57.

[30] It is also problematic where victims are unable for good reasons to act in protection of their own interests, as in cases of domestic violence (R McQuigg, 'The Victim Test under the Human Rights Act 1998 and its Implications for Domestic Violence Cases' (2011) European Human Rights Law Review 294) or cases involving vulnerable elderly persons in residential care (*R (on the Application of Broadway Care Centre Ltd) v Caerphilly CBC* [2012] EWHC 37(Admin)). Representative standing is currently permitted only in very limited circumstances, for example when a victim is a minor, lacks capacity, or is dead. See further Chapter 9 Section 9.2.

challenged on other public law grounds by anyone credibly representing the public interest, including a wide variety of representative organizations.[31] Wider representative standing rules that might increase the pool of qualified private enforcers were originally advised[32] but never enacted.

A popular recurring argument for limiting standing to victims is that they are less likely to be vexatious busybodies, but personal interest is no guarantee of proper public motivation or suitability to the enforcement role. One who has been personally harmed by a human rights violation is no more likely to be 'public spirited' (and may be less so) than one whose concern is solely for her community. Personal grievances may blind rather than enliven one to the interests of others and the litigation in question may just as equally be legally groundless. If vexatious litigation is a genuine concern (the evidence garnered in the last chapter was thin, remember), it would seem more appropriate for judges to tackle it by exercising their powers to terminate abusive suits in the normal way, after they have been launched, or (as in current applications for judicial review) to require public interest litigants to obtain judicial permission before proceeding with their claims. Either of these is a more desirable strategy from a rule of law point of view than limiting rights to bring public interest claims in the first place to only those with private 'skin in the game'.

B. Interests Protected

As the above discussion suggests, the State's duty under Section 6 is to protect both private and public interests,[33] so that either (or both) may be at stake in any given enforcement action. Most of the civil rights and freedoms safeguarded under Schedule 1 of the Act, such as the right to life, liberty, and the peaceful possession of property, very obviously protect private interests—interests that are already protected substantially (often, indeed, more strongly) by the private law of torts.[34]

[31] *R (on the application of Children's Rights Alliance for England) v Secretary of State for Justice* [2013] EWCA Civ 34; *Re Northern Ireland Commissioner for Children and Young People's Application* [2007] NIQB 115 (QB).

[32] It was suggested in the Labour's Party's own Consultation Paper in the run up to the Act's implementation: *Bringing Rights Home* (1996). See further J Wadham, 'Bringing Rights Home: Labour's Plans to Incorporate the European Convention on Human Rights into UK Law' [1997] Public Law 75.

[33] cf J Varuhas, 'Against Unification' in M Elliott and H Wilberg (eds), *The Scope and Intensity of Substantive Review: Traversing Taggart's Rainbow* (Hart 2015) Ch 5 (suggesting that human rights law and the law of judicial review should be more strongly contrasted, with private interests being the focus in the former case and public interests in the latter).

[34] The proper relationship between the development of human rights protection at common law and under the Act commands a vast literature. See eg D Oliver, 'The Human Rights Act and Public Law/Private Law Divides' [2000] European Human Rights Law Review 343; M Arden, 'Human Rights and Civil Wrongs: Tort Law Under the Spotlight' [2010] Public Law 140; D Hoffman (ed), *The Impact of the UK Human Rights Act on Private Law* (CUP 2011); J Wright, *Tort Law and Human Rights* (2nd edn, Hart 2017). Although it was at one stage thought that the most significant advances would take place under the Act, keeping the common law's logic distinct and conservative (on which see R Bagshaw,

The Act even sometimes protects private interests, like privacy,[35] which domestic tort law does not (or does not yet fully) protect. But other social and political rights secured by the Act—the right to free elections, association, or education, for example—safeguard interests that individuals share with others by virtue of their community membership. Indeed, on one view, it can be argued that, in addition to all of the specific public and private interests protected by the nominate rights listed in Schedule 1, the Act also aims to protect citizens' common interest in the State's observance of its international human rights obligations—an interest in the State's observance of the rule of law itself. On that view, *every* violation by the State of its protective obligations under the Act harms the public interest, as well as the private interests of persons personally affected by a breach.

The hybrid nature of the interests protected by the Act has, I suggest, implications for the proper modelling of enforcement rights. It is clearly morally appropriate to grant rights of action to victims where the State has breached an obligation to protect their private interests, but such rights should also be available to a broader group, where the relevant human rights are designed to protect the interests of a group, or society as a whole. *Any* member of the electorate should hence be entitled to challenge the validity of governmental restrictions on communal voting rights, whether or not the infringement of those rights has resulted in personal harm to him or her. *Any* member of the political community should be entitled to challenge public actions or policies that discriminate improperly against a minority group, whether or not they stand to be personally affected by a breach as a member of the minority in question. Enforcement of human rights laws is in such cases a matter of public as well as private concern precisely because the underlying rights are designed to protect interests that we share as a concerned community.

A wider test of standing, akin to that which we find below in the context of administrative law, is therefore appropriate for the private enforcement of human rights that are designed for the protection of public interests. In such instances, rights of action should be available to all community citizens. To safeguard against residual concerns about vexatious litigation and to ensure that a private enforcer is properly qualified to conduct the litigation, one could, if nervous, add a 'judicial permission' stage to the proceeding, as in cases of judicial review. An expansion of

'Tort Design and Human Rights Thinking' in Hoffman (ed), *The Impact of the UK Human Rights Act on Private Law* (n 34), 110; D Nolan, 'Negligence and Human Rights Law: The Case for Separate Development' (2013) 76 Modern Law Review 286, 117–28), there are signs of a common law resurgence: M Elliott, 'Beyond the European Convention: Human Rights and the Common Law' (2015) 68 Current Legal Problems 85; P Bowen, 'Does the Renaissance of Common Law Rights Mean that the Human Rights Act 1998 is Now Unnecessary?' (2016) European Human Rights Law Review 361.

[35] UK law does now recognize a right to the non-disclosure of private information through an adaptation of the law of breach of confidence—a development prompted by the European Convention even before the HRA came into force and now crystalized into a new tort: *Vidal-Hall v Google Inc* [2015] EWCA Civ 311. The types of interest protected via this action are nonetheless still narrower than those encompassed by the Convention Right.

the rights of action and resources of the Human Rights Commission's along the lines recommended by the Joint Committee in 2018 would helpfully reduce the need to rely on private enforcement in such cases and would undoubtedly be desirable in its own right, but there are good reasons to endorse rights of action for all citizens in public interest cases in any event as a safeguard against enforcement failure, on constitutional grounds. In so far as the effectiveness of the Commission's work is curtailed by resource concerns, there is also a pragmatic case for supplementing those resources with the initiative of private enforcers.

C. Remedies

The hybrid nature of the interests which the HRA protects has further implications for the remedies which enforcers can obtain. The Act's close ties to the European international law regime has had an unfortunate limiting effect upon these remedies, particular on the availability and quantification of monetary damages for persons harmed by a breach. Although it is often suggested that the HRA should be treated as if it were just another tort statute, and that damages should therefore be available standardly and on the same basis as in domestic tort law for the breach of a statutory duty,[36] this is not the case. Damages under the Act are discretionary and available only if necessary to afford 'just satisfaction' when other remedies fail and the possible consequences of making a monetary award have been taken into account.[37] This is precisely the opposite of the position in domestic tort law, where they are available as of right and specific relief is discretionary, and it shadows the position taken in respect of criminal compensation orders described at the end of the last chapter. Courts deciding on the availability and quantum of an award are also obliged to 'take into account' the 'principles' of the European Court, which has (perhaps too literally) been interpreted to mean that they must make only modest awards in line with European 'precedents', moderating them according to a 'public interest' rationale that is sensitive to State resource implications.[38] Although the

[36] The Law Commission (Law Com No 266) and The Scottish Law Commission (Scot Law Com No 180) *Damages under the Human Rights Act 1998* (Cmnd 4853) (HMSO 2000) [4.20] (the Act provides 'a form of action for breach of statutory duty'); R Stevens, *Torts and Rights* (OUP 2007) 239 (the Act 'creates a new statutory tort'); Varuhas, *Damages and Human Rights* (n 18) Chs 3 and 4 esp 207–08, 218 (human rights law 'is much closer to private law' than public law, creating 'individual rights' and protecting fundamental private interests, so that awards should be modelled on tort damages for infringement of torts that are actionable per se). The conclusion that damages should be calculated on a tort basis can also be reached, as it is in the text below, by those who take the view that the Act is public law; see eg A Burrows, 'Damages and Rights' in D Nolan and A Robertson (eds), *Rights and Private Law* (Hart 2012) 275, 292, 297–98. This possibility is reserved by Varuhas as a credible back-up position: *Damages and Human Rights* (n 18) 220–25.

[37] HRA s 8(3).

[38] HRA s 8(4); *Anufriejeva v Southwark LBC* [2003] EWCA Civ 1406 [52]–[59]; *R v Secretary of State for the Home Department ex parte Greenfield* [2005] 1 WLR 673; *Dobson v Thames Valley Utilities Ltd* [2009] EWCA Civ 28; *R (Faulkner) v Secretary of State for Justice, R (Sturnham) v Parole Board &*

European Court jurisprudence on its face expresses a commitment to corrective justice through a concept of '*restitutio in integrum*' that sounds reassuringly familiar to tort lawyers, the reality is therefore that its driving logic is closer to distributive rather than corrective justice—it provides compensation that is not full, but fair in the round, given its potential public costs.[39]

The more restricted approach to damages under the Act has been justified by Lord Bingham and others on the basis that the latter's aim is not (as it is in domestic tort law) to compensate private harm to victims, but instead to 'vindicate' public rights,[40] but the language of vindication does little to illuminate the intended contrast.[41] The basic idea appears to be that the protection accorded to human rights under the statute requires concessions that tort law does not because it reflects compromises struck between State and private interests at the international level.[42] But that does not, of course, justify or explain *why* the interests of victims of a human rights violation should be compromised to State interests in this way. Although criminal courts are sometimes required to make compromises between fully compensating crime victims, on the one hand, and imposing only tolerable financial punishments upon impecunious offenders, on the other, the arguments in the current context are surely very different. The State is not an impecunious offender whose proportionate punishment and rehabilitation must be borne in mind as moderating factors in determining how much it should pay the victim of a human rights violation.

The remedial compromise of victims' private interests to State financial interests in cases of public wrongdoing is certainly not inevitable. This much is evident from the remedies available for the common law tort of misfeasance in public office, considered in the next section, which compensates victims fully on

Anor [2013] UKSC 13. See generally J Edelman, *McGregor on Damages* (22nd edn, Sweet & Maxwell 2024) [51–139]-[51–161].

[39] F du Bois, 'Human Rights and the Tort Liability of Public Authorities' [2011] 127 Law Quarterly Review 589, 606–07. It should be noted, of course, that the principle of restitutio in integrum is moderated even in domestic tort law to some degree—for example, by caps on awards in many jurisdictions.

[40] *Greenfield* (n 38) [19] (Lord Bingham); *Watkins v Secretary of State for the Home Department* [2006] 2 AC 395 [9] (Lord Bingham); *Van Colle v Chief Constable of Herts Police* [2008] UKHL 50 [138] (Lord Brown).

[41] J Steele, 'Damages in Tort and Under the Human Rights Act: Remedial or Functional Separation?' [2008] Cambridge Law Journal 606; K Barker, 'Private and Public: The Mixed Concept of Vindication in Torts and Private Law' in S Pitel, J Neyers, and E Chamberlain (eds), *Tort Law: Challenging Orthodoxy* (Hart 2013) Ch 3, 65–66.

[42] This also explains the short limitation period of one year for claims to be brought. Note that other domestic human rights regimes not owing their provenance or detail to the European Convention also reflect this distributive justice compromise. For an analysis of the regime under the Canadian Charter of Rights and Freedoms (and supporting the compromise) see P Adourian, *Charter Damages: Private Law in the Unique Public Law Remedy* (Osgoode Digital Commons 2018) LLM Thesis 35 https://digitalcommons.osgoode.yorku.ca/llm/35 accessed 5 December 2025. For more comprehensive trans-jurisdictional coverage see K Cooper-Stevenson, *Constitutional Damages Worldwide* (Thomson Reuters 2013) and E Baginska (ed), *Damages for Violations of Human Rights—A Comparative Study of Domestic Legal Systems* (Springer 2016).

a corrective justice rationale. There may also, in fact, be sufficient wiggle-room in the Act's wording to permit courts more closely to follow domestic tort analogies and corrective justice norms if they wish, and there is much in Jason Varuhas's suggestion that they should do so where the aim of one of the Convention rights is to protect a victim's private interest.[43] By contrast, it will generally be inappropriate to award compensatory damages to a private enforcer where the aim of a Convention right is solely to protect a purely public interest (eg the right to free elections) and the only harm that has been caused by its violation is to the community. A declaration of the breach, the reversal of an improper public decision, or injunctive relief will be more appropriate in such instances.

D. Rationale

Why are private rights of action so dominant in respect of the enforcement of the State's duty under Section 6? There are several possible reasons. The first and perhaps most obvious is that the Act is partly designed to protect a core range of fundamental private interests. This yields a powerful moral case, which we unpack further in Chapter 8,[44] for granting rights of action to those whose protected interests are affected by a breach. To foreshadow the argument just briefly, one reason for protecting an individual's private interest—the desire to respect her autonomy—also provides a reason to grant her a power to litigate where the interest is harmed or threatened. Extending the late John Gardner's continuity thesis,[45] the reason for placing the State under a duty to protect her private interest in the first place feeds not just into the remedy when the duty is breached ('compensate the harm') but also into giving her a right of action ('empower her to bring a claim').

A second reason is that it is undesirable, from both a system design (capture) and constitutional (rule of law) point of view, to place the rights of action in respect of a State's human rights obligations in the State's own hands. Dracula is a poor custodian of the blood bank, and we are right not to trust him. So even if it were the sole purpose of domestic human rights law to protect public interests (which it is not), it would be both morally risky and constitutionally inadvisable to leave the enforcement of State duties entirely in the hands of State agents, or those funded and controlled by them.[46] These reasons for favouring private rights

[43] Varuhas, 'A Tort-Based Approach to Damages under the Human Rights Act 1998' (n 29); (n 18) Ch 3. See also Burrows (n 36) 296–303; Edelman, *McGregor on Damages* (n 38) [51-004], [51–150]–[51–161]. For the suggestion that there is room for awards to more closely follow the domestic approach, see also *R (Faulkner) v SS for Justice, R (Sturnham) v Parole Board for England and Wales* [2013] UKSC 23 [29] (Lord Reed).

[44] Chapter 8 Section 8.4(A)(ii), (iii).

[45] J Gardner, 'What is Tort Law For: Part 1: The Place of Corrective Justice' (2011) 30 Law and Philosophy 1.

[46] By contrast, at the international level, States can play a useful role as enforcers of other States' obligations without the same concerns about capture.

of action persist through all of the cases considered in this chapter, as well as other cases not considered here, in which individuals are granted the right to challenge legislation on constitutional grounds.[47]

A final, pragmatic justification is simply that once the State itself is excluded from enforcement for the reason just canvassed, there are currently no other credible enforcers in the game. Unless and until human rights commissions are granted wider rights of action, properly resourced and placed on a stronger and more independent footing, reliance on private enforcers is really our only option.

The downside of relying so heavily on private enforcement is that individual enforcers lack resources and experience. Even if they have funding of their own, their capacity to protect public interests is currently confined to cases in which where their own interests are coincidentally affected, and they lack the long-term strategic vision necessary to enable them to act effectively in the best interests of the community as a whole. These factors point to the need both for an expansion in private rights of action in public interest cases beyond the current range of 'victims', and for additional rights of action for independent human rights commissions and representative organizations. This would allow greater resources and better coordination to be brought to public interest protection, with commissions taking the lead in such cases and private citizens providing a valuable, secondary safeguard against system failure. But it would preserve as essential the right of action of any private party to sue where the right infringed was designed for the protection of private interests of theirs that have been (or stand to be) detrimentally affected.

6.3 Misfeasance in Public Office

Misconduct in public office is a crime that can be prosecuted publicly,[48] but public misfeasance is also a tort[49] with ancient common law roots[50] that is attended by private rights of action. The tort underwent judicial reinvigoration in the mid- to late twentieth century in response to the growth of the powers of the

[47] See eg *Imperial Tobacco Ltd v Lord Advocate* [2012] UKSC 61 (Scotland); *Flast v Cohen* 392 US 83 (1968) (USA); *Thorson v Attorney-General of Canada (No 2)* (1974) 43 DLR (3d) 1 (Canada); *Crotty v An Taoiseach* [1987] 1 IR 713 (Ireland).

[48] C Nichols and others, *Corruption and Misuse of Public Office* (4th edn, OUP 2024) Ch 5.

[49] *Northern Territory of Australia v Mengel* (1995) 185 CLR 307; *Sanders v Snell* (1998) 196 CLR 329; *Three Rivers District Council v Governor and Company of the Bank of England (No 3)* [2003] 2 AC 1 (HL); *Garrett v Attorney-General (NZ)* [1997] 2 NZLR 332; *Odhavji v Woodhouse* [2003] SCR 263 (SCC).

[50] *Ashby v White* (1703) 2 Ld Raym 938, 92 ER 126 is usually taken as the starting point of modern discussion, although some accounts reach further back to *Turner v Sterling* (1671) 2 Vent 25, 86 ER 287 and to earlier cases on the failure of judicial officers to execute judicial process in the fourteenth century: RC Evans, 'Damages for Unlawful Administrative Action: The Remedy for Misfeasance in Public Office' (1982) 31 International and Comparative Law Quarterly 640, 640; H Wruck, 'The Continuing Evolution of the Tort of Misfeasance in Public Office' (2008) 41 University of British Columbia Law Review 69, 71–72.

administrative State and the recent evidence is that private litigation is burgeoning, despite achieving very low rates of success.[51] The litigation spike may well, it has been suggested, be a reaction to the increased range of powers that public officials now wield in the administrative State, and the frustrating absence of other satisfactory legal means of holding the latter accountable for the harm caused by their maladministration.[52]

Although misfeasance is classified as a tort (because it gives rise to a private action for damages in respect of a wrong), it is unlike most others because it entails the breach of a public law duty owed by officers of the State—a duty not to abuse the powers of one's public office.[53] In its original early conception in Holt CJ's judgment in *Ashby v White*, it may have entailed the breach of a particular duty that was also owed by other private citizens[54] (a duty not to interfere with a person's proprietary right to vote), but it has since grown to encompass abuses of public power pure and simple, and is therefore now understood as attaching *only* to public officers. The concept of an 'abuse' of power is wide enough to encompass both the deliberate use of public powers to harm a citizen, and (more commonly) their use in circumstances in which the officer knows, or suspects, that he or she is acting illegally (beyond the powers in question) and that this is likely to cause a citizen harm. Although the duty was at one time a strict one of legality,[55] in its modern form it is therefore one of honesty and integrity in the exercise of public power. The shift away from strict liability no doubt reflects concerns about the impact that such a principle would have upon public finances in the age of the administrative State.

A. Enforcement Regime

A private right of action is available to anyone able to make out the elements of the tort, one of which is that the plaintiff proves actual, material damage[56] to a private interest protected by the law. This means some harm to his or her bodily integrity,

[51] K Barker and K Lamont, 'Misfeasance in Public Office—Raw Statistics from the Australian Front Line' (2021) 43 Sydney Law Review 315, 325. See also P Vines, 'Misfeasance in Public Office: Old Tort, New Tricks?' in S Degeling, J Edelman, and J Goudkamp (eds), *Torts in Commercial Law* (Lawbook Co 2011) Ch 11.

[52] Barker and Lamont (n 51) 340–46.

[53] The final definition of the tort is still work in progress. See, generally M Aronson, M Groves, and G Weeks, *Judicial Review of Administrative Action and Government Liability* (7th edn, Thomson Reuters 2022) 1260–76; M Aronson, 'Misfeasance in Public Office: A Very Peculiar Tort' (2011) 35 Melbourne University Law Review 1.

[54] *Ashby* (n 50) 953–58, 137–39. This interpretation is not universally accepted: *Pyrenees Shire Council v Day* (1998) 192 CLR 330 (HCA) 376 (Gummow J).

[55] In earlier times, liability flowed simply from the invalidity of the act: Evans (n 50) 642, 647–49.

[56] *Watkins* (n 40) (even where the wrong entails violation of a constitutional right).

liberty, property, psychiatric welfare, or (as is most frequently the case) an economic interest affected by the alleged wrong.

An important argument posited by Donal Nolan and others is that the current material damage requirement is not really a substantive element of the tort at all, but rather a separate standing rule, which limits the range of persons entitled to enforce an officer's public duties.[57] On this view, it serves the same function as the 'victim' test under the HRA, and should be relaxed in favour either of that, same test, or one which allows anyone 'personally adversely affected' by official misconduct to sue.[58] This would produce similar conditions for the exercise of a private right of action under the two regimes.

Following the logic of the preceding section, the acceptability of this idea turns on whether the tort is designed only to protect private interests harmed by official wrongdoing, or has a second, separate purpose in protecting the broader social interest in public trust and governmental legality too. If its sole purpose is to protect private interests, then it makes sense to require plaintiffs to prove actual or potential damage either as an element of the wrong itself, as (on conventional understandings) in cases of negligence, or as a precondition to establishing a secondary, remedial right to claim compensatory damages.[59] If, however, the tort has an additional and *independent* purpose in protecting the public interest that we share in the honest use of public powers (like the crime), then it would make sense to grant rights of action to a broader range of public interest litigants, even where personal damage cannot be proven. Something akin to the 'sufficient interest' approach that is taken in modern judicial review proceedings might be suitable as an alternative precondition to private rights of action in public interest cases, with wider representative standing being granted to public citizens and groups, and judicial permission being required to proceed. In Ontario, Canada, the rise in misfeasance litigation in recent years has been so sharp that the government has legislated to require litigants to obtain judicial permission even where their private interests have been harmed, which is a regressive and unfortunate development driven by defensive, short-term pragmatics.[60]

[57] D Nolan, 'A Public Law Tort: Understanding Misfeasance in Public Office' in K Barker and others (eds), *Private Law and Power* (Hart 2017) Ch 8 194. See also D Nolan, 'Tort and Public Law: Overlapping Categories?' (2019) 135 Law Quarterly Review 272. Support for this view can be found in Lord Steyn's reference to standing in *Three Rivers* (n 49) 193. For an earlier but different call for a standing rule, see E Chamberlain, 'The Need for a "Standing" Rule in Misfeasance in a Public Office' (2008) 7 Oxford University Commonwealth Law Journal 215.

[58] Nolan, 'A Public Law Tort' (n 57) 199–200.

[59] See J Murphy, 'Unpicking Torts: Elements, Conditions of Actionability and Standing Rules' (2024) Modern Law Review 1519, 1527.

[60] *Crown Liability and Proceedings Act 2019*, SO 2019, c 7, sch 17, s 17. The provision has since been declared to be unconstitutional and of no force in so far as it requires plaintiffs to seek permission by laying out their case without the Crown being under any obligation to provide discovery of key matters: *Poorkid Investments Inc v HMTQ* 2022 ONSC 883.

B. Interests Protected

In the past, the tort of misfeasance most certainly protected both the private interests of individual citizens harmed by official misconduct and the broader public interest in public accountability at one and the same time. This follows from the lack of any formal historical separation between the functions of the criminal law and the law of tort to which we referred in Chapter 4. Most commentators and many courts continue to advocate the tort's public accountability function in the modern day and to emphasize its strong connection to the protection of the public interest.[61] However, as the sophistication of public infrastructure for dealing with public misconduct has increased through the criminal law and the development of judicial review, and, as the boundaries of compensatory recourse against the State have expanded through the law of negligence, it might be asked whether we still need the tort action at all, let alone to extend rights of action to plaintiffs who have suffered no personal damage, as Nolan recommends. The English Law Commission, consulting in 2008, suggested that the tort is now both inadequate for the protection of private interests, on the one hand (because its requirements are so stringent), and unnecessary for the protection of public ones, on the other (owing to the separate crime), so that it should simply be abolished.[62]

As far as the protection of private interests is concerned, the suggestion that the action should be abolished because it only rarely succeeds is not good enough. However desirable a more generous system of compensation for the personal consequences of mere maladministration might be,[63] there is no reason to remove the protection currently provided by the tort when the other, more generous systems of compensation recommended by the Commission have not come to pass. The compensatory function of the tort is admittedly very fragile but remains significant in some of the worst instances of public maladministration. Where, however, the purpose of a private action is simply to protect the public interest in official accountability, the question whether it is still needed is much more real. There is, after all, an active jurisprudence (indeed a revival)[64]

[61] Nolan 'A Public Law Tort' (n 57) 200 (describing the accountability function as the tort's 'primary aim'). See similarly *Sanders v Snell* (n 49) 345–56 (Gleeson CJ, Gaudron, Kirby, and Hayne JJ); *Three Rivers* (n 49) 190 (Lord Steyn). Other modern commentators supporting a public interest role for the tort include: Aronson (n 53); J Murphy, 'Misfeasance in a Public Office: A Tort Law Misfit?' (2012) 32 Oxford Journal of Legal Studies 51; E Rock, 'Misfeasance in Public Office: A Tort in Tension' (2019) 43 Melbourne University Law Review 337.

[62] Law Commission, *Administrative Redress: Public Bodies and the Citizen* (Law Com CP No 187, 2008). None of the Commission's proposals made it into the final report, progress being hampered by lack of information about the costs of litigation against government: Law Commission, *Administrative Redress: Public Bodies and the Citizen* (Law Com No 322, 2010).

[63] Law Com CP No 187 (n 62) 75 [4.95] (proposing compensation in both public and private law where statutory powers were intended to benefit a plaintiff and the defendant was at serious fault).

[64] D Lusty, 'Revival of the Common Law Offence of Misconduct in Public Office' (2014) 38 Criminal Law Journal 337; UK Law Commission 'Misconduct in Public Office: Issues Paper 1, The Current Law' (Issues Paper, 20 January 2016) [1.15] (reporting a rise of cases from two in 2005 to 135 in 2014).

around the crime of public misconduct (which requires no proof of damage), as well as private rights of action in respect of the illegal use of public power through the modern processes of judicial review, to which we refer in the next section. It is even possible that the State itself[65] might have the power to sue wrong-doing officials for the tort in appropriate cases. Why, then, would one need a private misfeasance action in the modern day simply to keep State officials honest and to preserve the public trust?

Whether we do need the action for these purposes depends on the adequacy and efficiency of the various other systems of official accountability. On one view, the fact that private individuals already have rights to seek judicial review should be sufficient to protect this interest, and the sole focus of the modern tort should therefore remain on protecting private interests, with State accountability being merely a desirable side effect of a judgment where damage can be proven, not a key, *independent* purpose. However, a determination that an official has consciously *abused* power is qualitatively different to a declaration in review proceedings that his or her actions are invalid or illegal, and in this way the misfeasance action may achieve expressive condemnatory and public accountability functions that applications for judicial review actions currently do not. Whilst these aims are probably equally well (if not better) served by the criminal offence where it is successfully engaged, the rights of action in respect of the crime still lie predominantly with the State itself and the public processes leading to successful criminal prosecution can fail, as we shall see in the next chapter. Private parties do, in many jurisdictions, retain the right to mount a private criminal prosecution themselves when the public system will not (see, for example, the attempt to prosecute Boris Johnson in the United Kingdom in 2019),[66] but this either requires State permission, or is vulnerable to being extinguished at the motion of a public prosecutor. The crime also has different standards of proof and (possibly)[67] thresholds of seriousness; and in some jurisdictions, such as Australia, it has been replaced by a host of more specific offences, which can leave some instances beyond the criminal law's reach.[68] The criminal law may not therefore *always* be fully effective in holding abusers of public office properly to account.

[65] *Marin & Coye v Attorney-General of Belize* [2011] 5 LRC 209; A Holmes, 'Will Australia Courts Move to a Caribbean Beat? The Question of a State's Standing to Sue in the Tort of Misfeasance in Public Office' (2016) 41 University of Western Australia Law Review 155.

[66] *Boris Johnson v Westminster Magistrates Court* [2019] EWHC 1709 (Admin).

[67] In *Attorney General's Reference No 3* [2004] 2 WLR 451, 466, Pill LJ suggested that in English law the substantive requirements of the tort and the crime are the same. In Australia, the position is less clear, some additional level of seriousness 'meriting criminal punishment' of the relevant conduct being required: *R v Quach* (2010) 27 VR 310 [40] (approved in *Obeid v R* [2017] NSWCCA 221 [60]).

[68] P Finn, 'Official Misconduct' (1978) Criminal Law Journal 307, 308 (suggesting that the newer Australian offences cover 'little of the ground of the common law'. The common law offence now exists only in New South Wales and Victoria. The replacement statutory offence in the Australian Capital Territory (ACT) requires a dishonest intention to obtain a benefit or cause a detriment: Criminal Code 2002 (ACT) s 359.

All this being so, Nolan's point about the need to expand private rights of action within the tort of misfeasance if its public accountability function is to be taken seriously may well be correct, although it would seem logical, then, to extend rights of action further than he suggests, so as sometimes to grant them even to those who are not even 'personally adversely affected' by the wrong. Indeed, it might be more logical to adopt the same two-track system of standing recommended in respect of the HRA above, with those suffering actionable private damage having an automatic, unconditional right of action, and those representing the public interest in official accountability being required first to obtain judicial permission before being allowed to proceed.

The only qualification to this suggested vision is that recognizing additional private rights of action would only be needed as a residual safeguard in the small proportion of cases in which the other systems of public accountability that we have mentioned fall short of the mark. As things stand, however, the public interest function of the misfeasance action, although undoubtedly present in the background and often lauded as its primary *raison d'être*, is squarely contingent upon (and therefore in fact secondary to) its protection of private interests and this will necessarily remain the case for as long as actual damage remains a formal element of the tort. In this respect, public interests are currently only indirectly protected by the tort.

C. Remedies

The remedies available to a private enforcer reflect the tort's currently predominant focus on the protection of private interests. The full measure of compensation it provides demonstrates the strength of that commitment, contrasting dramatically with the weaker protections available against the State under the HRA, and arguably providing a better model, along with other torts, for the latter's development. An additional interesting point of contrast is that public misfeasance is currently the archetypal case for an award of exemplary damages (even when the liability is born vicariously by the State, rather than by an individual official)[69] whereas the availability of such damages under the HRA remains a matter of doubt,[70] even where a breach is deliberate. The availability of such awards, considered in greater detail in Chapter 8, enables the court to pursue public ends of condemnation and deterrence as secondary aims where the tort is made out and creates efficiencies of

[69] *Kuddus v Chief Constable of Leicestershire Constabulary* [2002] 2 AC 122 (HL).

[70] *Anufrijeva v Southwark London BC* [2003] EWCA Civ 1406 [55]. The issue was left open in *Kuddus* (n 69) [46], [92] and cf Edelman (n 38) [51–183]–[51–185] (such damages at domestic level have never been ruled out by the European Court and interferences with fundamental human rights are surely the best example of an appropriate case).

process by allowing both private and public interests to be protected in the same hybrid (private) proceeding.

D. Rationale

The exclusive reliance on private enforcement in the tort reflects the private interests that it is currently predominately designed to protect. Moral arguments, I suggested above, favour empowering those whose private interests are intended to be protected to seek recourse for the injury they have been caused. Two of the other arguments that we identified in the context of the HRA—the desirability of avoiding actual or perceived enforcement capture, and the constitutional argument in favour of permitting citizens to play a direct, participatory role in the curtailment of State wrongdoing and enforcement of State accountability—also clearly apply. From both perspectives, it would be inappropriate to allow the State itself exclusively to police public misfeasance, and the tort acts as a safeguard against gaps and failings in respect of prosecutions of the crime. Were the tort to be adapted to allow for the pursuit of pure public interest claims in the manner suggested above (which seems rather unlikely, despite Nolan's powerful arguments), these constitutional and enforcement capture arguments would become considerably more important and prominent as justifications for the private enforcement regime.

6.4 Judicial Review of Administrative Action

The third example of the private enforcement of State obligations considered in this chapter is perhaps the most important. It concerns the law of judicial review. This is a complex field and I focus here on the bare details of the law in just one jurisdiction—England and Wales—but much is still left out and, even then, there is considerable oversimplification.[71] In the United Kingdom, review applications by private citizens have increased dramatically over the last thirty years and the numbers quadrupled between 2000 and 2014 (before settling down again), partly as a function of particular public controversies surrounding the movement of peoples and decisions in the field of immigration, which have become points of intense pressure and sensitivity.[72] The latter development is interesting, because the greatest increase in Australia in misfeasance claims in recent times has also related precisely to this emotive and politicized field of government decision-making.[73]

[71] See generally I Hare and others (eds), *De Smith's Judicial Review* (9th edn, Sweet & Maxwell 2024); J Auburn, J Moffatt, and A Sharland, *Judicial Review Principles and Procedure* (OUP 2013); C Lewis, *Judicial Remedies in Public Law* (Sweet & Maxwell 2015); Aronson, Groves, and Weeks (n 53); P Cane, *Administrative Law* (5th edn, Clarendon 2011) Part III.

[72] *The Independent Review of Administrative Law* (CP 407 2021) (Faulks Review) [4.33]–[4.36].

[73] Barker and Lamont (n 51) 332.

In the same way that we saw the Canadian Province of Ontario in the last section attempting to check the rising tide of misfeasance claims, so the UK government has thrice in the last fourteen years sought to cap the availability and scope of judicial review on the grounds that applications cost the taxpayer too much, or interfere too extensively in the democratic process.[74] So far, it has backed away from its most far-reaching proposals, but changes were nonetheless made in 2015 that reduce the prospects of meritorious claims getting to trial in many instances,[75] and further limits came into force in 2022.[76] Since it is the nature of power to resist its own limitation, we should be extremely wary of such developments.

The laws underpinning actions for judicial review are public laws[77] because they describe either duties or conditions limiting the legal powers that exist between one public body and another, or between a public body (or decision-maker) and the State's citizens. They set the terms according to which public powers may be exercised validly and describe obligations (set out either in statute or statutory instrument) which public actors must observe when exercising them. Where the relevant public obligations are breached, or conditions for the exercise of the power not met, the conclusion of a court of law is not that what was decided was necessarily wrong, but that it was a decision that was not rightly made, so that it is invalid unless and until the point at which it can be made properly. Up until 1978, there was no unified process for making an application. Plaintiffs had to apply for one of the ancient 'public law' prerogative writs of *mandamus*, *certiorari*, and prohibition, on the one hand, or for the 'ordinary' private law remedies of injunction and declaration, on the other. It is only recently, therefore, that the enforcement process has been modernized and rationalized to any degree, with claims for the various remedies being channelled through a singular application for judicial review (AJR).[78]

A significant peculiarity of judicial review claims which is of special interest to us from the rights of action point of view, is that, whilst they have overwhelmingly been brought by individuals, they have until recently always been lodged in the

[74] Ministry of Justice, *Judicial Review: Proposals for Reform* (CP 25/2012); *Judicial Review: Proposals for Further Reform* (Cm 8703, 2013) [67]–[90]; Faulks Review (n 72). The last of these was independently commissioned. Whilst suggesting some changes, it rebuffed the government's most damaging proposals. See further Hare and others (eds) (n 71) [15-100]–[15-105].

[75] Criminal Justice and Courts Act 2015 (UK) s 84(2) introduces new sections into the Senior Courts Act 1981 which require courts to deny permission to bring a claim where it is 'highly unlikely' that the outcome for an applicant would have been different if the relevant illegality had not occurred, save in cases of 'exceptional public interest'. See further Hare and others (eds) (n 71) [16-050].

[76] Judicial Review and Courts Act 2022 (UK) ss 1, 2 (limiting the effects of quashing orders and excluding review of Upper Tribunals' refusals to grant permission to appeal). It has been suggested that government threats have in turn precipitated something of a 'climb down' by courts in recent cases: J Bell, 'The Resurgence of Standing in Judicial Review' (2024) 44 Oxford Journal of Legal Studies 313, 340.

[77] For a challenge to this classification on the basis that it hinders the law's capacity to protect individual rights see S Thomson, 'Judicial Review and Public Law: Challenging the Preconceptions of a Troubled Taxonomy' (2017) 41 Melbourne University Law Review 890.

[78] CPR Pt 54.

name of the Crown. The action hence took (and sometimes still takes)[79] the form *R v the Public Decision Maker (ex parte Citizen)*. This titular form suggests that the relevant underlying public law rights and the rights of action in respect of them are State rights, with individual applicants themselves only ever acting in a representative capacity in the proceeding, as in the 'relator' actions to which we shall come in the next chapter. The explanation for this probably lies with the old prerogative writs, which were indeed used by the King (administratively, from the thirteenth century) and then by his courts to prevent inferior courts from exceeding their jurisdiction, or to require courts or public officers to perform duties owed to the King.[80] There can be no doubt that the writs in such instances enforced 'public' rights of the nascent 'State' (although early on this process was really about protecting the personal rights and interests of the King—his jurisdiction being viewed as type of private property right). Nowadays, however—if this has not, in fact, long been the case[81]—the picture is more complicated. Some public duties owed by decision-makers under modern statutory provisions and instruments appear to be duties that are owed neither to a King, nor to the State (or the public as a whole), but duties owed to individuals, or groups. A good example highlighted by Joanna Bell is the right of a prisoner under rule 54 of the Prison Rules 1999[82] to be informed of a disciplinary charge made against her, which is specifically, Bell credibly suggests, a duty owed to *her* and to nobody else.[83] This account squares with an increased readiness amongst some commentators to rationalize the role of review proceedings as being to 'guard the rights of the *individual* against abuses of public power',[84] as well as to protect collective constitutional interests in good government and the rule of law. Such rationalizations are especially common in respect of norms of procedural fairness, where the relevant duties of the public decision-maker are arguably designed to protect the dignity and autonomy of those whose personal interests are liable to be affected by a decision, not *just* to promote better

[79] See eg *R (ex parte Gary Delaney) v The Parole Board of England and Wales* [2019] EWHC 779 (Admin).

[80] Auburn, Moffatt, and Sharland (n 71) [1.04]; E Jenks, 'The Prerogative Writs in English Law' (1923) 32 Yale Law Journal 523; E Henderson, *Foundations of English Administrative Law: Certiorari and Mandamus in the Seventeenth Century* (1st edn, Harvard University Press 1963); SA De Smith, 'The Prerogative Writs' (1951) 11 Cambridge Law Journal 40; C Langford, 'The Prerogative Writs and the Origins of English Administrative Law' (2014) 88 Australian Law Journal 567. For general histories see Hare and others (eds) (n 71) Ch 15; L Jaffe and E Henderson, 'Judicial Review and the Rule of Law: Historical Origins' (1956) 72 Law Quarterly Review 345.

[81] The long and ancient line of cases on rights to a fair hearing, such as those requiring service of a summons in a criminal proceeding, or notice to an affected individual before his property is distrained upon, or his licence or employment withdrawn (Hare and others (eds) (n 71) [8-012]–[8-019]) point strongly to duties owed historically to individuals, as well as the King, despite the language of the royal prerogative). The beginnings of this line lie with *Bagg's Case* (1615) 11 Co Rep 95b [77 ER 1271, 1275].

[82] Prison Rules 1999 (SI 1999/728). Another classic example is *Ridge v Baldwin* [1964] AC 40 (HL).

[83] J Bell, *The Anatomy of Administrative Law* (Hart 2020) 110.

[84] Hare and others (eds) (n 71) [1-016]–[1-017] (my emphasis); Thomson (n 77); S Nason, *Reconstructing Judicial Review* (Hart 2017).

governmental decisions in the round or ensure ethically robust systems of executive government.[85]

Despite the titular form of the proceeding, the underlying norms that must be observed by a public decision-maker if his or her decision is to be valid, are therefore not always (though they are usually) duties owed exclusively to the State or the public as a whole. Beyond this, however, even in cases in which duties are of this type, the State's involvement in review proceedings is nominal only. Indeed, in most jurisdictions in which streamlined statutory review processes have been introduced, its name no longer appears on the proceeding at all and the 'ex parte' formula has been dropped altogether in favour of reference only to name of the private applicant and the decision-maker as parties to the action.[86] The upshot is that whilst review applications are triggered by the breach of duties owed by decision-makers both to the State (or public as a whole) and (sometimes) separately to particular individuals, it is the individual applicant (*Citizen* in the above example) that now holds the right of action in *either* case.[87] Such proceedings are hence, in fact, the best and most important modern example of private individuals holding their *own* rights of action in respect of the breach of public law norms.

A. Enforcement Regime

(i) The Norms Enforced—Duties (sometimes) and Liabilities (often)

The norms that are enforced through review proceedings are often said to be the 'duties' or 'standards' according to which a public decision-maker must exercise its public powers legally, rationally, and with procedural propriety.[88] This statement is in turn shorthand for a far more complex textual description[89] and it needs to

[85] *R (Osborn) v Parole Board* [2013] UKSC 61 [68] (Lord Reed) cited in Bell, *The Anatomy of Administrative Law* (n 83) 88, 104; T Allan, 'Procedural Fairness and the Duty of Respect' (1998) 18 Oxford Journal of Legal Studies 497. This conception is not universally supported: cf D Galligan, *Due Process and Fair Procedures: A Study of Administrative Procedures* (OUP 1996); J Varuhas, 'The Reformation of English Administrative Law? "Rights", Rhetoric and Reality' (2013) 72 Cambridge Law Journal 369, 409–11 (the rights to which the duties correlate in such instances are collective, not individual rights).

[86] The 'ex parte' formula has hence not been used in Australia, except in Western Australia, since early in the new millennium. It persists in that jurisdiction because there is still no streamlined statutory review procedure.

[87] *R (on the application of Ben-Abdelaziz) v London Borough of Haringey Council & Anor* [2001] EWCA Civ 803 [29] (Phillips LJ, Pill and Arden LJJ agreeing).

[88] *Council of Civil Service Unions v Minister for the Civil Service* [1985] AC 374 (HL) 410–11 (Lord Diplock) (although the word duty is not used); 407 (Lord Scarman—the duty to act fairly); 414–15 (Lord Roskill—the duty to act fairly). De Smith [1001] prefers the word 'standards'—which reflects the customary uncertainty.

[89] The list of duties hence also includes avoiding fettered discretion, unauthorized delegations of power, bias, or the defeat of legitimate expectations that a decision-maker has engendered in particular persons. For the full range see Hare and others (eds) (n 71) [1-001]. As to whether these are true duties, or simply preconditions that must be met for the valid exercise of power, see further below.

be carefully refined. Many of the 'duties' (the duty to act legally and in accordance with the rule of law, for example) are ones owed by a decision-maker to the State or the public as a whole, as we said above, whilst others (in particular, some duties of procedural fairness, or duties to respect human rights when making decisions) may be owed to specific individuals or to groups whose interests are affected by a particular decision.[90] Whether the relevant 'duty' is owed to the public as a whole or to a particular individual (or to both) now turns on the precise terms of the legislation that grants the power in question.[91] It has become a highly nuanced question of statutory interpretation.

But the network of legal relationships enforced through judicial review applications is further complicated in another way. This is because most of the constraining legal incidents bearing upon a decision-maker's public powers are more accurately described not as duties but as Hohfeldian liabilities in the sense explained in Chapter 3. A mistake on the part of a decision-maker is not a breach of any legal *duty* owed to *anyone* but results in her liability to other agents of the State, or to individuals, to have the decision set aside.[92] Those who enforce the norms underpinning review proceedings are hence not *just* (or even very often) enforcing State duties with correlative claim rights, as they are in the tort of misfeasance, but State liabilities instead. Indeed, it is the enforcement of a public decision-maker's liability that is at stake in the greatest range of cases whenever litigants seek to overturn decisions that have been under some vitiating defect in the decision-maker's reasoning. Many of the 'duties' that public decision-makers have are not, on closer inspection, obligations the breach of which constitutes a wrong to anyone, they are merely preconditions of the valid exercise of a *power*—things a public official 'must do' *if* his or her decision is *to stand* as being *immune* to challenge. There are close analogies between such cases and private law examples to which we shall come in Chapter 8, in which individuals have the power to rescind private transactions that have been induced by mistake or misrepresentation.

Private rights of action in judicial review cases are hence important not just because they sometimes empower individuals to enforce duties that public decision-makers owe (eg a duty to do a particular thing enforceable by an order of *mandamus*) but because they enable those individuals to trigger changes in a broader Hohfeldian network of legal relations, unwinding legal consequences that have otherwise been brought about by the improper exercise of public power.

(ii) Rights of Action

Historically, it was the King, or his officials, who held the rights of action underlying the prerogative writs, because these writs, as I intimated above, enforced

90 Bell, *The Anatomy of Administrative Law* (n 83) 83–89, 103–106.
91 ibid 66–76.
92 Hare and others (eds) (n 71) [4-060] and [6-027]–[6-038].

rights than belonged to him, or to his courts. They were used as weapons in defence of his own private jurisdiction. Over time, however—and in some instances from the very start—they came to be enforceable also by private individuals on his behalf.[93] The exercise of the private right of action was always, as it is now, subject to obtaining judicial permission. In some instances, there appears never to have been any restriction on who might sue,[94] whereas in others (*mandamus* and *certiorari*) it came to be accepted that a suitor had to be a person 'aggrieved'.[95] The different stringency of the conditions attending the rights of action as between the writs at different times is an impenetrable historical puzzle, but its seems likely that it reflected the relative priority placed on the enforcement of the relevant underlying right (or jurisdiction—a power) on the one hand, and the perceived risk of vexatious private actions, on the other. The more important the King's right and the lower the risk of meddlesome private intervention that might overburden his courts, the wider he could cast the private right of action, consistently with his desire to reassert his jurisdictional power. If there is a discernible trend, it is that the extent to which total 'strangers' were permitted to enforce the prerogative writs (in particular *mandamus* and *certiorari*) shrank over time, probably in response to the growing number of cases in which such writs were sought post-1660, as more and more administrative powers were heaped on Justices of the Peace and ad hoc public authorities.[96] This understanding—that private rights of action in respect of the prerogative writs were initially cast pretty wide, but became increasingly

[93] Jenks (n 80) 527–31 (citing prohibition as an example in which private enforcers were used very early on, *quo warranto* also becoming available to common informers and then openly available to individuals with permission in the eighteenth century); SA De Smith, 'The Prerogative Writs' (1951) 11 Cambridge Law Journal 40, 50. *Certiorari* was available at the suit of individuals from about 1280: Langford (n 80) 570.

[94] This seems to have been the case in relation to the writs of quo warranto (which was designed to prevent usurpations of public office) and prohibition (E Coke, *Institutes of the Laws of England* (E and R Brooke 1797) 602 ('stranger')), although some have suggested that an applicant probably had to have some sort of personal interest: see Hare and others (eds) (n 71) [15-030]), as well as the writ of habeas corpus. For a more sceptical analysis suggesting that some form of special interest was probably always required, see Aronson, Groves, and Weeks (n 53) 818–19.

[95] Jenks (n 80) 528, 531. For the fuller picture, with all its glitches and uncertainties, see Hare and others (eds) (n 71) [15-028], [15-032]–[15-034], [15-040]–[15-043]; D Yardley, 'Certiorari and the Problem of Locus Standi' (1955) 71 Law Quarterly Review 388. According to R Berger, 'Standing to Sue in Public Actions: Is it a Constitutional Requirement?' (1969) 78 Yale Law Journal 816, 820–21, 824–27 there is at least some seventeenth- and eighteenth-century evidence that both *certiorari* and *mandamus*, like *quo warranto* and prohibition, were available at the suit of a stranger. See also L Jaffe, 'Standing to Secure Judicial Review: Public Actions' (1961) 74 Harvard Law Review 1265, 1270 (indicating that the author was unable to find any case in which standing has been disputed in respect of mandamus prior to the 1807 case of *The King v Archbishop of Canterbury*, 8 East 213, 103 ER 323). The language of a person 'aggrieved' has been retained by some statutory provisions that provide mechanisms for appeal or review outside of the new AJR procedure: Hare and others (eds) (n 71) [2-060]–[2-065].

[96] De Smith, 'The Prerogative Writs' (n 93) 48 mentions an 'inundation' of Kings Bench Courts by *certiorari* motions in this period. Jaffe (n 95) 1270 points to 1807 as the first *mandamus* case insisting on the need for a special legal right and identifies the highpoint of mandamus claims as the seventeenth century and early eighteenth (at 1272–1273), prior to the introduction of more satisfactory system of central administrative control.

constrained over time—corresponds with Louis Jaffe's observation that there was very little formal talk of any standing requirements in English courts before the beginning of the nineteenth century.[97]

By contrast, in the more limited number of instances in which final injunctions or declarations were sought prior to 1978, judicial permission to proceed was apparently always unnecessary, but rights of action were strictly confined to those who could show interference with some private right or special damage to a private interest of their own.[98] This apparent contradiction with the position in relation to the prerogative writs looks odd and the law was undoubtedly confused. A partial explanation for the confusion may be that although in these instances the remedies were always being sought against a public authority, the duties being enforced through the private action were not always duties that the authority *owed in its governmental capacity*. They were sometimes the same duties as were owed by private citizens. Some of the claims underpinning suits for injunctive or declaratory relief were hence probably properly classified as private law claims according to the definition furnished in Chapter 2, involving as they did the infringement of property, or other private rights of the plaintiff.[99] The insistence on a private right as a condition of enforcement in private law claims follows a well-established tradition in such cases that will be examined in detail in Chapter 8. Other claims were for the breach of public law duties that private individuals also have, such as duties not to commit a public nuisance.[100] In such cases, the next chapter will show, courts have historically insisted on private plaintiffs proving 'special damage' to their private interests, whether the defendant is a public body *or* a private person, as a way of safeguarding private defendants against multiple claims and crushing civil liability. Again, no 'State duty' as such is at stake in such instances and the strict rules governing rights of action were arguably a response (probably an exaggerated one, I shall later suggest) to concerns about multiple damages claims, which are inapposite where all that is sought is the declaration or restraint by injunction of some illegal public action.

[97] Jaffe (n 95) 1270.

[98] *Stockport District Waterworks* Co *v Manchester Corporation* (1863) 7 LT 545, 548; *Boyce* (n 6) 114; *Gouriet* (n 2). The origins of equitable intervention in the enforcement of public rights and duties are obscure. Equitable injunctive relief played probably no part before the nineteenth century and the declaration only really came into its own in the twentieth. On the history and respective standing requirements of the actions, see generally Hare and others (eds) (n 71) [15-047]–[15-073]; E Sykes, 'The Injunction in Public Law' (1953) 2 University of Queensland Law Journal 114.

[99] See eg *London Passenger Transport Board v Moscrop* [1942] AC 332 (HL) (right under employment contract); *Gregory and Another v London Borough of Camden* [1966] 1 WLR 899 (amenity rights). For similar cases where injunctions were hence sought against private parties for the infringement of private statutory rights, see *Cromford and High Peak Railway Co v Stockport, Disley and Whaley Bridge Railway Co* (1857) 24 Beav 74 (statutory rights to a monopoly); *Wyld and Others v Silver* [1962] Ch 561 (proprietary market rights).

[100] *Boyce* (n 6); *Attorney-General v Staffordshire CC* [1905] 1 Ch 336. That the 'special damage' requirement may indeed have been connected to public nuisance cases in this way was recognized by Brennan J in *Onus v Alcoa of Australia Ltd* (1981) 149 CLR 27, 71.

Whilst injunctive and (particularly) declaratory orders have hence come to be recognized as having a useful role in judicial review cases in recent years,[101] the apparent, historical requirement that an applicant possess an underlying private property right, or be able to prove 'special damage' to a private interest before having a right of action ('standing') to seek them to enforce the State's public duties and liabilities made no sense at all, and one would expect judicial permission to be required before an action is begun, as in the case of the other, prerogative remedies.

Under the new Application for Judicial Review procedure (AJR), this is now the position. Judicial permission is a universal requirement for enforcing the relevant public liability or duty in England, whatever the remedy sought. Anomalous cases such as those we have mentioned above, which do not actually concern the enforcement of the State's governmental duties and liabilities, are weeded out of the review process and rights of action are extended instead to all who have a 'sufficient interest in the matter to which the application relates'.[102] Although the Attorney-General in theory retains a right of action and may allow a private person to exercise it on his or her behalf by way of relation, that right is effectively redundant because individuals now have their own enforcement rights and do not need his *fiat* to exercise them. Aside from some instances under statute in which public authorities have legal capacity to apply for review on behalf their constituents,[103] enforcement in judicial review proceedings is therefore nowadays entirely a private business.

The question of what counts as a 'sufficient interest' for a right of action under the AJR procedure still tests courts. It is answered on a case-by-case basis, according to context. The content of the requirement appears to vary according to the deontic nature of the duty (or power) the breach (or excess) of which provides the basis for the action; as well as on the terms and purposes of any framing legislation.[104] The breach of a statutory 'due process' duty owed specifically to an individual (as in Bell's prisoner example) is hence actionable by the individual who is the holder of the correlative claim right (and usually by no other private person), but where the only duty or liability is to the public as a whole, an applicant need have no prior legal right of his or her own to make the application. This is what is meant when it is said that it is proof of 'interest' and not (individual) right that is

[101] The profile of the remedies has increased since the new AJR procedure was introduced: Hare and others (eds) (n 71) [15-048], [18-033]–[18-043]. Since the effect of an injunction is often no different from that of a mandatory or quashing order, it is the declaration that has in practice proven the more useful remedy: ibid [18-038]–[18-039]. This is particularly so in cases against the Crown, where the prerogative orders are excluded: Lewis (n 71) [2-179].

[102] Senior Courts Act 1981 (UK) s 31(3); *R v Inland Revenue Commissioners, ex p National Federation of Self-Employed and Small Businesses Ltd* [1982] AC 617.

[103] See eg Local Government Act 1972 (UK) s 222. The section grants capacity only, not necessarily standing.

[104] Hare and others (eds) (n 71) [2-025]–[2-029]. Just occasionally, the statute will expressly or impliedly stipulate who has the relevant right of action, but this is rare: [2-028]. See eg Local Government Act 1988 (UK) s 19(7) ('any potential contractor').

essential to a person's standing.[105] In contrast to the position under the HRA or the tort of misfeasance, an applicant's 'interest' need not be a private one, as evidenced by the many cases in which claims have successfully been brought by representative and public interest groups.[106] Indeed, it would be counterintuitive, I have suggested in this chapter, to make rights of action that are designed to protect public interests in good government dependent on the possession of an affected private interest of one's own. In such cases, proof of genuine, public motivation and of capacity competently to conduct the litigation in question is the key, and private interests are relevant only to the (questionable) extent that they establish that a plaintiff is not a 'busybody'—that is, someone who is intervening without good reason in the affairs of *others*. But there is no reason to think that a person with 'no particular [private] stake' in a decision is necessarily a 'meddler' when he or she seeks to enforce a duty that is owed to all citizens.[107] Indeed the basic presumption should probably be the reverse.

In practice, the increasingly liberal attitudes of English courts to standing in public interest cases signals their progressive acceptance of this reverse presumption and the result is that standing is now reportedly rarely a hurdle in any case that has apparent merit.[108] It is this, no doubt, that has rattled government and which led it in 2013 to propose a more restrictive 'direct and/or tangible interest' test for all judicial review proceedings.[109] The Australian approach to standing, incidentally, has historically been more conservative than that of English Courts, with the High Court generally insisting on the need for some special private interest (usually a financial one) to be at stake before an applicant will be granted standing even in a public interest case, although there are signs of greater liberality in recent years.[110] The historically conservative approach of the High Court (critically characterized by Justice Kirby as one that tended to treat public interest litigation as an 'evil')[111] was openly criticized by the Australian Law Reform Commission in 1996,

[105] *R (Bancoult) v Secretary of State for Foreign and Commonwealth Affairs* [2007] EWCA Civ 498 [61] (Sedley LJ); *AXA General Insurance Ltd v The Lord Advocate* [2011] UKSC 46 [169]–[170] (Lord Reed).

[106] *R v Inspectorate of Pollution and another, ex parte Greenpeace Ltd* [1994] 4 All ER 329 (No 2); *R v Secretary of State for Foreign Affairs, ex parte World Development Movement Ltd* [1995] 1 All ER 611; *R v Secretary of State for Trade and Industry Ex parte Greenpeace* [1998] Env LR 415.

[107] *R v Somerset County Council, ex parte Dixon* [1998] Env LR 111 (QBD) 121 (Sedley LJ).

[108] Hare and others (eds) (n 71) [2-030]; Auburn, Moffatt, and Sharland (n 71) [24.16]; Cane, *Administrative Law* (n 71) 284.

[109] Cmnd 8703 [67], [80]. The test is sometimes proposed in these different ways in the same paragraph. For criticism, see J McGarry, 'Importance of an Expansive Test of Standing' (2014) 19 Judicial Review 60.

[110] *Australian Conservation Foundation* (n 6) 530–31 (Gibbs J) (private 'advantage' or 'disadvantage'); *Onus v Alcoa* (n 100). Comments in *Bateman's Bay* (n 6) 263 [39] and the High Court formulations in more recent cases cited at n 6 appear more liberal, and there have been departures in environmental cases (see eg *North Coast Environment Council Inc v Minister for Resources* (1994) 55 FCR 492 (Sackville J)).

[111] M Kirby, 'Deconstructing the Law's Hostility to Public Interest Litigation' (2011) 127 Law Quarterly Review 537, 554–55.

but the Commission's proposals for a more generous 'open' standing rule in public interest cases[112] were studiously ignored by the government of the day, as it has been by all governments since.

The conditions attaching to enforcement rights in judicial review hence depend not just on the express or implied intention of Parliament in creating a particular governmental power, but also on the interests (public or private) which the various duties and preconditions attaching to the exercise of that power are designed to protect.[113] It should not depend on the type of remedy sought,[114] nor on the substantive merits of the claim. This is important, because individuals must have the power to enliven courts' jurisdiction to review government decisions, regardless of the remedy that may ultimately be considered best to redress any breach of duty (or excess of power) that is found. Moreover, the substantive merits of a claim are irrelevant to the possession of a right to initiate it. To the extent that there remains confusion over these matters and courts continue to consider them in determining whether a person has sufficient standing,[115] it is a sign, I venture to suggest, that they take the concept of standing to encompass a wider range of normative issues than just the question whether or not an applicant has a liberty and power to initiate an action in the way I suggested we should now think of the idea. This being so, there is no necessary inconsistency between courts' views and the position for which I argue here, but there is nonetheless a strong case for them distinguishing more clearly between rights of *action*, on the one hand, and *remedial* rights, on the other. This conclusion echoes the analytical point made at the end of Chapter 3, to which I promised to return. An assessment of the strength of a claim should obviously always be made and especially hopeless cases be struck out, but the point remains that ultimate lack of merit in a claim does not affect the appropriateness of vesting in a particular applicant the legal power to bring it.

[112] Australian Law Reform Commission (ALRC), *Beyond the Doorkeeper—Standing to Sue for Public Remedies* (ALRC 78 1994) [5.17]–[5.26], Rec 2 (the only restrictions being that standing does not contradict statutory intention or unreasonably interfere with another person's private rights).

[113] This appears to be borne out by Bell's observation that a different approach seems to prevail in respect of 'targeted' decisions 'about' an individual or corporation (such as a decision whether or not to grant them a licence) and more 'abstract(ed)', 'untargeted' decisions about the good of the nation, such as a decision to leave the European Union: Bell, 'The Resurgence of Standing in Judicial Review' (n 76) (on the definitions, see esp 318–19).

[114] Analytically, rights of action are independent of remedial rights in the same way that they are analytically independent of primary ones. Since they govern different questions (the power to bring a claim before a court and entitlement to a particular sort of relief, respectively) they should not be elided: see Chapter 3 Section 3.5. Note, however, that courts currently clearly insist that standing requirements vary according to the type of remedy sought: *Inland Revenue Commissioners v National Federation of Self-Employed and Small Businesses* [1982] AC 617 (HL) 648 (Lord Scarman); *Hobart* (n 6) [32] (Kiefel CJ, Keane and Gordon JJ); *Unions NSW v New South Wales* [2023] HCA 4 [16] (Gageler, Gordon, Edelman, Steward, Gleeson, and Jagot JJ).

[115] Hare and others (eds) (n 71) [2-030]; Auburn, Moffatt, and Sharland (n 71) [24.28].

B. Interests Protected

Although there are dissenters, it is therefore plausible to suggest that the public laws that underpin judicial review are designed for the protection of both public and private interests,[116] even if the former were historically prior, and even if they still dominate. The interests at stake in any given case in turn have a bearing on the conditions that are attached to private rights of action. It is partly this, Bell insightfully suggests, that explains the continuing flexibility and variation in courts' approach to the 'sufficient interest' test under the new AJR procedure.[117] Where public duties and liabilities are only to the public as a whole and designed solely to protect the public interest in legality and good government, any publicly motivated citizen of full age and capacity should logically have a right of action, subject only to obtaining judicial permission to proceed.[118] According to at least one study, vexatious litigation is a minor concern only,[119] and it can be struck out in the usual way. By contrast, where the purpose of a public law rule is to protect the private interests of a particular applicant, such as their dignity, reputation, economic interests, liberty, property, privacy, or a legitimate personal expectation that a public authority has engendered in them through its behaviour, it is logical that the right of action normally be confined to the person holding the relevant right or interest, or to a suitable personal representative, but court permission to proceed should in such instances probably not be required at all, or be automatically given, not discretionary.

[116] Bell, *The Anatomy of Administrative Law* (n 83); Thomson (n 77); T Cornford, *Towards a Public Law of Tort* (Routledge 2008) 17–19; cf contra Varuhas, 'Against Unification' (n 33) (taking a more clean-cut approach according to which judicial review is always about public interests); J Varuhas, 'Judicial Review at the Crossroads (2015) 74 Cambridge Law Journal 215; J Varuhas, 'The Public Interest Conception of Public Law: Its Procedural Origins and Substantive Implications' in J Bell and others (eds), *Public Law Adjudication in Common Law Systems: Process and Substance* (Hart 2016) Ch 4, esp 47–69; P Daly, 'Administrative Law: A Values-based Approach' in Bell and others (eds) ibid Ch 3 (also taking a pure public interest approach). For a detailed review of the ways in which judicial review structures can be modelled to accommodate collective public interest objectives see, classically, R Rawlings, 'Modelling Judicial Review' (2008) 61 Current Legal Problems 9. On the current modelling of public and private interests in Australia, see A Edgar, 'Public and Private Interests in Australian Administrative Law' (2013) 36 University of New South Wales Law Journal 202.

[117] Bell, *The Anatomy of Administrative Law* (n 83) Ch 6, esp 184–86, 191–95. See also Bell, 'The Resurgence of Standing in Judicial Review' (n 76).

[118] Whether leave should be needed even in these instances is questionable (eg there is currently no such requirement in the Federal Court in Australia) although the pragmatic arguments suggest it is likely to remain: AP Le Sueur and M Sunkin, 'Applications for Judicial Review: The Requirement of Leave' [1992] Public Law 102. For a suggestion that the Australian position now needs to be reconsidered, alongside the introduction of new powers to issue UK-style civil restraint orders, see J Griffiths, 'Is there Too Much Access to Administrative Justice? A Project for the Revived Administrative Review Council? (New South Wales Supreme Court Speech, 15 November 2024) <https://supremecourt.nsw.gov.au/documents/Publications/Speeches/2024-speeches/Griffiths_20241115.pdf> accessed 8 December 2025.

[119] Le Sueur and Sunkin (n 118) 124 (a maximum of three out of 86 cases in their study, in which leave was denied, were vexatious). cf Griffiths (n 118) [10] ('the problem (if there is one) should not be exaggerated' and most likely affects self-represented litigants).

This intuition corresponds loosely with proposals put forward by the Law Commission in 1994, which set out a two-track system of rights of action, with rights being automatic in private interest cases, but subject to some degree of judicial discretion where the interest is public.[120] It also corresponds, the reader will note, with suggestions made in earlier sections of this chapter as to the way in which private rights of action might potentially be modelled in cases under the HRA and, rather more tentatively, in the tort of misfeasance in public office, if the latter actions are ever to be given a broader public interest role than they currently have. There will always be practical difficulties for courts, of course, in determining whether the purpose of a particular law constraining the operation of public power is to protect public interests, private interests, or both, and the consequence is that decisions about standing will continue to be contingent upon the careful exercise of principles of statutory interpretation, but at least in this way courts might have a clearer sense of the underlying principles to apply.

C. Remedies

The discretionary 'prerogative' remedies that we have mentioned so far—now renamed 'quashing orders', 'mandatory orders', and 'prohibiting orders'—reflect the predominant conception of judicial review as protective of public and not private interests, the focus being on invalidation and compulsion in respect of key public duties and conditions for the exercise of power. Perhaps the key point of modern contention is whether or not breach of the relevant public duties, or excesses of the relevant powers, ought also to give rise to compensatory remedies for the harm that particular decisions cause to private interests, as they do in cases of misfeasance and under the HRA.[121] As things stand, damages can be claimed for such harm within the same review process, but only if a plaintiff is able to make out an independent cause of action in private law or under the HRA.

There is no reason in principle why damages should not be available for the breach of purely public, not private law duties, where the public duties are indeed genuine duties, the breach of which constitutes a wrong to the person injured. This much is clear from principles governing actions for breach of statutory duty and misfeasance in public office, but there are not likely to be very many such cases in respect of the laws underpinning judicial review. There is also nothing in principle to rule out compensation in cases in which a defect in reasoning or procedure leads to an invalid decision that prejudices a particular person's private interests even

[120] Law Commission, *Administrative Law: Judicial Review and Statutory Appeals* (Law Comm 226 1994) [5.20]–[5.22].

[121] P Craig, 'Compensation in Public Law' (1980) 96 Law Quarterly Review 413; D Cohen and JC Smith, 'Entitlement and the Body Politic' (1986) 64 Canadian Bar Review 1; P Cane, 'Damages in Public Law' (1999) 9 Otago Law Review 489.

where they were not owed a personal primary duty,[122] although the case may be less strong. The main concern is likely to be one about the potentially large size of the resulting liabilities, bearing in mind that the liabilities underpinning the judicial review regime are in many instances strict and large groups can be prejudiced by a single, invalid exercise of power.

If one is worried about this (I can already sense hesitations in the reader), there are several routes that could be taken to accommodate the concern. One option is to take the approach that is currently taken in cases of public nuisance considered in the next chapter, which is to make compensation available only to those who can show that their damage is 'special'—different in type or degree to damage caused to other members of the public. The unconscionable arbitrariness of this tactic is self-evident, however, and it should be discounted straight away.

A second option would be to keep the compensatory regime in cases involving invalid decisions discretionary and weak in all cases in the way that is done under the HRA, following the same spirit of compromise between private interests and State financial interests that currently infuses that Act. Compensation could in this way be made a measure of last resort and settled according to a distributive (not a corrective) justice rationale in cases in which a decision-maker has not breached a public duty that is specifically owed to a particular individual.

A third approach would be to make compensation available as of right only where the discernible intention of the legislation framing the relevant public duties or powers was to protect the private interests of particular individuals or groups (as, for example, in Bell's prisoner example to which I have constantly referred). This approach is logical and is supported to some degree by the approach taken in the tort of breach of statutory duty (as well in some cases involving the negligent exercise of public powers), although it may prove tricky to apply in practice because it involves staring into the crystal ball of legislative intention with limited interpretive tools.

A fourth approach, which was once proposed by the Law Commission,[123] would be to combine the third approach with a further restriction, according to which the relevant public illegality must involve 'serious' fault. This would narrow the compensation gap currently left by the tort of misfeasance, without going so far as to provide a public law remedy for common instances of careless administrative failure, or wholly innocent (faultless) illegality.

None of these proposals is under active consideration. The Law Commission's own proposals went down like a lead balloon with government departments and the result is that the perceived deficiencies in the remedies for harm to private

[122] Cane, 'Damages in Public Law' (n 121) 505, whilst not mentioning judicial review specifically, hence suggests that any exogenous loser in consequence of an exercise of governmental functions ought in principle to be entitled to a public law damages remedy.

[123] Law Comm CP No 187, 75 [4.95].

interests caused by excesses of administrative power are likely to continue to be met at best in an isolated way through *ex gratia* discretionary payment schemes in areas in which decision-making is causing special concern and proving too politically embarrassing for governments to sweep under the carpet. That nothing more than this is likely in the short to medium term is a function of the fiscal constraints existing in current economic conditions that we highlighted in the last chapter, and which continue to shape public liabilities across the board. Since turkeys rarely vote for Christmas, legislative measures exposing government to further financial liabilities also seem most unlikely in the short to medium term.

D. Rationale

In contrast to the two previous examples, the reliance on private enforcers in judicial review proceedings is predominantly now based on constitutional and enforcement-capture arguments, reflecting the public interest justifications that underpin a high proportion of the relevant public law rules. It is essential to the public good that the exercise of government power observes the rule of law, and it is both constitutionally appropriate and systemically logical that private citizens hold the power to enliven courts' jurisdiction to scrutinize those decisions. We cannot—and should not—rely solely upon the Attorney-General or other executive public enforcers to do the enforcement job.[124] Nor, in contrast to some of the cases that we examine in the next chapter, should we require executive consent to commence an action in any case. From the constitutional point of view, it is also important that judges retain control over questions of standing in respect of applications for judicial review, rather than Parliament allocating rights of action in a more limited way through legislation. The fact that Parliament is, in the British system of government, always under effective executive control, means that limiting private rights of action to cases in which they have been specifically granted by legislation is fraught with risk. It would mean, as Peter Cane has pointed out, that the consent of the governors would again in practice always be required before they could be held to account by the governed[125]—a consequence that we can be fairly sure that private rights of action in the modern age have been deliberately designed to prevent.

[124] ALRC 78 (1994) [4.15]. The same enforcement–capture arguments actually also sometimes justify granting standing to private persons other than those directly affected by a decision, where the decision is one that works to the latter's benefit, such that he or she has no incentive to question its legality: Bell, 'The Resurgence of Standing in Judicial Review' (n 76) 323–24.

[125] For this type of argument, see Cane, *Administrative Law* (n 71) 285: 'because Parliament is under the effective control of the government and is relatively ineffective as a forum for holding the executive accountable, courts can and should provide an alternative forum for the airing of widely held grievances . . . and for ensuring that public functionaries observe the law'.

It seems possible also that in some cases to which I have referred, the purpose of particular norms, especially those of procedural justice, is to protect the personal interests of those affected by a decision. Where this is so, there is an additional justification for according those with affected interests the power of suit. This rationale cannot, however, be relied upon in every case.

6.5 Summation

Citizens have always played a role in enforcing the duties and liabilities of the State and they continue to do so vibrantly in the modern law. Some of the most ancient Roman and medieval English examples of private enforcement were actions against corrupt public officials in respect of public extortions and abuses of office, with individuals being offered significant rewards for the prosecution of a suit.[126] Although rewards for taking action against the State or its officials are generally[127] no longer offered, this is not a field in which private enforcement has in any sense withered on the vine, but one where it continues to lead a vigorous modern life. The reinvention of the tort of misfeasance in public office in the middle of the last century has resulted in a groundswell of private litigation against State officers which persists defiantly despite an almost total lack of substantive success. The law of judicial review in England has similarly seen an exponential increase in private enforcement effort in the last thirty years and it is increasingly accepted that, whatever the titular form of the claim, the rights of action in such cases truly 'belong' to the citizen. The HRA provides entirely new private rights of action in domestic English law that were formerly only exercisable before the European Court of Human Rights.

The swell in private initiative in enforcing State duties and the conditions and limits of State power is clearly worrying for governments. It has political as well as fiscal implications and, in voicing protest, they like to emphasize the dangers for democracy and the costs to the taxpayer of the incoming tide. Some measures have been taken to stem that inflow. At the same time, those who believe in accountable government will see the greater use of private enforcement as an entirely proper manifestation of Newton's third law—an equal reaction to the burgeoning of State powers and responsibilities and as a desirable adjustment to traditional constitutional controls, placing important legal powers in the hands of the people when other controls are perceptibly, or potentially deficient. These powers supplement other public control mechanisms, rather than supplanting them. They form part of a complex set of checks and balances in which responsibility for the constraint of governmental power is distributed across a variety of different public and private

[126] See Chapter 4.
[127] But see n 11 above.

agencies. That configuration is in a constant state of adjustment and is not necessarily progressing in any singular, linear direction.

The explanations for the dominance of private rights of action in the respective legal regimes are, I have suggested, several. Aside from the important constitutional justification to which I have just referred, there are two other, critical factors. One is the risk of enforcement capture. It is most unwise to make anyone who owes a duty (or is subject to a liability) its sole or even primary enforcer. This is a basic matter of logical system design. The other is that the public duties and liabilities of the State are not always, though they are often, designed to protect public interests. The duties of public authorities under Section 6 of the HRA are often designed to protect private interests as well as public ones, and those owed by public officials in the tort of misfeasance in public office are primarily designed to protect private interests, with the protection of public interests currently featuring only as a secondary, contingent aim. The duties and liabilities enforced through judicial review are, by contrast, predominantly designed for the protection of public interests, but there is a degree of hybridity even here that flows from specific statutory provisions designed to give individuals themselves claim rights to notice, inclusion and dignity during the decision-making process. Wherever the purpose of the system of primary rights and duties is to protect particular private interests, there is a good, moral case for allowing those whose interests are harmed the liberty and power of a right of action.

The complex configuration of enforcement rights, interests and associated remedies in respect of the breach of the State duties that I have considered in this chapter can be summarized in the tabular way depicted in Figure 6.1. This rather butchers the subtlety of the various positions and preceding discussion, but may at least give the reader a satisfying sense of the main features of the landscape.

The fact that both public and private interests are protected through the various private enforcement regimes has logical implications, I have suggested, not just for the precise conditions that should be applied to the exercise of the relevant private rights of action but also for the remedial rights that one might expect the legal regime to grant to successful private enforcers. Where public law rules are designed primarily for the protection of particular private interests, one would expect private rights of action always to be unconditional on obtaining prior judicial permission. One would also expect compensation to be payable as of right in respect of any proven harm to those interests, preferably on a corrective justice rationale.

Where, on the other hand, the rule is designed for the protection of public, community interests, there is a good normative case for a right of action to be available to anyone who is suitably publicly motivated, although a requirement of judicial permission prior to commencing the action may be wise if there are thought to be serious concerns about vexatious litigation that cannot be met via ordinary case management processes. Compensation is not generally to be expected in pure,

Law(s)	**Duty or Liability**	**Interests Protected**	**Enforcement (right of action)**	**Private Enforcement Condition**	**Prior Executive Permission Required?**	**Judicial Permission Required?**	**Compensation Remedy?**
HRA s6	Public Duty + Liability	Private + Public	Private + Public	Victim rule: Personal Interest (Direct or Indirect)	No	No	Secondary, Discretionary Distributive Justice
Tort of Misfeasance in Public Office	Public Duties	Private (but contingently and indirectly also Public)	Private	Damage to Private Interest	No	No (but see Ontario)	As of Right Corrective Justice
Judicial Review (AJR)	Public Liabilities + Duties	Public (but sometimes also Private)	Public (Attorney General) + Private	Sufficient Interest (widely construed)	No	Yes (in the UK)	None

Figure 6.1 Enforcement Rights in Respect of State Duties and Liabilities

public interest litigation of this sort, if the only harm caused is suffered by the community itself and therefore born equally by all of its citizens.[128]

If the public interests protected under the HRA are to be fully protected, I have suggested above that the standing conditions currently attaching to actions under section 6 of the Act need to be relaxed in favour of more open standing rules; and the same will be true if one wishes to give the tort of misfeasance in public office a more significant public interest role in holding abusers of public office to account. In these instances, the practical need for the extension depends to some degree on the extent to which these public ends are being effectively pursued by other agencies, either governmental or independent of government, but there is nonetheless likely to be value in making the extensions in any event, on constitutional grounds, to guarantee the rule of law. In no instance, in any action against the State for the breach of one of its own duties (or to enforce one of its public liabilities), should private rights of action be conditional on executive *fiat*, whether or not that *fiat* is subject to judicial review. From this point of view, Lord Wilberforce's constitutional tenet, with which we opened this chapter—that the enforcement of public rights is nowadays a preserve of the State—must be heavily qualified where the rights in question are rights that citizens hold against the State itself. Furthermore, it is important that we cling determinedly to this qualification in the future if executive power is to be contained within proper constitutional bounds. There are worrying signs in some parts of the common law world that democracy is increasingly threatened by executive autocracy, and in such times the rights of citizens to invoke the jurisdiction of courts in protection of their rights and interests are especially crucial to both our individual and collective welfare.

[128] This should not be taken to preclude the possibility of compensation being made available persons who have suffered particular harm to their private interests where these have been harmed by the breach of a public law duty owed to the public as a whole, if the harm exceeds that which the community as a whole was expected to bear.

7
Public Law, Private Enforcement
Citizen Duties

The last chapter reviewed three cases in which private citizens have powers to enforce the State's duties and liabilities. This one engages in a similar exercise with regard to the enforcement of duties that are owed *to* the State *by* private citizens, focusing again on three examples: the law of public nuisance, a group of suits falling under the heading of 'popular actions', and private criminal prosecutions. Private rights of action are immediately more controversial in these instances because their persistence cannot be rooted in the same way in the constitutional value of State accountability before the law, and because citizens are potentially assuming a role in policing the behaviour of their fellow citizens that is now very widely considered an executive prerogative in most modern constitutions for all of the reasons discussed in Chapter 6.

7.1 Public Nuisances

The first example lies in the law of public nuisance. A public nuisance is a crime at common law[1] and under a variety of more specific, modern statutory provisions.[2] At common law, it consists in any unwarranted act or omission endangering the life, health, property, or comfort of the public, or which obstructs the enjoyment of rights common to all citizens.[3] As the breadth of this definition implies, 'the' wrong does not in fact consist in the breach of any single duty but rather in the violation of a ragbag of different public rights, the only common feature of which is that

[1] *R v Cross* (1812) 3 Camp 224.

[2] See eg Queensland Criminal Code 1899 s 230; Summary Offences Act 2005 (Qld) s 6. Whether it is *always* a crime is contested. Lord Bingham thought so in *R v Rimmington, Goldstein* [2005] UKHL 63 [7], but others disagree. For an ingenious reconstruction that attempts to disentangle the crime from a distinct (and narrow) private law tort based on private law rights to the communal use of public highways and fishing rights (akin to private easements and profits) see J Neyers, 'Reconceptualising the Tort of Public Nuisance' (2017) 76 Cambridge Law Journal 87; A Botterell and J Neyers, 'Tate & Lyle: Pure Economic Loss and the Modern Tort of Public Nuisance' (2016) 53 Alberta Law Review 1030.

[3] PJ Richardson, *Archbold Criminal Pleading Evidence and Practice* (Sweet and Maxwell 2017) 31–40. This definition was cited with approval in *Rimmington* (n 2) 470 [10] (Lord Bingham) and by the New Zealand Supreme Court in *Smith v Fonterra* [2024] NZSC 5 [109]. In the US, see, similarly, *Restatement (Second) of Torts* s 821B(1) (1979): 'an unreasonable interference with a right common to the general public'.

Enforcement Rights in Public and Private Law. Kit Barker, Oxford University Press.
DOI: 10.1093/9780191955006.003.0010

they are held collectively by all members of the community: it involves breaches of duties which a citizen owes to the State as the representative of the public as a whole.[4] Some of the earliest examples involved physical encroachments upon the royal domain, or the obstruction of public rights of way—inconveniences not so scandalous as to amount to breaches of the King's Peace but which were offences to the King personally, or the public nonetheless.[5] Additional, modern examples include violations of public decency, fishing rights, rights to health, safety, or (topically in the current climate and connected to public health) environment.

The breadth of the common law wrong and the vagueness of its definition historically allowed courts to control all sorts of antisocial behaviour that are now subject to more precise and carefully articulated forms of statutory regulation.[6] As regulation has grown, the role of the common law wrong has shrunk[7] but it has not entirely disappeared, and its versatility still sometimes gives it contemporary appeal. In America, there have hence been progressive attempts since the 1970s to vitalize it in the pursuit of a host of neglected regulatory goals, such as the control of firearms, tobacco, opioids, hazardous paint products, predatory lending practices, and the greenhouse gases that contribute to global warming.[8] Casting the offender

[4] J Joyce and H Joyce, *Treatise on the Law Governing Nuisances* (Bender & Co 1906) §5 ('an offense against the public order and economy of the State'); W Hawkins, *A Treatise of the Pleas of the Crown* (Walthoe 1716) Book I, Ch LXXV (an 'Offence against the Publick'). Despite what was said by Romer LJ in *AG v PYA Quarries* [1957] 2 QB 169, 187, a public nuisance is hence *not* simply a collection of individual private nuisances (which entail the violations of private rights)—it must bear on the 'community as a whole, rather than merely individuals': *Rimmington* (n 2) [44], [48] (Lord Rodger), [58] (Baroness Hale); Joyce and Joyce (n 4) §14; W Prosser, 'Private Action for Public Nuisance' (1966) 52 Virginia Law Review 997, 1001; *Restatement* (n 3) comment g to s 821B (1979). This does not preclude there being factual overlap between cases of public and private nuisance, where the public wrong also involves an interference with the use and enjoyment of a land right: *Colour Quest Ltd v Total Downstream UK Plc* [2009] EWHC540 (Comm) (rev'd on a different point [2010] EWCA Civ 180). There is also commonality in the origins of public and private nuisance actions—the assize of nuisance, which was a local jury process introduced in the late twelfth century largely for the purpose of settling disputes about private land rights being extended by a statute of 1285 to encompass violations of public rights. The idea that public nuisances were public wrongs '*ad commune nocumentum*' only emerged fully in the seventeenth century: D Gifford, 'Public Nuisance as a Mass Products Liability Tort' (2003) 71 University of Cincinnati Law Review 741, 793–97. Here as elsewhere, therefore, the public and private wrongs were originally dealt with via the same formal process and only gradually separated conceptually. Indeed, the assize of nuisance, although concerned originally with private land rights was still a 'criminal writ, affording incidental civil relief': Prosser (n 4) 997–98. It was replaced by the action on the case for what we now know as private nuisance.

[5] Hawkins (n 4) 197; JR Spencer, 'Public Nuisance—A Critical Examination' (1989) 48 Cambridge Law Journal 55, 58–66.

[6] J Murphy, *The Law of Nuisance* (OUP 2010) 132, 138. The vagueness of the offence led to its challenge under the European Convention of Human Rights, art 7, but it survived: *Rimmington* (n 2) [36] (Lord Bingham).

[7] It is now assumed that where Parliament has prescribed a more specific statutory offence, the conduct will only be prosecutable under the statute, not at common law: *Rimmington* (n 2) [30] (Lord Bingham).

[8] For sample contributions welcoming nuisance law in this role, see L Kendrick, 'The Perils and Promise of Public Nuisance' (2023) 132 Yale Law Journal 702; M Russo, 'Productive Public Nuisance: How Private Individuals Can use Public Nuisance to Achieve Environmental Objectives' (2018) University of Illinois Law Rev 1969; S Mullen, 'The Continuing Vitality of the Climate Change Nuisance Suit' (2011) 63 Rutgers Law Review 697 (noting however the possibility of such suits being

as the creator of a nuisance in such instances has been considered a convenient means to sidestep some of the deficiencies of State or federal regulatory agencies to which we alluded in Chapter 6, and to make progress on goals of public protection that legislators and executive public agents have let slip, or purposely ignored.

To be actionable, a public nuisance must 'affect' a 'representative cross-section' of the public in a substantial (non-trivial) way.[9] Provided that threshold is met, however, the wrong can be committed without fault—it is the unreasonable *effect* of a person's conduct upon the public's enjoyment of its rights that is key, not the standard of his or her conduct per se.[10] This makes it a potentially potent weapon.

A. Enforcement Regime

In early times, anyone might act (within reason) to remove a continuing public nuisance without prior recourse to law.[11] The liberty still exists in some cases of highway obstruction,[12] but it gradually gave way, in common with the general pattern identified at the start of Chapter 4, to rights of action before both local and the King's courts.[13] The process was usually initiated by the King, his sheriffs, or

ousted by federal regulatory schemes, as these are adopted); R Abate, 'Public Nuisance Suits for the Climate Justice Movement: The Right Thing and the Right Time' (2010) 85 Washington Law Review 197; R Abate, 'Automobile Emissions and Climate Change Impacts: Employing Public Nuisance Doctrine as Part of a Global Warming Solution in California' (2008) 40 Connecticut Law Review 591; J Zasloff, 'The Judicial Carbon Tax: Reconstructing Public Nuisance and Climate Change' (2008) 55 University of California Los Angeles Law Review 1827; D Antolini, 'Modernizing Public Nuisance: Solving the Paradox of the Special Injury Rule' (2001) 28 Ecology Law Quarterly 755. For more sceptical assessments see T Merrill, 'Is Public Nuisance a Tort? (2011) 4 Journal of Tort Law 1 (critiquing the use of the common law to these purposes without proper legislative authorization); T Merrill, 'Global Warming as a Public Nuisance' (2005) 30 Columbia Journal of Environmental Law 293; T Merrill, 'Public Nuisance as Risk Regulation' (2022) 17 Journal of Law, Economics and Policy 347; T Merrill, 'The New Public Nuisance: Illegitimate and Dysfunctional' (2023) 132 Yale Law Journal 985; V Schwartz and P Goldberg, 'The Law of Public Nuisance: Maintaining Boundaries on a Rational Tort' (2006) 45 Washburn Law Journal 541; Gifford (n 4).

[9] *Attorney-General v PYA Quarries Ltd* [1957] 2 QB 169, 184 (Romer LJ).

[10] Prosser (n 4) 1004: 'Nuisance . . . is not conduct, nor is it even a condition. It is the invasion of an interest.' With respect to the crime, it is sometimes suggested that an offender must always know or have means of knowing that a nuisance will be the consequence of his or her conduct (*Rimmington* (n 2) [40] (Lord Bingham), [57] (Lord Rodger), but even this has been doubted: Murphy, *The Law of Nuisance* (n 6) 136. The standard of liability probably varies according to the source of the nuisance and type of right violated: Spencer (n 5) 75.

[11] *James v Hayward* Cro Car 184, 79 Eng Rep 761 (KB 1630); Hawkins (n 4) 199; E Garrett, *The Law of Nuisances* (Clowes & Sons 1897) 350.

[12] *Clerk and Lindsell on Torts* (23rd edn, Sweet and Maxwell 2020) 29–32 (citing nineteenth-century authority). It is assumed by that authority that the private party must be able to prove special damage, in the same way that he or she must if she now brings a civil action, on which see further below.

[13] Sir F Pollock and FW Maitland, *The History of English Law Before the Time of Edward I* (CUP 1968) Vol 2, 520; D Ibbetson, *A Historical Introduction to the Law of Obligations* (OUP 1999) 101. Local courts included those of sheriffs, local magnates and, later, justices of the peace at quarter sessions: Spencer (n 5) 59–61.

local presenting juries,[14] but individuals were also sometimes given incentives to prosecute through systems of reward,[15] as they had been in earlier Roman times.[16] From the sixteenth century onwards, private individuals then acquired their own rights of action, enabling them to obtain first damages and then injunctive relief where they could prove 'special damage' (see below). This is the point at which it is sometimes said that the crime of public nuisance also became a tort,[17] although of course those classifications were not at that stage developed in that way we now think of them.

As the State's policing and prosecutorial machinery grew, the enforcement process solidified into the now predominantly 'public' mould. By the late nineteenth and early twentieth centuries, it is hence estimated that the ratio of public to private enforcement action in respect of public nuisances in the United States was about nine to one.[18] In England, the State now has powers of criminal prosecution by indictment or information, both at common law and under statute, and these are supplemented by extensive powers for public authorities to restrain specific statutory nuisances through summary procedures. The Attorney-General also retains a historic right to seek injunctive relief *ex officio* at his or her discretion.[19] This right has largely fallen into disuse in England, but it has been put to more determined work in the United States and Canada by State law officers seeking to curtail the harmful activity of drugs companies responsible for widespread opioid addiction, and polluters contributing to greenhouse gas emissions.[20] In practice, the overwhelming prosecutorial initiative in respect of day-to-day environmental and health hazards now lies in the hands of the police, local government officers, and public agencies.[21] There are nonetheless three, remaining instances in which private enforcement can potentially play a role.

[14] Ibbetson (n 13) 101.

[15] L Radzinowicz, *A History of the Criminal Law and its Administration from 1750* (Stevens & Sons 1956) Vol 2, 143.

[16] See Section 7.2A.

[17] Whether it should have been so recognized is contested (see eg Neyers (n 2); Merrill, 'Is Public Nuisance a Tort?' (n 8)) but there is no doubt that private individuals can sue for compensatory damages: D Bullock, 'Public Nuisance is a Tort' (2022) 15 Journal of Tort Law 137. Confusion is caused by the term 'tort', which is often used to indicate that the primary duty breached is one owed to an individual, not the State, which is not the case here.

[18] Gifford (n 4) 805.

[19] See generally, J Ll J Edwards, *Law Officers of the Crown* (Sweet & Maxwell 1968) Ch 14.

[20] The jurisdiction has been used to claim both injunctive relief and damages for public harm. See C Jones, 'The Attorney General's Standing to Seek Relief in the Public Interest: The Evolving Doctrine of Parens Patriae' (2007) 86 Canadian Bar Review 121, esp 138–48. US litigation has until recently met with little success and all federal common law nuisance claims in respect of greenhouse gas emissions have now been held by the US Supreme Court to be impliedly precluded by the Clean Air Act 1970 (which assigns primary responsibility for regulating emissions to the Environmental Protection Agency): *American Electric Power Co v Connecticut* 564 US 410 (2011). Recent State opioid litigation has been more successful: see eg M Richards, 'Pills, Public Nuisance and Parens Patriae: Questioning the Propriety of the Posture of the Opioid Litigation' (2020) 54 University of Richmond Law Review 405.

[21] On the powers of the Environment Agency in the UK, see Chapter 5 Section 5.2, n 11.

(i) Relator Actions with Permission

At common law, private persons may still bring a 'relator' action on the Attorney-General's behalf to restrain a nuisance in the public interest, with the latter's consent. Such actions are more common than the Attorney-General acting *ex officio* at his own initiative,[22] but are still vanishingly rare. Although they were popular for a period from the mid-eighteenth century as an alternative to criminal prosecution,[23] consent is nowadays granted in only a handful of cases,[24] and consent decisions are not judicially reviewable,[25] which is controversial in jurisdictions (like Australia and Canada) where the Attorney-General is a serving member of Cabinet and therefore potentially open to the distorting influence of party politics. There are suspiciously few, if any, examples of an Attorney-General granting consent to relator proceedings against his or her own government.[26]

Where consent to proceed is given, there has been some ambiguity historically as to who it is that 'holds' the right of action—the private 'relator', or the Attorney-General himself. Practical control over the running of proceedings has fluctuated from time to time.[27] The best analysis appears to be that a relator does hold an enforcement power of his own, but that the exercise of the power (along with the right to appeal, or terminate the action) is always subject to the *fiat* of the Attorney-General,[28] who can not only withhold his initial consent to the exercise of the right but bring the action to an end at any time against the relator's wishes,[29] or indeed

[22] JA Jolowicz, *Civil Procedure* (CUP 2000) 135.

[23] J Baker, *An Introduction to English Legal History* (5th edn, OUP, 2019) 463; Spencer (n 5) 70 (corporations were initially hard to prosecute). The origins of the relator action are commonly attributed to the Attorney-General's jurisdiction to proceed *parens patriae* in cases involving charitable trusts: Edwards (n 19) 287 and Chapter 9 Section 9.3.

[24] C Saunders and P Rabbat, 'Relator Actions: Practice in Australia and New Zealand' (2002) 13 Public Law Review 292 suggest that, of a total of thirty-seven *fiats* sought at federal and State level in Australia between 1992 and 2002, only eight were granted. In Queensland, twelve permissions were sought, one of which was granted. Only a very small proportion of *fiats* sought related to public nuisances. In England, only two relations were apparently sought in respect of such nuisances between 1973 and 1982, one of which was subsequently withdrawn—Spencer (n 5) 81, fn 14.

[25] Non-reviewability is assumed in *Gouriet v Union of Post Office Workers* [1978] AC 435, although the point was conceded on appeal. It is possible that decisions under the Attorney-General Act 1999 (Qld) s 7(1)(g) are subject to judicial review (*Sharples v Shea* [2002] QSC 94 [8]) and it has been suggested that a more flexible approach in respect of his or her quasi-judicial functions is appropriate and available in some jurisdictions: B Hough, 'Judicial Review Where the Attorney General Refuses to Act: Time for a Change' (1988) 8 Legal Studies 189; C McCormick, 'Reviewing the Reviewability of the Attorney General for Northern Ireland' (2018) Public Law 22.

[26] For refusals, see *Helicopter Utilities Pfy Ltd* v *Australian National Airlines Commission* [1962] 1 NSWR 747; *Bateman's Bay Local Aboriginal Land Council v Aboriginal Community Benefits Fund Pty Ltd* (1998) 194 CLR 247.

[27] *Gouriet* (n 25) 462–63 (counsel). See also Spencer (n 5) 69.

[28] The power is hence always subject to the Attorney-General's own perpetual Hohfeldian power to revoke it. An alternative view is that the right of action (like the primary public right) is vested throughout in the State and the relator is effectively mandated by the State to exercise it, going through the motions on the AG's behalf. It is hard to know which view is technically correct. In England, little seems in practice to turn on the issue, but it is more important in the context of American *qui tam* actions and citizen suits for Constitutional reasons discussed further in Section 7.2(C)(ii).

[29] *Gouriet* (n 25) 478 (Lord Wilberforce); GS Robertson, *Civil Proceedings by and against the Crown* (Stevens & Sons 1908) Bk V, Ch II; Garrett (n 11) 360–62.

continue it after the latter's death. Whilst the State may hence play no visible, practical part in a proceeding at all, its role, as Lord Wilberforce pointed out in *Gouriet*, is neither fictional, nor limited to weeding out vexatious litigants.[30] It retains absolute control over the exercise of the relator's right to proceed.

The rarity of relator actions these days no doubt reflects the conventional view of most Attorneys-General that the enforcement of public rights is the State's own business. It may also reflect the fact that many public nuisances are now actionable by private individuals relying upon independent rights of action of their own that are exercisable without State consent. Many environmental or public health hazards simultaneously infringe a person's private law rights (eg one's right not to be negligently injured in one's person, or the right to the reasonable enjoyment of the amenity of one's land),[31] and anyone suffering 'special damage' can now sue for public nuisance without the Attorney-General's permission, as we shall see below.

For all intents and purposes, the relator action is therefore redundant in the modern day. If it is to persist at all (and it is hard to think of many cases where it is needed),[32] it would seem to be essential to ensure that consent decisions are handed over to a statutory law officer (such as the Director of Public Prosecutions) who is more independent of government so as to safeguard against political capture, and that private citizens can seek a review, perhaps initially in the same way that they can ask the CPS to review public decisions concerning the prosecution of other forms of crime. A more radical approach taken in Wisconsin is to abandon the State *fiat* altogether and require only that a relator first obtain judicial permission to proceed,[33] which is the approach currently taken in England in private applications for judicial review.

(ii) Special Damage

The more common case in which private parties continue to exercise rights of action in public nuisance is where they have sustained—or stand to suffer—'special' private damage. The right is thought to have been recognized in 1535, although neither the propriety of the suit nor its precise origins are free of contention.[34]

30 *Gouriet* (n 25) 478 (Lord Wilberforce).

31 *Halsey v Esso Petroleum* [1961] 1 WLR 683 (QBD).

32 The case would have to be one in which: (1) the Attorney-General was unwilling to act; (2) public systems of statutory regulation offered no recourse; (3) the public nuisance was not coincidentally infringing any private law rights (or the right holder was unprepared to sue); and (4) no member of the community affected by the nuisance had suffered special damage in the required sense examined below. In such an instance, a private relator claim might still directly protect a public interest that is otherwise unprotected, assuming that an Attorney-General who was himself not willing to act would nevertheless be prepared to give permission for a private person to do so on his behalf, which seems rather unlikely. The only way around the obstacle of the *fiat* would be to abolish it, or implement a mechanism for its review, as envisaged in the text.

33 M Rothstein, 'Private Actions for Public Nuisance: The Standing Problem' (1974) 76 West Virginia Law Review 453, 469.

34 The first suggestion that a private person might have a right of suit in respect of a public nuisance is reported by W McRae, 'The Development of Nuisance in the Early Common Law' (1948) 1 University of Florida Law Review 27, 36 to be in a case in 1411: Y B 12 Hy 4 p 43. The idea that an action might be

The right has never been conditional upon State consent and is considered a right of action 'in tort',[35] as in the cases of public misfeasance that we examined in the previous chapter. Special damage does not require a plaintiff's *private law rights* to have been infringed—the proceeding is still based on the breach of *public* rights that she holds in common with all other members of the community.[36] She must nonetheless prove both that (1) she suffered direct, substantial harm to a recognized private interest, such as her person, property or a protected financial interest; and (2) the harm is different to that suffered by other members of the public with whom she holds the relevant right in common. These preconditions have (controversially, for reasons discussed further below) been assumed to apply whether the plaintiff is seeking damages or, as later allowed from about 1816, injunctive relief.[37]

The first requirement of 'damage to a protected private interest' is a sensible precondition for granting a plaintiff a *compensatory remedy* for a public nuisance, since it stands to reason that, for damages to be payable, an individual must suffer some harm and, in determining what counts as harm, it is logical for public law to take its cues from private law's recognized list of compensable ('protected') interests. It makes no sense, however, to insist on damage if the plaintiff is seeking an injunction to protect the *public* interest.

The second requirement—that the damage must be 'special'—is harder still to fathom. It has variously been taken to mean that a plaintiff must suffer harm that is of an entirely different *type* to that sustained by other members of the public, or (more liberally) harm that is of the same type, but notably greater in its *extent*—distinctions which are hard to draw in practice, easily manipulated, and which no one has been able convincingly to defend.[38] The rule originates in cases involving

conditioned on special damage appears in Fitzherbert J's judgment in an anonymous case of 1535—YB Mich 27 Hy 8, f 26 pl 10. Although recovery in this case was denied, Fitzherbert's idea was repeated in later cases (for the details of which see Prosser (n 4) 1005, fn 75) and clearly founded recovery in the 1617 case of *Fowler v Saunders* (1617) Cro Jac 446, 79 ER 382 (Spencer (n 5) 74). In Merrill's view (n 8) 13–15, all of these more recent cases are based on a misinterpretation of Fitzherbert J, so that there never was, nor should be, any private right to sue for public nuisance.

[35] It is unclear what people mean when then say this. If they mean that the action is for a private wrong, the definition does not apply, because the duties breached are public law duties. If they mean it is one by a private individual for harm caused to his or her private interests, then it is rightly applied.

[36] cf Merrill 'Is Public Nuisance a Tort?' (n 8) and Neyers (n 2) who in effect argue that private rights of action should be confined to cases in which there is a violation of private law, not public law rights.

[37] *Crowder v Tinkler* (1816) 19 Ves Jun 618, 34 ER 645 (cited in Spencer (n 5) 69). For the extensive American authority taking this line (concerning highway obstructions) see Joyce and Joyce (n 4) §218, fn 29, 31. The same rule applies where the plaintiff exercises the liberty to abate: Prosser (n 4) 1006; Garrett (n 11) 352 (citing Jessell MR in *Bagshaw v Buxton* LB (1875) 1 Ch D 220). Its correctness was questioned by John Wade during the redrafting of the *Restatement (Second) of Torts*, under pressure from environmentalists, with the consequence that it was dropped: Merrill (n 8) 28; *Restatement (Second) of Torts* § 821C(2)(c) (1979).

[38] The approach currently appears to differ as between the UK and US, with the former accepting the more flexible 'difference in extent' approach and the latter generally clinging to the stricter 'different type of harm' approach. Courts have also sometimes required difference in *both* type *and* extent: *Clabaugh v Harris* 27 Ohio Misc 153, 273 NE 2d 923 (CP 1971). For comprehensive discussion and criticism, see J Smith, 'Private Action for Obstruction to Public Right of Passage' (1915) 15 Columbia

the obstruction of public highways and waterways,[39] where a good many members of the public could be inconvenienced at once, so that it is often rationalized as a blunt device for preventing a 'multiplicity of actions'[40]—a way of protecting either courts against administrative overload or wrongdoers against crushing liability[41] for widespread harm caused by a single event. In either formulation, it lacks convincing logic. For one thing, if public nuisance law is designed to protect public interests, it makes no sense to confine the pool of private enforcers to those who happen to suffer a unique form, or amount, of personal damage.[42] There is indeed an interesting and cryptic footnote in Ibbetson's distinguished history, alluding to the case of *Westbury v Powell*,[43] which suggests that the requirement never applied in the early years in cases in which a public nuisance was not, for one reason or another, prosecutable by way of presentment in the leet courts, and that in such cases anyone 'grieved' might sue. This suggests that the action was at one time open in the public interest—where public prosecution failed—to *anyone* potentially affected. The senselessness of the special damage rule from the public interest point of view resulted in textual changes to the US *Restatement (Second) of Torts* that were specifically designed to expand the class of enforcers able to seek injunctive relief in public nuisance cases, in response to key environmental concerns.[44] The problem has also been noted by the New Zealand Supreme Court in the recent *Fonterra*

Law Review 1 (favouring any 'actual damage'); G Kodilinye, 'Public Nuisance and Particular Damage in the Modern Law' (1986) 6 Legal Studies 182 (proof of 'any actual damage' should do); Antolini (n 8) 790–857 (advocating an 'actual community injury' test); Rothstein (n 33) (favouring total abolition of the special injury rule). cf GHL Fridman, 'The Definition of Particular Damage in Nuisance' (1953) 2 University of Western Australia Law Review 490 (preferring the 'difference in kind' test).

[39] Joyce and Joyce (n 4) §424; Garrett (n 11) 19–22; Smith (n 38) 142.

[40] *Walsh v Ervin* [1952] VLR 361 (SC Vict) 368 (Shall J); *Fonterra* (n 3) [149] (Williams and Koss JJ); Prosser (n 4) 1007: 'defendants are not to be harassed, and the time of courts taken up, with complaints from a multitude who claim to have suffered'; Antolini (n 8) 762. The rule has sometimes been construed as a way of preventing defendants being exposed to multiple punishment (Y B Mich 27 Hy 8, f 27 pl 10 (1536) (Baldwin CJ); W Estey, 'Public Nuisance and Standing to Sue' (1972) 10 Osgoode Hall Law Journal 563, 563) but this concern, even if historically valid, cannot apply today, given that damages are compensatory, not punitive in nature: Spencer (n 5) 73.

[41] In America, it has been reported that courts were reluctant to extend the reach of public nuisance actions against railroads and industrial enterprises in the nineteenth century for fear of exposing them to 'ruinous damage judgments', which reflects this sort of logic: Gifford (n 4) 803.

[42] Spencer (n 5) 73. Antolini (n 8) 761–62, 789 rightly describes the approach as 'paradoxical' because it limits those who are entitled to enforce public rights to those who have the least in common with their community. See also Russo (n 8) 1995–96.

[43] Ibbetson (n 13) 106 fn 65. *Westbury v Powell* is cited in the case of *Fineux v Hovenden* (1599) Cro El 664, 78 Eng Rep 902 (KB 1681): 'where there is not any remedy to be had other than by [private] action, there every one may have his action who is grieved.'

[44] *Restatement (Second) of Torts* § 821C(2)(c) (1979); J Bryson and A Macbeth, 'Public Nuisance, the Restatement (Second) of Torts, and Environmental Law' (1972) Ecology Law Quarterly 241. The change was designed to equiparate the approach taken in public nuisance claims to that those taken in administrative law and public interest 'citizen suits' but is said to have 'utterly failed to penetrate the case law' and to have gone unnoticed or ignored by judges and practitioners: Antolini (n 8) 762–63. One of the few jurisdictions to have adopted it is Hawaii: *Akau v Olohana Corp* 65 Haw 383, 652 P 2d 1130 (1982).

case, which identified the rule as a public law standing rule that will have to be reconsidered if citizens are ever to make meaningful use of public nuisance law to meet the modern challenges of environmental pollution for the public good.[45]

It is therefore illogical to require a person to prove special damage as a precondition of exercising a right of action to protect public interests.[46] But it makes even less sense if, as I suggest below, the rights underpinning public nuisance actions are in part designed to protect private interests too. For if the purpose of a law is to protect a person's private interest, anyone who suffers *actual* damage to that interest should morally be empowered to sue, whether or not her damage is different in type or degree to that being suffered by anyone else.[47] If this gives rise to concerns about big polluters or other offenders being exposed to excessive financial liability, the solution is to restrict the damages recoverable in private actions, as in private law,[48] not arbitrarily to limit the range of persons granted standing. Concerns about a defendant's *remedial exposure* are logically irrelevant, I suggested in Chapter 3, to the conditions governing a plaintiff's right of action—her power to initiate a claim.

On its face, the law governing private rights of action 'in tort' in respect of public nuisances therefore make little sense. There are two paths to greater rationality, but they lead in diametrically opposite directions. The first option is to wind the clock back five centuries and bar private individuals from suing in their own name for public nuisances altogether at common law, leaving all enforcement to the State and abandoning private parties to such rights in respect of their own interests as they are able to muster in private law.[49] This is similar to the path advocated by the Law Commission in the last chapter, when it recommended abolishing private actions for misfeasance in public office altogether. In practice, it has been suggested, this would not cause great hardship to those whose private interests are harmed by public nuisances because private law now provides significant independent protection for those interests. There would, however, still be gaps in compensation (personal injury and property damage in private law almost always require proof of fault, remember)[50] and citizens would have no independent power at all

[45] *Fonterra* (n 3) [151].

[46] O Reynolds Jr, 'Public Nuisance: A Crime in Tort Law' (1978) 31 Oklahoma Law Review 318.

[47] For this reason, I struggle with John Murphy's view that the special damage rule is a rational precondition to having a secondary right to a damages remedy—what he calls a condition of 'actionability': J Murphy, 'Unpicking Torts: Elements, Conditions of Actionability and Standing Rules' (2024) 87 Modern Law Review 1519, 1528. Actual, not special damage is surely the logical precondition to such a right?

[48] On the private law devices used to limit liability for indirect economic harm, see K Barker, 'Relational Economic Loss and Indeterminacy: The Search for Rational Limits' in S Degeling and J Edelman (eds), *Torts in Commercial Law* (Thomson Reuters 2011) Ch 9. Statutory capping is another option.

[49] Merrill (n 8); Spencer (n 5) 81–83 (concluding that private law rights of action cover most of the ground already and that, to the extent that they do not, granting individuals the right to claims damages or an injunction in respect of the public wrong is anomalous); Neyers (n 2).

[50] Spencer (n 5) 82–83; Murphy (n 6) 154–56. Some compensation might now be available through criminal compensation orders. See further Chapter 5 Section 5.5A.

at common law to protect the public interest. They would be limited to doing so where they are either expressly authorized by Parliament (considered below) or where they have been given ad hoc permission by a State law officer to sue in the State's name in a relator action (above). That would put a serious dampener on progressive attempts to use public nuisance law to engage modern problems of global warming or more generally to progress the public good.

The second option is to keep private rights of action for public nuisances at common law, but to place them on a more logical footing. In cases in which plaintiffs seek damages for personal harm suffered, they would need to prove actual damage to a protected private interest as a remedial matter but would not need to prove their damage was any different to that suffered by anyone else in order to initiate a claim. Courts would determine the extent of a defendant's liability for damages in each case by using normal causation and remoteness of damage principles. The concern that multiple damages claims are oppressive to wrongdoers is unprincipled and should generally be disregarded by courts[51] (although there is nothing to stop legislatures intervening to cap the strict liability of particular industry sectors if this is really necessary for pragmatic, policy reasons), and the fear that courts themselves will be overwhelmed by their number is almost certainly either imaginary,[52] or as the court in *Fonterra* accepted, likely to be met by modern class action and case management procedures.[53]

Where, by contrast, the aim is to restrain a defendant's nuisance in the public interest, rules could be relaxed under the second approach so as to extend rights of action to a wider range of enforcers, along the lines suggested by the *Second Restatement.* If vexatious public interest litigants are a serious concern (again, I doubted this in Chapter 5), they can be dealt with via the usual case management processes, or public interest actions could be made subject to an additional, judicial permission stage.[54] The practical effect of this would be to kill off the already moribund relator action altogether, since there would be no reason for private litigants

[51] FH Newark, 'The Boundaries of Nuisance' (1949) 65 Law Quarterly Review 480, 483 (if a hundred wrongs have been done, then a hundred actions should lie); Smith (n 38) 5 (what claim can a tortfeasor have to pity where he has injured multiple persons?). If there are pressing concerns about the exposure of a particular industry sector, legislatures can always intervene to cap compensation on pragmatic, policy grounds.

[52] Antolini (n 8) 888–90 ('largely imaginary and rhetorical'); Rothstein (n 33) 479 (the law would be 'neither difficult to administer, nor likely to result in over-congested dockets'); Smith (n 38) 4 ('imaginary'); Bryson and Macbeth (n 44) 253 (pointing out that the requirement that plaintiffs prove substantial harm already negates this concern).

[53] *Fonterra* (n 3) [151] (Williams and Kos JJ); Antolini (n 8) 889; Neyers (n 2) 110; D Hogas, 'Private Actions for Public Nuisance: Common Law Citizen Suits for Relief from Environmental Harm' (1989) 16 Ecology Law Quarterly 883, 889–90.

[54] Some may object that this places decisions whether to sanction private enforcement of public rights in the hands of judges, not the executive, but this may well be appropriate and to the point, providing a more robust guarantee that public rights will be enforced when public mechanisms are ineffective or politically compromised. It would also remove the workload regarding permissions from the hands of a single executive law officer and distribute it more evenly amongst the entire judicial workforce.

to seek permission to restrain a public nuisance in the State's name, when they have a more liberal right at common law to do so in their own, subject to court approval. The State's own public interest in the action could be protected by requiring that the Attorney-General be notified of any such suit, so that the State retained the opportunity to intervene in the action and terminate it, if it were considered seriously inimical to the public good.[55]

On the second model, then, citizens would retain unlimited rights of action at common law to protect their own interests against public nuisances where the protection of these interests was a purpose of the underlying public right and those interests were harmed or threatened. But they would also have an independent right of action, contingent on court approval, to restrain a nuisance in the public interest, where public enforcement mechanisms have failed for lack of resource, prosecutorial initiative, or (where the State itself is the creator of the nuisance in question, or is heavily invested in a polluting industry) political capture. The State's legitimate interest in the action would be protected not by requiring its permission for an action to be commenced in the first place, but by allowing it to intervene and terminate it at a later stage.

(iii) Statutory Authorization

The third case in which private parties enjoy private rights of action in respect of a public nuisance is where the right is expressly granted by statute. An English example is the current power of private 'persons' (which includes incorporated and unincorporated groups) to initiate summary proceedings in respect of statutory environmental nuisances before magistrates under Section 82(1) of the Environmental Protection Act 1990 (EPA). The right of action here connects to a variety of US statutes, examined below, which allow private parties to launch 'citizen suits' to seek the imposition of penalties upon offenders for breaching environmental laws and committing other types of public nuisance.

The Act allows 'any person . . . aggrieved by' the nuisance to sue. This again does not require any interference with the person's private law rights,[56] only that their private interests (typically health, comfort, or enjoyment of their land) be affected, or threatened. Merely being subjectively annoyed is insufficient, and 'mere busybodies' or those prosecuting for 'purely tactical' or 'abusive' reasons are excluded.[57] The approach to standing is therefore somewhat similar to the private 'victim' test under the Human Rights Act. It stops short of the open standing rules of the American environmental citizen suit provisions examined below, which allow *all* citizens to sue, whether 'aggrieved' or not, but there is no requirement, at least,

[55] As, for example, under the False Claims Act (Section 7.2B(ii) this chapter) and suggested by the Justice Committee in respect of private criminal prosecutions (Section 7.3A n 166 this chapter).
[56] *Watkins v Aged Merchant Seamen's Homes* [2018] EWHC 2410 (Admin).
[57] ibid [34], [41]–[42].

that an aggrieved person suffer 'special damage' as he or she must at common law. A possible explanation is that, in contrast to the common law tort, the Act provides no right to compensation, so that there are none of the traditional concerns about private actions resulting in crushing financial liabilities for offenders. Successful private prosecutions under Section 82, being primarily public interest actions, usually result in orders prohibiting the nuisance, or requiring it to be abated, and fines, although a criminal compensation order can be granted if a private party suffers harm as a result of an offender's failure to abide by a court abatement order.[58]

The EPA is a classic, contemporary example of a statute that expressly empowers both public and private enforcers to enforce public laws. The normal constitutional concerns about citizens taking on law enforcement roles that are not rightly theirs to prosecute are neatly kicked into touch—at least in England and Wales—because the creation of such rights is expressly authorized by Parliament.

B. Interests Protected

The common law of public nuisance, I have suggested at various points above, protects a mixed range of different interests. Some were originally private interests of the King. Others, such as the liberties of passage we enjoy across communal land or waterways, are interests that we enjoy by virtue of our community membership and are therefore public. Others again, such as those protected by the right to the enjoyment of a healthy environment, have both public and private dimensions; the public dimension being the shared interest we have in living in a society that is free of unreasonable levels of discomfort or disturbance, and the private dimension lying in our entitlements not to be injured (in our property, person or purse) by the 'antisocial' activities of others.

Now that there are more ways of protecting the public interests at stake through statutory regulation—and many more, independent private law rights protecting the private interests harmed by nuisances—it would certainly be possible to achieve a cleaner break in enforcement arrangements, along Blackstonian lines. We could exclude the common law right of private enforcers to act in protection of the relevant public interests altogether and leave protection for their private interests to private law, or to statutory compensation provisions in environmental and criminal law statutes. Before we finally embraced this choice and excised the private common law action for public nuisance, however, we would need to be certain both that our public regulatory systems provide complete protection for the public interest, and that courts, or Parliaments, would be prepared to extend the protections for private interests that currently exist in the 'tort' of

[58] See Chapter 5 Section 5.5A (compensation orders); R McCracken and others, *Statutory Nuisance* (Bloomsbury 2019) Ch 7 esp [7.101]–[7.120].

public nuisance through other common law torts and statutory causes of action. Otherwise, we would be embracing a form of 'purity' in enforcement matters that left the underlying substantive purposes of public nuisance law unfulfilled. As things stand, the fact that modern governments continue actively to *legislate* private enforcement rights in respect of a variety of specific types of public nuisance attests to a continued perception on the part of the State itself that such rights are valuable in targeting areas of public risk and in supplementing public enforcement efforts in the public interest; and the residual common law right of action continues, on occasion, to fill other enforcement gaps that the legislature may have missed.

C. Rationale

There are several possible understandings, therefore, of the continued existence of private rights of action in public nuisance law. One is simply that they are anomalous, the product of a historical gap in public enforcement that has now been—or which could be—fully closed by statutory regulation and its associated public enforcement systems. On this view, private enforcement rights are on their way out and their extinction is just a matter of time. But this would not explain the creation by statute of *new* private enforcement rights in some of the domains of public nuisance (eg environmental risk) traditionally covered by the common law. These new rights suggest that there is a useful modern role for private enforcement to play in protecting the public interest, although it suggests that the modern preference is for such rights to be placed on a democratic, statutory footing.

A second view is that private enforcement rights persist in spheres in which the allotted public mechanisms are failing, despite the expansion of central State, local authority, and public agency enforcement systems. This logic could explain the recent invigoration of private enforcement in the environmental context, where the detection and suppression of public wrongdoing often lies beyond the full reach of State capacity, or (sometimes) political inclination. It allows private parties to use courts to enforce laws for the public good that the executive cannot or will not itself enforce.

A third possible rationale for the private right of action is that it is in part a function of public nuisance law to protect private as well as public interests. There would then, I have suggested, be a moral logic in granting legal powers of suit to those whose protected interests have been—or stand to be—harmed by the public wrong. The protection of these private interests is also undertaken by private law, but the responsibility is shared. This logic is strong in respect of the common law tort, which dishes out compensatory remedies to those 'specially' damaged, and less strong in respect of statutory nuisances under the EPA, where compensation rarely features.

On this last understanding, private enforcers at common law are sometimes acting in defence of their own protected interests, not those of anyone else, so there is no reason why State permission for the suit should ever be required. Whether they have an enforcement right depends solely on whether it was a purpose of the public right that has been infringed to protect their private interests. It is not always easy to tell whether or not this is the case. The exercise is rather like the process of interpretation that is required when one is trying to work out whether a statute containing a public duty intends also to confer a private law right of action on individuals harmed by its breach in cases of breach of statutory duty, only it is directed at ascertaining the purposes of the traditional common law rights underpinning public nuisance law (rights to use the public highway, to breathe clean air, and so on) instead. The former task is hard enough, you might think and determining the purposes of a common law rule harder still. There would nonetheless be nothing irrational (and potentially even something morally satisfying) in granting private rights of action in cases in which the protection of a person's private interests could clearly be determined to be a purpose of the relevant public law right, as I suggested in the last chapter. On this view, there will always be a place for private enforcement in public nuisance law wherever a purpose of the relevant law is to protect private interests of a particular type and a private plaintiff has suffered harm of that type, even if plaintiffs are given no independent public interest enforcement role.

7.2 'Popular Actions' and 'Private Attorneys-General'

We turn next to two types of private action—actions '*qui tam*' and 'citizen suits' that are in one way simpler than private suits for public nuisance, because, in their modern manifestations at least, their purpose is to protect *only* public interests. No compensation for private harm is involved. In both instances, private parties are construed as 'private Attorneys-general',[59] enforcing public laws on the State's behalf. Such actions are sometimes considered modern examples of the Roman '*actio popularis*'—'popular actions' in which private enforcers act in the interests 'of the people'. Another difference from common law public nuisance actions is that they are, generally speaking (and subject to some questions about Federal Court jurisdiction in the United States to which we shall come), open to *all* citizens *without proof of damage*. The main difference between the two types of action is that in the former (actions '*qui tam*'), the private enforcer is granted not just a right of action but the right to a reward if the claim is successful, so that diligent private

[59] The term stems from the judgment of Justice Jerome Frank in *Associated Industries of New York State Inc v Ickes*, 134 F 2d 694, 704 (2d Cir 1943), 320 US 707 (1943) but is used in a far greater range of cases than those considered in this Part and can refer to public interest enforcers with a wide range of different profiles: W Rubenstein, 'On What a "Private Attorney General" Is—And Why It Matters' (2004) 57 Vanderbilt Law Review 2129.

enforcement is actively incentivized. Both groups are nonetheless disparate and there is a good deal of variation within—and between—the actions populating the two categories, so it is important to be cautious about overgeneralization. I have again had to be very selective in choosing my examples.

A. Roman Origins—The '*Actio Popularis*'

The language of the 'popular action' or, the '*actio popularis*' is much used in modern law,[60] but it must be treated with care. It is derived from the Roman law, but Roman law in fact offered no general right for private citizens to enforce public laws, as noted in Chapter 4. What it did offer under the label of the '*actiones populari*' was a variety of different actions of praetorian origin in respect of a number of different wrongs (some awkwardly classified 'quasi-delicts')[61] the common feature of which was that they could be brought by anyone.[62] Most of these actions were penal in nature and therefore had 'public' ends, and most allowed the private prosecutor to keep the relevant penalty, so that they offered powerful incentives to launch the suit. Some, interestingly, involved what modern lawyers would recognize as classic examples of public nuisances, where matter was ejected from a building onto a public highway,[63] or a dangerous obstruction was suspended above it.[64] Others could be brought in respect of wrongs as varied as the falsification of praetorian edicts, the violation of tombs, causing damage to aqueducts, or the enslavement of free men.

The *actiones populari* can usefully be viewed as precursors to later equivalents in Scotland[65] and to the actions '*qui tam*' that at one time existed in England[66]—and which persist to this day in the United States—which I examine below. It is seems likely, however, that they were only rarely used.[67] They were also a disparate

[60] It is especially common in the context of third-party claims in international law, but the language is also used to signal, or advocate, open standing in administrative, constitutional or competition law claims.

[61] On the classification see P Birks, 'The Problem of Quasi-Delict' (1969) Current Legal Problems 164. Since these cases fall outside the neat division of Roman wrongs in Chapter 4 into *delicta* and *crimena*, they were omitted from coverage there. There is probably no substantive distinction between delicts and quasi-delicts, the latter simply having been added by praetors at a later date: J MacKintosh, *Roman Law in Modern Practice*, Tagore Law Lectures 1933 (Green 1934) 169.

[62] See generally, J van der Vyver, 'Actiones Populares and the Problem of Standing in Roman, Roman-Dutch, South African and American Law' (1978) Acta Juridica 191, 191–93; P Mercer, 'The Citizen's Right to Sue in the Public Interest: The Roman Actio Popularis Revisited' (1983) University of Western Ontario Law Review 89, 97–99; W Nippel, *Public Order in Ancient Rome* (CUP 1995) 19–21.

[63] The *actio de effusis vel deiectis* (giving rise to a collectible penalty of fifty solidi and actionable by anyone where leading to the death of a free man).

[64] The *actio de positis ac suspenis* (ten solidi penalty in all cases).

[65] J Pfander, 'Standing to Sue: Lessons from Scotland's Actio Popularis' (2017) 66 Duke Law Journal 1493, 1520–27) (noting a decline in the provision of bounty incentives in the relevant period).

[66] Radzinowicz (n 15) 138–47; Chapter 4 Section 4.4(B)(iii) this book.

[67] Mercer (n 62) 98.

group in terms of their operational mechanics. Some allowed the private prosecutor to keep the whole penalty. Others—the action for damaging an aqueduct is identified as one such in Berger's *Encyclopedic Dictionary*[68]—divided it between the State and the prosecutor, which is a pattern we encounter below in the modern American action under the Federal False Claims Act 1863 (FCA). Whilst most actions protected public interests, some, such as the *interdictum de libero homine exhibendo*, also clearly protected a citizen's private interest in liberty at one and the same time.[69]

The other interesting feature of all of the *actiones populari* was that if more than one private prosecutor volunteered to bring the claim, there was a preliminary process via which the praetor determined which should be allowed to direct the proceeding, preference reportedly being given to anyone with a personal interest in the matter.[70] Whilst harm to some private interest was only absolutely required for standing where the plaintiff was a woman or a child,[71] it therefore still played a role in any case in which a choice had to be made between different enforcers. Here, as in many of the other cases we have looked at, proof that one's private interest had been affected by a wrong was therefore considered a helpful indicator—if not necessarily a guarantee, or a precondition in all cases—of suitability to the public prosecutorial office.

B. Actions '*Qui Tam*'

(i) Examples Ancient and Modern

The two, distinctive features of the *actiones populari* were hence the availability of the right of action to everyone and a positive incentive to exercise it in the form of a penalty collectable in whole, or in part, by the enforcer. Both of these features are shared by a group of (now entirely) statutory actions, commonly labelled actions '*qui tam*', featuring (historically) in English and (still, and controversially) in both modern US law[72] and in a rarely invoked section of the Australian Constitution.[73] The most widely used contemporary example in the United States is the action

[68] A Berger, *Encyclopedic Dictionary of Roman Law* (American Philosophical Society 1953) 347.
[69] Justinian Digest 43.29.1.
[70] Justinian Digest 47.23.3.
[71] Justinian Digest 47.23.6.
[72] For the full history of actions *qui tam* in England and the United States; see 'Note, The History and Development of Qui Tam' (1972) 1 Washington University Law Quarterly 81; J Beck, 'The False Claims Act and the English Eradication of Qui Tam Legislation' (2000) 78 North Carolina Law Review 539; M Beresford, 'The Common Informer, the Penal Statute and Economic Regulation' (1957–8) 10 Economic History Review (2nd ser) 221.
[73] Australian Constitution, s 46. Plaintiffs are now barred from suing on s 46 itself but provided instead with an equivalent statutory right to sue for a penalty of AUS $200 for every day that a person sits in Parliament whilst disqualified: Common Informers (Parliamentary Disqualifications) Act 1975 (Cth), s 3(1), s 4.

under the FCA for frauds perpetrated against the federal government, and it is this action that forms the main focus of my analysis.[74] Another highly controversial contemporary example, however, is the 'Texas Heartbeat Law'[75] which, at a single stroke in 2021, both made it a strict liability offence for a person to aid or abet any abortion contravening the prescribed 'fetal heartbeat rule' and permitted any private party to prosecute offenders, and to receive the prescribed (minimum) US $10,000 penalty in full (plus costs and attorney's fees) for each illegal abortion performed. The law is arresting not simply on account of its subject matter, but because it was purposely designed *only ever* to be enforceable privately—*never* by the State itself[76]—in order to minimize the possibility of it being challenged constitutionally on the grounds formerly recognized in *Roe v Wade*.[77] The Texas legislature's tricky sidestep is technically now otiose, since *Roe* itself has controversially been reversed by a conservative majority of the Supreme Court in the *Dobbs* decision,[78] but the statute remains on the books[79] and has precipitated a storm of criticism and public concern. The *complete* statutory delegation of the enforcement of a public law to private citizens is, to my knowledge, unprecedented, and its use to avoid basic constitutional guarantees of human rights both cynical and dangerous.[80] It is also unwise to create private rights of action in respect of laws as socially divisive, ideologically laden, and emotive as those relating to abortion.[81]

[74] 31 USC §§ 3729–33. The literature is vast. For seminal contributions with contemporary references, see Beck (n 72); J Boese and T Baruch, *Civil False Claims and Qui Tam Actions* (5th edn, Wolters Kluwer 2021); P Bucy, 'Private Justice' (2002) 76 Southern California Law Review 1, 43–54; C Broderick, 'Qui Tam Provisions and the Public Interest: An Empirical Analysis' (2007) 107 Columbia Law Review 949; C Doyle, 'Qui Tam: The False Claims Act and Related Federal Statutes' *Congressional Research Service Report* R40785 (26 April 2021).

[75] Tex Health & Safety Code Ann § 171.208(a)(2) (West 2023), inserted by Texas Heartbeat Act, ch 62, 2021 Tex Gen Laws 125, § 3. The law is often referred to as 'SB-8'. See further J Wall, 'The Margins of Private Law: SB-8 and the Private Enforcement of Abortion Law' in K Falconer, K Barker, and A Fell (eds), *Life and Death in Private Law* (Hart 2024) Ch 3.

[76] Tex Health & Safety Code Ann § 171.207.

[77] *Roe v Wade* 410 US 113 (1973); *Planned Parenthood v Casey* 505 US 833 (1992). As to whether the law was wholly successful in this aim, the jury is sceptical, but out. See eg A Lindvall, 'Texas, Abortion, and State Action' (2021) 74 SMU Law Review Forum 139 (no, because private parties act as State delegates, so that State action is involved); A Pfeffer-Gillet, 'Civil Disobedience in the Face of Texas's Abortion Ban' (2021) 106 Minnesota Law Review Headnotes 203 (yes, but civil disobedience to the law would trigger State action, in turn facilitating challenge). On the three main barriers to challenge (standing, sovereign immunity, and the State action doctrine), see A Zunski, 'Ducking the System: Examining the Efficacy of Bounty Hunting Statutes that Stifle the Free Exercise of Constitutional Rights' (2022) 31 William & Mary Bill of Rights Journal 267 (also endorsing the view that the attempted evasion should be regarded as ineffective).

[78] *Dobbs v Jackson Women's Health Organization* 597 US 215 (2022).

[79] It has also given rise to copycat laws in some other jurisdictions (Oklahoma and Idaho, although in the latter State the pool of enforcers is restricted to family members); and to an equivalent law in California giving citizens the exclusive right to enforce certain gun control laws: Cal Bus & Prof Code 22949.65(a).

[80] A Huq, 'The Private Suppression of Constitutional Rights' (2023) 101 Texas Law Review 1259; J Michaels and DL Noll, 'Vigilante Federalism' (2023) 108 Cornell Law Review 1187.

[81] J Brobst, 'Perilous Private Enforcement Strategies: From Posses and Citizen's Arrest to Texas Heartbeat Statutes' (2022) 14 ConLawNOW 11. Criminal laws touching on matters as personal and

The twin private litigation drivers of religious fealty to the perceived will of a god (on the one hand) and handsome monetary rewards (on the other) create a heady cocktail of distorted motivation and risk to the public interest; and the total absence of any right for the State to intervene in the action[82] to terminate it leaves that risk uncontained.

Stepping back a little, the label '*qui tam*' is a shortening for Blackstone's historical reference to an early set of actions in English law that were brought by a private person '*tam pro domino rege . . . quam pro se ipso*',[83] meaning 'as much for the King as for himself'. The reference in the phrase to the interests of both the plaintiff and the King being *combined* in the proceeding appears to contradict the statement I made above about such actions now being *purely public* interest actions and therefore requires further explanation. Part of the explanation could be that some early common law examples of actions *qui tam* indeed involved a plaintiff suing simultaneously for both a private wrong (usually a trespass) to himself and a public wrong in the form of a breach of the King's peace, the plaintiff choosing to sue on the King's behalf for the public as well the private wrong in the same action simply in order to access the superior system of justice then available in the King's courts. However, the need to piggyback private law claims on public law ones for procedural advantage in this way declined as the King's justice became available to private parties for the infringement of their own private law rights in the fourteenth century.[84] So this cannot really be the answer.

A second potential explanation for Blackstone's allusion to the *combination* of public and private interests in *qui tam* actions could be that, in the specific cases to which he was referring when using the Latin phrase, the penalty payable by a wrongdoer on a successful prosecution was *split* between State and the private prosecutor,[85] as under the old Roman action for damaging an aqueduct. Perhaps he meant that the actions were 'as much for' the private enforcer as the State (King) because the *spoils* of the actions were divided between them. But this is not a full explanation either, because statutory penalties were not always divided and were, in fact, quite often kept entirely by the private enforcer, as they are now under the Texas Heartbeat Law.[86]

emotive as this are commonly only enforceable in England with State consent. See Section 7.3A(ii) this chapter. There are nonetheless previous precedents: 18 USC §1531(c)(1) (2003) (right of father or maternal grandparents to bring civil suit for psychological injury plus three times the cost of an illegal partial-birth abortion).

[82] 171.208 (h).
[83] William Blackstone, *Commentaries on the Laws of England* (Robert Bell 1773) Book 3, 160.
[84] 'History and Development of Qui Tam' (n 72) 85.
[85] Blackstone (n 83) 160.
[86] ibid: 'more usually' the penalty was payable to the common informer alone.

Whatever the position had been at common law or under some early statutory provisions,[87] the purpose of *qui tam* actions under the 'common informer' statutes of medieval and later times came to be understood as enforcing the State's rights alone, not those of the 'informer', and as being designed to protect purely public interests, even when the plaintiff kept the whole statutory bounty for himself. In so far as such actions persist in the modern law, this is the way that they are now understood, so that the only sense in which an enforcer's own interests are implicated in them is through the reward to which she is entitled if the claim is successful. Private parties suing *qui tam* therefore have a financial 'interest' in a *motivational* sense in the enforcement of a public law, but the purpose of the enforcement process is not the protection of their private interests. This is a third way of understanding what Blackstone meant, and the one that best fits actions in the modern day.

Actions *qui tam* featured in early Anglo-Saxon law, one of the first examples relating to bans on Sunday trading.[88] They waxed and waned in England through the medieval and Tudor periods until they were finally abolished in 1951.[89] Although plaintiffs were often dubbed 'informers', the rights which they held were never simply what I have called 'information' rights[90]—the informer's right was not just a liberty to tip off public prosecutors for a fee, as under many modern whistle-blower provisions,[91] but a true right of action (a legal power to 'lay information' before the court) combined with an entitlement to all, or some, of the action's fruits. The first informer to sue obtained the right of action, thereby excluding others from seizing control.[92]

The combination of open rights of action with rewards is the most powerful private enforcement cocktail that public law has devised to date. It creates risks for both public and other private interests, which, whilst not unique to actions *qui tam*, are intensified by the money on offer.[93] The risks are elevated where informers club

[87] Even after the decline of actions at common law, there were some statutory provisions that allowed for the recovery by private parties of both compensation for private injury and penalties payable to the King: 'History and Development of Qui Tam' (n 72) 90–91; *Vermont Agency of Natural Resources v US ex rel Stevens* 529 US 765 (2000) 775.

[88] Chapter 4 Section 4.4B, n 139 and text.

[89] Common Informers Act, 14 & 15 Geo 6, ch 39 (1951) (Eng). For the full detail, see Beck (n 72) 567–608.

[90] Chapter 2 Section 2.3A.

[91] See F Lipman, *Whistleblowers: Incentives, Disincentives, and Protection Strategies* (Wiley 2012) Ch 9.

[92] E Freund, *Legislative Regulation* (Commonwealth Fund 1932) 326. Contrast the Roman *divinatio* system, according to which decisions were made as to the most suitable rival enforcer: Chapter 4 Section 4.3B(ii) n 65.

[93] See Chapter 5 Section 5.3B; 'History and Development of Qui Tam' (n 72) 89; M Davis, *The Enforcement of English Apprenticeship: A Study in Applied Mercantilism 1563–1642* (HUP 1956) Chs 2, 3; Beck (n 72) 579–85, 608–20; Radzinowicz (n 15) Ch 6. Similar problems reportedly attended the *actiones populari*: Nippel (n 62) 20–21.

together into prosecution associations,[94] engage professionals to act on their behalf, and operate on a commercial basis. They reach an alarming peak when there is no State oversight in respect of their exercise, as under the Texas legislation.

Successive monarchs and Parliaments in England tackled the most serious concerns arising from *qui tam* actions by enacting measures to prohibit collusion, harassment, and vexatious actions, by limiting the time and venue within which claims could be brought, licensing only certain persons to sue, or requiring bonds from them for costs, so that it is said that by the seventeenth century most of the problems had been addressed and the controversy of such actions was somewhat reduced.[95] The commercial funding of private enforcement was also for a long time restrained by the laws of maintenance and champerty. The risks were nonetheless still very much in the minds of legislators when the actions were finally abolished in England in 1951,[96] and the potential tension between public interests and private reward remains a concern.

(ii) The False Claims Act 1863

All of this makes it all the more extraordinary to English eyes that *qui tam* actions are enjoying a dramatic resurgence in the United States. Although the Texas Heartbeat Law provides the most controversial recent example, the most widely used is a provision of the FCA that grants private parties ('relators') the right to prosecute frauds committed against the federal government in the State's name, using a civil standard of proof.[97] Triple damages awards are available, together with penalties, and private enforcers can claim up to 30 per cent of the total spoils. The right of action was first introduced in March 1863 to tackle scams perpetrated by commercial suppliers to Union forces during the Civil War,[98] but its wings were then clipped during the Second World War and it dwindled until 1986. At that point, however, the relevant enforcement incentives were ramped up—and the action revived—in response to revelations about the widespread nature of defence procurement fraud.[99] The scandal of taxpayers being defrauded into paying

[94] D Philips, 'Good Men to Associate and Bad Men to Conspire: Associations for the Prosecution of Felons in England, 1760–1800' in D Hay and F Snyder (eds), *Policing and Prosecution in Britain 1750–1850* Ch 3 (Clarendon 1989).

[95] See 'History and Development of Qui Tam' (n 72). On the different forms of control, see Davis (n 93) Ch 3.

[96] Beck (n 72) 605–06: the risks dominated debate about the proposed abolition, which attracted support across the political spectrum. The disruption that *qui tam* provisions in English Sunday trading laws might have inflicted on plans for the 1951 Festival of Britain were probably also a factor in pushing legislation through.

[97] 31 US § 3730.

[98] *United States ex rel Marcus v Hess* 317 US 537, 547 (1943). Unlike England, the US has never had *qui tam* suits at common law. All are the products of statute, the first appearing in 1791: H Krent, 'Executive Control Over Criminal Law Enforcement: Some Lessons from History' (1989) 38 American University Law Review 275, 296.

[99] Doyle (n 74) 8 (90 per cent of the largest US defence contractors were under criminal fraud investigation in 1985). Changes included: increasing the percentage of penalties recoverable to a maximum of 30 per cent (up from the 25 per cent limit imposed in 1943, but down from the original 50 per cent

US$435 for a hammer was too acute to be ignored.[100] Since this time, claims have exploded, netting over US$75 billion for federal coffers, with returns of more than US$5.6 billion in the 2021 fiscal year alone.[101] The system has been used to target deceptions upon the public health system by the pharmaceutical industry, royalty frauds by oil and gas corporations, and even false claims upon disaster relief funds in the wake of the 2005 Hurricane Katrina disaster, as well as a range of more traditional defence procurement scams.[102]

From the State's point of view, the private right of action has boosted public finances and cracked down on forms of public wrongdoing that are secretive and hard to detect. Indeed, statutory measures were introduced in 2006 to ensure that the right of action is widely publicized to employees of potential fraudsters and to encourage them to use it as part of a determined public deficit reduction strategy.[103] The risks to which we alluded above have not been ignored, but they have been moderated through a subtle crafting of the jural architecture surrounding the right of action, described below.

Some twenty-nine States have followed the federal lead and enacted their own False Claims Acts at the time of writing.[104] Despite what one might think, the signs are that private enforcement efforts generally align with government interests and advocates have suggested extending the model to cover antitrust and securities fraud,[105] environmental protection laws and national financial regulation.[106]

maximum in 1863); providing additional protections for informers against reprisal by their employers; and (most importantly) weakening bars introduced in 1943 on the use of public information already within the government's possession. On the ups and downs of the public information bar and its further weakening, see R Salcido, 'Screening Out Unworthy Whistleblower Actions: An Historical Analysis of the Public Disclosure Jurisdictional Bar to Qui Tam Actions Under the False Claims Act' (1995) 24 Public Contract Law Journal 237; A Harmon, 'Interested, but Not Injured: The Compromised Status of Qui Tam Plaintiffs under the Amended False Claims Act and the Return of the Citizen Suit' (2014) 43 Public Contract Law Journal 423 (pointing out that the bar can be freely waived by the State); B Cohen, 'Kaboom—The Explosion of Qui Tam False Claims under the Health Reform Law' (2011) 116 Penn State Law Review 77.

[100] Beck (n 72) 561.

[101] https://www.justice.gov/opa/pr/justice-department-s-false-claims-act-settlements-and-judgments-exceed-56-billion-fiscal-year accessed 5 December 2025.The 2023 figure was lower (US $2.68 billion) but claims and settlements are at an all-time high: <https://www.justice.gov/opa/pr/false-claims-act-settlements-and-judgments-exceed-268-billion-fiscal-year-2023> accessed 5 December 2025.

[102] D Engstrom, 'Harnessing the Private Attorney General: Evidence from Qui Tam Litigation' (2012) 112 Columbia Law Review 1244, 1270–71.

[103] Deficit Reduction Act of 2005 Pub L No 109-171, 120 Stat 4 (2006), 6032.

[104] J Barger Jr and others, 'States, Statutes, and Fraud: An Empirical Study of Emerging State False Claims Acts' (2005) 80 Tulane Law Review 465.

[105] D Kwok, 'Does Private Enforcement Attract Excessive Litigation? Evidence from the False Claims Act' (2013) 42 Public Contract Law Journal 225; A Rose, 'Better Bounty-Hunting: How the SEC's New Whistleblower Program Changes the Securities Class Act Debate' (2014) 108 North Western University Law Review 1235; J Fisch, 'Class Action Reform, Qui Tam, and the Role of the Plaintiff' (1997) 60 Law & Contemporary Problems 167; W Kovacic, 'Antitrust Analysis of Joint Ventures and Teaming Arrangements Involving Government Contractors' (1990) 58 Antitrust Law Journal 1059, 1076–77.

[106] Bucy (n 74) 76–79, Appendix A-2, A-3; R Kafin and N Needleman, 'The Use of Qui Tam Actions to Protect the Environment' (1971) 17 New York Law Forum 130.

A number of States are at this time either implementing, or contemplating, similar legislation in respect of tax fraud (which currently lies outside the FCA regimes) and the violation of workplace- and consumer-protection laws.[107] These moves are a purposeful response on the part of States to their frustration with the ineffectiveness of public agencies, and to restrictions upon their own budgets for proper public enforcement action.[108]

(iii) Enforcement Regime under the False Claims Act

As in public nuisance claims, there has been some confusion regarding who it is that holds the right of action under the FCA—the private 'relator', or the State.[109] The relator has an express power to initiate the claim[110] without first obtaining the State's consent. The exercise of the power is nonetheless attended by a legal duty on the relator's part to serve a copy of the proceeding on the State so as to give it an opportunity to intervene and take the action over within sixty days,[111] and the relator may not serve the claim on the wrongdoer until the court has given its permission, the matter remaining under seal until that time.[112] If the State does not intervene, the relator then has a liberty to proceed.[113]

If the State does intervene (which occurs in only a very small minority of cases but results in the highest rates of successful prosecution)[114] it obtains practical control of the action, together with the legal powers of appeal and settlement, but the relator is entitled to claim between 15 per cent and 25 per cent of the spoils if the action succeeds, together with attorney costs. If it does not intervene, it is not a party to the action and the relator has the right to conduct the proceeding[115] and

[107] M Gilles and G Friedman, 'The New Qui Tam: A Model for the Enforcement of Group Rights in a Hostile Era' (2020) 98 Texas Law Review 489, 492–94. Attempts to extend the statute in California to cover tax frauds were reportedly defeated by dubious lobbying and scaremongering tactics on the part of businesses: D Ventry, 'False Claims in Fight of California's False Claims Act' (4 November 2019) Tax Notes State (2019) <https://ssrn.com/abstract=3491996> accessed 5 December 2025.

[108] Gilles and Friedman (n 107) 490–91, 497–512.

[109] V Park, 'The False Claims Act, Qui Tam Relators, and the Government: Which Is the Real Party to the Action?' (1991) 43 Stanford Law Review 1061.

[110] 31 US § 3730 (b)(1) ('a person may bring a civil action').

[111] 31 US § 3730(b)(2).

[112] ibid.

[113] 31 US § 3730(b)(4).

[114] Broderick (n 74) 971 cites official Justice Department statistics showing that the number of occasions in which the State declined to intervene between 1987 and 2004 outnumbered the number of interventions by about 4:1. A more recent study estimates intervention in less than 4 per cent of cases: F Engstrom, 'Public Regulation of Private Enforcement: Empirical Analysis of DOJ Oversight of Qui Tam Litigation Under the False Claims Act' (2013) 107 Northwestern University Law Review 1689, 1717. State interventions nonetheless account for the vast bulk of recovery: Engstrom (n 114) 1720 (94 per cent of all recoveries between 1986 and 2011); Civil Div, US Department of Justice, *Fraud Statistics—Overview* (30 September 2021) <https://www.justice.gov/opa/press-release/file/1467811/download> accessed 5 December 2025.

[115] 31 US §3730(b)(4)(B). The State is hence not a party to the action unless it intervenes: *United States ex rel Eisenstein v City of New York* 566 US 928 (2009).

press on alone. In the event of success, the relator has the right to an increased share of between 25 per cent and 30 per cent of the proceeds.

Even if the State initially declines to take the action over, it retains significant powers. It can hence still: (1) intervene and take over later on, if showing good cause;[116] (2) terminate the proceeding at any time and against relator's wishes, providing it gives the latter an opportunity to be heard;[117] (3) settle the claim without the relator's consent, provided the court considers the settlement to be fair;[118] and (4) (probably) prevent the relator settling the action in a way of which it disapproves, by withholding its consent.[119]

The upshot is that although the relator holds the initial right of action, the right is attended by a complex array of duties and liabilities, so that the balance of power remains very much with the State. This was not always so—under the original provisions of 1863 the State had no right of intervention at all—but the shift has enabled the Department of Justice to assess, on a case-by case basis, the extent to which an action meets the public interest. Although the absolute veto which it enjoys over settlement has been questioned (judicial approval of such settlements might perhaps be safeguard enough),[120] it probably makes the system more resistant to challenge under Article 2, Section 1 of the US Constitution, which, it has been suggested, requires all enforcement powers ultimately to lie in the hands of the executive for reasons associated with the separation of powers.[121]

Some suggest that even this level of State control is insufficient and that private enforcers should be barred from bringing any action which the Department

[116] 31 US §3730(c)(3) (this is without prejudice to the relator's rights). The intervention can sometimes be years later: *United States ex rel Teresa Ross v Independent Health Corp* et al, 12-cv-299, 2021 WL 3492917 (WDNY Aug 9 2021) (7 years).

[117] 31 US §3730(c)(2)(A). The issue of new internal DOJ guidance in 2018 in what has come to be known as the 'Granston Memorandum' suggests that this power will now be used more often in response to the rising number of claims (about 600 a year in 2018): 'Factors for Evaluating Dismissal Pursuant to 31 USC § 3730(c)(2)(A)' (Jan 10 2018) <https://assets.documentcloud.org/documents/4358602/Memo-for-Evaluating-Dismissal-Pursuant-to-31-U-S.pdf> accessed 5 December 2025. For an analysis of the current approach and suggestions for its variation, see N T Tschepik, 'The Executive Judgment Rule: A New Standard of Dismissal for Qui Tam Suits under the False Claims Act' (2020) 87 University of Chicago Law Review 1051.

[118] 31 US §3730(c)(2)(B).

[119] 31 US §3730(b)(1). Courts and commentators are split on this question. On the one hand, if the State could prevent settlement, it could effectively force the relator to continue the proceeding against its wishes and the incentives for relators to bring the action would be reduced. On the other, if had only the right to raise an objection rather than to veto settlement, the public interest might be prejudiced by the relator settling on terms that favoured himself over the public good. A compromise might be to leave the power to approve the settlement to the court, as in cases in which the State itself wishes to settle the relator's action. See further G Forney, 'Qui Tam Suits: Defining the Rights and Roles of the Government and the Relator under the False Claims Act' (1997) 82 Minnesota Law Review 1357.

[120] Forney (n 119).

[121] On the art 2 challenges (and concluding that the Act survives them) see R Bales, 'A Constitutional Defense of Qui Tam' (2001) Wisconsin Law Review 381, 403. A 2019 challenge to the Act based on the 'appointments clause' (US Const art 2, s 2) went nowhere (*Intermountain Health Care, Inc v United States, ex rel Gerald Polukoff* No 18-911 (14 January 2019)) but see now the discussion at n 128 below.

of Justice itself declines to prosecute.[122] This would effectively confine the role of the relator to commencing the proceeding and supplying information for such enforcement action as the Department chose to take, ensuring that such claims as are pressed are conducted and settled by public agents. It would also, however, exclude private initiative in cases in which the Department lacks the resources to proceed, which are likely to be the cases in which such actions are potentially most useful.

Standing under the provisions of the FCA is unrestricted, with rights of action extending to any private 'person'.[123] The question is hence not whether a relator is 'aggrieved' or privately affected,[124] but simply whether or not she has information which has either not already been publicly disclosed, or which is nonetheless materially useful to the prosecution of the claim, and even this requirement can be now waived by the government.[125] This open standing provision has been challenged on the basis that it places claims before courts that they have no jurisdiction to hear, the Supreme Court's view now being that such jurisdiction is limited to cases in which plaintiffs have been caused an actual or imminent (and redressable) 'injury in fact'.[126] It has nonetheless survived, on the theory that the State itself suffers a relevant financial 'injury' through the financial fraud and the relator is merely acting as its assigned representative in bringing the action.[127] The fact that the relator can initiate proceedings as of her own right, without formal 'appointment', assignment, or prior executive approval, makes this analysis questionable and has given rise to the suggestion that it may eventually meet its demise,[128] but it has not hitherto been considered fatal to the constitutionality of the action.

[122] Beck (n 72) 638–39; *United States ex rel Berge v Board of Trustees of the Univ of Alabama* 104 F 3d 1453 (4th Cir 1997). For the suggestion that the State should have still more control over the running of the action even where it does not intervene, see Broderick (n 74) 997 et post.

[123] 31 US §3730(b)(1). There are some limited exclusions.

[124] Some of the more recent State-based *qui tam* provisions are more restricted in this regard: see eg the California Labor Code Private Attorneys General Act 2004 Cal Lab Code §§2698–2699 ('aggrieved' employees': §2699(c)).

[125] 31 US §3730(e)(4)(A), (B). The effect of 2010 amendments is that the State may allow the claim to proceed even where the plaintiff has no new or useful information of his own at all to bring to the table. On one view, this changes provision from a qui tam provision to a mere 'citizen suit' provision and raises additional concerns about the action's propriety: Harmon (n 99). On the weakening of the original source requirements and the consequent upswing in litigation, see Cohen (n 99).

[126] *Lujan v Defenders of Wildlife* 112 S Ct 2130 (1992); 504 US 555 (1992). The limitation is purportedly based on US Const art 3, but has a decidedly weak jurisprudential basis and has been cogently criticized: C Sunstein, 'What's Standing After Lujan? Of Citizen Suits, 'Injuries' and Article III' (1992) 91 Michigan Law Review 163, 170–79.

[127] *Vermont Agency of Natural Resources v US ex rel Stevens* 529 US 765, 773–74 (1999). The Constitutionality of the action was initially strongly doubted: W Barr, Memorandum Opinion for the Attorney-General, 'Constitutionality of the Qui Tam Provisions of the False Claims Act' (18 July 1989). On the controversy, see T Lee, 'The Standing of Qui Tam Relators Under the False Claims Act' (1990) 57 University of Chicago Law Review 543; J Blanch, 'Note, The Constitutionality of the False Claims Act's Qui Tam Provision' (1993) 16 Harvard Journal of Law and Public Policy 701 (unconstitutional); S Hamer, 'Lincoln's Law: Constitutional and Policy Issues Posed by the Qui Tam Provisions of the False Claims Act' (1996) 6 Kansas Journal of Law & Public Policy 89, 93–97 (constitutional); E Caminker, 'The Constitutionality of Qui Tam Actions' (1989) 99 Yale Law Journal 341 (constitutional).

[128] There are recent rumblings and a possibility that the issue will be considered by the Supreme Court in the wake of *United States ex rel Zafirov v Florida Medical Assocs, LLC*, No 8:19-CV-01236-KKM-SPF

The FCA is intriguing because it provides a resurgent modern example of the more ancient systems of incentivized private enforcement which have generally gone out of fashion. It both compensates the State for harm to its financial interests and splits penalties for public wrongdoing between the State and private enforcers. It carries some of the traditional risks of private bounties, as well as certain challenges to the constitutional order in the United States, but both challenges have so far been managed by locating the private right of action within a broader network of State rights and powers that operates as a check upon the private power so as to ensure that it is exercised in ways that are consistent with the public good. It is the lack of these checks and balances in the Texas Heartbeat Law which renders its enforcement design so perilous, even ignoring the illiberal, regressive, and socially divisive nature of the substantive rules that it is designed to enforce. The FCA model also provides a possible modern template for splitting penalties between private enforcers and the State which could usefully be replicated, I suggest later in Chapter 8, in cases involving punitive damages in private law. If one of the main complaints about such damages awards is that they allow private parties to keep the benefit of public interest awards, then a solution, the FCA suggests, is to divide the spoils in such a way as to ensure that a significant proportion of such awards finds its way to the public purse.

C. 'Citizen Suits'

(i) Environmental Suits and the Clean Air Act 1970 (CAA)

The second set of 'popular' actions existing in the United States is titled 'citizen suits'. This is also a very broad and disparate group[129] and I again confine myself to modelling just one example in outline. To highlight parallels and contrasts with some of the cases of public nuisance examined above, I have chosen actions

(MD Fla, 30 September 2024) (which held the Act to violate US Const art 2, s 2, despite four previous contrary decisions of US Circuit Courts of Appeal). *Zafirov* follows Justice Thomas' dissent in *United States ex rel Polansky v Executive Health Resources Inc* 599 US 419 (2023). See further (suggesting ways that the problem may be avoided) E Mitchell, 'The New Constitutional Challenge to Qui Tam' (2025) 74 Emory Law Journal 759.

[129] Citizen suit provisions can be divided broadly into three groups: (1) those, like the ones examined here, which exist for the protection of *purely* public interests, whose rationale is therefore similar to modern *qui tam* provisions; (2) those which create private rights of action for harm to private interests (eg the American Disabilities Act 42 USC § 12188(a)(1) (1995); Consumer Product Safety Act 15 USC § 2072 (1997) and the Civil Rights Act 1964 Title VII 42 USC § 2000e–5(f)), where breaches of the relevant provisions give rise to private rights to compensation; and (3) those which primarily protect private interests by allowing injured individuals to claim for personal harm, but which also have a public interest component, in so far as they allow plaintiffs to claim triple damages by way of punishment or deterrence, as under the Clayton Antitrust Act 15 USC § 15 (2012), or Racketeer Influenced and Corrupt Organizations (RICO) Act 18 USC §§ 1961–68 (2000).

available under federal environmental protection laws, in particular the Clean Air Act of 1970 (CAA).[130] This is a gross under-representation of the enormous range of modern citizen suit provisions (which historically includes statutory rights to prosecute a significant range of 'moral nuisances', such as prostitution)[131] but it accurately highlights an area in which they have been most widely and enthusiastically used since the early 1970s. The power of such suits is increased because they can be used not just to enforce the duties that private polluters owe to the State but also the duties that State agencies owe to citizens to ensure proper enforcement of the relevant laws.[132] Indeed, recent empirical analysis suggests that it is the use of citizen suit provisions to police the actions of the State—to force public agents such as the Environmental Protection Agency (EPA) to observe their own legal duties in rule-making or implementation—that is often at the forefront of private litigation activity in the environmental field.[133]

The key point of distinction between citizen suits and the popular *qui tam* provisions examined above is that the rights of action that they provide are unaccompanied by any formal reward. A successful private enforcer under the CAA can hence seek injunctive relief to prevent further infringements, together with civil penalties payable to the State and costs (including reasonable attorney fees, in

[130] Clean Air Act 42 USC § 7604 (1982). Virtually all modern federal environmental statutes contain citizen suit provisions, including the Water Pollution Control Act (Clean Water Act) 33 USC § 1365 (1972), Endangered Species Act 16 USC § 1540 (1973), Surface Mining Control and Reclamation Act of 1977 30 USC § 1270 (1982) and the Toxic Substances Control Act, 15 USC § 2619 (1988). See further B Boyer and E Meidinger, 'Privatizing Regulatory Enforcement: A Preliminary Assessment of Citizen Suits Under Federal Environment Laws' (1985) 34 Buffalo Law Review 833; J Austin, 'The Rise of Citizen-Suit Enforcement in Environmental Law: Reconciling Private and Public Attorneys General' (1987) 81 Northwestern University Law Review 220; M Axline, *Environmental Citizen Suits* (Butterworths 1991); B Thompson Jr, 'The Continuing Innovations of Citizen Enforcement' (2000) 2000 University of Illinois Law Review 185; J May and others, 'Environmental Citizen Suits at Thirtysomething: A Celebration and Summit' (2003) 33 Environmental Law Reporter News & Analysis 10721; D Adelman and R Glicksman, 'Reevaluating Environmental Citizen Suits in Theory and Practice' (2020) 91 University of Colorado Law Review 385. There is also a raft of similar provisions at State level: J May, 'The Availability of State Environmental Citizen Suits (2004) 18 Natural Resources & Environment 53. Most academic commentaries welcome citizen suits as responses to regulatory failure, but there are also abundant, negative views: see eg M Greve, 'Private Enforcement of Environmental Law' (1990–1991) 65 Tulane Law Review 339 (the provisions create an 'off-budget entitlement program' for environmental protection group 'cartels'); S Driscoll, 'Environmental Private Actions: Are Special Interest Groups Hobbling Comprehensive Programs Without "Standing" Themselves?' (1993) 24 Rutgers Law Journal 469, 503–06 (private suits produce overdeterrence and undermine EPA enforcement); M Stephenson, 'Public Regulation of Private Enforcement: The Case for Expanding the Role of Administrative Agencies' (2005) 91 Valparaiso Law Review 9 (greater agency control over private rights of action is needed for reasons of efficiency and political accountability). Recent empirical evidence suggests that both the hopes of optimists and the fears of critics may have been exaggerated: D Adelman and J Reilly-Diakun, 'Environmental Citizen Suits and the Inequities of Races to the Top' (2021) 92 University of Colorado Law Review 377, 43.

[131] For the history and a new phase of modern examples in the US see S Stern, 'Moral Nuisance Abatement Statutes' (2022) 117 Northwestern University Law Review 613.

[132] 42 USC § 7604(a)(2). The duty in question must be strict in the sense that it is non-discretionary.

[133] Adelman and Reilly-Diakun (n 130) 382–83, 407, 410, 416, 437 (about 85 per cent of environmental citizen suits filed between 2001 and 2016 were directed at federal government, with 88 per cent of litigation under the CAA directed at obtaining 'wholesale' review of EPA regulations).

theory at least),[134] but it does not receive any share of the penalties in question. An inventive aspect of the remedial regime is that the penalties collected are placed in a designated Treasury fund that can be used by the EPA for improving air quality and compliance,[135] which makes wrongdoers directly subsidize the costs of environmental regulation and may increase the incentive for private environmental enforcers to sue. I am more likely to act where I know that the penalties collected will be put to ends of which I approve ideologically rather than disappearing into an anonymous central reserve that could be used for some rival, or even antagonistic public purpose. A proportion of the deterrent penalties collected (currently up to US$100,000) can also be diverted, at the court's discretion, directly into 'beneficial mitigation projects' after consultation with the EPA.[136] There are direct analogies here with the sorts of private redress solution that are now available at the suit of a number of UK regulatory agencies, which we examined in Chapter 5, and with some more inventive schemes for the distribution of punitive damages awards in private law cases, analysed in Chapter 8.

The CAA was the first environmental provision in US federal law to be privately enforceable. It was innovative because it enabled private enforcers to protect public interests of an intangible sort, not just the State's financial interests, as under the FCA. Like *qui tam* provisions, it had English precedents dating back to at least the fourteenth century.[137] The private right of action was originally designed as a prompt to the EPA to do a proper job of enforcing air quality standards at a time when there were serious concerns about agency capture and ineffectiveness,[138] but the suit then took off in its own right as a means for private enforcers to enforce the relevant standards directly against polluters.[139] The concerns about agency capture that prompted the private action were real and remain valid

[134] 42 USC § 7604(d). On the obstacles see S Dunne, 'Attorney's Fees for Citizen Enforcement of Environmental Statutes: The Obstacles for Public Interest Law Firms' (1990) 9 Stanford Environmental Law Journal 1. Recent studies suggest that as few as 10 per cent of litigants were awarded fees in two-thirds of the Circuits in which cases were filed between 2001 and 2016 and that awards have declined 'dramatically' in the last decade: Adelman and Reilly-Diakun (n 130) 423, 436.

[135] 42 USC § 7604(g)(1).

[136] 42 USC § 7604(g)(2).

[137] Nuisances in Towns Act 12 Rich 2, c 13 (1388) (water pollution by dung and filth). There was a flurry of similar US State legislation in the environmental space in the period 1970–1975, starting in Michigan: Stern (n 131) 637–44.

[138] Boyer and Medlinger (n 130) 843–44. After an initial period of relative vigour under the Carter administration in the 1970s, the EPA was plunged into a period of demoralization and organizational turmoil under the Reagan administration, and the rate of case references to the Department of Justice dropped: ibid 870–79.

[139] Thompson (n 130) 200; Boyer and Medlinger (n 130) 852, 864–66. Private actions under the CAA started to accelerate after 1990 amendments to the Act which made it easier for plaintiffs to detect infringement and meet the required standards of proof, and which made civil penalties available in private suits for the first time: D Buente, 'The Clean Air Act Amendments of 1990: Closing the Enforcement Loop' (1991) 21 Environmental Law 2233. Note, however, the recent observation that most private actions are directed to ensuring proper agency enforcement, rather than being directed at private industry: Adelman and Reilly-Diakun (n 130).

today.[140] President Trump's appointment of the climate change sceptic Scott Pruitt, to head up the agency during his first term of office, provides a particularly crass example of the realpolitik and he is carrying the same blunt strategy into effect today, but subtler processes of industry influence have long plagued public agency enforcement in this space[141] and their risk persists, as I suggested in Chapter 5. Even excluding the problems of agency capture, there will tend always to be a gap between regulatory promises in the environmental space and the public budgets necessary to keep them, which provides modern governments endorsing environmental agendas with obvious incentives to harness private resources to the public enforcement effort. A further factor behind the enactment of the CAA was ideological—the political prerogative of 'democratically empowering' citizens by increasing their opportunities to participate in the implementation of important environmental goals.[142]

Although there is formally no reward for the enforcer under the Act, the tension between private and public interests that was noted in *qui tam* actions is not completely absent because enforcers still have the power to settle actions privately with polluters. These powers can be used as levers to exaggerate other private claims being pursued by an enforcer against the same defendant in respect of private harm caused by an infringing activity, so that the terms of settlements need to be watched carefully. There is also potential for the enforcement priorities of the EPA and private enforcers to clash, resulting in distortion of the former's planned activity that may not, on balance, be to the greater benefit of the public overall. A recent empirical study notes this concern, but interestingly tends to dismiss it on the basis that the use of environmental citizen suits largely tracks public commitment to environmental objectives in the jurisdiction in which the claims are brought, so that they map local values and public policy, rather than contradicting them.[143] Private actions against polluters themselves are also still only a tiny proportion of enforcement actions overall,[144] and there do not appear to be the same concerns about litigation levels as there are in respect of actions under the FCA.[145] The small number of cases in which private enforcers directly enforce the Act against their fellow citizens could be considered either a sign of failure (if the objective is to fully 'democratize' citizen participation in the implementation of

[140] M Zinn, 'Policing Environmental Regulatory Enforcement: Cooperation, Capture, and Citizen Suits' (2002) 21 Stanford Environmental Law Journal 8; L Dillon and others, 'The Environmental Protection Agency in the Early Trump Administration: Prelude to Regulatory Capture' (2018) 108 American Journal of Public Health 92.

[141] Boyer and Medlinger (n 130) 840–41.

[142] Adelman and Reilly-Diakun (n 130) 395; Thompson (n 130) 209–11.

[143] Adelman and Reilly-Diakun (n 130) 396, 425–30. Perhaps unsurprisingly, the State in which most suits are filed is California, with the litigation rate being between 4.5 and 10 times the median for all jurisdictions: ibid 414.

[144] ibid 433 (litigation against private polluters is only about 3 per cent the rate of formal federal enforcement action).

[145] ibid 393.

environmental policy) or a sign of success in so far as it might imply that private actions are meeting their original, intended goal of spurring public enforcers toward more significant enforcement efforts of their own. The pattern according to which private enforcement action plays second fiddle to public enforcement is repeated in other citizens suits in the United States,[146] in the UK Environmental Protection legislation we considered above (which is still overwhelmingly enforced publicly), and in standard criminal prosecution arrangements in England, considered below. It is not, however, necessarily any the less successful for playing this secondary role. Private rights of action in respect of the breach of citizens' public duties can act as conscientious nudges to public action, as much as they are statistically significant in their own right.

(ii) Enforcement Regime under the CAA

Aside from the absence of any formal reward, the basic mechanics of the right of action under the CAA are similar to those under the FCA, with some key differences. As under the FCA, no State consent is required to initiate an action against a polluter, but it can only be commenced sixty days after notice has been provided to the EPA administrator and the State,[147] and plaintiffs are barred from initiating a claim if the State or administrator is already diligently pursuing enforcement action, so that active public enforcement always trumps and displaces private enforcement.[148] A key difference from the FCA is that, although the State can add itself as a party at any time, it has no power to terminate the private action if it fails to do so within the initial sixty-day period. Another is that it lacks any absolute veto over private settlement, being confined instead to a right to be served with a copy of any proposed compromise and to intervene and present its objections to the court within forty-five days.[149] Although the State and the EPA therefore have the opportunity to run the action themselves if they wish, they lose control if they don't and it is the court that acts as ultimate arbiter of the public interest in assessing the fairness and desirability of any settlement of the action. The State therefore has less control than it does in the FCA *qui tam* action.

Rights of action under the CAA are again available to any person, as they are under the FCA. However, the Supreme Court's conclusion that courts only have jurisdiction under Article 3 of the Constitution to hear claims where the private enforcer can prove an actual 'injury in fact' has here proven more problematic and has restricted the capacity of private parties and environmental organizations to pursue claims. This is because plaintiffs under the CAA are regarded as exercising rights of action 'on their own behalf', not as 'relators' suing for State injury, so they

[146] Stern (n 131) 647–66.
[147] 42 USC § 7604(b)(1) (A).
[148] 42 USC § 7604(b)(1) (B).
[149] 42 USC § 7604(c)(3).

have to prove that a wrong has caused (or will cause) them some 'concrete' injury of their own. This has narrowed the class of persons entitled to sue polluters to those whose own private interests are affected, or likely to be affected, by the pollution, which, at the very least, complicates and increases the costs of litigation, but which also seriously restricts the capacity of private enforcers to pursue public interest actions.[150] The Supreme Court's concerns about jurisdiction are actually—and despite the form of their expression—concerns about the separation of powers. They reflect the conservative view expressed by the late Justice Scalia that private citizens have no place protecting public interests and that community law enforcement is exclusively an executive prerogative.[151] This view directly contradicts the will of Congress expressed in the Act but remains a continuing obstacle.

It has ironically been suggested that one way to avoid the jurisdictional problem would be to shift the model of private enforcement under the Act from 'citizen suit' to '*qui tam*' so that private enforcers could claim a private interest of their own to be at stake in the claim, but whilst this is pragmatic, it is uncertain to succeed and is, in any event, a very technical way of sidestepping the more fundamental constitutional concerns about the impropriety of private 'public interest' enforcement, which should really be met head on. The introduction of a reward element to claims for the sake of bolstering their constitutionality also elevates moral risk and the danger of conflict between public and private interest. As things stand, there is a palpable tension between Congress' clear plans to recruit private enforcers to the protection of the public interest and the constitutional objections of the Supreme Court to the use of judicial power to that end. The jurisdictional distinction that is currently drawn between the action *qui tam* and citizen suits also looks pretty fragile, since the reality is that in *both* instances the plaintiff has his or her own right of action and is enforcing the rights of the State, not primary rights of his or her own, albeit that the State enjoys different levels of control over the action in each case, once it has been started.

D. Rationale of 'Popular Actions'

None of the modern 'popular' actions examined above—either *qui tam* or environmental citizen suits under the CAA in the United States—can be justified on the basis of some moral interest that litigants have in being entitled to seek recourse for

150 See eg *Washington Env Council v Bellon* 732 F 3d 1131 (2013); *Spokeo Inc v Robins* 578 US 330 (2016); *Center for Biological Diversity v University of North Carolina*, No. 1:19-CV-1179, 2021 US Dist LEXIS 163459 (MDNC 30 August 2021). Most recently, attempts by ExxonMobil to further tighten the injury in fact requirement have been rejected, and the constitutionality of the citizen suit provision affirmed by the US Court of Appeals (5th Circuit): *Environment Texas Citizen Lobby, Inc v ExxonMobil Corporation* No 17-20545, 2024 (USCA 5th C 11 December 2024).

151 G Nichol, 'Justice Scalia, Standing and Public Law Litigation' (1993) 42 Duke Law Journal 1146.

a harm that a public wrong has done to one of their own private interests. All such actions are pure public interest actions in pursuit of penalties and harm to State interests—personal harm is not in point.[152] A requirement of private injury may have developed in the United States as a constitutional constraint upon the class of persons entitled to exercise the respective statutory rights—and a private incentive to sue is provided in actions *qui tam*—but private interest does not itself underpin the power of suit under the FCA, the Texas Heartbeat Law, or the citizen suit provision of the CAA.

The rationale of private actions under these statutes is therefore more pragmatic. In some instances (the FCA) the potential financial benefits for the State have proven very hard to resist. Here we see detectable shadows of the more ancient tendency of Kings to construct devices to fill their own coffers.[153] Private actions are also thought to be efficient at bringing to the fore information about infraction that it would be difficult for public enforcement agents to secure on their own. This cannot be the only reason for granting rights of action to private individuals, however, since giving them 'information rights' (plus rewards) to inform State agents about public frauds or environmental infractions could achieve similar ends, as under weaker whistle-blower laws.[154] There are also sometimes deficiencies in the effectiveness of public enforcement even where public infractions are obvious—either in consequence of an agency's capture or as a result of the sheer scale of the relevant regulatory task and the paucity of public resource available to meet it.

Finally, there are clearly deep-rooted constitutional and political factors in play. The modern US actions under the FCA, the Texas Heartbeat Law and citizen suit provisions form part of a long and complex saga in which private enforcement has been embraced as a modern solution to political hesitations and stalemates about the merits of public regulation.[155] At the federal level, Sean Farhang's fascinating recent work has shown beyond reasonable doubt that private enforcement provisions have been used by Congress from the 1960s onwards as a tool for sidestepping presidential opposition to bureaucratic regulation.[156] Within Congress, it has

[152] It is therefore especially ironic, and probably misconceived, for the Supreme Court to have held that the existence of the enforcement regime under the Clean Air Act precludes recourse by private plaintiffs to the law of public nuisance for private harm occasioned to them by breaches of the Act's provisions: *American Electric Power Co v Connecticut* 564 US 410 (2011) and n 20 above.

[153] Chapter 4 Section 4.2 nn 10, 11, and text therein.

[154] For the view that *qui tam* systems are nonetheless more efficient in bringing forward higher-quality information and better lawsuits than mere reward provisions under whistle-blower laws, see A Casey and A Niblett, 'Noise Reduction: The Screening Value of Qui Tam' (2014) 91 Washington University Law Review 1169. See also Bucy (n 74).

[155] JM Glover, 'The Structural Role of Private Enforcement Mechanisms in Public Law' (2012) 53 William and Mary Law Review 1137. See also, on the historical, cultural, and political factors that have fostered private enforcement strategies, S Burbank, S Farhang, and H Kritzer, 'Private Enforcement' (2013) 17 Lewis and Clark Law Review 637; R Kagan, *Adversarial Legalism: The American Way of Law* (2nd edn, Harvard University Press 2019).

[156] S Farhang, *The Litigation State: Public Regulation and Private Lawsuits in the US* (Princeton University Press, 2010) 4–6, 32–39 and see generally Chs 1–3 (positing that the main factors behind the use of private enforcement are institutional, relating to the particularly stark separation of powers

come to represent an acceptable political compromise for Republicans and fiscal conservatives who are opposed to public regulation and who therefore resist any extension of public agency enforcement powers. For welfarists and believers in the regulatory State, on the other hand, private enforcement is better than no enforcement at all (or better than under-enforcement) and it may help to prompt public awareness and incentivize agencies that are dragging their feet to do a better job.

At the level of constitutional theory, private enforcement can further be seen as a mechanism of citizen empowerment in the constitutional order—a way of increasing democratic participation. If one takes this view, it is not simply a default enforcement mode, applying as a last resort in the absence of proper public alternatives, or a type of pragmatic political compromise dictated by institutional factors, but a potentially desirable feature of a system of public laws in its own right, placing legal power in the hands of the people and enlisting their resources to ensure community fidelity to the rule of law, accountability, and the implementation of legislatively endorsed community goals.[157]

In the case of the Texas Heartbeat Law, the realpolitik has become sinister. Private initiative has been chosen as a means of removing the State entirely from public law enforcement precisely to avoid constitutional safeguards for fundamental human rights—a phenomenon (rightly) derided by Jon Michaels and David Noll as exhibiting a form of populist 'vigilante federalism' that is both a symptom and an accelerant of the corrosive political dynamics of a far-right agenda in the United States and which undermines the rule of law.[158] In this instance, the conscious choice by a State legislature of private over public enforcement is far from being a sign of constitutional health, but is more representative of a seismic fracture in the landscape of modern US federalism and the core values on which it is built.

7.3 General Rights of Private Criminal Prosecution

This brings us to our final and perhaps the most important example of the private enforcement of citizen duties—the residual, general right of any private person to initiate a criminal prosecution without prior State permission. Such a broad right

between legislature and executive and oppositional politics in the US). For an earlier summation of the thesis and empirical evidence, see S Farhang, 'Public Regulation and Private Lawsuits in the American Separation of Powers System' (2008) 52 American Journal of Political Science 821.

[157] L Norris, 'The Promise and Perils of Private Enforcement' (2022) 108 Virginia Law Review 1483 (but noting the perils of recent private enforcement forms in the US). See also S Lawrence, 'Justice, Democracy, Litigation, and Political Participation' (1991) 72 Social Science Quarterly 464 (emphasizing the educative role of litigation as a mechanism for engaging citizens in the discussion of justice and the public good). For a detailed defence of the merits of litigation in advancing democratic values such as adherence to the rule of law, accountability, participation in self-government, transparency (access to information), and social equality, see A Lahav, *In Praise of Litigation* (OUP 2017) esp 19–20, 142.

[158] Michaels and Noll (n 80). See also Norris (n 157); Huq (n 80) 1259.

of action is rare (if not unheard of) in civilian jurisdictions[159] and also (now) in the United States,[160] but it persists in many common law and mixed jurisdictions, including England and Wales.[161] I focus on the last of these because it is here that there has been a sharp uplift in the private prosecution rate in recent years, spawning a thriving new litigation industry with its own private prosecutors' association and voluntary code of practice.[162] It is also here that a series of catastrophic miscarriages of justice have hit the headlines, stemming from the Post Office's personal prosecution of over 700 of its former employees for fraud and similar offences since 1991. The saga, which is rooted in the failings of the institution's own defective electronic accounting system (Horizon),[163] resulted in a large number of unsafe convictions, over 100 of which were set aside judicially before the government—in a rising sense of public embarrassment following a television dramatization of the scandal in early 2024 ('Mr Bates v The Post Office')—took extraordinary, legislative measures to quash the rest *en masse*.[164] The miscarriage

[159] This is an attribute of their inquisitorial tradition. See Y Ma, 'Exploring the Origins of Public Prosecution (2008) 18 International Criminal Justice Review 190, esp 196–98. An important exception prevails in Spain in the form of the *acusación popular*, which provides a right for any citizen (subject to some exceptions) to prosecute almost all types of crime in his or her own name, with free legal assistance. The right was guaranteed in the Constitution (Title VI, art 125) in 1978 as a reaction to the popular oppression of the Franco regime: J Pérez Gil, 'Private Interests Seeking Punishment: Prosecution Brought by Private Individuals and Groups in Spain' (2003) 25 Law and Policy 151, 152.

[160] See generally J Bessler, *Private Prosecution in America* (Carolina Academic Press 2022). For an accessible, but highly detailed history of the demise of private prosecution in the US (which really only accelerated after the Civil War and was completed in the early twentieth century with the advent of unprecedented Attorney-General powers) see J Barth, 'Criminal Prosecution in American History: Private or Public?' (2022) 67 South Dakota Law Review 119. See also M O'Neill, 'Private Vengeance and the Public Good' (2010) 12 Journal of Constitutional Law 659. The origins of the public system are sometimes attributed to Dutch influence in New Amsterdam (Manhattan) and other colonies but are probably more complex than this. For a recent call to rethink the model, see E Kaufman, 'The Past and Persistence of Private Prosecution' (2024) 173 University of Pennsylvania Law Review 89.

[161] See eg Prosecution of Offences Act 1985 (UK) s 6; Criminal Procedure Act 2011 (NZ) s 15; Criminal Code RSC 1985 (Canada) s 504; Crimes Act 1914 (Cth) (Aus) s 13. The unconditional right persists in Australia in all States and Territories, with exceptions in Western Australia (where prior executive authorization is always required: Criminal Procedure Act 2004 (WA) s 20) and Tasmania (where it is required for any prosecution under the Criminal Code: Justices Act (Tas) 1929 s 27). Some States (eg Queensland) require judicial permission in respect of indictable offences: Criminal Code Act 1899 (Qld) s 686. Certain Commonwealth offences (crimes against humanity) have been held not to be privately prosecutable at all on the construction of the relevant legislation: *Taylor v Attorney-General* [2019] HCA 30. In Scotland, judicial permission is always required in the form of a grant by the High Court of Justiciary of a bill of criminal letters, and the Lord Advocate can oppose the application (although there appears to be no power of veto as such). The last permission in Scotland was granted in 1982 and private prosecutions are vanishingly rare. There are also some residual cases in England and Wales, where the DPP's permission is required, on which see further below. For a broad, international review, see J Mujuzi, 'The Right to Institute a Private Prosecution' (2015) 4 International Human Rights Law Review 222.

[162] <https://private-prosecutions.com/> accessed 5 December 2025.

[163] On which, see *Bates v The Post Office* (No 6) [2019] EWHC 3408 (QB). The scandal precipitated a subsequent independent inquiry (which became a full public inquiry in 2021): <https://www.postofficehorizoninquiry.org.uk/> accessed 5 December 2025. Payments of compensation to victims have been scandalously slow.

[164] Post Office (Horizon System) Offences Act 2024 (c 14) (24 May 2024) (capturing convictions for all relevant offences between 1996 and the end of 2018). For a critique of the legislation as an unprecedented violation of the doctrine of separation of powers and dangerous example of political

of justice has been described by the Criminal Cases Review Commission as the most widespread it has seen since it started work in 1997.

The dramatic recent increase in the number of private prosecutions in England has been noted judicially[165] and by the Justice Committee of the House of Commons, which was charged in 2019 with reporting on it and proposing additional safeguards to offset its risks.[166] Most explanations point the finger at the cuts made to police and CPS resources since 2010. Figures provided by the Institute for Government show that central government spending on law and order decreased by 16.2 per cent in real terms between 2009 and 2016–17 and that whilst there was an uplift in 2019, spending in 2023 remained below 2009 levels. Funding for the CPS itself dropped by a third.[167] Charging rates declined significantly in the period 2013–2023[168] and the rate at which rape in particular was prosecuted dropped from (a small) 15 per cent in 2015–2016 to (a scandalous) 3 per cent in 2019–2020. Alongside these funding cuts, the costs of publicly investigating and prosecuting crime have reportedly increased as a result of changes in the types of offences being committed, with a shift toward complex fraud and online, computer-related activity (now accounting for up to half of all reported crime),[169] and scarce police resources are also reportedly being consumed by growth in their responsibilities for safeguarding and mental health protection.[170] Beyond these short-term factors, there are also longer-term explanations for the decline in charging rates that have applied since the early 1980s, when DPP policy (later formalized in the terms of the 1994 CPS Prosecution Code)[171] changed the criteria for taking cases forward to trial, so as to require a greater than 50 per cent chance of conviction in all cases. This shift was itself partly driven by fiscal considerations. If there were any remaining doubt at all that the recent spike in private litigation stems from public enforcement deficit, it has been dispelled by the

interference in judicial decisions about guilt and innocence, see H Quirk, 'The Post Office Scandal and the Separation of Powers' (2024) Criminal Law Review 91.

[165] *R (on the application of Virgin Media Ltd) v Zinga (Munaf Ahmed)* [2014] EWCA Crim 52 [10] (Lord Thomas CJ) (pointing to the 'retrenchment of state activity').

[166] House of Commons Justice Committee (HCJC), *Private Prosecutions: Safeguards*, 9th Report, 2019–21 (29 September 2020). The number of prosecutions each year has been estimated as in the thousands: C de Than and J Elvin, 'Private Prosecution: a Useful Constitutional Safeguard or Potentially Dangerous Historical Anomaly?' (2019) 8 Criminal Law Review 656, 657.

[167] Institute for Government (IFG), *Performance Tracker 2023* (30 Oct 2023) 194; Rt Hon Geofrey Cox QC AG, evidence to the House of Commons Justice Committee HC 1887 (23 January 2019).

[168] IFG (n 167) 193.

[169] ibid 196.

[170] ibid 196–97 (up to 20 per cent of front-line policing is allocated to incidents requiring mental health engagement, according to one study).

[171] A Ashworth and J Fionda, 'The New Code for Crown Prosecutors: Part 1: Prosecution, Accountability and the Public Interest' (1994) Criminal Law Review 894, 895 identify the 1994 Code as the first explicitly to refer to a 51 per cent rule. D Wolchover and A Heaton-Armstrong, 'It's Time to Modify the "50 per cent' Threshold Test' (2021) (July) New Law Journal 17 at 17 nonetheless indicate that the policy was in operation from the early 1980s.

evidence provided to the Justice Committee by professional private prosecutors themselves, who openly admitted that their business models respond to public failure. One of them referred to the government's austerity measures as the direct cause of its rising fortunes.[172]

A. Enforcement Regime

The gradual shift from private to public enforcement in respect of (what we now call) crime was charted in Chapter 4. It occurred late in the day, as official police forces were established from 1829[173] onwards and gradually took over from private individuals and the great number (some suggest as many as four thousand) private prosecution associations that were formed from about 1760 onwards to cope with the perception that crime rates in the late eighteenth and early nineteenth centuries were rising.[174] The founding statutes of these forces never actually accorded them any formal prosecutorial function, so that police officers were technically always private prosecutors in uniform. As the police stepped up and public resourcing increased, actions by private associations and individuals declined. Police officers then became the prosecutors of first resort (although they increasingly enlisted professional legal assistance to do the job) until the establishment of the CPS in 1985. There were some early rumblings about police corruption and oppression in the mid-1800s and associated calls for the introduction of professional State prosecution services at that stage, but the disquiet reportedly settled by the 1880s, although it is not entirely clear why.[175] Some suggest that the English failure to develop a more comprehensive system of public prosecution at an earlier

[172] HCJC 9th Report (n 166) [26]. For a vision in which private enforcers play a greater role in fraud prosecutions to make up for the deficit in public enforcement, see C Lewis and others, 'Evaluating the Case for Greater use of Private Prosecutions in England and Wales for Fraud Offences' (2014) 42 International Journal of Law Crime and Justice 3.

[173] Although this date is commonly cited, private forces, at first voluntary but later paid, coalesced in magistrates' offices from the 1750s: J Beattie, *Crime and the Courts in England: 1660–1800* (Princeton University Press 1986) 66. For the state of play in 1816, see House of Commons Committee on the State of the Police of the Metropolis, Report (William & Charles Clement 1816).

[174] K Lidstone, R Hogg, and F Sutcliffe, *Prosecutions by Private Individuals and Non-Police Agencies* (HMSO 1980) 2–3; D Hay and F Snyder, 'Using the Criminal Law, 1750–1850: Policing, Power and the State' in Hay and Snyder (eds) (n 94) 3, esp 36–47. On the history of private prosecution associations, see Philips (n 94) 113; M Koyama, 'Prosecution Associations in Industrial Revolution England: Private Providers of Public Goods?' (2012) 41 Journal of Legal Studies 95. Koyama personally collected the names of 534 associations between 1750 and 1850, but points to another study for the figure of up to 4,000 in this time frame: at 103 and fn 18.

[175] Although the creation of the office of the DPP in 1879 might appear to be a factor, the office had very few staff and played little practical part in the prosecution of offences prior to the creation of the CPS in in 1985: *R (on the application of Gujra) v Crown Prosecution Service* [2012] UKSC 52 [93]–[95] (Lord Mance SJC). A better explanation may be that officers had handed the actual conduct of prosecutions in court over to solicitors and counsel by this stage: Hay and Snyder, 'Using the Criminal Law, 1750–1850: Policing, Power and the State' (n 174) 45.

stage was due at least in part to a deep-seated distrust of State authority,[176] which, if true, is interesting because it chimes loudly with reported American attitudes in the modern day.

(i) The Range of Prosecutors

Modern 'public' prosecutors now include not just the Director of Public Prosecutions (since 1879) and the CPS but a surprisingly wide variety of other public agencies including the Civil Aviation Authority, Serious Fraud Office, Health and Safety Executive, local authorities, the Immigration Office, His Majesty's Revenue & Customs, National Crime Agency, and (still) the police. Whenever any of the last four of these agencies initiates proceedings, the CPS must (and does) immediately take over the proceeding.[177] Whilst there are therefore multiple public rights of action, the CPS exercises its own right (and terminates those of others) in a high proportion of cases, bringing greater independence and coordination[178] to the prosecution than existed when the relevant powers lay in the hands of individual police officers. Although it is sometimes suggested that the CPS should be required to take over *all* public prosecutions, the expertise and experience of the other agencies is thought to be valuable in the particular contexts in which they operate, and they take financial pressure off the service.[179] For these reasons, the CPS itself remains a strong supporter not just of other public agency rights of action but also, ironically, of the supposedly rival, residual right of private prosecution. Whatever they may think of their constitutional prerogative, Crown prosecutors do not want all of the additional work that private prosecutors currently do.[180] Nor is the government keen to impress further responsibilities upon them.[181]

The body of modern private prosecutors is more diverse still than that that of public agencies.[182] It includes individuals (usually victims, and mostly in cases of common assault),[183] but also private organizations such as retailers (shoplifting

[176] A May, *Advocates and Truth-Seeking in the Old Bailey Courtroom* (2005) 26 Journal of Legal History 71, 76–77. For a full history of the background to the creation of the CPS in 1985, see T Hetherington, *Prosecution and the Public Interest* (Waterlow Publishers 1989) Chs 1–4.

[177] Prosecution of Offences Act 1985 (UK) s 3(2).

[178] Although central coordination was part of the original design, in practice the service has been decentralized through division into forty-two different areas, each with its own Chief Crown Prosecutor.

[179] Although an argument of principle exists for universal CPS take-over, resourcing was thought by a Royal Commission to preclude the possibility even in 1981: Royal Commission on Criminal Procedure (RCCP) Cmnd 8092 (1981) [7.41]–[7.44].The financial pressures have increased since them.

[180] HCJC 9th Report (n 166) [50].

[181] HCJC, Private Prosecutions: Safeguards: Government Response to the Committee's Ninth Report, 10th Special Report 2019–21 (HC 1238 2021). The government's general unwillingness to implement anything other than a central prosecutions register and cuts in funding for private prosecutors has fuelled renewed calls for the abolition of the right altogether: S Colman, 'Evaluating Private Prosecutions: Reform or Abolition? (2023) 11 Criminal Law Review 692.

[182] See generally L Leigh, 'Private Prosecutions and Diversionary Justice' [2007] Criminal Law Review 289.

[183] Lidstone, Hogg, and Sutcliffe (n 174) 95 (2.4 per cent of cases prosecuted by non-police agents; 82 per cent of these involving assault).

cases), the RSPCA (since 1824), the National Society for the Prevention of Cruelty to Children (NSPCC), the Federation Against Copyright Theft (FACT), and—the oldest and currently most controversial for reasons already mentioned—the Post Office (since 1683). Until 2013, postal operations in the United Kingdom were almost entirely State-owned,[184] which explains why the government has scrambled so visibly to deal with Horizon's fallout. The RSPCA has historically handled 85 per cent of all prosecutions under the Animals Welfare Act 2006, and secured 1,432 convictions in 2019 alone,[185] but it recently signalled its intention to stop prosecuting and to feed cases to the CPS instead, citing concerns about the increasing complexity of cases and the involvement of organized criminal gangs.[186] It is hard to imagine, given the financial pressures on the CPS, that the same number of animal cruelty cases would have been brought to book over the years without the RSPCA's private efforts.[187] As long ago as 1980, the Society was investigating 24,000 complaints a year.[188] A serious increase in CPS resources and training will therefore be required if the State is to make up the prospective enforcement deficit in the animal welfare field, and the likelihood in the current fiscal environment is that such cases will be deprioritized and fall by the wayside.

The exact, relative proportions of public and private prosecution today is hard to assess, since there has until recently been no register of who is prosecuting a case in any given instance, and cases prosecuted in the Crown Court are always brought in the State's own name. The last, detailed statistical breakdown (itself limited in scope) was commissioned in 1980, prior to the CPS' birth. It estimated that 75 per cent of prosecutions were then being brought by the police, with the remainder initiated by private individuals, associations, and other State agencies.[189] Private

[184] The picture is complicated. Prior to 1969, what I have referred to as the Post Office was a State department (the General Post Office). It became a statutory public corporation under the Post Office Act 1969 (UK). The public corporation then became a public limited company in 2001 (Consignia, then renamed Royal Mail Holdings) and split between post office operations (Post Office Limited—which still remains in Crown ownership and is subject to government oversight, although 99 per cent of offices have been franchised to private operators) and postal delivery services (the Royal Mail Group Ltd—comprising the Royal Mail and Parcelforce) which have been entirely in private ownership since 2015, following the passage of the Postal Services Act 2011 (UK).

[185] See the CPS' submission (PPS0044, [29–30]) to the HCJC, referenced in the HCJC 9th Report (n 166) [50].

[186] H Sherwood, 'Top Lawyer urges MPs to Review Private Prosecutions after Post Office Scandal' (*Guardian*, 12 January 2024) https://www.theguardian.com/uk-news/2024/jan/12/top-lawyer-urges-mps-to-review-private-prosecutions-after-post-office-scandal accessed 5 December 2025. It has also been under political pressure for some time, its processes being criticized for lacking in accountability and transparency: S Wooler CB, *The Independent Review of the Prosecution Activity of the RSPCA* (24 September 2014). See also Environment, Food and Rural Affairs Select Committee, 3rd Report (2017–18), *Animal Welfare in England: Domestic Pets* 38 (advocating its withdrawal from the role of prosecutor of first resort).

[187] Wooler (n 186) 127: 'society depends on the RSPCA to enforce a difficult aspect of the law'.

[188] RCCP (n 179) 88.

[189] Lidstone, Hogg, and Sutcliffe (n 174) 33 (the figures relate to the prosecution of adults for non-traffic offences in 1977 in just twelve Magistrates Courts and assume some underreporting of non-police prosecutions); A Samuels, 'Non-Crown Prosecutions: Prosecutions by Non-Police Agencies and by Private Individuals' (1986) Criminal Law Review 33, 35.

individuals ranked ninth (out of eighteen) in the list of non-police prosecutors, local authorities fourth, the RSPCA thirteenth, and the Post Office topped the list with some 4,000 prosecutions in a twelve-month period (the vast majority of which related to television licensing infractions).[190] Private individuals' conviction rate (60 per cent) was one-third lower than that of non-police public agencies, and that success rate roughly halved again (to 35 per cent) wherever a prosecution was contested.[191] Ninety per cent of individual prosecutions were conducted without legal representation.

(ii) Private Prosecutions—Risks, Conditions, and Constraints

The private right of action is a common law right held by all citizens. Its exercise remains[192] unconditional upon obtaining either prior State or judicial permission, save in a number of seemingly random instances prescribed by statute, where the *fiat* of either a Crown prosecutor,[193] or the DPP personally,[194] is necessary. Historically, such cases probably included instances in which the risk of a private prosecutor having prejudicial motivation was perceived to be especially high (eg cases of assisted suicide or family incest), as well as some in which the interest harmed was entirely public (such as breaches of the Official Secrets Act or cases of tax evasion). In 1998, the Law Commission described the remaining list as 'haphazard'[195] and took the view that consent conditions are an improper way of weeding out either weak cases, or vexatious litigants.[196] It recommended reducing the number of cases requiring State consent and placing them on a logical footing.[197] Whilst, however, the number of consent conditions has now dropped by about 60 per cent, no greater logical order is apparent in their profile. If it is impossible to find any logical basis for discrimination, the better approach might be to remove the conditions altogether and mediate the State's public interest in preventing a prosecution entirely through post-initiation controls, in particular by reconfiguring the architecture surrounding State rights of intervention and termination in ways discussed further below. For now, however, governments are simply happy to live with the mess.

[190] Lidstone, Hogg, and Sutcliffe (n 174) 15.

[191] ibid 28.

[192] Historically, the right was always unconditional, the first impetus toward State control being taken from the mid-nineteenth century: Edwards (n 19) 237–46.

[193] Prosecution of Offences Act 1985 (UK) s 1(7) (48 statutes).

[194] Seven statutes (eg the Bribery Act 2010 and tax evasion offences under the Criminal Finances Act 2017).

[195] Law Commission, *Consents to Prosecution* Law Comm No 255 (TSO 1998) [4.16], Appendix A (153 statutes).

[196] ibid [6.17], Rec 9.

[197] ibid Recs 11–13 recommended only three categories of case—those in which a prosecution may infringe human rights, national security cases, and cases in which there is a high risk of both abuse of process and irreparable harm.

Even in standard cases in which permission is not required, the right of private prosecution is attended by significant limits, duties, and liabilities. First, a magistrate before whom an information is laid has no absolute duty to issue a summons and may refuse to do so if any improper motive is detected, if crucial information remains undisclosed, or the facts asserted are legally incapable of proof.[198] This protection is limited, because the court's information is restricted and it has no obligation to make further inquiry.[199] Second, if the magistrate decides to issue the summons on overly weak evidence, the decision can be challenged by judicial review, as in the case in 2019 in which Boris Johnson successfully sought the quashing of a decision to allow his prosecution for the crime of misconduct in public office.[200] Third, both the DPP and Crown Prosecutors have powers to take over the prosecution and terminate it. Applying its modern criteria, the CPS will do this in any case of which it is aware, the prospects of which it assesses to be less than 51 per cent. This resulted in 2019 in it terminating twenty-nine of forty-nine prosecutions referred to it for review.[201] This is stricter than its old, pre-2009 approach (which was to terminate only if there was 'clearly no case to answer')[202] and stricter also than the approach in Australia, where the Commonwealth's policy is to allow a private prosecution to continue unless there is 'no reasonable prospect' of a conviction.[203] The policy was nonetheless upheld by the UK Supreme Court in 2012 as being consistent with the liberty of citizens to prosecute that is preserved in the 1985 Act.[204] An unlimited power to *initiate* a private prosecution does not, the Court found, mean an unlimited power to *continue* it.[205] A claim can be terminated in this way simply by a Crown prosecutor making an appearance in the case and offering no evidence, and defendants may request a CPS review of any private prosecution in order to achieve this end, at any time.

A fourth limit is that the CPS' powers to terminate or continue a proceeding are themselves subject to a liability that any decision it makes can be set aside in proceedings for judicial review. This means that there is a further private check available to a defendant if the CPS review of a case results in an irrational, illegal, or procedurally improper decision to allow it to continue in private hands.[206] Fifth, the Attorney-General can issue a *nolle prosequi* at his own motion at any stage (in the Crown Court). Sixth, courts retain the power to stay proceedings for

[198] Criminal Procedure Rules 2020, Part 7, R 7.2(14).

[199] Colman (n 181) 698.

[200] *Boris Johnson v Westminster Magistrates Court* [2019] EWHC 1709 (Admin).

[201] <https://www.lawgazette.co.uk/practice/cps-drops-more-than-half-of-its-private-prosecutions/5107989.article> accessed 5 December 2025.

[202] *R v Director of Public Prosecutions Ex parte Duckenfield* [2000] 1 WLR 55 [63] (Laws LJ).

[203] CDPP, *Prosecution Policy of the Commonwealth, Guidelines for the Making of Decisions in the Prosecutions Process* (2021) 4.10(a).

[204] *Gujra* (n 175).

[205] ibid [21] (Lord Wilson JSC).

[206] As in *Duckenfield* (n 202) (although the application was in that instance unsuccessful).

an abuse of process, again at any time.[207] Seventh—and this is admittedly highly exceptional—courts can strip vexatious prosecutors of their right to bring future proceeding without first obtaining judicial permission, as we saw in Chapter 5. Abusive actions might also give rise to private liability for malicious prosecution, where malice can be proven.[208]

Significant as these protections are, an important gap identified by the Justice Committee was the absence of any duty on the part of a private prosecutor (or indeed the courts service) to notify the State about the existence of a private prosecution. This contrasts with the position under both the FCA and the CAA in the United States. Whilst it is always, of course, open to the accused himself to notify the CPS and seek the latter's intervention, it became clear during the Horizon scandal that some defendants did not even know that their prosecutions were being conducted privately. The result is that actions have been able to proceed for many years in a blind spot, beyond State oversight. Nor, on the current law, does either the private prosecutor, or the court, have any duty to notify the accused of his or her right to seek CPS intervention. The government's apparent distaste for notification duties is based on the self-serving logic that once the CPS is aware of a prosecution, it may come under a duty to review it, which will simply consume further, already scare resources.[209] The State is therefore not overly keen to know about private prosecutions, lest it has to spend time and money doing something about them.[210]

The State's willingness to control private prosecutions in the wake of the Post Office scandal hence currently extends little further than enforcing existing procedural safeguards, a new requirement that summonses identify the existence and identity of a private prosecutor,[211] the creation of a central prosecutions register (which accused persons and the CPS could try and consult if they wish, but which is in practice proving very hard for members of the public to access),[212] and a willingness (indeed a keen appetite) to cut the costs recoverable by private prosecutors to the same (legal aid) rates as are available to public prosecutors. It has ignored the

[207] See eg *R (on the application of Kay) v Leeds Magistrates' Court* [2018] EWHC 1233(Admin) (private prosecutor failed to disclose that proceedings in respect of the same matter had been dismissed by Polish courts); *Morjaria v Westminster Magistrates' Court* [2023] EWHC 2936 (Admin); *Asif v Ditta and Riaz* [2021] EWCA Crim 1091 (prosecutor motive in both cases improperly to force accused to settle a civil suit, or pay an alleged debt).

[208] See eg *A v New South Wales* [2007] HCA 10.

[209] HC 1238 (n 181) 6.

[210] If CPS termination of private prosecutions became the general rule it is also arguable that the statute's purpose in preserving the right of private prosecution might be undercut in a way not in issue in the *Gujra* decision itself: HCJC 9th Report (n 166) [50]; CPS PPS0044 (n 185) [29].

[211] Criminal Procedure Rules 2020, No 759 Part 7, R 7.4(2)(c)(iii) (as inserted by the Criminal Procedure (Amendment No 2) Rules (SI 2022/815).

[212] A freedom of information request address to HM Courts and Tribunals Service for access to records on 22 May 2022 was declined on the basis that Court records are exempt from the provisions of the Freedom of Information Act: <https://www.whatdotheyknow.com/request/private_prosecutions_register_fo?utm_campaign=alaveteli-experiments-87&utm_content=sidebar_similar_requests&utm_medium=link&utm_source=whatdotheyknow> accessed 5 December 2025.

call for a formal system of licensing or inspection of corporate prosecutors, or for the creation of a binding private prosecution code, preferring to leave regulation to private associations themselves on a purely voluntary basis.[213] The requirement that private prosecutors be identified in any summons is an important step, but whether it results in a greater number of CPS interventions in the absence of notification duties remains to be seen.

Whilst private prosecutions often cost more than public ones,[214] the government's enthusiasm for capping costs at legal aid rates is controversial. Private claims are low in volume compared to public ones; they are inevitably unable to realize the efficiencies that are possible where high volumes and centralized public agencies are concerned. On the current understanding to which we refer further below, they also help to plug holes in the State's enforcement operation, often focusing on the prosecution of complex cases (such as financial fraud) which the State does not have the resources to pursue. They are therefore *bound* to cost more in some instances and may just be worth the additional premium. The government's speculative suggestion that no costs *at all* might be recoverable unless a private prosecution is successful,[215] if further pursued, seems likely to kill off a high proportion of actions. The better view is that if the State thinks that a private action is contrary to the public interest, then it should step in and terminate it, but that if it allows the action to continue then the prosecution must be presumed to serve public ends and should be sponsored at reasonable rates, even if no conviction is ultimately secured. Courts can regulate the costs recoverable in such instances in the normal way. A requirement that the CPS be notified early of any private prosecution would also facilitate decisions about intervention being made before the costs heap gets too high.

There may therefore be a case for dealing with the recently documented hazards of private prosecution not by abandoning the practice altogether,[216] by imposing a universal requirement of prior State consent,[217] or by removing the right to prosecute from corporations,[218] but rather by requiring proper State notification of any such prosecution, so that the CPS has a meaningful opportunity to exercise

[213] <https://private-prosecutions.com/ppa-code-foreword/> accessed 5 December 2025. For determined suggestions that such a code is needed, if the right remains in being, along with pre-trial reviews and a statutory duty on the part of the CPS to terminate any action not in the public interest, see de Than and Elvin (n 166).

[214] Precise comparative figures are hard to find. The HCJC 9th Report (n 166) [35] concluded only that 'many' private prosecutions cost the taxpayer more but conceded that this may in part be a product of the complexity of the cases taken on privately. This would seem to map the profile of cases (many of them involving financial fraud) in which private prosecutions are increasingly common.

[215] HC 1238 (n 181) 5.

[216] Colman (n 181).

[217] *Report of the Royal Commission on Criminal Procedure* (Cmnd 8092, 1981) [7.50] (subject to the right to apply for judicial permission if the consent is refused). The existence of such a requirement in Scotland did not prevent the problem regarding Horizon.

[218] <https://www.theguardian.com/uk-news/2024/jan/09/post-office-scandal-could-rules-change-private-prosecutions> accessed 5 December 2025

its powers to intervene and terminate proceedings that are contrary to the public interest, as occurs under the False Claims Act in the United States. This will almost certainly lead to the CPS reviewing more cases and requiring additional funding in order to do so, but some of the expense could be met by allowing criminal profits confiscated in consequence of a successful private prosecution to be ringfenced for that purpose, rather in the way that penalties can be sequestered to the enforcement efforts of the EPA under the Clean Air Act.[219] Notification duties could be combined with changes in the relevant CPS guidance so as to create a presumption of State take-over in some higher-risk cases in which the private prosecutor is simultaneously engaged in civil litigation with the alleged offender and might therefore be using the prosecution as an illegitimate spur to civil settlement.[220] Another possibility is to introduce a licensing system for corporate prosecutors and dispense with notification requirements where a private prosecutor holds a prosecution licence.[221] In any event, the additional costs of engaging the CPS review process more often and more meaningfully will be a lot less than the costs of taking up all of the prosecutorial slack that would be left by abolishing the private right of action altogether, or limiting it solely to individuals.

B. Interests Protected

Blackstone construed crimes to be public wrongs in the sense that they infringe rights and duties owed not to private individuals but to the community as a whole.[222] This accurately describes who it is that owes the duties and holds the relevant legal rights in the criminal law, but it would be wrong to think that criminal laws consequently only protect public interests. This thesis was already disproven at the end of Chapter 5 in the section discussing criminal compensation orders.

If this insight was not shared by Blackstone himself,[223] it is by many modern commentators, although they tend to express the point a little differently in so far

[219] See n 138 and text above. The sums can be considerable, as in *Somaia v R* [2017] EWCA Crim 741 (£20 million).

[220] J Rogers, 'Private Prosecutions and Safeguards' (2020) Criminal Law Review 769, 771.

[221] Law Comm No 255 (n 195) [1.28], [7.9].

[222] Blackstone (n 83) Book 4, 5 ('violation of the public rights and duties due to the whole community, considered as a community, in its social aggregate capacity').

[223] It is hard to be sure. There are some passages in the text (ibid 5–6) suggesting that crimes such as murder and robbery are both an 'injury done to individuals' (harming their private interests?) and that they 'strike at the very being of society' (impacting upon the public interest?). At one point, he even says that 'every public offence is also a private wrong' and that it 'affects' both the individual and the community. I am not sure, however, that he was saying that *criminal* laws of which he wrote protected both public and private interests, as opposed to saying that the same act could be both a criminal law wrong against society (injuring public interests) and (independently) a private law wrong to individuals (injuring their private ones) at the same time. The difficulty stems from the fact that the term 'injury' could be taken to refer on the one hand to the violation of a primary legal right (thereby identifying the person wronged by the breach of a criminal law) or, on the other, to the interest harmed by virtue of

as they say that many crimes are 'wrongs to' *both* the public and the private individual at one and the same time. For Duff and Marshall, the crime of rape is hence both a wrong to the victim and a wrong to the community because it 'properly concerns' any community standing in solidarity with the individual.[224] It is the second normative dimension (the fact that the wrong 'concerns the community') that distinguishes crimes against individuals from private wrongs to them, which feature in our legal landscape as torts. Owing to my own particular analytical perspective, I prefer to say that crimes are always and *only ever* wrongs *to the State*, but that the State's substantive rights are often designed to protect both the public and private interests of its citizens. In some cases, a criminal law (treason for example, or a tax law) protects only an interest shared by the political community, but in others (murder, rape, robbery) it is designed to protect both the interests of the community and the individual victim.

On the Duff and Marshall view, the fact that crimes frequently have this hybrid nature—and are not *just* wrongs suffered by the State—justifies private victims retaining prosecutorial rights of action in some instances, and it could even—in the case of less serious crimes that do not significantly engage the concern of the community—justify making offences *only* prosecutable by the victim, or granting the latter a veto over any public prosecution, by requiring his or her consent for it to proceed.[225] On this logic, the precise configuration of rights of action in the criminal law and their various conditions, constraints, and attendant liabilities are a function of the wrong's effects on a victim's private interests ('what was done to them'), as well as of its broader normative political implications for the community itself.

This view meshes well with the observation made elsewhere in this and the preceding chapter that private rights of action in public law often coalesce around

that violation. On balance, it seems likely that Blackstone saw crime as a wrong to the King and harm to his (public) interests; but that he considered the protection of *private* interests a matter entirely for the *civil* law.

[224] SE Marshall and RA Duff, 'Criminalization and Sharing Wrongs' (1998) 11 Canadian Journal of Law and Jurisprudence 7; RA Duff and SE Marshall, 'Public and Private Wrongs' in J Chalmers, F Leverick, and L Farmer (eds), *Essays in Criminal Law in Honour of Sir Gerald Gordon* (Edinburgh University Press 2010) 70, 71–72; A Duff, 'Torts, Crimes and Vindication: Whose Wrong is it?' in M Dyson (ed), *Unravelling Tort and Crime* (CUP 2014) 146, 163–64. For further explanation and defence of this conception of public wrongdoing as a violation of the civil order, see, RA Duff and SE Marshall, 'Crimes, Public Wrongs and the Civil Order' (2019) 13 Criminal Law and Philosophy 27; RA Duff, *The Realm of Criminal Law* (OUP 2018) Ch 7. Ashworth expresses similar intuitions in A Ashworth, 'Punishment and Compensation: Victims, Offenders and the State' (1986) 6 Oxford Journal of Legal Studies 86, in so far as he recognizes that many serious crimes involve both public and private wrongs (at 111) and that it is a legitimate function of the criminal law itself to require offenders to compensate victims, irrespective of whether the victim has a right to compensation in private law (at 109, 111–12).

[225] Duff and Marshall, 'Public and Private Wrongs (n 224) 80–82; Duff, 'Whose Wrong Is It?' (n 224) 171–72. The authors acknowledge that none of these options is free of difficulty, or controversy. cf contra Ashworth (n 224) 108, maintaining the view that prosecution is exclusively a public function, although victims and 'interested citizens' should be able to appeal prosecution decisions.

cases in which the law's underlying purpose is to protect citizens' private interests. To the extent that Duff and Marshall express a view about the way in which rights of private prosecution should ultimately be configured, it seems to be that rights of action (or powers of veto over public prosecution) should lie exclusively in the hands of victims where their private interests are impacted in ways that are not of serious public concern, but that in other instances (where *only* community interests are protected by the criminal law in question) it is proper that they lie solely in the hands of the State. That does not map the current configuration of rights of action because the existing law extends such rights not just to victims but to *anyone* in respect of *all* crimes. It is nonetheless illuminating in suggesting that we need to be more discriminating in our understanding of crimes and potentially even prepared to adjust the configuration of rights of action in ways that are responsive to the types of interest that a particular criminal law is designed to protect.

C. Rationale

The above discussion discloses several possible reasons for the persistence of the general right of private criminal prosecution in England and Wales. Despite what Lord Bingham said in *Jones v Whalley*,[226] it is not simply an historical anomaly. The suggestion that it is anomalous flies flat in the face of the legislative commitment made to retaining the right in 1985 and the vigour with which it is currently being exercised in English courts. One explanation, mooted above, might be that some criminal laws are designed for the protection of private, not just public interests, so that the right replicates the sort of moral logic I suggested sometimes supports private rights of action (and damages remedies) under the Human Rights Act. But this explanation is clearly inadequate, because the right of action extends to *all* citizens—whether or not personally affected by a crime—and to *all* offences, even those, like tax evasion, that protect purely public interests. The same difficulty thwarts claims that the right of action embodies a victim's historic moral entitlement to be personally involved in the fate of his or her offender. Ways to involve and empower victims do now exist at several stages of the criminal process[227] and are valuable for a host of good reasons that relate to respect for their dignity and healing (as well as the rehabilitation of the criminal), but the general right of

[226] [2007] 1 AC 63 (HL) 73 ('a somewhat anomalous survival').

[227] The key example is the right of victims (since 2013) to seek a review of public decisions not to prosecute: Crown Prosecution Service, *Victims' Right to Review—Policy and Guidance* (2020); T Kirchengast, 'Victims Rights and Right to Review: a Corollary of the Victim's Pre-Trial Rights to Justice' (2016) 5 International Journal for Crime, Justice and Social Democracy 103. Others include the right of victims to make victim impact statements prior to an offender's sentencing, and opportunities for victims to meet with their offenders at the post-sentencing stage to attempt reconciliation.

private prosecution, not being restricted to victims, is again not explicable on this rationale.

The second and more convincing explanation is therefore that the right is a constitutional safeguard against actual or perceived failures in the public enforcement process—whether these stem from public prosecutorial bias, selectivity in charging processes flowing from resourcing constraints, risk aversion, or straightforward incompetence. There are a host of public statements supporting this understanding—judicial,[228] academic,[229] and in the public debates leading up to the enactment of the 1985 Act.[230] In this way of thinking, the right supplements other checks upon the efficacy of the public prosecution system, such as the police complaints system (which is bizarrely still not truly independent in many jurisdictions in Australia) and rights to seek CPS review, and the rules of administrative law that bind prosecutorial decision-making. But it is much more powerful than any of these because it grants citizens the power to force an offender to answer a legal claim without any executive involvement at all. Despite the independence of the CPS from the police service, concerns about public agency capture also justify the safeguard in some instances, as, for example, when a prime minister, or other official with public power and influence, is the identified object of a controversial criminal complaint. It is also possible that ignorance and involuntary bias plague public prosecutorial attitudes in certain types of case, including (still!) some of the most terrible instances of domestic violence.[231] This being so, private rights of action can again potentially act as a nudge to public agents to reformulate prosecutorial policy, or to take a more interested and energetic approach in particular cases, even where a private prosecution fails.

If, however, the statistics to which I have alluded above are correct, agency capture and involuntary bias are not the main explanation for the continued use of the safeguard in England and Wales. The real problem is resourcing. And if this is the problem, nudging public prosecutors to engage in more vigorous action through private enforcement is not going to help, because they have no space to move. If money and time are so short that our public system can no longer cope with the regulatory task we have given it, then private rights of action can do nothing to impel public agents toward greater diligence. Instead, they are acting once again as a primary, front-line resource. The resourcing issue is not a product of more crime

[228] *Gujra* (n 175) 496 (Lord Wilson JSC), 504 (Lord Neuberger MR), 509 (Lord Mance JSC), 520 (Baroness Hale JSC); *Whalley* (n 226) 79 (Lord Mance); *Gouriet* (n 25) 477 (Lord Wilberforce) 498 (Lord Diplock). Judicial views are, however, not universally supportive: see *Whalley* (n 226) 71, 73 (Lord Bingham) (Lords Rodger, Carswell, and Brown agreeing).

[229] See eg V Michel, *Prosecutorial Accountability and Victims' Rights in Latin America* (CUP 2017) (private prosecution acts as a tool of public accountability in respect of the public system and contributes to the rule of law 'from below').

[230] Hansard (HL Debates), 29 November 1984, col 1068 (Lord Simon of Glaisdale).

[231] For a notorious recent example in Queensland, see <https://www.theguardian.com/australia-news/2020/feb/24/man-pleads-guilty-to-petrol-splashing-despite-queensland-police-refusal-to-lay-charges> accessed 5 December 2025.

per se, because overall crime rates have been falling since the mid-1990s.[232] Rather, it lies in public financing restrictions during the recent economic downturn and a political deprioritization of justice relative to other social ends.

The possibility that we might once more genuinely need private citizens as supplementary primary enforcers of the criminal law and protectors of the public interest is confronting. At the same time, it may suggest that the best solution to the current private prosecution controversies and scandals is not reactively to ban private actions, or further restrict the costs recoverable by private prosecutors, but to think again about the resources needed for public ones. If the history of private prosecution associations tells us anything, it is that if we fix the public enforcement deficit, the market for private enforcement solutions will dry up of its own accord. That would then leave the private right of action to be what it was intended to be when it was left in place in 1985—a residual constitutional check on the State's enforcement monopoly and a prompt for public agents constantly to assess their own practices for the public good, rather than a genuinely weight-bearing prop in a prosecutorial enterprise, the walls of which are visibly cracking.

7.4 Summation

The examples forming the focus of this chapter have been limited in number, but their detail, I realize, has been intense, so it is again worth drawing out the themes. Across all of them—public nuisance, actions *qui tam*, citizen suits, and the residual right of criminal prosecution—there is a much higher level of controversy about the persistence of private rights of action than we encountered in the last chapter. The idea that private citizens should enforce each other's observance of public laws is simply more threatening to modern legal constitutions than the idea that they should have rights to sue the State for the breach of its own public law duties, or to enforce the State's own public liabilities. Where the serious sanctions and social stigma of a criminal conviction are at stake, the controversy is especially acute on account of the greater fallout and moral risk associated with an improper prosecution.

Nonetheless, the main point is that there is no sign of private rights of action disappearing across the areas we have examined. In fact, clear attempts have been made to reinvigorate them, or even to introduce them *de novo* in particular contexts. The rise in private prosecutions in England, the explosion of suits under the Federal Claims Act, and the great number of federal regulatory statutes in the United States now containing citizen suit provisions all signal a fresh, twenty-first century enthusiasm for harnessing of citizens to the service of the public good. This represents a startling reversion of sorts to more ancient patterns. Most of the

[232] Office for National Statistics, *Crime in England and Wales: Year ending September 2023*.

rights of action we have examined (save those in respect of the common law wrong of public nuisance) now have a statutory basis and therefore sit upon a properly democratic footing, which reduces their constitutional controversy in most (but not all) jurisdictions. Figure 7.1 again provides a snapshot of the various enforcement patterns, checks and interests at stake, which may serve as a summative aid.

An easy provisional conclusion is that persistence of the rights we have examined is not explicable on any single rationale. Sometimes, the laws enforced privately are designed to protect private as well as public interests. This may help explain, I suggested, why private parties have their own rights to sue for damage done to them by a public nuisance at common law in many cases. In a significant proportion of the instances we have examined, however, the interest protected through the private action is purely public and the reasons for empowering citizens are pragmatic—private actions are either nudges[233] to reticent officials to engage in better public enforcement, or they meet residual concerns over public agency capture; or they provide additional front-line prosecutorial resources at times when public money is short, or they provide private initiative in the prosecution of particular offences (such as financial fraud, the breach of environmental regulations, animal cruelty, and so on) that are impossible, or prohibitively expensive, for State agents to discover on their own. Whether full rights of action are necessary to solve the last of these (informational) problems is open to question: if information were the *only* problem, then rewards for providing it to public agents might be enough to deal with the issue. On any of these pragmatic hypotheses, however, the existence of private rights of action is a function of a public enforcement deficit of one sort or another and the result is that one can expect the extent to which the rights are *actually used* to vary greatly and across time, according to the ratio between a State's regulatory ambitions, on the one hand, and the resources available to it to meet them, on the other. The greater the ambition and the smaller the public resource, the more probable it is that private enforcement will feature in the picture.

Finally, we have seen that in some jurisdictions—the United States in particular—private rights of action represent complex political compromises between competing models of the regulatory State, one maximal and one minimal, in a constitutional framework in which power is highly fragmented and Congressional politics so oppositional that neither vision has been fully allowed to prevail.

Whatever the explanation for the existence of a private right of action in a given case, it is clear that wherever it is used to protect a public interest, the State is closely involved in controlling its exercise in a way that it is (for very good reason) *not* involved where its own duties are being enforced. In some instances, the control

[233] A nudge is helpfully described, in Sunstein's lexicon, as being a liberty-preserving measure that steers its object in a particular direction, but which nonetheless leaves him or her free to go his or her own way: C Sunstein, 'Nudging: A Very Short Guide' (2014) 37 Journal of Consumer Policy 583, 583.

Law(s)	Duty	Interests Protected	Enforcement (right of action)	Private Enforcement Condition	Prior Executive Permission Required?	Judicial Permission Required?	Compensation Remedy?
Public Nuisance (Common Law)	Public	Public + Private	1. Public (AG ex officio) +	1. N/a	1. Yes	1. No	1. No
			2. Private (Relator) +	2. Anyone	2. Yes	2. No	2. No
			3. Private ('Tort')	3. Special Damage	3. No	3. No	3. As of Right Corrective Justice
Statutory Nuisance (EPA 1990)	Public	Public	1. Public + 2. Private	Private Interest ('aggrieved')	No	No	Discretionary (compensation orders) Distributive Justice
False Claims Act	Public	Public	1. Public + 2. Private (incentivised)	Anyone – fresh/useful information relevant, but requirement waivable by State.	No (but State may terminate at any time)	No	No (no compensation for enforcer – compensation goes to the State)
Clean Air Act 1970 §7604	Public	Public	1. Public + 2. Private	Anyone (but 'injury in fact' required for court jurisdiction)	No, but State may terminate w/n 60 days)	No	No. Costs only.
Criminal Laws (General)	Public	Public + Private	1. Public + 2. Private	Anyone	No (subject to some exceptions) but state may terminate at any time	No	Discretionary (compensation orders) Distributive Justice

Figure 7.1 Enforcement Rights in Respect of Citizen Duties

consists in a prior executive permission requirement, but this strategy has proven too restrictive for private actions to have any real (as opposed to a purely symbolic) function, so that this approach is not favoured in recent statutory examples. A more common approach under the statutes we have examined is hence for the private right of action to be accompanied by key notification duties, and by post-initiation powers for the State to intervene in the action for good public reasons. In all cases in which serious criminal sanctions are threatened, these powers of intervention persist even when the State has initially declined to be involved in running the action, but in others that threaten only civil penalties, State control diminishes once it has first allowed the action to proceed. Where the State does exercise power to intervene and terminate an action, that decision is itself often subject to the power of an interested individual to seek review, so that each exercise of private power is subject to a public one and vice-versa. There is a complex and subtle distribution of power.

I have stated the view that a private right of action in the criminal law should only be granted to a citizen or association if it is accompanied by a liability to yield to the State in this way and that a duty to notify the State of an action is a key and necessary precaution in the mix. Whatever else one thinks about the Texas Heartbeat law, the complete absence of State powers to intervene and terminate the private action is therefore a highly problematic feature, irrespective of the issue of personal reward. I have also suggested that State powers of intervention and termination are in principle a more desirable form of control than prior consent conditions, or rights of action that are so constrained in terms of their standing requirements ('special damage', for example) as to be of no practical use to the majority of publicly interested parties that could usefully be yoked to the common weal. Open standing rules, accompanied by normal court powers to deal with vexatious or ill-motivated litigants seem to me to be a better model for most of the public interest actions that we have examined.

A final preliminary conclusion is that the use of reward incentives in combination with rights of action is a dangerous mix and usually a mark of some desperation. The satisfaction of doing public good (and recoupment of the full costs of so doing) should generally be incentive enough for the ethical use of private initiative. If, however, the need for law enforcement is urgent and public exigencies require it, the risks of such reward systems can be moderated to some degree if careful thinking (and public resources) are dedicated to the architecture of accompanying public checks. The False Claims Act appears to me still to provide the best template we have for moderating these risks, if this choice is made in the modern era.

8

Private Law, Private Enforcement

We turn now to rights of action in private law.[1] Private law, as I defined it in Chapter 2, comprises all the legal relations (rights, duties, powers, liabilities, and so on) that exist 'horizontally' between 'private' persons. These are typically described by property law, contract, most of the law of unjust enrichments,[2] trusts and fiduciary obligations, and most (but not all)[3] of the modern law of torts. Private law primarily protects private interests and was historically always enforced privately. Subject to some limited exceptions to which we turn in the next chapter, this remains the case today.

8.1 Preview

This chapter takes a closer look at the dominant private enforcement paradigm across some of these fields, mapping the location of rights of action within them and the limited conditions attaching to their exercise. The basic rule, we shall see, is that enforcement rights are granted to those—and only those—who hold the primary rights that are at issue in the relevant proceeding ('right-holders'), but that there are some exceptional instances in which they are accorded to third parties. This is usually with the right-holder's permission, but not always. In some instances, other persons who are able to show a sufficient private interest in the enforcement of the right-holder's rights are permitted the right of suit. We examine possible justifications both for the basic 'right-holder' rule and for the various exceptions.

The final part of the chapter tackles a residual controversy about the types of interest protected by the private enforcement process, which is evident in the continuing availability of exemplary or 'punitive' damages in some cases. Like the private right of criminal prosecution examined at the end of the last chapter, the right of plaintiffs to claim exemplary damages is proving obstinately resistant to

[1] For a detailed exposition of some of these rights in contract, tort and the law of trusts see T Liau, *Standing in Private Law* (OUP 2023); L Smith, *The Law of Loyalty* (OUP 2023) Ch 8.

[2] Exceptions are the peculiar liabilities of the State for overpayment of tax made by private citizens (*Woolwich Equitable Building Society v Inland Revenue Commissioners* [1993] AC 70 (HL)) and the peculiar liability of citizens to repay ultra vires overpayments made to them by government, both at common law (*Auckland Harbour Board v R* [1924] AC 318 (PC)) and under statute.

[3] Exceptions are the torts of public nuisance and misfeasance in public office.

Enforcement Rights in Public and Private Law. Kit Barker, Oxford University Press. © Kit Barker 2026.
DOI: 10.1093/9780191955006.003.0011

abolition, despite being clearly out of kilter with the prevailing view that public interests should be protected through public law by public agents. Public law's lingering appetite for the use of private initiative in the protection of public interests is hence carried through into private law. Rather than questioning the continuing availability of exemplary damages here, I instead pause to examine the logical implications of remaining committed to their public interest rationale for the structure of enforcement rights and the proper distribution of awards. If private enforcers are in such cases really involved in protecting public interests and punishing wrongdoers, why is it, I ask, that the State has no right to intervene in the proceeding, as it does in criminal prosecutions, to ensure that such awards promote the public good? I also ask why it is that the benefit of awards is almost always permitted to inure to private enforcers, rather than to the broader community whose interests they purportedly serve, and explore ways in which the current pattern of distribution might be changed for the better.

8.2 The Dominant Enforcement Regime—Rights of Action for 'Right' Holders

A. Holders of All Types of 'Right'

The basic paradigm of private law enforcement is that it is those who hold the primary (substantive) 'rights' that hold the rights of action.[4] Those entitled to enforce a contract are hence the contracting parties holding the rights to its performance; it is the libelled celebrity who has the power to sue for the tort of defamation, no one else; it is the beneficiaries of a trust who presumptively have the power to enforce the trustee's duties; and the person with the right to sue for restitution of a mistaken payment in unjust enrichment law is the person at whose expense the payment was mistakenly made.

Although the right of action in these instances is usually vested in the holder of a primary claim right, this is not always the case. In the mistaken payment example, for instance, the payer seeking restitution has no primary claim right in respect of the money at the time her action is initiated, since her legal title to it technically passed to the payee with the payment, notwithstanding the mistake. Her right of action is therefore thought to be paired instead with either a *remedial* claim right to get the money (actually, its value) back that exists from the moment the payment is received, or, possibly, with a legal *power* to bring that consequence about. There is some disagreement about which (if either) of these

[4] *Bateman's Bay Local Aboriginal Land Council v Aboriginal Community Benefit Fund Pty Ltd* (1998) 194 CLR 247 [43] (espousing a 'general' equation between standing and the 'elements of a cause of action').

analyses is correct,[5] but whichever view one takes, the payer's right of action is clearly no longer paired with a primary claim right, because that primary claim right has gone.

The same is true where a person initiates proceedings to rescind a voidable contract or gift that has been induced by another's misrepresentation, duress, undue influence, or unconscionable dealing. Here again, she asserts no claim right in the action, but a legal power to set the transaction aside, exercisable at her election.[6] This is also the case where the beneficiaries of a trust seek to impugn a transaction that a trustee has entered into with a third party (or himself, in a case of self-dealing) in excess of administrative authority.[7] In such instances, the beneficiaries are again wielding legal powers and enforcing a defendant's *liability* to having his or her contractual or property rights altered. The fact that only a power and not a claim right is involved is clear from the fact that the plaintiff must take active steps to exercise the power to rescind, before the defendant's rights or duties change.

Rights of action are also sometimes exercised by persons asserting legal liberties, or immunities. The examples are less visible, since it is unusual for a person with a liberty or immunity to initiate an action to 'enforce' it, as opposed to *defending* an action initiated by someone else who is intent on asserting the 'opposite' duty or liability against her. It is nonetheless clearly possible. Imagine, for example, that

[5] For variants of the view that the restitutionary plaintiff has a 'power only' see P Jaffey, 'Hohfeld's Power–Liability/Right–Duty Distinction in the Law of Restitution' (2004) 17 Canadian Journal of Law & Jurisprudence 295, esp 301–04; S Smith, 'A Duty to Make Restitution' (2013) 26 Canadian Journal of Law and Jurisprudence 157, 166; S Smith, 'The Restatement of Liabilities in Restitution' in C Mitchell and W Swadling (eds), *The Restatement Third: Restitution and Unjust Enrichment: Critical and Comparative Essays* (Hart 2013) Ch 10, 227. A potential problem with this view is that it struggles to explain why D has an *immediate* duty to repay the money as soon as it is received (indicated by his or her obligation to pay interest as from that date) without P first having *exercised* the power. A third analysis, which connects to the argument set out in Chapter 3 Section 3.3B (this book), is that P has neither an immediate remedial claim right nor an immediate legal power to impose a remedial duty on D at the time the payment is received, and that the power to create the restitutionary duty always lies with the court once P's claim has been lodged. On this view, all that P has at the time the action is launched is a bare right of action—a power to enliven the court's power (and duty) to grant a restitutionary remedy. When the remedy is granted, an award of interest compensates for the fact that remedy could not be granted instantaneously. Parallel controversies arise in cases involving wrongdoing, where there is an active debate as to whether D has an immediate secondary (remedial) duty to P when a wrong is committed, or is simply liable—once P has initiated the action—to the court's power to impose a duty to pay damages through its order. For the former view see J Gardner, 'What Is Tort Law For? Part 1: The Place of Corrective Justice' (2011) 30 Law & Philosophy 1; J Gardner, 'Damages without Duty' (2019) 69 University of Toronto Law Journal 412 (the wrongdoer's remedial duty substitutes immediately for the primary one as the 'next best thing' to performing it); S Steel and R Stevens, 'The Secondary Duty to Pay Damages' (2020) 136 Law Quarterly Review 283; Liau (n 1) 6, 64 fn 61.

[6] See generally, D O'Sullivan, S Elliot, and R Zakrzewski, *The Law of Rescission* (3rd edn, OUP 2023). At law, the plaintiff's election is still thought to effect rescission without any requirement for a court order—the plaintiff has a right of action that accompanies a legal power herself to alter the defendant's rights and duties. In equity, the position is more confused owing to the existence of court discretion and a level of conflict in the authorities—see Ch 11 ibid esp 266–68, 268–84. In such cases, the exercise of the plaintiff's right of action vests the court itself with the power to alter the parties' rights and duties.

[7] Smith (n 1) 285. In such instances, although the beneficiaries clearly do have claim rights, it is not these that they assert in the action but powers to set the transaction aside.

a doctor wishes to obtain an advance declaration from a court that she is under no duty to administer treatment to a patient who is demanding it, or (as is more often the case) whose relatives are demanding it.[8] The doctor may bring an action to obtain a declaratory order, but the primary 'right' she seeks to protect in so doing is a liberty, the point of the action being to establish that she is *free* of a particular obligation to the patient. There are similarly a great many cases in which plaintiffs regularly ask courts to declare the non-existence of: a debt;[9] another's contractual power to make deductions from their wages;[10] easements over their land;[11] or other adverse interests that might affect the sale, lease, or distribution of property that they own, or are charged to administrate. Landowners may seek a declaration of their liberty to exclude others from entering upon it,[12] or of their immunity to the purported exercise by someone else of an option to purchase it.

The upshot is that, although it is often considered to be a rule in private law that rights of action are wedded to primary claim rights,[13] the basic paradigm actually connects them to a much wider group of 'rights'—in fact, to the entire group of Hohfeldian 'advantages' (claim rights, powers, liberties, and immunities) that we identified in Chapter 3.[14] Although this was not made explicit in previous chapters, the same is true of rights of action in public law: a private party may, for example, seek a declaration of her legal liberty or immunity in respect of a public law that is constitutionally invalid,[15] or claim an immunity to some change in her public

[8] *Portsmouth Hospitals NHS Trust v Wyatt* [2005] EWCA Civ 1181 (application for declaration of liberty not to continue treatment of a child against the wishes of its parents); *Aintree University Hospital NHS Foundation Trust v David James and Ors* [2013] EWCA Civ 65 (application for declaration of liberty not to resuscitate a child against the wishes of the parents).

[9] See eg *Chapman v Michaelson* [1908] 2 Ch 612; *Collins v Marinovich* [2021] QSC 141; *Macks v Viscariello* [2017] SASCFC 172 [11]; *Kenny v Carkeek* [2007] FMCA 510.

[10] *Collette v Lochie, Pemberton & Co* 63 Sol J 24 (Ch 1918); *Lofthouse Colliery v Ogden* [1913] 3 KB 120.

[11] *Clark v Barnes* [1929] 2 Ch 368; *Treweeke v 36 Wolseley Road Pty Ltd* (1973) 128 CLR 274; *Weigall v Toman* [2006] QSC 349.

[12] *London & North-Eastern Railway Co v Chester & Son* 147 LTR 308 (KB 1932).

[13] See eg B Zipursky, 'Substantive Standing, Civil Recourse, and Corrective Justice' (2011) 39 Florida State University Law Review 299, 306; A Goldberg and B Zipursky, *Recognizing Wrongs* (Harvard University Press 2020) 112 (correlating powers to obtain redress with the infringement of a plaintiff's rights and the breach of legal duties owed to him or her); Liau (n 1) 81, 92: the general rule in private law is that 'only the primary right-holder has the standing . . . to sue to enforce his rights (and no-one else)', 'enforcement is generally exclusive to the right-duty relation'. Goldberg and Zipursky's focus on claim rights stems from the context (tortious wrongs) that they are primarily concerned to investigate, where actions are invariably brought in respect of an actual or threatened breach of a defendant's primary legal duty, so it is hard to know whether they would correlate rights of action with other primary legal incidents outside this context.

[14] See Edelman and Steward JJ (dissenting) in *Hobart International Airport Pty Ltd v Clarence City Council* [2022] HCA 5 [79], where their Honours said that a person normally only has standing to bring a claim where they have a 'right', the term 'right' meaning a Hohfeldian claim right, power, privilege (liberty), or immunity, 'or their correlative concepts'. The alignment of rights of action with all of the Hohfeldian incidents is most obviously revealed in applications for declaratory relief, where the truth was recognized long ago by E Borchard in *Declaratory Judgments* (2nd edn, Banks-Baldwin Law Publishing Co 1941) esp 19–22, 211–12, 229.

[15] *Unions NSW v NSW* [2023] HCA 5 (provided she has a sufficient interest).

duties (perhaps a duty to pay more in tax) by seeking judicial review of an unlawful public decision.

B. No Permission Required

The key distinction between cases in which private parties enforce private laws and the exceptional cases in which they are permitted to enforce public laws that we examined in the last two chapters, is that neither executive nor court permission is required for the exercise of a plaintiff's right of action. *Executive* permission to exercise the right is unnecessary on the traditional analysis because the private law claim protects private interests, not public ones, and the liberal State has no business controlling the assertion of our interests against one another. Even where the remedy claimed by a plaintiff has a public interest dimension (as in the case of exemplary damages, to which we shall come) the State's consent is unnecessary because the plaintiff is simultaneously (and primarily) protecting a private interest of her own in the same proceeding. The fear of vexatious litigation that sometimes generates requirements for *judicial* permission to commence public law proceedings, while not entirely absent, is also less prominent in private law, precisely because litigants are generally restricted to those whose own private rights are implicated. Concerns about ill-motivated or unfounded claims are handled through courts' powers to terminate actions for abuse of process at the post-initiation stage, not by policing the initiation of actions in the first place.

The consequence, John Gardner observed, is that rights of action in private law are in one way more potent than in public law, because they are 'radically discretionary'.[16] By this, he meant that the conditions attending their exercise are 'few and pro forma' and that the rights can legally be exercised unreasonably against 'anybody . . . for anything'.[17] Whether the discretion is quite as radical as this sweeping phrase suggests is doubtful for reasons we addressed in Chapter 3,[18] but it is certainly true that the absence of permission requirements sets private claims in private law apart from most (but not all) of those in public law. Private law rights of action are also paired with powers to terminate a proceeding at any later time (and for any reason) that are again not subject to court or State *fiat*. Gardner expressed concern about their 'illiberal' oppressive potential,[19] and with some justification.

[16] J Gardner, *From Personal Life to Private Law* (OUP 2018) 201.

[17] ibid 200–201.

[18] Chapter 3 Section 3.4. See also L Katz and M Shapiro, 'The Role of Plaintiffs in Private Law Institutions' in H Psarras and S Steel (eds), *Private Law and Practical Reason* (OUP 2023) Ch 14, 247–49 (suggesting that Gardner's own continuity thesis suggests that private litigators have reasons to use their powers only for the (corrective justice) reasons that they were accorded those powers, not for abusive or collateral purposes, and noting that this yields some tension with his expressed view that they can be exercised for any reason at all).

[19] Gardner, *From Personal Life to Private Law* (n 16) 202.

Not only do rights of action fix courts with public powers and duties to hear a claim but they also, remember, saddle defendants with public liabilities and duties to respond to them, and this can be a burdensome business. The cost of defending defamation actions, for example, is well known to be crippling, and the onus of proving the truth of a defamatory statement lies in both England and Australia on the defendant, so that a well-funded plaintiff may despotically wield its right of action to deter all but the boldest from exercising their liberty to speak the truth.[20]

8.3 Rights of Action without Primary 'Rights'

Although rights of action in private law usually vest in primary right-holders, they can also be held by other persons. Proving this point has been one of the aims of Tim Liau's excellent recent work on 'standing' in private law,[21] and the chain of analytical reasoning that I have previously articulated, and which now appears in Chapter 3,[22] strongly supports that position. Here, I address some of the examples discussed by Liau and others. Many of these are true examples of the point, but some, I suggest, are false, or so open to alternative interpretations that the thesis cannot safely be rested upon them.

A. Agents, Private Guardians

Agency and guardianship are true exceptions that are perhaps so uncontroversial that they have tended to pass notice.[23] In both instances, a right of action is exercised by a representative of the right-holder to enforce the *latter's* primary or secondary rights. Agency is a liberal arrangement that enables right-holders to 'contract out' the enforcement task; and guardianship grants others (parents, for example) the power to act where right-holders themselves lack legal capacity. These cases are not greatly troubling to those taking the traditional view that a person's private rights are his or her 'own business', since the stranger's power of suit is either consistent with the right-holder's consent (in the former case) or protective of their interests when they are legally incapable of giving it (in the latter).

[20] The power of large, commercial corporate entities to do this is now restricted in Australia by the removal of their right of action in defamation proceedings through Uniform legislation (see eg Defamation Act 2005 (Qld) s 9), but this does not remove the problem entirely.

[21] Liau (n 1).

[22] K Barker, 'Rights of Action in Public and Private Law: The Analytics of Enforcement' (1 June 2021) <http://dx.doi.org/10.2139/ssrn.3883088>.

[23] But see Smith (n 1) 285–87. Guardianship arrangements can vary greatly, but guardians of a person's personal affairs (such as his or her healthcare arrangements) are not generally transferees of the represented person's primary rights, instead being given powers in relation to those rights. On the origins of guardianship and modern practice see further Chapter 9.

B. Class Action Representatives

A third example lies in modern class action procedures, which enable representative plaintiffs to enforce the rights of other right-holders in the same litigant class.[24] Sometimes this requires the right-holder's prior consent through an 'opt-in' procedure, but increasingly these days, the onus is on the latter to 'opt out' instead.[25] The consent of the right-holder is hence ultimately respected under both models,[26] but in the latter instance, she must assert a negative choice if she is to prevent another asserting her rights, which has implications for her freedom of action. The aim of the procedure is to promote the collective interests of the victim class while overcoming the difficulties that would otherwise arise, if the prior consent of every similarly affected plaintiff were required before the action could be launched. It addresses a collective action problem. This system of private, *ex post* right-holder veto is similar to the State's power to terminate private prosecutions in the criminal law. In both instances, the right-holder has the last word on any third party's use of the right of action.

C. Indemnity Insurers Exercising Subrogation Rights

A fourth example is provided by cases in which an insurer may 'take over' and enforce an insured's existing primary right against a debtor, where it is itself contractually liable to cover the debt. The process is (beguilingly) known in Charles Mitchell's language as 'simple' subrogation.[27] The insurer's action is brought in the name of the insured; and the debt itself is never formally 'assigned' to the insurer, so that the substantive right asserted belongs to the insured.[28] Dennis Ong explains:

[24] See generally, R Mulheron, *The Class Action in Common Law Legal Systems: A Comparative Perspective* (Hart 2004); P Karlsgodt (ed), *World Class Actions: A Guide to Group and Representative Actions Around the Globe* (OUP 2021). Another example of a representative right of action exercised to protect the rights of a broader class is that enjoyed by a petitioning creditor in a company's liquidation, where the petitioner represents the rights of all creditors, not just his or her own: *Re International Tin Council* [1987] Chs 419, 456 (Millett J). The petitioner in such instances must meet distinct standing rules: R Goode, *Principles of Corporate Insolvency Law* (2nd edn, Sweet & Maxwell 1997) 110–14.

[25] Mulheron (n 24) 29–38. These are just two models in a more complex range. Other, more controversial possibilities allow no opt out, opt out at the court's discretion, or for flexible judicial decision as between opt in and opt out, depending on the facts. Currently, opt in is still the more common model in the UK (although things are changing) and opt out in the US.

[26] There is sometimes an exception, where the final relief sought is injunctive or declaratory only, in which case there may be no opt-out option. This is the position under US Federal Civil Procedure rules: Fed R Civ P 23 (b)(2) (cited in Mulheron (n 24) at 31–32). It remains controversial: S Cottreau, 'The Due Process Right to Opt Out of Class Actions' (1988) 73 New York University Law Review 480.

[27] C Mitchell, *The Law of Subrogation* (OUP 1995) Chs 6, 13. For full discussion, see C Mitchell and S Watterson, *Subrogation Law and Practice* (OUP 2007) 5–6, Ch 10; D Ong, *Ong on Subrogation* (Federation Press 2014) Ch 3, esp 88–129; C Mitchell, P Mitchell, and S Watterson (eds), *Goff and Jones on Unjust Enrichment* (10th edn, Sweet & Maxwell 2022) Ch 21.

[28] For the insurer to sue *in its own name* it must have received a full assignment of the primary debt, whether by way of contract, or statute: *Esso Petroleum Co Ltd v Hall Russell & Co Ltd* [1989] AC 643,

> Subrogation is 'the equitable doctrine' that confers on A (without the necessity for B to *assign* to A the right of B as against C) the right to exercise, for A's sole benefit, this right of B as against C. However, the right so conferred on A merely entitles A to exercise, for A's sole benefit, B's right as against C. Subrogation does not *transfer* to A the right of B as against C.[29]

True it is, in this instance, that the indemnifying insurer (A) has a primary (contingent)[30] contractual right *as against the insured* (B) of its own that *explains and undergirds* its entitlement to enforce the insured's primary right against the debtor (C). But the existing primary right that the insurer's action enforces against the debtor when 'subrogating' is still the insured's right, not the insurer's.[31] The point is that private law sometimes, in the interest of protecting one person's rights (here, the insurer's) against another, gives that person the power to assert the rights (and collect in the debts) of the other. Where this is by agreement with the right-holder, as in this particular case,[32] it is again consistent with the latter's consent.

D. Contract: Third Party Rights

Superficially (but this time probably *only* superficially) one of the strongest examples of a right of action held by someone other than a primary right-holder is the right that a third-party beneficiary of a contract enjoys under the Contracts (Rights of Third Parties) Act 1999 (UK) (CRTPA) to enforce the contract.[33] The right of action in this instance is not, on its face, based on the beneficiary's own

663 (Lord Goff). For discussion, see further Ong (n 27) Ch 1, Ch 8 esp 90–99; Mitchell, Mitchell, and Watterson (eds) (n 27) [21.114]–[21.119].

[29] Ong (n 27) 1.

[30] One condition is that the indemnity first be paid by the insurer: Mitchell and Watterson (n 27) 326–27.

[31] *Blaauwpot v Da Costa* (1758) 1 Eden 130, 131; 28 ER 633, 634. This may in turn explain why (1) defences that would have been available as against the insured are also available to the debtor in the action by the insurer (*Lister v Romford Ice & Cold Storage Co* [1956] 2 QB 180, 191 (Lord Denning MR); (2) the insurer cannot bring a subrogation claim where the insured is a company that has been wound up (*MH Smith (Plant Hire) Ltd v DL Mainwaring (t/a Inshore)* [1986] 2 Lloyd's Rep 244; and (3) the claim will fail if the insured has previously released the debtor from liability. There is nonetheless some ambiguity on this point in the authorities stemming in part from the confusion of cases involving subrogation and assignment of the insured's right, and from certain procedural aspects of the subrogation claim. See further Ong (n 27) 88–114; Mitchell, Mitchell, and Watterson (eds) (n 27) [21.37]–[21.92].

[32] Insurance contracts do not always contain a subrogation clause, so that the right may sometimes exist even without the right-holder's consent, by operation of the law of unjust enrichment: Mitchell and Watterson (n 27) 6; Mitchell, Mitchell, and Watterson (eds) (n 27) [21.04]–[21.06]. There is an analogy in such instances with cases in which liquidators have rights to collect debts owing to debtors in order to satisfy the latter's obligations to their creditors. This again requires no consent. See further Chapter 9 Section 9.4D text to n 138.

[33] CRTPA s 1(1); Liau (n 1) Chs 6, 7 esp 112–15; 'Privity: Rights, Standing and the Road Not Taken (2021) 41 Oxford Journal of Legal Studies 803.

primary claim right to performance, since he has no such claim right at common law. Instead, it looks like a right to enforce a primary claim right belonging to the promisee.

The basis of the third party right of action is not clearly stated in the statute, but its most plausible justification is that the right promotes the autonomy of the contracting parties and the commercial facility of the contracting mechanism more generally.[34] Private parties are permitted, at their own volition, to extend rights of action to others to enforce an agreement's terms where it suits them. This rationale explains why the right of action extends not just to potential beneficiaries of the contract—those who have a personal interest in its performance—but to *anyone* identified by the parties by name, description, or class.[35]

Although the statute appears to create a private right of action for third parties who lack primary contractual rights, there is nonetheless a puzzle that complicates the analysis and which probably defeats it in all but the most exceptional case.[36] As Liau notes, for the third party to have a right to bring an action for *damages* in respect of his *own* loss (as he does), the Act must also be providing him with a new, secondary, *remedial* right that he did not previously have.[37] That means either that the Act is vesting *in the third party* a new and additional primary right to performance upon which to base that secondary, remedial right, or—oddly—that it is granting him a right to claim damages for loss suffered as a result of a wrong done to *someone else*: the promisee. Since secondary rights to damages in private law presumptively only vest in P in respect of the breach of primary claim rights *held by* P, it is then tempting to conclude that the Act in fact gives *both* rights of action *and* (silently) new primary contractual claim rights to named third parties. And if this is so, the Act does not actually provide an example of private rights of action uncoupled from primary claim rights after all—the third party holds *both* a primary claim right *and* a right of action at one and the same time. The traditional right-holder paradigm is vindicated, not refuted.

The thought that the Act gives new primary claim rights to a third-party seeking damages for breach of the contract's terms could simply be a consequence of the very assumption about the necessary correlation between rights of action and primary rights that Liau suggests we should be questioning. It also runs into complications of its own, including the fact that it involves *duplicating* the promisee's right

[34] Other justifications suggested by Liau (n 1) at 134–39 are a 'policy of anti-circumvention' that prevents promisors reneging on their promises; the inability of a promisee to sue; and the avoidance of 'lacunas' or remedial 'black holes'.

[35] Privity legislation in Australia differs in so far as the contract must also purport to confer a *benefit* on the third party: see eg Property Law Act 1974 (Qld) s 55 (1); Property Law Act 1969 (WA) s 11 (2).

[36] Assuming that the third-party enforcer is not a person who is suing for his own loss, or to protect his own interest in performance, and is just an agent who has been appointed to enforce the contracting parties' own respective rights and duties, his right of action will indeed be severed from any primary or secondary right, as Liau intimates. In practice, it is hard to find such a case, perhaps because appointing a solicitor as an ad hoc agent to act on one's behalf in a proceeding achieves exactly the desired result?

[37] Liau (n 1) 108–09, 113.

to performance in the third party,[38] and, as Liau says, it changes some of our fundamental inception doctrines of contractual obligation, because it sidesteps both the doctrine of privity and the doctrine of consideration in one go.[39] It is also at odds with the apparent purpose of the statute as stated in the preamble, which suggests that it is designed to provide a new means of 'enforcing' rights not (explicitly) of *creating* new ones.[40]

If, however, the Act does *not* grant new primary claim rights to third parties, but *does* give new remedial rights to claim damages, then we are left with the uncomfortable conclusion that it is not just rights of action that can be severed from primary claim rights in private law but remedial rights too. The third party not only gets her own right to sue under the Act, but a right to claim damages for losses she has suffered as a result of a wrong done to someone else. We did come across some examples of this in public law: plaintiffs in the law of public nuisance have secondary rights to seek damages for harm suffered as a result of a defendant's violation of primary public duties that are owed to the community as a whole, *not* specifically to the plaintiff, and individuals can now seek discretionary statutory compensation in many jurisdictions for criminal injuries caused by offenders' violation of duties that those offenders technically owe to the State.[41] It is therefore not *impossible* that this is the intention and effect of the privity statute, but such a construction is clearly controversial in a way that these examples are not. Why would one want to give a third party a right to claim compensation for a *personal* wrong done to someone else?

The public law examples, although superficially similar, do seem to be different. In cases of public nuisance, the injured plaintiff is at least one member of a community to which the primary public duty was owed and therefore intended to benefit by it; and criminal compensation schemes simply confer primary rights to seek financial support from the State on the occurrence of particular events. This is a compassionate exercise of distributive justice, a bit like handing cash out to the victims of a natural disaster. By contrast, the idea that A is entitled to damages for the violation of a private right vested in B is entirely alien to the norms of corrective justice that are generally instantiated in private law. This is Liau's point, of course—the Act could be an interesting exception. But the implications of that exceptionalism are so great that one must hesitate to accept it, if there are other viable explanations.

What Liau successfully shows, I think, is that third-party rights of action *could* and sometimes *should* exist in isolation from primary contractual rights, not that they generally[42] *do* under the English legislation. The more likely construction

[38] ibid 113 and fn 57.
[39] ibid 112–15.
[40] CRTPA, preamble. There is admittedly a latent ambiguity in the term 'enforce.'
[41] See eg Criminal Injuries Compensation Act 1995 (UK).
[42] See n 36 above.

of the Act, in my view, is that it grants third parties new primary contractual rights, liberties, and immunities, as well as rights of action. This is implied by the fictional (substantive) equation of the third party's rights with those of the parties themselves,[43] and by the provisions of the Act that give the promisor the right to assert a substantive defence (or counterclaim) to any claim brought by the third party that would have existed if the third party were actually a party to the contract.[44] True, this construction does upset traditional thinking about the inception doctrines of contractual obligation in so far as the third party need be neither a party, nor give consideration in order to obtain primary contractual rights, but the short answer is that it is open to Parliament to make limited changes to those doctrines if it thinks that doing so is useful to those using the contracting mechanism, and provided that it is consistent with the intentions of the contracting parties themselves.[45] Furthermore, while this does, as Liau says, replicate for the third party a primary performance right already held by the promisee, there is no reason why a promisor cannot owe two contractual duties of identical content to two different persons at one and the same time. This can cause problems if the parties wish to dissolve—or change the content of—the replicated duty, or if both promisee and third party sue the promisor simultaneously, but it remains a logical possibility and the Act contains provisions, however awkward, that are designed to accommodate challenges of this type.[46] Although the question we are considering is a specific one relating to the construction of the English statute, the suggestion that third-party beneficiaries have primary rights under the contract is consistent with the view expressed in the American *Restatement of Contracts*.[47]

Fortunately, there is a much clearer example than the CRPTA of the severance of rights of action from contractual claim rights, which can make Liau's point very nicely. In *Hobart International Airport Pty Ltd v Clarence City Council*,[48] a majority of the High Court of Australia held that a third-party council that was the nominated beneficiary of payment provisions under a Commonwealth lease had 'standing' to seek a declaration of the proper meaning of the lease's terms, even where that meaning was not disputed by the contracting parties themselves.

[43] CRTPA s 1(5).

[44] CRTPA s 3.

[45] It is ironic from this point of view that commercial parties regularly contract out of the provisions of the Act: H Beale, 'A Review of the Contracts (Rights of Third Parties) Act 1999' in A Burrows and E Peel, *Contract Formation and Parties* (OUP 2010) 229, 230–31. A likely reason is that there is a risk latent in the Act's presumption that it is the parties' intention to allow for third-party enforcement where the contract purports to confer a benefit on the third party (s 1(1)(b)): P Davies, 'Excluding the Contracts (Rights of Third Parties Act 1999' (2021)137 Law Quarterly Review 101. The risk might be moderated by the substitution of an express provision in the Act requiring the intention always to be objectively manifested.

[46] CRTPA s 2 (variation and rescission), s 5 (protection of promisor from double liability).

[47] *Restatement of Contracts* (2nd) § 304, § 302. I am grateful to Lance Green for drawing this to my attention.

[48] *Hobart* (n 14).

The majority accepted the conventional position that a person seeking such a declaration must normally be the holder of the claim rights or liabilities declared, but did not consider the rule absolute. There is no bright line, it said, that divides the approach to standing in public law from that in private law.[49] Provided the third party has a 'sufficient' and 'real interest' in the question, it may enliven the powers of the court to seek declaratory relief, even if it not itself privy to the contract. Kiefel CJ and Keane and Gordon JJ concluded:

> Although lack of privity is a factor relevant to standing and a reason for a court approaching the question of the standing of an outsider with considerable caution, an outsider to a contract may, 'for other reasons'—what might be described as 'exceptional circumstances'—have a 'sufficient' or 'real' interest to seek declaratory relief as to the meaning and effect of a contract between contracting parties. As the Full Court put it below, 'there is reason to be concerned as to the potential for what might be described as unfounded intermeddling by a third party to a contract. But, in the context of declaratory relief, the solution to that concern is not the doctrine of privity of contract.'[50]

The point was reiterated in the separate judgment of Gageler and Gleeson JJ:

> That conception of standing has involved recognition that a person who does not claim to have a legal right or equitable interest to be vindicated by a declaration or other order that would resolve a controversy about a right or obligation may yet have a material interest in seeking the order. In this context, an interest will be 'material' if the person 'is likely to gain some advantage, other than the satisfaction of righting a wrong, upholding a principle or winning a contest, if [the order is made] or to suffer some disadvantage, other than a sense of grievance or a debt for costs, if [the order is not made]. Depending on the totality of the circumstances, the material interest that the person has in seeking the order may be sufficient to justify a court entertaining the proceeding in which the order is sought.[51]

On the facts, the plaintiff council had no primary legal right to performance of the lessee's payment obligations at common law, nor any equitable claim right (or power) under a trust of the lessee's promise to pay, but nonetheless had both a *real commercial interest* in seeking the declaration (as an intended beneficiary of the payments) and a *practical* one (because the terms of the contract described for it an active role in notifying the lessees of the proper payment amounts).[52] While a

[49] ibid [34]–[35] (Kiefel CJ, Keane and Gordon JJ). See also [67], [70]–[71] (Gageler and Gleeson JJ). cf contra Edelman and Steward JJ at [82], [84]–[99].

[50] ibid [34]–[35] (Kiefel CJ, Keane and Gordon JJ).

[51] ibid [65].

[52] ibid [38]–[39] (Kiefel CJ, Keane and Gordon JJ). See also [65], [74] (Gageler and Gleeson JJ): the plaintiff's interests were 'distinctive, substantial and squarely within the scope of those third-party

'mere' commercial interest in another's contract is not enough for a right of action, Kiefel CJ, Keane and Gordon JJ hence thought that a combination of exceptional circumstances may suffice.[53] They deliberately reserved their position in respect of cases in which the third party is seeking a remedy other than a declaration,[54] but there is, in fact, no logical reason why the preconditions of a person holding a *right of action* should differ according to the type of *remedy* sought, even if the conditions attaching to the availability of the remedies themselves vary. The contrary supposition confuses and conflates rights of action with remedial rights in a way that I have suggested is inappropriate in other parts of this book.[55] The grant of damages or injunctive relief to a third party to a contract clearly has consequences for the rights and liberties of those parties that the mere grant of a neutral declaration does not, so that coercive remedies of this type should probably only be awarded where the third party has herself been accorded a primary *right* to performance under the contract. This distinction, I nonetheless suggest, should go to a third party's entitlement to remedies at the end of a proceeding, not to his or her standing to bring a claim.

All of this, it must be admitted, was said in the context of the tricky and decisive question whether the *court* had *jurisdiction* (liberty and power) to hear the plaintiff's claim.[56] It also involved a suit to declare the claim rights of the Commonwealth government and their financial implications for local councils, so that the council's application for a declaration of the rights and obligations of the contracting parties might be construed as having an important *public* interest component. Gageler and Gordon JJ considered this to be a 'weighty' consideration in accepting the council's standing on the facts.[57] We have seen in previous chapters the way in which private rights of action are granted in public law precisely to ensure independent scrutiny of governmental action, and we shall witness a

interests that were sought in the public interest to be advanced through entering into the contractual obligation'; *Aussie Airlines Pty Ltd v Australian Airlines Ltd* (1996) 139 ALR 663.

53 *Hobart* (n 14) [41].

54 ibid. See, similarly, Gageler and Gleeson JJ at [57] (to have standing to seek a common law damages remedy, a plaintiff would have to be able to make out the elements of a substantive cause of action).

55 See eg Chapter 3 Section 3.5 and Chapter 6 Section 6.4A(ii) n 114 and text thereto, this book. The same confusion also materializes from time to time in the law of torts. Arguing strongly for the distinction in that context, see J Murphy, 'Unpicking Torts: Elements, Conditions of Actionability and Standing Rules' (2024) 87 Modern Law Review 1519, although Murphy labels the distinction in this context as one between 'standing' and 'conditions of actionability' (the latter being preconditions to 'obtaining a remedy') and ultimately concludes that there is no real evidence of any separate standing rules in the law of torts.

56 The question was whether the claim raised a 'matter' triggering the court's jurisdiction, a constituent part of which requires there to be a 'justiciable controversy'. That was in turn understood to depend on the plaintiff having standing to assert the claim.

57 *Hobart* (n 14) [69], [76] (Gageler and Gleeson JJ). Similar thinking may underpin *Aussie Airlines* (n 52). By contrast, in the reasoning of Edelman and Steward JJ at [134]–[136], standing premised on a public interest would have to be based some public *right* of the council (which may have existed, on their view, in *Aussie Airlines*).

similar pattern in cases involving claims for punitive damage in the final section of this chapter. This clearly adds some weight to this point of view. By contrast, however, the public interest in the dispute was not thought by Kiefel CJ, Keane and Gordon JJ to be key to the council's right of action, so that, as a matter of precedent, the case must be understood as having implications for third party rights of action beyond cases involving government contracts. It suggests that there may be exceptional instances in which third parties may have a right of action in respect of *any* type of contract, where a purpose of the contract is to protect or implicate the third party's own *private interests.*

The significance of this conclusion being drawn by the Court at common law is that the separation of the third party's right of action from any primary claim right held by her is crystal clear in a way that is it not under the CRTPA for reasons already discussed. An interesting difference in the foundation of the third-party right of action as between the CRTPA and the common law action in *Hobart* is that it is the expressed or implied intention of the contracting parties to create a right of action that gives rise to it in the former case, whereas in the latter it is the third party's private *interest* in the contract's performance. In so far as an interest-based model of standing creates a greater risk of vexatious 'busybodying' on the part of third parties, the threat is limited in *Hobart* by restricting the pool of sufficiently 'interested' parties to those who were intended to receive—and who were directly implicated in—performance of the contract. Concerns about the further implications of allowing third parties to seek coercive remedies that have more serious implications for the autonomy of contracting parties—such as orders that one or other of them pay damages, or for specific performance of the contract—can be met by limiting plaintiffs' remedial rights to declaratory relief, independently, I suggest, of questions of standing.

E. Trusts and Estates

(i) Discretionary Purpose Trusts

A sixth, genuine exception exposed by Lionel Smith concerns discretionary purpose trusts. In common law systems, such trusts must generally be charitable to be enforceable, as we shall see in the next chapter. But in Quebec and an increasing number of offshore and American jurisdictions, Smith points out, they need not be.[58] In such instances, neither the settlor nor anyone who is a potential object of the trust's purpose has any obvious claim right either in respect of the settled

[58] Smith (n 1) 293–95. See also P Matthews, 'The New Trust—Obligations Without Rights?' in AJ Oakley (ed), *Trends in Contemporary Trust Law* (OUP 1996) 1; L Smith, 'Massively Discretionary Trusts' (2017) 70 Current Legal Problems 17, 22–24; L Smith, 'Give the People What They Want: The Onshoring of the Offshore' (2018) 103 Iowa Law Review 2155, 2167, 2170–71 (doubting the propriety of the massively discretionary private trust (MDT) on the ground that it enables settlors to shield assets from their creditors whilst potentially continuing to benefit from them). Note that non-charitable

property, or against the trustee personally, but both may nonetheless enforce the trustee's duties[59] and recover property to the trust that has been distributed beyond its purposes. By definition, the potential object of a mere power of distribution in respect of which there is some discretion has no claim right as against the distributor with regard to the *precise pattern* of distribution: one with a '*discretion* to X' has a multital liberty—they owe *no duty* to anyone either *to* X, or *not*-X.[60] The point is even more obvious when the object of a discretionary purpose trust is a dog called Dick.[61] This does not mean, however, that a distribution that exceeds the terms of a discretionary power under a purpose trust or which is made in bad faith (or without genuine consideration) cannot be impugned at the suit of a sufficiently 'interested person', amongst whom both the settlor and potential human objects of the purpose can count.[62]

In many of the (five or so) American jurisdictions listed by Smith that now recognize non-charitable purpose trusts, the enforcer of the trust need not even be 'interested' in its performance, either as settlor or as a potential object. He or she can simply be nominated in the terms of the settlement (rather in the same way that contracting parties can nominate a third-party enforcer under the CRTPA) or be appointed by a court.[63] The result is that these jurisdictions entertain the possibility of entirely 'disinterested' private 'trust protectors'. These provide a pragmatic

purpose trusts are now recognized in the US as valid under the Uniform Trust Code adopted in many States, subject to time limits on their enforcement that typically vary from twenty-one to ninety-nine years: see eg Unif Trust Code (2000) 7C ULA § 409 (twenty-one years). A trust for the care of an animal is also valid and enforceable during its life: § 409.

[59] Smith (n 1) 294. The 'duty' identified by Smith (112–14) is one of loyalty to the trust's purpose, which is consistent with the language used in respect of the duties of administrators of charitable purposes: *Children's Investment Fund (UK) v Attorney General* [2020] UKSC 33, [20] [29], [44]–[50], [104] (Lady Arden JSC).

[60] Some cases suggest that objects of a discretionary trust (albeit not in this case a pure purpose trust) may have (claim) 'rights' to be considered: see eg *Gartside v Inland Revenue Commissioners* [1968] AC 553 (HL), 617–18 (Lord Wilberforce). It has similarly been argued (again outside the context of pure purpose trusts) that the objects of both exhaustive and non-exhaustive discretionary trustee powers may have claim rights to due administration of the trust property which correlate to the trustees' duties, without having any beneficial rights in respect of the trust property: J Hudson, 'Mere and Other Discretionary Objects in Australia' in Y Liew and M Harding (eds), *Asia-Pacific Trusts Law: Theory and Practice in Context* (Hart 2022) 19. Whether the same analysis can be extended to potential objects of a pure purpose trust is unclear, but if this is so then some objects may well have claim rights upon which rights of action are based. In more recent work, Hudson has argued, with Charles Mitchell, that trusts never have right-holders and that the duties of trustees are all 'undirected', so that trust duties are more akin to public law than private law duties: C Mitchell and J Hudson, 'Standing in Trusts Law, the Beneficiary Principle and the Juridical Nature of Trustee Duties' (2026) 142 Law Quarterly Review (forthcoming).

[61] *Willett v Willett* 247 SW 739 (Ky 1923).

[62] Civil Code of Quebec, art 1290, cited in Smith (n 1) 294. Although this is traditionally thought to be controversial in respect of charitable trusts—the assumption being that it is only the Attorney-General (or a relator) who may enforce—this was not so historically and is certainly not the case today. See further G Jones, *History of the Law of Charity 1532–1827* (CUP 1969) 8–9, 16–21; Charities Act 2011 (UK) ss 115 (1)(c), (d); and Chapter 9 Section 9.3B, this book.

[63] Uniform Trust Code (2000) 7C ULA, § 408 (b), §409 (2).

solution to the enforcement gap that is otherwise created by the absence of persons with vested primary equitable claim rights (or powers) to press the purposes of the trust.[64]

The furthest that English law has ever been prepared to go to close the enforcement gap in respect of non-charitable purpose trusts (other than simply declaring them invalid and returning the settled property to the settlor on resulting trust, which hardly seems to be a solution) is the suggestion that the residuary legatees of a will might sometimes have enforcement rights in respect of the administrator trustee's duties.[65] However, even if this were exceptionally so, it would put the power of enforcement into the hands of those who have an interest in seeing the trust *fail*, not succeed in its design, which makes it not just an incomplete solution, but structurally problematic. It replicates the type of enforcement capture problem that we encountered in public law contexts when enforcement agencies are run by persons who have no real interest in seeing the enforcement job done. Another solution suggested in *Re Astor*, which was rightly dismissed by Roxborough J as nonsensical—that the trustee might proceed *ex parte* to enforce a purpose trust against himself[66]—suffers the identical handicap.

(ii) *Vandepitte*

Beyond the case of discretionary purpose trusts, there are further instances discussed by Liau in which the beneficiaries of a normal trust for persons exceptionally have powers to enforce the trustees' claim rights against third-party debtors of the trust, when the trustees themselves fail to do so.[67] The beneficiaries exercising the right of action do, of course, hold their own claim rights against the trustees in such instances, but it is again not these rights that they are asserting in the action,

[64] D Hayton, 'Developing the Obligation Characteristic of the Trust' (2001) 117 Law Quarterly Review 96, esp 98, 107; R Ausness, 'Non-Charitable Purpose Trusts: Past, Present and Future' (2016) 51 50 Real Property Trust & Estates Law Journal 321, 369; L Frolik, 'Trust Protectors: Why They Have Become "The Next Big Thing"' (2015) 50 Real Property Trust & Estates Law Journal 267. There is a dispute as to whether such persons fully solve the enforcement problem, since it is uncertain whether they have any *duty* to enforce and, if so, who can in turn enforce *that* duty: K Low, 'Non-Charitable Purpose Trusts—The Missing Right to Forego Enforcement' in R Nolan, K Low, and HW Tang (eds), *Trusts and Modern Wealth Management* (CUP 2018) 486, 491–92, 496. The concern may have been overstated: M Harding, 'A Fresh Look at Purpose Trusts' in S Degeling, J Hudson, and I Samet, *Philosophical Foundations of the Law of Express Trusts* (OUP 2023) 201, 221; Hayton (n 64, fn 26) (suggesting that it is unimportant whether or not the enforcer has a duty to enforce). If a settlor nominates himself as having a power of enforcement, it would certainly seem unlikely (as per Hayton's view) that he should be under any duty to exercise it against his own will.

[65] *Re Thompson* [1934] Ch 342 (obiter—residuary legatees would be 'at liberty to apply' if the trustee undertakes to apply funds to the relevant purpose and they are then used for a different purpose). The validity of the trust in *Re Thomson* was clearly regarded as exceptional and anomalous in *In Re Astor's Settlement Trusts* [1952] Chs 534, 547 (Roxbourgh J).

[66] *Re Astor* (n 65) 542.

[67] Liau (n 1) 177–80; *Vandepitte v Preferred Accident Insurance Corporation of New York* [1933] AC 70 (PC); *Roberts v Gill* [2010] UKSC 22. See, similarly, the procedure under the Fatal Accidents Act 1979, s 2(1) for dependants to obtain their own right of action where an executor fails to enforce their rights in a timely fashion: n 83 below.

but rather the *trustees'* claim rights against the third party. For the beneficiaries' right of action to arise, there must be more than simply a refusal by the trustee to act —the latter must be guilty of some 'failure, excusable or inexcusable' to perform his duty to do so in protection of the trust estate.[68] Clearly accepted examples include cases in which the trustee (or the executor of a will) is insolvent, colluding with the third party debtor, or conflicted, but it is possible that they may extend as far as any instance in which there is a serious practical impediment to enforcement by the trustee or executor.[69] An obvious explanation for the existence of the beneficiary's right of action in such instances is pragmatic—the need to safeguard against the risks of enforcement capture, a refusal by the primary enforcer to do his or her enforcement duty, or some other insuperable deficit in the latter's enforcement capacity. Another is that it is a purpose of the trust arrangement that the trustee holds its claim rights for the express purpose of protecting the beneficiaries' private interests and the trustee is under an obligation to protect those interests.

F. Tort: Third Party Rights?

Outside the cases involving representative class action proceedings mentioned above (and similar cases in which a tort victim's executor brings a representative action on behalf of a deceased's estate), I know of no clear examples (save perhaps one)[70] of persons other than primary right-holders having rights of action in the substantive common law of torts. This accords with the general perception.[71]

(i) *White v Jones*

Liau suggests that *White v Jones*[72] might be one, but I again have my doubts. In that case, the intended beneficiary of a will was held to be entitled to sue a solicitor in the law of negligence for the loss of a testamentary gift when the latter carelessly failed to ensure that the testator's wishes were given proper legal effect before the testator died. Like Stevens,[73] Liau's view is that the beneficiary was in this instance not allowed to sue for any violation of her own right to reasonable care for her economic interest in the clearly intended gift, but for harm caused to her by the

[68] *Hayim v Citibank* [1987] AC 730 (PC) 747–49 (Lord Wilberforce). Technically, this case involved an estate, not a trust, but the principle is the same.
[69] *Ramage v Waclaw* (1988) 12 NSWLR 84, esp 91–94 (Powell J); *Roberts v Gill* [2010] UKSC 22 [46] (Lord Collins JSC) ('the underlying question is whether there are sufficiently special circumstances to make it just for the beneficiary to have the remedy').
[70] See Section 8.3F(iii) this chapter.
[71] For Goldberg and Zipursky, this is a key feature of what they refer to as the 'substantive standing' rule, or 'proper plaintiff' principle in the law of torts: see eg B Zipursky 'Substantive Standing' (n 13); J Goldberg and B Zipursky, 'Torts as Wrongs' (2010) 88 Texas Law Review 917, 957–58; Goldberg and Zipursky, *Recognizing Wrongs* (n 13) 198–203; R Stevens, *Torts and Rights* (OUP 2007) 173.
[72] [1995] 2 AC 207 (HL); Liau (n 1) 214–28.
[73] Stevens (n 71) 176–82.

solicitor's breach of his contractual duty to the testator. Understood in this way, tort law gave the plaintiff both a right of action and a remedial right to expectation damages in respect of a wrong done to someone else, following the same logic that Liau suggests underpins the third-party claim for damages under the CRTPA, discussed above.[74] If this is so, then the case provided an even more radical exception to the doctrine of privity of contract than is embodied in the CRTPA, because it allowed the plaintiff to sue for harm caused by the breach of another's contractual right even though neither party to the contract intended to provide her with any contractual performance at all (the solicitor's services, remember, were being provided to the testator) and (more crucially) because neither expressed any intention to give her any right to enforce the contract (because the relationship between solicitor and client normally excludes contract duties being owed by the solicitor to any third party).

This analysis of *White* extends the contractual model of liability a very long way but is not completely implausible. The obvious point, however, is that if one accepts it, then the case is not really a tort case at all and so does not provide an example of tort law departing from the basic enforcement paradigm.[75] Tort is simply contract in disguise. By contrast, if *White* is indeed a 'true' tort case in which the law extended a duty of reasonable care to an identified plaintiff for harm culpably and directly caused to her pure economic interests, then it is an outlier in terms of the substantive law,[76] but it fits the normal enforcement paradigm, because both the beneficiary's right of action and her remedial right are based on her own primary claim right against the solicitor. She is the one who was wronged.

(ii) Rights of Dependants and the Unborn

The other possible 'tort' examples discussed by Liau are statutory—the right of dependants to sue (normally through a deceased's executor) for financial loss of dependency under the Fatal Accidents Act 1976 (UK) (FAA), and the right of a child to sue for pre-natal injury under the Congenital Disabilities (Civil Liability) Act 1976 (UK) (CDCLA). The form of the respective provision in each case certainly supports his thesis that the plaintiff is being given rights to sue the tortfeasor for damages for a wrong done to someone else (the deceased, or the parent, respectively) because both statutes require the plaintiff to prove a wrongful injury *to the deceased (or parent)* as a precondition to being entitled to recover.[77] The result,

[74] Liau (n 1) 225–28.

[75] As much is conceded by Liau (n 1) 236–37.

[76] What makes it an outlier in tort is not that pure expectation losses are compensated, since this occurs in the torts of interference with trade and interference with contractual relations, but that they are protected against careless, rather than intentionally harmful conduct. See further K Barker, 'Are We Up to Expectations? Solicitors, Beneficiaries and the Tort–Contract Divide' (1994) 14 Oxford Journal of Legal Studies 137, 146–48. Another case which demonstrates the possibility of plaintiffs having their *own* rights to protection in the law of negligence for their economic interests, where harm has been caused to them by physically injuring another, is *Barclay v Penberthy* [2012] HCA 40.

[77] FAA s 1(1); CDCLA s 1(3).

Liau argues, is that, although there are clear difficulties with the Act, dependants under a tweaked FAA could be regarded as enforcing (and having rights to damages for a defendant's infringement of) a primary right that the *deceased* had to his own, future income stream and his associated right to choose to dispose of that income to his dependants if he wanted.[78] Similarly, the injured child, he suggests, could be understood to be enforcing and claiming damages for the breach of its *parents'* right to receive proper pre-natal treatment.[79] Giving the dependant, or child, a right of action could then be regarded as a morally attractive solution to the same type of 'enforcement gap' that we encountered in the trusts examples in the previous section, and in some of the public law cases considered in previous chapters. The gap is created either by the absence of a living enforcer capable of enforcing his or her own rights at the time an action for loss of dependency is initiated (FAA),[80] or by the fact that the child suffering the relevant congenital physical injury (CDCLA) was not alive when the wrong was done.

I confess that it is hard to be sure of the correct analysis in these instances. The Acts are known to be conceptually problematic, and they aim to provide practical compensation solutions, not to elucidate the underlying rights architecture for private law theorists. The requirement in each instance that the deceased (FAA) or parent (CDCLA) would have succeeded if they had sued for their *own* injury as a precondition of the plaintiff's own claim *could*, I think, simply be a pragmatic device for avoiding any inconsistency that might otherwise arise between the duties owed by the tortfeasor to the deceased and the dependant (FAA), or to the parent and the child (CDCLA). The problem of 'inconsistent' or 'incoherent' duties is one with which the common law is already familiar and deals without much fuss. In *Stuart v Kirkland-Veenstra*,[81] for example, it was accepted by the parties without argument that police officers could not owe any duty of care to avoid causing psychiatric harm to the wife of a suicide victim, unless she first proved that they owed her *husband* a duty to prevent him harming himself. This was not, however, taken to imply that any successful action the wife *did* bring would be an action for the officers' wrong *to her husband*. If they were liable to her, it would be because they owed a duty of care *to her* in respect of her own injury. They just could not be expected to take *more* care for her than for him. Although the Acts' reference to a prior wrong to the deceased or parent might therefore appear to support Liau's view that the action is based on a wrong to another, it seems to me that the language is readily explicable in another way.

[78] Liau (n 1) 199–214. Liau accepts that the legislation is unjustifiable as it stands. He nonetheless takes the view that the best conception is that the dependant's action is 'parasitic' on, or 'derived' from, the deceased's primary right, and achieves the closest position possible to a world in which the wrong to the deceased has not occurred.

[79] Liau (n 1) 230 ('the tort is to the parent, a tort which then has negative effects on the child subsequently born').

[80] ibid 212 ('the exceptional situation is created by the right-holder's *death*').

[81] [2009] HCA 15.

Looking past the language for a second, is it likely that these provisions grant third parties the right to sue and obtain damages in respect of breaches of the primary rights of others? Or do they, as I have suggested the CRTPA does, create independent, *primary* rights for dependants and unborn children, as well as rights of action, upon which plaintiffs can base their remedial rights? The FAA could, and in my view probably should, be understood as granting exceptional, primary statutory rights in respect of relational (ricochet) economic losses suffered by the dependants of a tort victim. One reason for thinking that this might be the case is that there are already common law precedents recognizing the primary rights of a person, A, not carelessly to be made to suffer the economic consequences of an injury to another, B, upon whom they rely.[82] Why would one then assume that the Act is doing anything different in respect of dependants? If anyone *were* to be given rights to enforce the rights *of the deceased*—including his or her right to dispose of future income as he wished—this would surely be his personal representative: the executor of his estate. If it is the dependants that have the right of action, as under the FAA,[83] it therefore seems to me much more likely that the law is granting them exceptional primary rights of their own, albeit rights that cannot impose more extensive duties on a defendant tortfeasor than the duty he or she owed to the deceased.

In a similar vein, the CDCLA could simply be understood as sidestepping in a practical way the messy political controversy (and, on some views, the deontic impossibility) of recognizing unborn children as 'holders' of primary rights that are separate to their parents. One can quite understand why people may be uncomfortable to think of persons having primary rights when they are not alive at the time of the wrong allegedly done to them. If, however, the 'legal agency' paradox is suspended, there seems no reason to doubt that a parent's doctor might owe a duty to take care to protect the interests of a child that will later be born,[84] that pairs with the latter's right of action, acquired at birth.[85] On one view at least, P can

[82] For example, a duty can be owed to an employer in respect of economic loss suffered as a result of having to replace an injured employee. The duty exists in Australia both through the *actio per quod servitium amisit* and the law of negligence: *Barclay* (n 76). The *actio per quod* (which is now anomalous) recognizes the employer's own quasi-proprietary right in the labour of the injured employee, which is *collateral* to the employee's own primary right as against the tortfeasor, rather than being *consequent* upon it: ibid at [33] (my emphasis). The negligence action imposes a duty of care on the tortfeasor that is owed directly to the employer, thereby creating in the employer a correlative, qualified right to reasonable care in respect of his own financial interests.

[83] Technically, it is the deceased's executor that has the right in the first instance (FAA s 2(1)), but the executor is in this instance representing the collective rights of the dependants (not the deceased), who can sue in their own right if he or she refuses to enforce their rights. This architecture serves the purpose of coordinating collective action.

[84] The fact that the unborn have legal interests is evident from the fact that the Attorney-General may be appointed to represent those interests in legal proceedings: *Hamersley v Newton* [2005] WASC 221[16].

[85] Liau (n 1) 234 (duties may potentially be owed to a future class), citing N McBride, 'Duties of Care—Do they Really Exist?' (2004) 24 Oxford Journal of Legal Studies 417, 434. See also C Wellman, 'The Concept of Fetal Rights' (2002) 21 Law & Philosophy 65, 91. Liau nonetheless cites a possible additional problem, namely that the child cannot claim to have been 'damaged' by what the doctor

have *interests* without P being in existence at the time to 'hold' those interests; and if there is a reason for D in particular to protect such an interest of (future) P, then D is under a duty to (future) P to protect the interest, and (future) P has a corresponding right as against D that D do so.[86] While Liau's view of the right of action under the CDCLA is therefore again feasible and his argument finely reasoned, this case seems to me to be so overshadowed by philosophical uncertainty and political controversy about the interests and/or rights of the unborn and the dead as not to provide a very reliable example. The paradoxes presented by life and death make for poor precedents and solutions.

(iii) Bailee Rights—*The Winkfield*

This leaves us with very few clear exceptions to the 'right-holder rule' in the law of torts, but it is possible that there may be some. One, which might provide an example of both a right of action and a secondary right to claim damages for wrongful harm done to another person, is the right enjoyed by a bailee of goods to bring an action for the goods' value when they are converted, devalued, or destroyed by a third party—the rule in *The Winkfield*.[87] In such a case, the bailee has a primary right to possession of the goods, but it is not simply this possessory right that she is permitted to assert in the action, but also the owner's primary patrimonial right; and the loss in respect of which she can recover in the action includes the owner's loss, which explains why she must normally account to the owner for such damages obtained in the action as reflect harm to the owner's own interest. Significantly (and not uncontroversially)[88] the action may be initiated without the consent or knowledge of the owner; and the recovery of full damages by the bailee prevents any further action against the third party by the owner himself. The rule is traditionally explained by saying that the chattel is 'deemed' to belong to the bailee and that, as between the bailee (or anyone else entitled to possession) and a

did, since he or she never existed in anything other than the 'damaged' state. This, implies, incorrectly I think, that there is no qualifying counterfactual or baseline of entitlement as against which the child's position at birth can be measured—no hypothetical state of being *other than the state that he or she is in* with which to compare her current position. I doubt this. The relevant hypothetical state with which to compare the live child's condition is the position she would have been in had the doctor not acted negligently—which is a state of being *without* the abnormality.

[86] For this argument in the context of discussing the rights of the dead, see A Fell, 'The Rights of the Dead' in K Falconer, K Barker, and A Fell (eds), *Life and Death in Private Law* (Hart, 2024) Ch 6, esp 106–107, 110–13.

[87] [1902] 1 P 42. I am grateful to Rick Bigwood for this example. For discussion see N Palmer, *Bailment* (2nd edn, Law Book Co 1991) 308–17.

[88] E Warren, 'Qualifying as Plaintiff in Conversion' (1936) 49 Harvard Law Review 1084; Comment, 'A Re-Examination of the Winkfield Case' (1940) 9 Fordham Law Review 247 (both criticizing the lack of any requirement for obtaining the consent of the owner where the latter's interests are asserted). For further, contemporary criticism, see *Shipping Gazette and Lloyd's List* (Saturday 21 December 1901) 9–10 (denoting the rule to be 'artificial and unsound'—potentially preventing the owner from recovering for his full loss of profit, where the property bailed is a profit-earning chattel, such as a ship that has been chartered).

stranger, 'possession gives title'[89] (that is, full rights of ownership). If this explanation is accepted, the example is of course not an exception to the normal right-holder rule, since the bailee is to be regarded, vis-à-vis anyone but the owner, as the holder of the full and sole title to the goods.[90] But the deeming in this case must be called out for what it is—a legal fiction. The original reason for the bailee's right of action in the twelfth century may simply have been that the owner of the goods lacked one.[91] There are other, more obvious, pragmatic reasons of convenience for the rule that have greater purchase in the modern day. It enables both a claim for possession of the goods (protecting the interest of the bailee) and a claim for their devaluation or destruction (protecting the patrimonial interest of the owner) to be consolidated efficiently in a single action; and the bailee may more often than not be in a better position than the owner to know of the third-party's wrong, especially where it takes place in a jurisdiction foreign to the owner.[92] It may be a peculiarity of the common law that cases such as this are dealt with via the law of torts, rather than the law of property,[93] and there are no doubt those who would prefer the latter classification, the acceptance of which would obviously further crop the list of exceptions that 'tort' offers up to the normal right-holder rule.

The main conclusions about the private law enforcement regime to which we are drawn are these. First, the general requirement that those granted rights of action must hold primary 'rights' is clearly firmly embedded in our law. Second, properly understood, the enforcement paradigm extends rights of action not simply to claim right-holders but to holders of any of the primary Hohfeldian 'rights'—claim rights, powers, liberties, and immunities. The strongest evidence of this lies in the law relating to declaratory relief. Third, Liau is quite right to say that exceptions to the paradigm are not just analytically possible but do in fact exist, even if I have doubted some of the particular examples he gives. Tort law seems to me to be improbable ground for the growth of exceptions to the dominant paradigm, precisely because any third party right of action is unlikely in this context to be consistent with the prior consent of the primary right-holder, whereas consensual exceptions to the rule are more likely in the law of property, trusts, and contract, which are facilitative institutions that are designed to be adaptable by those using them to suit their preferences and ends. Third-party enforcement rights may also increase the private utility of those institutions and the autonomy of those who use them in ways that third party rights generally do not increase the autonomy of those holding rights to the person, to liberty, or to reputation. Fourth (and following

[89] [1902] 1 P 42, 60 (Collins MR).

[90] ibid 60–61; Palmer (n 87) 313.

[91] Note, 'The Bailee's Rights to Recover Full Damages: Historically and Critically' (1950) 25 St John's Law Review 51, 52–53 (although it is hard to be sure of this).

[92] ibid 55.

[93] Common law systems lack a *vindicatio*: S Douglas, *Liability for Wrongful Interferences with Chattels* (Hart 2011) 9.

on from this point), in most of the cases in which a person other than a primary right-holder has a right of action in private law, it is with the right-holder's consent, or the right-holder retains a legal power to veto the use of the right of action. Fifth, there is nonetheless a range of other, rare exceptions in which private law grants rights of action to non-right-holders even without their first obtaining right-holder consent. This tends to happen where the right-holder lacks legal capacity, where there is no primary right-holder at all (or he or she is dead, or insolvent), or where the right-holder is improperly failing, or refusing, to use his or her enforcement powers, in breach of obligations that he or she owes to the third-party. The primary right-holder's failure to enforce can result from her insolvency, the lack of any relevant legal incentive to sue, her self-interest, or some other insuperable, practical obstacle. These, pragmatic explanations for departures from the basic enforcement paradigm chime with some of the cases in which private rights of action are exceptionally allowed to operate in public law, as, for example, where private parties retain the right to enforce criminal laws that the State itself is refusing to enforce.

8.4 Rationale of the Enforcement Regime

What, then, are the candidate justifications for the basic rule in private law that primary-right-holders are the ones with the power to enforce their rights? The reason might seem obvious, given that private law rights are primarily designed to protect right-holders' own interests. But the question is more difficult than it seems. We also need to understand why one might depart from the basic paradigm. The arguments are broadly divisible as between moral or deontic arguments, on the one hand, and pragmatic, instrumental ones, on the other.

A. Moral and Deontic Justifications

One justification for giving rights of action to right-holders[94] that can be quickly dismissed is that rights of action are analytically 'entailed' by primary rights. Primary rights and rights of action are *not* simply the same right 'seen from different ends'.[95] This point was made in Chapter 3.[96] It is not, therefore, necessarily

[94] For additional arguments relating to moral standing, see Liau (n 1) 270–77. I omit fuller reference to these because the analogy between questions of moral and legal standing seems to me to be inexact, and I lack the space to do justice to the relationship between them.

[95] This language was famously used by Peter Birks to describe the relationship between primary and secondary rights: P Birks, 'Definition and Division: A Meditation on Institutes 3.13' in P Birks (ed), *The Classification of Obligations* (Clarendon 1997) 1, 24. It is sometimes said to describe a 'monist' view.

[96] See, similarly, Zipursky, 'Substantive Standing' (n 13), 330; Gardner, *From Personal Life to Private Law* (n 16), 19, 204; Goldberg and Zipurksy, *Recognizing Wrongs* (n 13) Chs 3, 4, esp 112–13: a system without rights of action would be 'deficient, not incoherent'.

'in the nature of' a primary right that it involves a right of action for the person holding that right (and no one else) even if we think this to be desirable, as many do.

What we are looking for, then, are *good normative reasons* as to why a person, A, who holds any of the primary Hohfeldian rights as against another person, B, should also have an associated power of enforcement. We are also asking whether these reasons are reasons that *exclude* the possibility of enforcement by a third party, C.

(i) Control and Will

For some, a primary right is *only* a 'right' because it gives its holder control over others' duties and liabilities, and one only has control if one has the exclusive power to enforce or waive them. This is the essence of Hart's well-known approach to the *definition* of legal rights.[97] That definition is not one that I personally endorse because it assumes exactly the sort of necessary analytical connection between primary rights and rights of action that I have claimed does not exist. However, even if one does not *define* primary rights in terms of control, it is clearly possible to argue that those who have them *ought* to control their enforcement.

The strongest proponent of this position is Arthur Ripstein, who, recall from the end of Chapter 3, takes the view that rights of action in private law are *necessarily normatively implied* by primary rights. The two sorts of rights come as an indivisible normative 'package', the justifications for which are rooted in one and the same Kantian norm: the will of one person is not unilaterally to be subordinated to the purposes of another.[98] This conception of freedom is quite specific. For a primary right-holder, A, not to be subjected to B's will, it is essential that A has an enforcement power that enables her to 'stand on' or be 'in charge of' her primary right against B. It is also essential that *no one else* can officiously interfere by enforcing A's primary right for her,[99] or by vetoing A's decisions about enforcement.

In this account, control (sometimes called 'independence' or 'negative freedom') is a distinct moral value, not something that is valuable simply because it contributes to the welfare or autonomy of the right-holder in the broader sense canvased in the next section.[100] Kantian freedom is a narrower and more limited conception

[97] HLA Hart, 'Legal Rights' in HLA Hart, *Essays on Bentham* (Clarendon 1982) esp 182–84.

[98] A Ripstein, *Private Wrongs* (Harvard University Press 2016) 11–12. 271–73; A Ripstein, 'Private Order and Public Justice' (2006) Virginia Law Review 1391. See also E Weinrib, 'Corrective Justice and Civil Recourse' (2011) 39 Florida State University Law Review 273, 284–85.

[99] A Ripstein, 'Civil Recourse and Separation of Wrongs and Remedies' (2011) 39 Florida State University Law Review 163, 200–01. This is disputed. For the suggestion that the Kantian premise does not in fact prevent C being able to enforce A's rights, provided the enforcement process is omnilateral in the sense of being overseen by a public body, see R Stone, 'Who Has the Power to Enforce Private Rights' in P Miller and J Oberdiek (eds), *Oxford Studies in Private Law Theory* Vol 2 (OUP 2023) Ch 2, 25, 30.

[100] If it is only valuable to the extent that it promotes autonomy then the argument because ones about autonomy (below).

of freedom than autonomy in the latter sense. It is almost certainly also, as Liau says, a 'zero-sum game'—you either have it, or you don't, so that it is impossible for A and C to *share* control over the enforcement of A's rights.[101] The sole instance in which C could have a right of action in respect of A's rights would hence be where A had personally given her one, or consented to her being given one, so that A's dominion over her own is properly preserved. A mere interest on the part of C in the enforcement of A's rights would not be enough, any more than A's own interest in C's enforcing the right would be.

This rationale could, therefore, justify the normal right-holder enforcement rule and some prior-consent-based exceptions, but it cannot justify all of the exceptional instances we identified above. It struggles to accommodate the suggestion in *Hobart*, for example, that a third party's interest in another's contract can justify a right of action even where the right is not intended by the primary right-holder and no permission for the action has been given. It also struggles with cases, like the class litigation example, where rights of action are created to solve a collective-action problem, with only a later (or indeed no) opt-out opportunity for the right-holder, or, as under the *Vandepitte* procedure or in *The Winkfield*, cases where the right-holder's permission for the action is simply irrelevant. In a footnote, Ripstein appears to accept guardianship as an exceptional case in which a third party may enforce, but this is premised on the idea (questionable I think) that it is not really an exception to the basic right-holder enforcement paradigm at all. Since the guardian acts on the child's behalf, he says, the guardian's right of action still 'accompanies' the child's primary rights.[102] The subtext of this brief comment seems to be that the guardian holds the child's primary rights as well as the right of action and therefore expresses the child's will on its behalf. If that is the idea, it is problematic, since the child, lacking capacity, can express no 'will' and the guardian cannot therefore be expressing it either. Even if the child could express will (perhaps he or she is sufficiently mature, despite being below the legal age of consent), a guardian's decision to enforce could sometimes be taken against that will, if it were nonetheless in the child's best interests. Enforcement by a child's guardian cannot therefore easily be explained as consistent with the expressed will of the child, or the child's right to 'control' his or her rights.

[101] Liau (n 1) 249. Note the similar conclusion of Hohfeld in Chapter 3 Section 3.3B n 21, that whilst both A and C may have volitional control over rights, only one of them ultimately has the 'power' to change them—the person whose control is 'paramount'. If control can be shared, then the argument again becomes one about the extent to which the sharing arrangement promotes or diminishes the choices open to the respective enforcers—ie it concerns their respective autonomy.

[102] Ripstein, *Private Wrongs* (n 98) 12, fn 19. There is equivocation in the footnotes, it being said both that the right of action and primary right 'come apart' in this case and that that they 'accompany' one another.

(ii) Personal Autonomy

A different argument which I have previously sketched in outline[103] is that primary right-holders have the rights of action because this promotes their autonomy in a specific sense that is most commonly associated with Joseph Raz. Anything that increases the range of valuable options open to a person increases their autonomy, and anything that reduces their valuable options, decreases it.[104] Since private law rights protect one's private interests, and these interests are morally valuable goods that contribute to one's personal well-being, a power to enforce such rights can itself clearly be morally valuable. Rights of action enable a right-holder to protect and prevent others from diminishing those goods, as well as to obtain certainty from a court as to the way they may be dealt with (as, for example, where a declaration is obtained). The liberty *not* to initiate a claim is also valuable in enabling one to forgive a wrong done by another (forgiveness and magnanimity themselves being morally valuable), to avoid the additional reputational harm that might be involved in airing a private wrong that has been done to one, and to keep sensitive private information away from the public eye. By enabling the right-holder to settle the dispute privately, the liberty also accords a right-holder the option of avoiding the emotional distress and additional psychiatric consequences that are commonly associated with litigation. That is very often in the right-holder's interest. Having the right to enforce or waive the enforcement of his or her primary rights could be a source of personal dignity for A (here meaning self-esteem) and of respect from others.[105]

From the autonomy point of view, there is nothing *necessarily* to prevent third parties enforcing one's own rights, if this promotes one's interests and enhances one's valuable options in life. Respect for C's autonomy might also justify granting C a right of action to enforce A's rights where C's own valuable interests and options are potentially implicated by B's infringement, provided that it does not unduly impact upon A's own range of choices. Autonomy, unlike control, is not a 'zero-sum

[103] K Barker,' Modelling Public and Private Enforcement: The Rationality of Hybridity' (2018) 37 University of Queensland Law Journal 9, 21.

[104] J Raz, *The Morality of Freedom* (Clarendon 1986) Ch 14, esp 372–78, 407–12. Gardner, *From Personal Life to Private Law* (n 16) 208–09 clearly accepts this as a good argument in favour of giving a right-holder a right of action, whilst concluding that it cannot justify excluding others from enforcement. For a distinct approach presenting rights of action as important to the realization of a wronged person's 'self-authorship' and the pursuit of their 'ground projects and comprehensive goals', see A Gold, *The Right of Redress* (OUP 2020) esp 39–41, 66–68, 73–79, 155–59. Whilst Gold suggests that a personal right of redress has positive effects for autonomy (as well, potentially, for efficiency), the difference is that it is not valuable just for this reason. It is valuable in its own right in affirming and expressing *who one is*, allowing one to exercise sovereignty and coercive power unilaterally without the grace of the State: ibid 66–68, 76–78. It follows that a right of action premised on self-authorship of this type belongs to the person wronged: 73.

[105] J Feinberg, 'The Nature and Value of Rights' in J Feinberg, *Rights, Justice, and the Bounds of Liberty: Essays in Social Philosophy* (Princeton University Press 1980) 143, 151, 156–57; J Feinberg, 'Duties, Rights and Claims' in Feinberg ibid 130, 141–42; Gold (n 104) 76–77. On different types of respect for self and others, see L Darwall, 'Two Kinds of Respect' (1977) 88 Ethics 36.

game'. The enforcement of A's rights by C might even exceptionally have such significant repercussions for group (or societal) interests and wellbeing as to justify the State, or the group, enforcing A's rights in order to increase the autonomy and well-being of all concerned. Since autonomy can be shared, decisions about the location of rights of action can therefore be based on balancing the autonomy interests of the right-holder against those of third parties who also have an interest in the enforcement of his or her rights.

The arguments from autonomy therefore also strongly support rights of action for the right-holder, A, but can support additional rights of action for C, where either A's or C's interests are implicated. Where there is no implication for C's interests at all, one would normally expect the right of action *only* to vest in the right-holder, A, as the control model suggests. But there can be no hard and fast rule. Interventions by C might be justified in some instances. The first, clear case is again where A consents, because in such instances we have the best evidence that C's intervention promotes A's own interests. A second is where A's capacity to protect her own private interests is diminished (children, those lacking mental or physical capacity), even if no formal legal consent has been, or can be, given. That seems to me to be a potentially better explanation of guardianship than that briefly provided by Ripstein.

More controversially, enforcement of A's rights by C might also be permissible in a third case, where it promotes C's interests, provided those interests are *consistent* with A's own interests. Examples might be where a contract was made by A with B in order to benefit C,[106] or where A is otherwise bound by law to protect C's interests, as where A is a trustee or executor of property for C's benefit.[107] The need for consistency between C's interests and A's is important, so that promotion of C's autonomy is not permitted to operate unduly to the detriment of A's own options. Group litigants might enforce A's rights on his or her behalf so as to ensure that litigation has enough momentum to guarantee the protection of the group's interests, again providing that this does not unreasonably diminish A's own choices. And so on. Taken as a whole, the argument from autonomy therefore again strongly supports the general rule of right-holder enforcement, but it is capacious enough to justify and explain a greater number of the current exceptions than the argument from right-holder 'independence' or 'control'.

(iii) Reason Continuity—A Limited Argument

The argument from autonomy, we saw, supplies a loose way of connecting rights of action to primary right-holders, but the connection is defeasible. It cannot justify the complete exclusion of rights of action for others. A similarly loose connection between primary rights and rights of action can be made by deploying a

[106] *Beswick v Beswick* [1968] AC 58 (HL) and see this chapter, Section 8.3D.
[107] See Section 8.3E, this chapter.

very extended version of John Gardner's continuity thesis.[108] This thesis suggests that, while A's primary rights may not survive their violation by B, the reasons for A having them continue, and have normative implications for A's secondary rights against B. The reasons for our primary rights 'echo' forward into the form of our remedial rights. The same type of argument ('reason continuity') can, I think, justify a loose normative association between primary rights and rights of action. The argument is best set out in stages in the following way, using a claim rights example:

1. A reason (R1) for creating a primary private law claim right in A is to protect A's private interests. A private interest is a *private* good—a good that *A has* as an individual.
2. The fact that the primary right is vested *in A as against B*, says something further about its justifications. A's private interest *could* theoretically have been protected by giving C (or the State) a primary right as against B that B not harm A's interest. That would be one way of doing things. But A's private interest is *not* protected in that way in private law: it is protected by vesting the primary right against B *in A*. While we cannot be sure of the reason (it could be moral, or pragmatic), we *can* be pretty sure that there *is* such a reason (R2), assuming the law to be a rational practice.
3. If there is a reason (R2) to vest the primary right to the protection of A's interest *in A*, that reason—whatever it is—is likely also to be a *pro tanto* reason to permit *A* to *enforce* that right as against B, all other things being equal. It provides a pro-tanto reason to give a right of action to A, on the violation of A's primary right by B.

Let us make this more concrete, to test it out. Assume that I have a primary right not to be defamed because the law recognizes that I have a moral interest in my reputation. Private law does not choose to protect my interest by giving my *mother* the right that you not defame me, although she might well be a fierce protector and in the best position to ensure that the defamation does not occur. It gives *me* a claim right as against you that you not defame me. In so doing, it recognizes that you have a particular reason and therefore a particular duty *to me* not to call me a liar and that *I* can call upon you to avoid doing so. Given the personal nature of this duty *to me*, is it surprising, then, that when you do call me a liar, the law gives *me* a right to initiate a claim, so as to impose upon you the public duty to answer it? Not

[108] Gardner 'What is Tort Law For' (n 5) 28–48; Gardner, *From Personal Life to Private Law* (n 16) 98–124. For discussion and defence of Gardner's thesis, as well as other forms of continuity argument, see S Steel, 'Compensation and Continuity' (2020) 26 Legal Theory 250; J Oberdiek, 'Wrongs, Remedies, and the Persistence of Reasons: Re-examining the Continuity Thesis' in H Psarras and S Steel (eds), *Private Law and Practical Reason* (OUP 2023) Ch 10; Gold (n 104) Ch 2, esp 46–49 (the 'persistence' thesis: post-wrong rights to enforce redress are echoes of one's pre-wrong rights to prevent the violation of one's primary rights through acts of self-defence).

really: the reason (R2) for *my* having a primary right as against you that you protect my private interest is likely also to be a reason, when the right is infringed, for *me* to have a power to sue when you don't.

I do not want to press this argument too far. All it really says is that, whatever the reason we had to make the *primary* right a 'personal' affair *as between you and I*, that reason is also likely to feature as a *pro-tanto* reason for giving *me* a right of action exercisable against you that takes a similar form. If the reason for giving *me* a primary right against you is a moral reason, it may also provide a moral reason for giving me a right of action.[109] We might then say that there is at least a rational basis for giving private right-holders rights of action. The right of action provides an echo of a reason (R2) that underpins the personal nature of the basic primary right. But that, again, does not exclude the possibility of there being *other* good reasons, moral, constitutional or pragmatic, for giving rights of action to persons other than the right-holder.

It will come as no surprise that this type of argument occurred to Gardner, but this time he did not buy it.[110] He thought that it sentimentally obscures a variety of independent, pragmatic arguments (to which we shall come) that furnish the real reasons for giving right-holders the right of action.[111] He also thought that the argument that there might be a rational echo from the personal nature of A's primary right against B into his possession of right of action is misconceived because a right of action is not (as is the primary right) a right *as against B*—it is a permission and a claim right *as against the general community* that others ('strangers') help him to enforce his right and themselves keep out of the enforcement of the right.[112] I nonetheless think that in the form that I put the argument here, there could still be something in it. For one thing, the type of personal reason for A's primary right that I suggest echoes into his right of action (R2) is not necessarily, as Gardner envisages, a reason to stop others from enforcing—it is just a pro-tanto reason to allow *A* to enforce. Moreover, although rights of action are indeed rights (powers) between A and courts (because they enliven court jurisdiction), they are *also*, on the analysis presented in Chapter 3, rights (powers) *as against B* to impose public

[109] I take John Oberdiek to be endorsing something like this sort of argument in suggesting that personalized, relational duties between parties are especially morally attractive and that they provide the 'only basis' for recognizing 'persons . . . as sources of claims': J Oberdiek, 'It's Something Personal: On the Relationality of Duty and Civil Wrongs' in P Miller and J Oberdiek (eds), *Civil Wrongs and Justice in Private Law* (OUP 2020) 301, 319–20. For a similar (meta)ethical claim that 'bipolar' obligations give rise to a special form of discretionary authority and power in an obligee to hold the obligor personally responsible, see S Darwall, 'Bipolar Obligation' in R Shafer-Landau (ed), *Oxford Studies in Metaethics* Vol 7 (OUP 2012) 333, 346–47; S Darwall and J Darwall 'Civil Recourse as Mutual Accountability' (2011) 39 Florida State University Law Review 17, esp 24–26. Note that Darwall's account does not preclude third parties from holding the obligor accountable, but their authority to do so is different in not being a personal one.

[110] Gardner, *From Personal Life to Private Law* (n 16) 212–14.

[111] ibid 213.

[112] ibid 213–14 (although he ultimately remains agnostic as to the existence of the claim right).

liabilities or duties on B to answer the claim. If this is so, Gardner is not quite right, I think, in saying that rights of action are not rights against B in the way that primary rights are. They do involve powers exercisable against B that have some consequences for B, and they therefore do, to some extent, weakly mimic the form of the primary, personal right.

While my suggestion is that this argument may help rationally to explain the grant of rights of action to right-holders, it does not help much in identifying precisely what exceptions to the basic paradigm might be made. This, the argument says, will depend weakly on the reason (R2) or reasons (R1, R2, R3, R4) why A was given the primary right against B in the first place. Like the argument from autonomy, however, it does suggest that the linkage between right of action and primary right can potentially be looser than anything akin to the 'control' model of rights suggests. Even if we are weakly observing the reasons for creating bilateral primary rights when we create rights of action, we can still always *add* additional good reasons (R5, R6, R7) for giving rights of action to third parties; or we could find sufficiently strong contrary reasons to justify suspending or qualifying a right-holder's right of action[113] or (although it is really hard to think of a good case these days)[114] denying a right-holder a right of action at all.

(iv) Right to Civil Recourse

One of the influential views canvassed in Chapter 3 was Goldberg and Zipursky's claim that right-holders *must* have rights of action because the State has a duty (both political and legal) to provide them with an avenue of civil recourse to enforce their primary rights and obtain remedies for personal wrongs that have been done to them. Before further considering this view, it is important to remember that what the authors mean by a right of action is different to what I have claimed it to be. For them, it is not just a power to enliven a court's jurisdiction and subject a defendant to public law duties to respond to a claim, but also a power to impose personal *remedial* duties on her, so as to hold her accountable for a private wrong she has done.[115] This, as I have previously said, threatens to conflate A's right of action with his or her remedial rights against a defendant, B, when the two types of right should really be kept analytically distinct. Nonetheless, the arguments about a citizen's 'right' to civil recourse can be used to support the State's provision of rights of action for right-holders, whichever of these definitions one prefers. If the argument is good enough to justify giving right-holders rights of action on their conception, it is certainly good enough to justify doing so on my own.

[113] This is sometimes done in the case of prisoners: Public Trustee Act 1978 (Qld), s 95(1)(b) (those sentenced to three or more years are only entitled to sue with the permission of the Public Trustee), and those deemed to be 'vexatious litigators' where court permission must first be obtained before action will be permitted.

[114] Historically, women were often denied rights of action.

[115] *Recognizing Wrongs* (n 13) 98. For the earlier literature, see Chapter 3 Section 3.3.

In its most recent articulation, the argument from the right to civil recourse is that any private claim right-holder must have a right of action as part of his or her compact with the liberal democratic State.[116] The idea of a compact is weak, and the key point is that the State's provision of a right of action to its citizens is one of the preconditions of it claiming legitimate political authority over them, a bit like giving them the right to vote.[117] It is a necessary *quid pro quo* for them giving up their right to take measures to protect themselves—their rights of self-defence.[118] Why, you might ask, could the State not meet its obligation to its citizens by giving someone else (even itself) the power to enforce a private right-holder's rights? The answer, Goldberg and Zipursky say, is that it could, but that a liberal democratic State's obligations to its citizens are informed by its values. Putting rights of action in the hands of right-holders reflects liberal democratic values because it promotes equality and fairness in the systemic protection of citizens' primary rights, it respects their 'independence' in respect of these rights, and it promotes their 'individual sovereignty'.[119] The language of independence (control) will sound familiar, because it is Ripstein's. The idea is the same. Individual sovereignty means something similar, but this time different—the value of being able to hold others personally accountable for the wrongful injuries they do to us, which Goldberg and Zipurksy insist is an important, embedded social norm.[120] Both independence and sovereignty (in this special sense) are aspects of the broader value of self-determination endorsed in liberal societies.

In referencing these values as the basis for providing rights of action for primary rights-holders, the argument also appeals to a type of continuity argument. One of the reasons for giving right-holders rights of action (independence or control) is that this echoes the reason for granting them certain types of primary right (such as the ownership of property).[121] More broadly, right-holders' rights of action reflect the 'relational' directives[122] that exist in private law. I interpret this to mean that that they map the way in which primary rights against B are vested in private law in the right-holder, A, and therefore that they potentially echo the moral reasons that underpin *interpersonal* rights and duties of this sort, along the lines suggested in the previous section.

Since a State with liberal democratic values such as these is only meeting its obligation of civil recourse if it allows the right-holder *herself* to enforce her private

[116] ibid Ch 4. Compare Andrew Gold's account, in which the State's obligations of in respect of 'redressive' justice are grounded not in social contract but in its *sui generis* fiduciary status and its (general) prohibition of self-help: Gold (n 104) Ch 6.

[117] ibid esp 123, 127–28, 130.

[118] ibid 119, 123. On the right to self-defence, see further Liau (n 1) 253–55.

[119] Gold (n 104) 134–35, 144–46.

[120] ibid 141, 143–45. See similarly S Darwall and J Darwall (n 109) 24–26 (bipolar obligations give the obligee a distinctive moral authority and standing to hold the obligor accountable, or not).

[121] *Recognizing Wrongs* (n 13) 112, 140.

[122] ibid 139.

rights, there does not seem to be much space in this account for enforcement by others. Right-holder independence and sovereignty are compatible with third-party enforcement where a right-holder gives her consent. But it is hard to see much beyond this in terms of specific exceptions. The values of equality and fairness might, I would have thought, leave space for third-party rights of action where this is necessary for the protection of the interests of vulnerable right-holders, who cannot give their consent and who lack autonomy, but the implications of the values of equality and fairness are not fully extrapolated and it is unwise for me to speculate too much. All that one can say is that if autonomy *were* a value sufficiently strongly socially embedded in a particular society (as it might potentially be in ours),[123] one might expect that value to feature in the way in which rights of action are allocated. The line drawn in the sand, however, is that the connection between rights of action and primary rights is, as under previous arguments, *not* instrumental. A right of action could not, for example, be given to a third party to enforce a contract simply because this made the contracting mechanism more reliable,[124] or because it incentivized the keeping of promises. Nor, presumably, could outside parties be given rights to enforce the duties of a trust administrator just because this ensures the utility or efficient functioning of the trust institution.

B. Instrumental Reasons

The final group of justifications for right-holder enforcement is instrumental.

The first is what I have previously referred to as the 'default' argument.[125] It suggests that a good reason to use private right-holders to enforce private law rights is the lack of State machinery to enforce them instead. Historically, the absence of State agents can certainly explain why virtually all law (both private and public) was enforced privately, but it does not explain why enforcement powers would be restricted to private right-holders, as opposed to any other private person who was well positioned to enforce the right, such as a member of the victim's family. The argument also has little force today. State enforcement of private law rights might be expensive, difficult, or morally undesirable from any of the points of view previously articulated, but it is no longer *impossible* in the age of the administrative State. In fact, we shall see some examples of this in the next chapter.

123 For a vision of private law in which this value is realized see H Dagan, 'The Challenges of Private Law: A Research Agenda for an Autonomy-Based Private Law' in K Barker, K Fairweather and R Grantham (eds), *Private Law in the 21st Century* (Hart 2017) Ch 4; *A Liberal Theory of Property* (CUP 2021). cf J Penner, 'Taking Raz Seriously: On the Value of Autonomy and Its Relation to Private Law' in P Miller and J Oberdiek (eds), *Oxford Theory in Private Law* Vol 2 (OUP 2023) Ch 4 (pointing out that the Kantian conception of negative freedom is the one more consistently protected in private law).

124 *Recognizing Wrongs* (n 13) 131–32.

125 Barker (n 103) 20. For more expansive discussion, see Chapter 10 Section 10.4A.

A second and better argument is therefore that right-holder enforcement is likely to be more efficient because the right-holder has the best access to information about the relevant infraction[126] and is generally the person best motivated to sue. It is more time-consuming and expensive for a third party to identify a past (or prospective) private wrong, and third parties lack the same type of motivation to enforce, perhaps even when they are paid. Moreover, whereas in public law a private enforcer's private interest can act as an obstruction to efficient enforcement by setting up a potential conflict between the interests of the enforcer and the public interests that public law is generally designed to protect, in private law, the private interests of the private right-holder and the interests protected by the private right are generally[127] one and the same. This, direct alignment between the interests of the enforcing right-holder and the interest protected by the primary right minimizes the risk of improperly motivated action,[128] or, as economists might frame it, 'moral hazard'. While there might be third parties who are equally well motivated to act in protection of the right-holder's interests, this is likely to be sufficiently uncommon (and the costs of determining who might qualify to enforce so high)[129] as to justify the basic right-holder rule.

These sorts of efficiency argument certainly suggest that the general right-holder enforcement rule is sound, and that adding third-party rights of action will usually be needlessly duplicative and add extra complication (and cost) to the enforcement system as a whole. They are nonetheless empirically contingent, so that exceptions can be justified. Allowing a right-holder to contract the enforcement of his or her rights out to an experienced agent can reduce costs. A parental guardianship exception makes sense because the child cannot act, the parent is in a good position to identify the legal wrong done to her and to gather relevant information; and the parent's motivations are closely aligned with the child's interests. Allowing an interested third party to enforce a contract designed for her benefit will also make economic sense, if the promisee lacks the incentive or capacity to enforce it, to ensure that losses caused to the third party by the promisor's breach are internalized by the promisor. The third party is in a better position than the promisee right-holder to determine her losses, and her interests align with those of those of the promisee in so far as the latter intended to benefit her. Similarly, if purpose trusts are to function in the manner intended by a settlor, *someone* must be eligible to enforce them, or their economic facility is lost—either the State or a qualified third party may be allowed to step up. If the trustees of a trust for persons will not fulfil their obligations to protect the interests of trust beneficiaries by gathering in

[126] Barker (n 103) 20. See also Liau (n 1) 262–63.

[127] Because private rights generally protect private interests. But see Section 8.5, this chapter.

[128] Barker (n 103) 20 (the argument from 'interest alignment'). The risk is obviously not fully eliminated, since private right-holders may still abuse their enforcement rights, but the structure of enforcement rights reduces the risk.

[129] Liau (n 1) 260.

trust debts because they are captured, the beneficiaries themselves have (or can easily obtain) the information required to enforce the debts on the trustees' behalf, and they are motivated to do so by their equitable interest in the fund. Opt-out representative enforcement techniques in class action proceedings yield the efficiencies of scale necessary to overcome collective-action problems. And so on. It is impossible to delineate the full range of possible exceptions that could be justified by considerations of efficiency here, but it is potentially extensive, varying contextually and in response to a wide variety of variables relating to information costs, enforcer capacity and capture, expertise, and motivational alignment.

A possible normative objection to allowing efficiency arguments such as these to influence the configuration of rights of action in private law is that it is inconsistent with private law's purpose in doing corrective (or interpersonal) justice. The criterion according to which rights of action should be distributed in private law should reflect the moral precepts underpinning the primary rights, not ones of efficiency or overall social cost, otherwise enforcers are just the means to an end, not moral agents acting in defence of private rights. This, I think, is to take an extreme point of view and there is much to be said for the more balanced position that there is nothing wrong in combining aims of justice and efficiency, if efficiency is ranked a secondary, and not the primary, aim.[130] It is perfectly sensible to think of private law as a system of *interpersonal* rights and simultaneously to try to ensure that such rights are enforced in the most cost-effective way.

A final instrumental argument canvased by Gardner, which I mention only because it resonates with the reasoning of two of the judges in the *Hobart* case, is that there is a special public interest in using private enforcers as a check on State authority and monopoly in respect of law enforcement.[131] This is especially important where the State's own obligations are concerned. It cannot independently justify or explain the basic right-holder enforcement rule in private law. If we wanted private parties to police the State's private transactions in the public interest, or to break up its monopoly on law enforcement more generally, any private enforcer would potentially do, subject to the normal conditions that apply in public law cases to prevent administrative overload and vexatious litigation.

[130] See generally K Mathis (trans Shannon), *Efficiency Instead of Justice? Searching for the Philosophical Foundations of the Economic Analysis of Law* (Springer 2009) esp 78–79, 195. See similarly Gardner, *From Personal Life to Private Law* (n 16) 210–14 (the various instrumental efficiency arguments are 'not alien, but subsidiary' to the aim of doing corrective justice, counting in favour of the basic allocation of rights of action to right-holders). At least one commentator has observed (with a note of surprise) that Kant himself considered efficiency in the administration of private law rights was relevant in defining their substance: I Englard, *Corrective and Distributive Justice* (OUP 2009) 181, fn 776 (citing cases of bailment, and the rule of market overt).

[131] Gardner, *From Personal Life to Private Law* (n 16) 210.

C. Conclusions

To sum up: the current presumption in favour of right-holder enforcement in the modern day is potentially explicable by a variety of quite different arguments from right-holder control, autonomy and efficiency. There is also a viable argument that the allocation of rights of action to right-holders is a rational reflection of one or more of the reasons why primary private-law rights are given to those who hold them in the first place. That is not the same as saying that rights of action and primary rights are analytically entailed by one another, or even that the former are *necessarily* normatively *required* by the latter, when all reasons are considered. But it suggests that a reason for me having a primary right as against you in respect of my private interests is likely also to be a pro-tanto reason, all other things being equal, for me being accorded the right to sue you where my right is violated or threatened, or where its precise content needs to be determined and declared by a court of law.

When it comes to exceptions, the arguments diverge in terms of the range that they are able to justify, and this in turn may say something about which of them provides the best overall explanatory account of the legal rules we have identified. Arguments from right-holder control and independence, as well as the particular form of 'individual sovereignty' argument supported by Goldberg and Zipursky, suggest that right-holder consent (and prior consent at that) is key. The protection of private interests in private law is on this type of view very much a personal business in which no one else should be involved unless the right-holder wants them to be, even though the protection of those interests may be sufficiently important to others to give rise to public law protections for those interests that are also enforceable by public enforcers. Arguments from autonomy are less clear-cut and allow for third-party enforcement where this promotes the interests of the right-holder, or others, provided that this does not unduly compromise the right-holder's own options. A general rule of thumb would seem to be that right-holder consent should generally be sought, but that if the right-holder is incapable of giving it, third-party intervention is permissible where it is consistent with the purposes and interests of the right-holder, or where the right-holder was under a duty to protect the third party's interests, but not otherwise. The various instrumental arguments are likely to support a still greater range of exceptions, some of which are entirely independent of prior right-holder consent. The full range of exceptions implied by these arguments is hard to assess without very detailed modelling and the varied empirical challenges to which pragmatic exceptions often respond are likely to mean that new possibilities are always on the cards. If arguments about efficiency are subordinate to those of interpersonal justice, however, as I personally think they should be, then they should not be allowed to greatly extend the reach of third-party rights of action beyond the boundaries supported by the other models I have mentioned. Third parties should not, for example, be permitted to enforce just because a right-holder chooses not to, even if this leaves unwholesome or damaging externalities unaddressed, or wrongdoers undeterred. Efficiency in the allocation of rights of action in private law should therefore generally be made to serve the interests of right-holders and their purposes, not the other way around.

8.5 Interest Hybridity Again—Exemplary and Punitive Damages

Everything in this chapter so far has assumed that the interests that private enforcers of private law are protecting are private interests, either those of private right-holders, or of others implicated by private injustices. This is a great deal of the truth. There is, however, a well-known exception, in so far as private enforcers are still able to claim exemplary or 'punitive' damages awards at the end of the enforcement process in some cases of wrongdoing. Whether such awards really are 'punitive' these days I have doubted,[132] *if*, by this, one means that their object is to permit a plaintiff to exact vengeful retribution upon a wrongdoer. Yet, while it is sometimes claimed that such awards are simply doing corrective justice or compensating for some harm done to private interests that has historically been missed,[133] or that they 'substitute' for private rights infringed,[134] this is not the whole truth either. One clear purpose of such awards, in the modern judicial understanding, is to protect public interests by expressively condemning and deterring acts that concern the community, and which the community must been seen to disavow.[135] According to some courts, they also still serve a vestigial public order function, reducing the risk of private acts of revenge,[136] although this seems rather unlikely given that such acts will nowadays most certainly attract the penalties of the criminal law. And in the US Supreme Court jurisprudence, retribution is still clearly understood to be a primary aim.[137]

The public interest motivation of awards is especially evident in cases against State agents—a pattern presaged in those ancient, Roman law statutes that gave

[132] K Barker, 'Punishment in Private Law—No Such Thing (Any More)' in E Bant and others (eds), *Punishment and Private Law* (Hart 2021) Ch 2.

[133] E Weinrib, 'Punishment and Disgorgement as Contract Remedies' (2003) 78 Chicago-Kent Law Review 55; A Beever, 'The Structure of Aggravated and Exemplary Damages' (2003) 23 Oxford Journal of Legal Studies 87; A Beever, 'Justice and Punishment in Tort: A Comparative Theoretical Analysis' in CEF Rickett (ed), *Justifying Private Law Remedies* (Hart 2008) 249. For the evidence and the extensive literature suggesting that punitive awards were indeed at one time (and sometimes still do) compensate private losses, see Barker (n 132) 47–50.

[134] Stevens (n 71) 60 (awards are the 'next best substitute for the primary right').

[135] *Lamb v Cotogno* (1987) 164 CLR 1 (HCA) 8; *Rookes v Barnard* [1964] AC 1129 (HL) 1228 (Lord Devlin).

[136] *Lamb* (n 135) 9.

[137] C Sharkey, 'Punitive Damages Transformed into Societal Damages' in Bant and others (eds) (n 132) Ch 7, 159–60, citing *Phillip Morris USA v Williams* 549 US 346 (2007). See also *Gertz v Robert Welsh Inc* 418 US 323 (1974), 350. This best explains why the Supreme Court has brought constitutional due process protections to bear on excessive awards: *BMW of North America Incorporated v Gore* 517 US 559 (1996).

private enforcers incentives to prosecute official extortion,[138] which was present in some of the earliest English cases of the eighteenth century,[139] and which remains clear today in claims against the police.[140] Awards are not, however, confined to such cases and cannot therefore be rationalized solely as another way of making the State accountable for abuses of governmental power. They have a wider public interest role, engaging plaintiffs as private Attorneys-General to sanction the conduct of other citizens.[141] This connects them loosely to the cases of private criminal prosecution examined at the end of the last chapter; to the various *qui tam* actions and statutory citizen-suit provisions triggered by the violation of regulatory provisions examined in Chapter 7; and to the numerous instances in which public agencies are now empowered to seek penalties according to a civil standard of proof for a variety of regulatory offences, the object of which (in Australia at least) is specific and general deterrence.[142] The main difference between cases involving punitive damages in private law and the other cases just listed is that the plaintiff's public interest role is always secondary and contingent, because it depends always on a plaintiff's own private right having first been violated.

The object here is not to revisit the debate about the public interest role of exemplary awards, which I will take as established. Admittedly, it is controversial. The deterrence value of such awards is very questionable in jurisdictions in which liability is either modest (as in England)[143] or insurable;[144] the suggestion that they prevent victims taking the law into their own hands is so antiquated as to seem faintly ridiculous in modern conditions; retribution, if it is an aim at all, is so sensitive a matter as surely to require the procedural protections of the criminal law if it is to be permitted at the initiative of private citizens; and the expressive value of exemplary awards is doubtful when they can easily be settled privately behind

[138] See Chapter 4, 4.3B(ii) text to nn 73–76 (these included the *Lex Acilia*).

[139] *Wilkes v Wood* (1763) Lofft 1, 98 Eng Rep 489; *Huckle v Money* 2 Wils 205, 95 Eng Rep 768 (KB 1763); *Beardmore v Carrington* (1764) 2 Wils 244, 95 Eng Rep 790.

[140] F Maher, 'An Empirical Study of Exemplary Damages in Australia' (2020) 43 Melbourne University Law Review 694 (the highest proportion of awards in Australia are against the police); A Kildea, 'Power and Punishment: A Closer Look at Exemplary Damages as a Response to Tortious Conduct of Police Officers in Western Australia' (2021) University of Western Australia Law Review 10; M Fielding, 'Exemplary Damages and Police Wrongdoing: An Empirical Analysis' (2024) 29 Tort Law Journal 53.

[141] One of the more common uses in England is to sanction wrongful evictions by landlords: J Goudkamp and E Katsampouka, 'An Empirical Study of Punitive Damages' (2018) 38 Oxford Journal of Legal Studies 90, 112–13.

[142] D Kayis, E Gluer, and S Walpole (eds), *The Law of Civil Penalties* (Federation Press 2023); *Australian Building and Construction Commissioner v Construction, Forestry, Mining and Energy Union* [2018] HCA 3 [116] (Keane, Nettle, and Gordon JJ). See further Chapter 5 Section 5.2, this book.

[143] On the modesty of awards in the UK, see Goudkamp and Katsampouka (n 141). For a more general assessment, see J Goudkamp and E Katsampouka, 'Punitive Damages: Ten Misconceptions' in Bant and others (eds) (n 132) Ch 8, 193–98.

[144] This is most often possible in jurisdictions such as the US, where awards are available for even some types of grossly negligent conduct. See generally K Barker, '*Lamb v Lotogno* (1987): Insured Punishment' in J Goudkamp and E Katsampouka (eds), *Landmark Cases in the Law of Punitive Damages* (Hart 2023) Ch 6, 112–17.

closed doors. English and Australian courts maintain that exemplary damages are a remedy of last resort[145] and awards are rare, even in the United States.[146]

Despite this, however, there is no sign of law-makers pressing for their abolition.[147] English courts have relaxed their approach to the types of case in which they can be granted,[148] and one civilian jurisdiction (France) has even recently flirted with the idea of introducing them for the first time, as an alternative to a civil penalties regime.[149] This is extraordinary, given the traditional opposition of civilian systems to using private law to punish, but is a response to rising pressure and reflects a growing trend.[150] It is no coincidence that the French proposal came at a time when public finance was short, that it focused specifically on wrongs done for profit, and that it contained measures for a proportion of the relevant award to be redirected to the Public Treasury. There are gains to be made by government through any such scheme, as in *qui tam* actions. In any event, the point is that exemplary damages are far from withering on the vine. Unusual they may be, but anomalous they are certainly not. They form part of a set of private enforcement tools designed to fill increasingly large gaps in public interest protection that are left by a creaking framework of public laws and public enforcers.[151]

The question here, then, is not whether punitive damages serve a public interest role but what the implications of this might be for the conditions attaching to a private enforcer's right of action—and for the way in which remedial rights are structured—if that role is taken seriously. Why would the victim of a *private* wrong

145 See eg *Thompson v Metropolitan Police Commissioner* [1998] QB 498, 517 (Lord Woolf MR).

146 One analysis of 2005 State Court data collected in forty-six of the US's seventy-five most populous counties suggests that awards are made in only 3.4 per cent of civil jury trials: T Eisenberg and M Heise, 'Judge–Jury Difference in Punitive Damages: Who Listens to the Supreme Court? (2011) 8 Journal of Empirical Legal Studies 325, 330. But some specific types of case undoubtedly show much higher rates, with rates in case of intentional tortious wrongdoing as high as 24 per cent: C Sharkey, 'Punitive Damages as Societal Damages' (2003) 113 Yale Law Journal 347, 351, fn 12.

147 The Law Commission, *Aggravated, Exemplary and Restitutionary Damages* (Law Comm No 247, 1997) recommended their expansion. Note, however, that awards have been abolished in some Australian jurisdictions in cases of unintentional personal injury (where they are unlikely to have played much of a role anyway) and where the State's liability is vicarious; and in all jurisdictions in defamation cases: Maher (n 140) 700–03; Barker (n 144) 103.

148 *Kuddus v Chief Constable of Leicestershire Constabulary* [2002] 2 AC 122 (HL).

149 See S Rowan, 'Punishment and Private Law: Some Comparative Observations' in Bant and others (eds) Ch 3 (n 132). The original 2005 proposal (Code Civil Draft Article 1371) was never implemented and abandoned in 2017 in favour of one for a civil penalties action at the suit of either the citizen or the State in respect of deliberate tortious wrongs for profit (Draft Article 1266-1). The latter is not yet in force but thought 'likely to be enacted' by Rowan (ibid 71).

150 ibid 64. The rise in civilian interest is wider than just France: see M Parker, 'Changing Tides: The Introduction of Punitive Damages into the French Legal System' (2013) 41 Georgia Journal of International & Comparative Law 389; M Alles, 'Punitive Damages: Reorienting the Debate in Civil Law Systems' (2019) 10 Journal of European Tort Law 63; J Zekoll and W Vop, 'The Conflict Between American Punitive Damages and German Public Policy—A Reassessment' (2020) 61 Virginia Journal of International Law Online 3, 33; M Sossamon, 'Split the Difference: A Civilian Thesis for Punitive Damages' (2023) 98 Tulane Law Review 219, 239–48 (citing a softening of attitudes in Italy, France, Argentina, Mexico, and Louisiana).

151 Law Comm No 247 (n 147) [1.15]; *ACB v Thomson Medical Pte Ltd* [2017] SGCA 20 [173].

be possessed of a wholly unrestricted right of action that enables her to protect broader community interests? And why, if the relevant damages award is protective of this public interest, would she be allowed to pocket those damages for herself?

A. Implications for Rights of Action and State Intervention

The first question is easier to answer than the second. From a court's point of view, the wrong to the plaintiff identifies her as most likely possessing a proper motivation for the exemplary damages claim, and a private interest that is sufficiently distinct to those of other members of the community to eliminate any floodgates concerns. Of all members of the community concerned by a tortious excess of police power[152] or private assault,[153] the victim is the most obviously 'qualified' and highly motivated person to make an example of the tortfeasor and deter any repetition of the wrong to himself, or others. Allowing the plaintiff to sue is consistent with other instances in which private persons are permitted to act in protection of public interests, falling as it does within the 'private law right' exception identified at the start of Chapter 6.

This may explain why courts are satisfied as to the plaintiff's standing to assert the public interest: it reassures them that she is unlikely to be a 'busybody'. But does it explain why the State, as representative of the public good, lacks any *fiat* or right of intervention in respect of that aspect of the claim? Why does it not, at the least, retain a power to strike out the remedial claim post-initiation, as it does the whole action in private criminal prosecutions and actions *qui tam*? Why does it not have the power to prevent a punitive damages claim being privately settled on disadvantageous terms, or even to settle the claim itself, as it can under the Federal Claims Act? Why can it not join the plaintiff's action and add its own claim for an exemplary award? The reasons are not immediately obvious.

One answer may simply be that the State delegates the relevant public interest judgement to courts. What is at issue, after all, is not the plaintiff's right to initiate a suit at all (which is clear, since she has been wronged) but simply her right to seek an additional type of judicial remedy. Remedial rights fall within a court's jurisdiction and the court can assess the need for deterrence and condemnation itself, allowing or denying the remedy accordingly. But that response rather too neatly sidesteps the issue, I think. It does not explain *why* the executive would leave the public interest judgement to a court and would not reserve a power to intervene in the plaintiff's remedial rights if it thought that the public interest was not being served by them.

[152] *New South Wales v Zreika* [2012] NSWCA 37.

[153] *MacDougal v Mitchell* [2015] NSWCA 389; *Zorom Enterprises Pty Ltd v Zabow* [2007] NSWCA 106.

A second, entirely pragmatic explanation is that the range of instances in which a plaintiff can seek exemplary damages is potentially so great as to make State supervision wholly impractical. Public agents are hard pressed enough, we saw in the last chapter, to monitor the relatively small number of private criminal prosecutions that citizens bring. If they had to be notified of every case in which a claim for exemplary damages was made and consider whether or not to supervise or veto it, the resource implications would be mind-boggling.

A third, good reason of both a constitutional and pragmatic kind is that a significant proportion of punitive awards these days are made against State agents, so that the danger of enforcement capture weighs heavily against any State *fiat*, or intervention. But that would not, or course, preclude State intervention in 'punitive' damages claims brought by one citizen against another.

The final possibility is that the function of punitive damages has historically been so indeterminate as between retributive, deterrent, compensatory and expressive ends, and that it still not entirely clear that it *only public* interests that are at stake when an award is made. The English Law Commission clearly took this view, describing awards as *primarily* public interest awards, but nonetheless 'hybrid'.[154] To the extent that doubts persist and there is some continued leaching of compensatory or private 'vindicatory' purposes into punitive awards, the State will inevitably be reluctant to interfere, lest its intervention prejudice the operation of private justice. This argument would drop out, of course, if the purpose of such awards were finally settled as being *always* and *only* public. For now, however, it yields a credible additional explanation for the State's reluctance to get more involved.

The upshot is that if one were to take the public function of punitive awards as firmly established and as the only end in view, a private right-holder's right to seek them in addition to compensation would still be logically justifiable as a matter of standing, but one might, if resourcing allowed, expect some requirement that the State be notified of a claim, and give the State a power to intervene so as to veto the remedy, or control the terms of any settlement, if it considered the award to be contrary to the public interest. That it does not do so is probably a reflection of the practicalities and the remaining uncertainty about the true purpose of judicial awards.

B. Implications for the Distribution of Awards

The second question is more vexed. Assuming again that awards are truly public interest awards, they should presumptively inure to the benefit of the public, not to the purse of a plaintiff who has already been fully compensated for the wrong.

[154] Law Comm No 247 (n 147) Part V, [1.143].

The point has long been recognized in the common law authorities.[155] Windfalls are inappropriate from the point of view of corrective justice and can also be inefficient.[156] Unless one thinks that making the plaintiff *better off* is actually necessary as an aspect of retributive justice (which seems to me unlikely, despite a novel recent argument to this effect),[157] the only reason for allowing a private plaintiff to retain any part of the award himself would be to ensure that he or she has sufficient incentive to bring the claim.

Historically, this point has been taken seriously from time to time. There is evidence, we noted previously, that the penalties payable under Roman law may sometimes have been split between the State and the citizen prosecutor, rather than being left exclusively in the latter's hands.[158] This also happened under the English *qui tam* statutes mentioned by Blackstone, where portions of the relevant fine were 'given to the crown, the poor, or some public use'.[159] It is the modern pattern, we saw, in respect of frauds upon the State under the False Claims Act in the United States (where the State gets between 70 per cent and 85 per cent of any penalty award), under the proposed civil penalties regime in France (which can be enforced privately as well as publicly), and in respect of punitive damages awards in at least ten jurisdictions in the United States at the time of writing.[160]

The splitting of punitive damages awards in the United States began in the 1980s and is customarily effected by statute,[161] although courts have sometimes also made the split at their own motion.[162] The statutory provisions were ironically motivated either by the desire to reduce the attractiveness of claims for plaintiffs in

[155] See eg *Bass v Chicago & NW Ry Co* 42 Wis 654, 672–73 (1877).

[156] Sharkey (n 146) 371–72; Note, *An Economic Analysis of the Plaintiffs Windfall from Punitive Damage Litigation* (1992) 105 Harvard Law Review 1900, 1907.

[157] For such a thesis (based on the idea that proper retribution requires a counter-message about the defendant's wrongdoing in which the plaintiff is seen to bounce back better than before— 'retributive resilience') see E Encarnacion, 'Resilience, Retribution and Punitive Damages' (2021) 100 Texas Law Review 1025. This concept of retribution seems to me to be distinct to the classical understanding of retribution (which involves hurting a person as a matter of desert in just proportion *to the wrong done*) and is best understood as an extension of expressive theories of punishment. For a brief account of such theories, see Barker (n 144) 123–27.

[158] Chapter 4 Section 4.3(ii) text to nn 75,76.

[159] William Blackstone, *Commentaries on the Laws of England* (Robert Bell 1773) Book 3, 160.

[160] Alaska (Alaska Stat § 09.17.020(j)), Colorado (Colo Rev Stat § 24-75-201.7), Georgia (GA Code § 51-12-5.1(e)(2)), Illinois (Ill Comp Stat Ch 735 § 5/2-1207), Indiana (Ind Code § 34-51-3-6), Iowa (Iowa Code § 668A.1), Missouri (Mo Rev Stat § 537.675), Oregon (Or Rev Stat § 31.735), Pennsylvania (Pa Stat tit 40 § 1303.505) and Utah (Utah Code § 78B-8-201(3)). At one time, there were four more (Kansas, California, Florida, and New York), but the legislation was allowed to lapse without renewal.

[161] The literature is vast. For a representative range of views (and references to many more), see Sharkey (n 146), 372–86; B Rabe, 'The Constitutionality of Split-Recovery Punitive Damage Statutes: Good Policy, but Bad Law' (2008) Utah Law Review 333; L Goldstein, 'Split-Recovery Statutes Do More Harm than Good' (2009) 38 Colorado Law Review 105; S Sanders, 'Uncle Sam and the Partitioning Punitive Problem: A Federal Split-Recovery Statute or a Federal Tax?' (2013) 40 Pepperdine Law Review 785; A David, 'The Problem of State Split-Recovery Statutes: Why Punitive Damages Should be Taxed as Windfalls' (2015) 68 The Tax Lawyer 715.

[162] *Dardinger v Anthem Blue Cross & Blue Shield* 781 NE 2s 121 (Ohio, 2002). For other cases where this has been done or contemplated, see Sharkey (n 146) 382–386.

response to insurance industry lobbying about the size and incidence of claims, or to raise State revenue.[163] Courts' efforts, by contrast, seem to have been generated more by the moral concern about the impropriety of leaving the plaintiff with an improper windfall. In most cases, the percentage creamed off to public purposes under the statutes is fixed (between 50 per cent and 75 per cent) and the splitting mechanism is triggered whenever a punitive damages award is made, irrespective of the claim type. One scheme (Pennsylvania) nonetheless targets a particular type of wrongdoing (medical malpractice),[164] and one (Illinois) gives judges a general discretion to set the proper split between the plaintiff and the relevant public fund, rather than predetermining it.

The schemes also vary in so far as they either require the relevant public cut to be paid to the State's general treasury, or ringfence it for payment to special purposes such as the compensation of criminal injuries or tort victims, civil reparations and legal aid programmes, the remediation of environmental hazards, property tax relief, or the compensation of medical accidents. Judges have proven more flexible and inventive still, with one Ohio court famously sequestering funds to a charitable purpose chiming directly with the sort of social harm likely to have been caused by the offender's conduct, requiring a health insurer that had cynically withheld payments from a cancer patient to pay US$20 million into a court-established cancer-research fund.[165]

All of these redistributive solutions are refreshingly creative and chime with the statutory schemes that are sometimes now available at the suit of public enforcers to force wrongdoers to redress their wrongs, which we examined at the end of Chapter 5. Judicial redistribution raises serious concerns, since it is not the role of an unelected judge to determine social policy in respect of the use of public funds. Judges cannot simply give damages awards away to their favourite charity.[166] However, schemes that are legislatively sanctioned are immune to that critique and can simultaneously eliminate a significant proportion of the plaintiff's windfall and apply a portion of the public interest award to its most logical end—the protection of public interests. They may also (although this is characteristically unclear) create more efficient incentives to suit by removing the excessive temptations of private reward that can otherwise yield overenforcement in jurisdictions where damages awards are high.[167] In the United States, it is admittedly sometimes suggested that damages-splitting is unconstitutional because it involves a State 'taking' some of a plaintiff's property, imposing an excessive fine on a defendant

[163] Sharkey (n 146) 375–77.

[164] Pa Stat tit 40 §1303.505.

[165] *Dardinger* (n 162), discussed in Sharkey (n 146) at 381–82.

[166] Sharkey (n 146) 427.

[167] S Dodson, 'Assessing the Practicality and Constitutionality of Alaska's Split-Recovery Punitive Damages Statute' (2000) 49 Duke Law Journal 1335, 1348. The efficiency of split-recovery scheme in the US is (as always) disputed, with the consequence that 'no consensus emerges': Sharkey (n 146) 387–89.

or exposing him to the risk of double punishment, or because due process is prejudiced by jurors making awards when they know that part of the award is destined indirectly for their own benefit (as taxpayers), or to a charitable purpose.[168] However, with one exception, none of these concerns has so far proven fatal[169] and they do not translate clearly to other jurisdictions,[170] so that the introduction of similar schemes outside that constitutional context appears both perfectly possible and, in principle, a good idea.

When it comes to determining the appropriate destination of the relevant funds, much might perhaps be learned from recent research considering the best use of confiscated criminal profits. Thinking in that field suggests that dedicating funds to purposes that resonate with, and move society forward from an offence (rather than simply confiscating the funds to general State revenue) is beneficial in helping to regenerate some of the social cohesion lost in consequence of the wrong.[171] From this point of view, a scheme that allowed punitive awards for cynical environmental torts to be ploughed into an environmental remediation fund might have both an important social purpose and the ring of poetic justice[172] in respect of the polluter's conduct, in the same way that the Ohio court's divergence of the

[168] For the arguments and relevant case law see Sharkey (n 146) 434–39 (suggesting that the concerns can be greatly mitigated by reconceptualizing many awards as compensating *societal* damage, not punishing defendants for harm done to a particular plaintiff); C Stevens, 'Split-Recovery: A Constitutional Answer to the Punitive Damage Dilemma (1994) 21 Pepperdine Law Review 857, 871–91 (concluding that the greatest risks relate to excessive State punishment, double jeopardy, violation of equal protection—where schemes allow splitting in some cases but not others—and due process, but that these can be avoided through suitable statutory drafting); V Schwartz, M Behrens, and C Silverman, 'I'll Take That: Legal and Public Policy Problems Raised by Statutes That Require Punitive Damages to be Shared with the State' (2003) 68 Missouri Law Review 525, 548–57 (raising all of the above concerns as giving rise to a risk of constitutional litigation, whilst acknowledging that Courts have not as yet struck the legislation down); Dodson (n 167) 1353–68 (acknowledging the concerns but concluding that none of them is fatal to the Alaskan statute, and pointing out that some at least are now met by the general constitutional restriction now placed upon the size of awards).

[169] The only example of a court striking down legislation (on the basis that it involved an unconstitutional taking) is *Kirk v Denver Publishing Co* 818 P 2d 262 (1991) (in respect of Colorado legislation that no longer exists, and which had the peculiarity of only allowing distribution to the State after judgment had already been given in a plaintiff's favour).

[170] Due process concerns are less in jurisdictions in which juries have no involvement in making awards. The allocation of this function to judges in England and Australia also results in awards that are modest, not 'excessive'. Whilst the Australian Constitution does prohibit State taking of property without compensation, it is most unlikely that exemplary damages, being entirely discretionary, are a prior right of the plaintiff, so as to count as property.

[171] The Queensland Crime and Corruption Commission appears recently to have accepted in principle academic criticism that the current criminal assets confiscation scheme operating in the State (which simply gathers all such assets in to the consolidated revenue) is unimaginative and may require rethinking so as to redirect funds to victims of fraud or property-related crime, or even offender rehabilitation schemes: Queensland Crime and Corruption Commission, *Modernising Queensland's Asset Confiscation Regime: A Reform Agenda for the Criminal Proceeds Confiscation Act 2002* (Qld) (April 2024) 38–41, Rec 8. See more generally on the psychology surrounding confiscated asset distribution: G Dale, *Crime, Confiscation and Emotion*, PhD Thesis, Faculty of Law, Monash University, Melbourne (2022) esp 210–21.

[172] M Galanter and D Luban, 'Poetic Justice: Punitive Damages and Legal Pluralism' (1993) 42 American University Law Review 1393 esp 1436–38 ('expressive defeat').

wrongdoer's funds to cancer research did. Behavioural science research completed in 2011 in relation to split-recovery systems appears to support solutions with this type of social resonance, finding that distributing the 'public' share to an 'organisation somehow related to the problematic issue in the trial' was preferred by 90 per cent of participants in the study to straightforward disbursement to State coffers.[173] This resonance is missing if the State takes its cut by taxing a plaintiff's punitive damages award as part of his or her reportable income.[174]

Setting up and administering particular purpose funds does, of course, take more time and effort, and one view is that it can overly constrain public judgments about how public money should be used, which should always be responsive to governmental needs and priorities of the moment, not fixed in advance. However, even if ringfencing is generally thought too expensive and inflexible, it would clearly help to overcome the specific difficulty that otherwise flows from redistributing punitive damages awards that have been made against State agents back to the general public treasury: requiring money to be paid from a policing budget to an independent police complaints authority, or to a discretionary public compensation scheme for the compensation of victims of domestic violence, solves the otherwise jarring problem of a court in a split-recovery system being seen to give the State some form of 'cash back' whenever it pays out for one of its agents' egregious violations of a citizen's private rights.

Why, then, have jurisdictions such as England and Australia not followed the American lead? On first blush this is puzzling. One concern voiced in America—that split recovery systems encourage juries to make larger awards in the knowledge that the money will in part inure to the public good[175]—clearly does not apply in jurisdictions where awards are judicial and generally modest in amount. Another—that reducing the plaintiff's take will undermine her incentive to sue because she needs the full sum to help cover the costs of bringing the action—again has less purchase in systems in which costs follow the event and can be averted by allowing the plaintiff to retain some portion of the fund. It also tends to ignore the point that a plaintiff seeking a punitive award already has the incentive of compensatory damages for his or her own loss. The worry that splitting awards will increase squabbles between plaintiffs and their contingency-fee lawyers (who may now have to accept a smaller slice of the pie)[176] is a headache caused by the contingency-fee system itself, and lawyers' fees are closely scrutinized in England and Australia to ensure that they do not exceed a fair arrangement.

[173] P Fox, T Wingrove, and C Pfeifer, 'A Comparison of Students' and Jury Panelists' Decision-making in Split Recovery Cases' (2011) 29 Behavioural Sciences and the Law 358, 370.

[174] An alternative solution to the split-recovery system sometimes suggested, which is said to be more efficient and to avoid some of the problems of incentives and voluntary settlement: David (n 161); Sanders (n 161) esp 827–32.

[175] Schwartz and others (n 168) 538 (and see also 548–51 as regards the implications for due process).

[176] ibid 544–45.

The key issue for the English Law Commission, when considering the possibility of a split system that might divert one third of awards to the State, therefore came down to the pragmatic question of whether the public costs of splitting would in practice outweigh the benefits.[177] Three issues contributed to the Commission's concern about this matter—a worry that exemplary awards are generally so modest in the English system that the State's receipt of a share might not cover the public cost of their diversion;[178] a worry that the State's share of a judgment award might go unexecuted and therefore unrecovered because the plaintiff would have no incentive to execute it on the State's behalf;[179] and a fear that the State might lose out on its proper share as a result of settlement collusions between plaintiffs and defendants, with plaintiffs negotiating higher compensatory measures of damages in exchange for settling correspondingly much lower exemplary awards.[180]

Although full-scale costings would need to be done in each jurisdiction in which the possibility is considered, none of these concerns is conclusive. Giving the State an independent power of joinder, and a power to intervene in settlement (as under the False Claims Act) could in principle tackle the second and third concerns respectively (although close court supervision of settlements would surely itself also solve that problem at much lower cost). The costs to the State of a diversionary scheme are also very much dependent on the type of diversion that is envisaged and on the identity of the organization responsible for overseeing it. It costs little for a court officer to order part payment to the public treasury, rather than the private plaintiff, although this is the least imaginative of public disbursal arrangements. The setting up of a more specific, tailored scheme and its oversight costs more, but the diversion could be made to existing public arrangements, such as criminal injuries compensation schemes, or, in Australia, the National Disability Insurance Scheme (NDIS), which is terribly short of funding. The Law Commission is hence clearly right to observe that awards in Australia and England do nothing to rival the billions of dollars sometimes awarded against corporate giants in blockbuster cases in the United States,[181] which give legislators in that jurisdiction such a powerful incentive to get into the diversion game, but this does not mean that there is no social value—in either cash or in kind—in split-recovery punitive damages regimes in systems in which awards are not as eye-wateringly high. That such schemes have waxed, waned, and waxed again across the broader span of our legal history should come as no surprise, since their incidence and form is

[177] Law Comm No 247 (n 147) [5.146], [5.158].
[178] ibid [5.146].
[179] ibid [5.148]–[5.149].
[180] ibid [5.150].
[181] See W Viscusi, 'The Blockbuster Punitive Damages Awards' (2004) 53 Emory Law Journal 1405. Such awards less common than one might think, it being suggested that only about 14 per cent of cases in one study were above US$1millon, and half of awards less than US$100,000: C Sharkey, 'Economic Analysis of Punitive Damages: Theory, Empirics and Doctrine' in J Arlen (ed), *Research Handbook on the Economics of Torts* (Edward Elgar 2015) Ch 19, 486, 500.

responsive always both to the background regulatory environment (where gaps may be bigger or smaller as the regulatory ambitions and capacities of the State expand and contract), and to the social and economic conditions of the day.

8.6 Summation

The private enforcement of private law is the securest part of the classical enforcement paradigm that I identified at the outset of this book. It is indeed mainly private parties that enforce its rules in the sense of holding the rights of action—and in the main, these private enforcers are holders of claim rights that have been violated by others. In the main again, the interests that private right-holders protect when suing for violations of their claim rights are their own private interests. There are potentially very good reasons—both moral and pragmatic—for each of these basic features of the enforcement system. But none of these tenets, we have seen in the preceding pages, is fully secure. Adjustments to the classical paradigm are necessary to present a more accurate picture.

The first adjustment, which is a minor but important clarification, is that rights of action are not always paired in private law with primary claim rights—they can be coupled with any of the basic types of right that you and I have—claim rights, powers, immunities, or liberties. This is morally reassuring.

The second, bigger shift for which we are indebted to Tim Liau, Lionel Smith, and others, lies in the observation that sometimes private persons other that right-holders have rights of action that enable them to enforce the rights of others. In most cases—and consistently with the liberal premises of the jurisdictions from which the examples in this chapter have been drawn—this is with the consent of the right-holder, but not always. Sometimes such rights are provided to overcome incapacities in the right-holder (or the lack of such a right-holder), to avoid problems of enforcement capture, to overcome collective action problems, to enable the actions of persons with more than one type of private interest in property to be consolidated into a single proceeding, or to protect the interests of third parties who hold no primary rights at all, where the protection of those interests was a purpose of the right-holder and consistent with the right-holder's own interest. These exceptional cases all test models of private rights of action that understand them as instruments of a right-holder's exclusive personal sovereignty or control over what is hers. But they can be supported in so far as they promote the autonomy of the right-holder, or of others whose interests are consistent with those of the right-holder, as well, potentially, as by the more pragmatic types of argument which we have encountered in previous chapters.

The third adjustment is that private enforcers in private law are sometimes protecting not just their own private interests, or the interests of other private persons, but the public interests of the community too. In private law, this role is secondary, sporadic, contingent, and contested. It is an 'add-on' job served by the exemplary damages remedy (as well, potentially, as by others).[182] This not a new insight by any means and it could obviously be challenged, but if it is correct, the point is that its implications are probably not be being taken sufficiently seriously in so far as the process via which exemplary awards are made still lies entirely outside the State's (executive's) supervisory oversight, and in so far as the beneficial consequences of successful enforcement are still overwhelmingly permitted to inure to the enrichment of the private enforcer. Pragmatically, this might be justified by considerations of convenience and cost, but solutions adopted elsewhere in cases in which private enforcers have rights to enforce public laws in the public interest (actions *qui tam*, for example) suggest that closer State involvement in the process via which awards are made and settled might be expected (if practical), and the fruits of personal enforcement initiative might be shared in more imaginative and socially productive ways. Fruit sharing could be done most simply by taxing punitive awards, or by diverting money to the general revenue, but the intangible social benefits would probably be greater if we were deploy the funds to more creative, particular uses. Diverting punitive awards into general State revenue is clearly unacceptable where awards are made against the State itself, but this is no reason necessarily to leave the proceeds entirely in the hands of private victims who have already been fully compensated for the wrong. Distributive choices in all these instances are political judgments and the way we decide to distribute the fruit available ultimately depends on its size, the cost of dividing it up, and the public appetite. Perhaps the most flexible arrangement—and the one therefore best suited to the varied types of case—would be one that granted judges a discretion to allocate a fixed proportion of any exemplary damages award either to the public treasury, or to one of a list of designated public benefit schemes, such as criminal injuries compensation, disability insurance schemes, environmental protection schemes, or legal advisory services. An approved list of such arrangements is not beyond the reach of our collective imagination, and some level of consultation with the plaintiff in any given case as to which destination scheme might be preferred could also increase the incentive for claims to be made.

The final adjustment is the topic of the next chapter, for we shall see that it is not only private parties that have enforcement rights in private law. Sometimes the State gets involved in enforcing their rights, either paternalistically for the protection of their private interests, or in the pursuit of public ones. Rare as this is, it is a final truth to which we must now turn our attention if our understanding of enforcement rights is to be complete.

[182] The remedy of account of profits for a breach of fiduciary duty may be another example, an object being to protect the institution of trust itself by guaranteeing that no personal gain can be made from fiduciary status without proper authorization: *Boardman v Phipps* [1967] 2 AC 46 (HL).

9

Private Law, Public Enforcement

9.1 Four Exceptions to the Private Enforcement Rule

There are not many exceptions to the general rule that private law is enforced privately. Private law rights, we saw in the last chapter, are almost always enforced by private right-holders or by other persons or corporations. There is generally no reason to involve the State, save in so far as to insist on its provision of an accessible system of justice through which private parties can resolve their own disputes. Whilst public laws often exist to protect private interests as well as public ones and thereby potentially invite the addition of affected private parties to the list of possible enforcers, the reverse does not hold true: private laws do *not* generally exist in order to protect public interests.[1] There is therefore no equivalent reason why the State, as representative of the community, should be accorded a right of suit in private law—save, of course, where it is acting in its own private capacity as property owner, the promisee under a contract, or the like.

There are nonetheless some exceptions, in which the State has enforcement powers in private law in something other than its own private capacity. We examine three below in some detail: (1) where it acts *parens patriae* in the protection of incapable citizens; (2) in the enforcement of charitable trusts; and (3) where it acts as an official liquidator (in a broad sense—the language gets more technical)[2] of the assets of an insolvent corporation, or bankrupt individual. In the first instance, the relevant private right-holder lacks capacity for autonomous action and the State steps in to protect his or her interests when no private individual is available, willing, or suitable to do so. In the second, there are—as we saw in the last chapter when considering purpose trusts more generally—no private right-holders to do the enforcement job and the State therefore again acts as a default enforcement agent, alongside an increasingly wide range of non-right-holding private enforcers. In this case, however, there is an additional reason for State involvement that

[1] This is not to say that private law ignores public interest arguments. It recognises them through public interest defences to private law claims (illegality, for example) as well as in moderating remedial principles—either by deflating damages awards through statutory intervention, or (as we saw at the end of the last chapter) by inflating them through exemplary awards. The point, then is that public interests are not the driving justificatory logic of private law claims.

[2] The term here is used to refer to any agent responsible for taking control of, maximizing, and then distributing an insolvent debtor's assets to creditors. In Australia, trustees and receivers deal with the assets of bankrupts; liquidators and receivers with those of insolvent corporations.

Enforcement Rights in Public and Private Law. Kit Barker, Oxford University Press. © Kit Barker 2026.
DOI: 10.1093/9780191955006.003.0012

does not exist in the case of other purpose trusts. Charitable trusts have public interest implications in so far as they benefit the community as a whole (or a section thereof) and consequently attract special public privileges, such as exemptions from the normal taxation regime, suspension of the customary trust rules concerning certainty and perpetuity, and rescue from failure through the device of cy-près administration.

In the third example—which I shall refer to generically as 'insolvency'—the State is a legal actor of last resort in a process designed to protect and reconcile the competing interests of private debtors and creditors when debts have become too large for the debtor to bear. Whilst the bulk of both personal and corporate insolvency work is done by private agents, there are still some cases in which government officers get involved in collecting in property belonging to the debtor and enforcing the latter's claims, as well as in seeking directions from courts as to how to dispose of the debtor's assets. They also have rights sometimes to trigger compulsory insolvencies in protection of the public interest. In doing all of this, they contribute to the logistics of a system which aims to do both public and private good by rehabilitating debtors (where possible), or by maximizing and then distributing the debtor's assets amongst competing creditors (where it is not). In practice, the system achieves a blunt, second-best measure of distributive justice for those whose private interests have been adversely affected by an insolvent, preventing what would otherwise be an unseemly free-for-all in which the first (or strongest) creditor to the kill picks clean what remains of the debtor's private carcass at the expense of the rest of the pack.

There is a fourth case, that I mentioned fleetingly in Chapter 5, in which public agencies are sometimes authorized to enforce the private law rights of individuals and corporations under modern consumer-protection legislation.[3] This usually requires the permission of the right-holder and is therefore consistent with their prior consent, but not always.[4] In such instances, the agency's action on behalf of a consumer helps to solve a collective action problem (as in other representative proceedings), recovering compensatory damages for losses that are widely spread and

[3] See eg the power of the Australian Securities and Investments Commission (ASIC) to commence civil proceedings for damages under the Australian Securities and Investments Commission Act 2001 (Cth) s 50 and the National Consumer Credit Protection Act 2009 (Cth) s 275. Proceedings will only be commenced where the agency is already conducting an investigation and the decision to do so is discretionary, turning on a number of factors, including: the potential of the proceedings to advance regulatory aims, their cost, the size of the affected class of consumers and the size of their losses, whether the proceedings might prejudice other public enforcement action or carry a risk of harm to individuals (such as whistleblowers), and the alternatives open to those suffering loss, such as dispute resolution processes and their involvement in individual or representative proceedings: ASIC, *ASIC's Approach to Involvement in Private Court Proceedings, Information Sheet INFO 80* (June 2013). Note that both ASIC and the ACCC also have distinct powers to seek orders for private redress (not damages) for consumers for the breach of public laws: Chapter 5 Section 5.4 (B).

[4] A corporation's consent is not required for the exercise of ASIC's powers, but is normally sought: *INFO 80* ibid 6.

sometimes too small for individual consumers to have the incentive to sue in their own right. From the public interest point of view, the action can contribute to an agency's public investigation and to its broader regulatory aims in protecting the interests of all consumers, not just those on whose behalf it launches a particular civil proceeding. In fact, the Australian Securities and Investments Commission (ASIC) will generally only exercise its right to sue on behalf of an individual consumer where it thinks that broader public interests of this type are likely to be advanced.[5] From the consumer's point of view, however, such actions are nonetheless a useful, cost-free alternative to the modern representative class-action proceedings mentioned in the last chapter. They provide another example of a hybrid enforcement system in which public enforcers are able to protect both public and private interests at one and the same time.

9.2 Private Incapacity—Guardianship *Parens Patriae*

The State has long had the power to protect the private interests and enforce the legal rights of infants and those suffering from mental incapacity '*parens patriae*' (as 'parent of the nation'),[6] although this power was ironically all too often used in the early years not to benefit them, but instead cynically to line the pockets of kings.[7] The wardship that the King exercised over the infant heirs of his feudal tenants from the time of Edward I onwards was hence cynically milked for his own financial advantage, not used to advance the interests of the child.[8] The abuse of

[5] ibid 4–5.

[6] The origins of the doctrine of *parens patriae* are murky, separate Crown prerogatives originally having existed in respect of infant heirs of the King's feudal military tenants, on the one hand; and insane persons (divided into idiots and lunatics) on the other. The prerogatives were exercised (at least) from the reign of Edward I (1272–1307) and set out in the reign of Edward II in *de Praerogativa Regis* (1324), but the first reference to the idea of the Crown as a 'parent' does not appear until 1567: L Custer, 'The Origins of the Doctrine of Parens Patriae' (1978) 27 Emory Law Journal 195, 201–02. The first judicial reference to the King as 'Pater Patriae' comes later still in *Falkland v Bertie* 23 Eng Rep 814, 818 (Ch 1696) (Somers LC). On the historical subtleties and complexities, see further J Seymour, 'Parens Patriae and Wardship Powers: Their Nature and Origins' (1994) 14 Oxford Journal of Legal Studies 159; M McGlynn, 'Idiots, Lunatics and the Royal Prerogative in Early Tudor England' (2005) 26 The Journal of Legal History 1; L Brereton, 'The Origins and Evolution of the Parens Patriae Jurisdiction' (Lecture delivered to Sydney Law School, 5 May 2017); H Theobald, *The Law Relating to Lunacy* (Stevens & Sons 1924).

[7] Brereton (n 6) 1–3: the financial exploitation of the King's wardship over the affairs of the minor heirs of his feudal tenants extended from Edward I's reign right through to the abolition of the Court of Wards in 1660. His wardship of adult idiots (those deemed incapable from birth) and lunatics (suffering later mental incapacity) seems not to have been exploited in quite the same way, with families in practice also having a significant role and the King's patrimony gradually being moderated in the light of new social expectations and conceptions of the kingship role in Tudor times: McGlynn (n 6) 2. For a modern warning in the US (where the doctrine has expanded considerably beyond its origins) see G Curtis, 'The Checkered Career of Parens Patriae: The State as Parent or Tyrant?' (1976) 25 De Paul Law Review 895.

[8] Seymour (n 6) 165. See further S Bottomley, 'Institutional Change and Property Rights Before the Industrial Revolution: The Case of the English Court of Wards and Liveries, 1540–1660' (2023) 83 Journal of Economic History 242.

this particular prerogative eventually came to an end when feudal tenure practices were abolished and courts of equity assumed jurisdiction from the seventeenth century onwards,[9] and public guardianship has thankfully since then been generally[10] benevolent in spirit. That philosophy of paternal protection now underpins all modern guardianship arrangements, as well as the continuing *parens patriae* jurisdiction that courts of equity enjoy in many jurisdictions to act in the interests of vulnerable persons, sometimes even in opposition to the actions of their appointed guardians.[11]

Modern guardianship works by courts or (increasingly) public tribunals appointing persons, often private but sometimes also public, to manage the affairs of those adjudged incapable of managing them for themselves.[12] The system modelled below is that which exists in Queensland, but it is similar in other jurisdictions. For reasons of space, I have focused mainly on the set-up in respect of incompetent adults. The terminology of 'guardianship' can be slippery, since the word is sometimes used—as I have used it thus far and in the title of this subsection—to reference any case in which a person is accorded protective control over another's affairs. Some thirteen different types of infant 'guardian' were identified by Simpson at the beginning of the twentieth century.[13] Usually, however, the word 'guardian' is used to refer to those managing a person's personal affairs (for example their education, or a child custody arrangement) and the term 'trustee' ('estate guardian',[14] 'conservator' in the United States, or 'administrator'[15]) to refer

[9] The demise of feudal tenure in favour of socage was key. The time frame is contested. Seymour (n 6) indicates that the equitable jurisdiction in respect of affairs affecting infant heirs existed as early as the fifteenth century, but that it is unclear whether it went so far as to enable a court of equity to act in a full guardianship role. He concludes pragmatically that, whatever the truth, the Tenures Abolition Act of 1660 nevertheless gave 'particular impetus' to the development of Chancery's jurisdiction over infants and 'paved the way' toward the modern concept of protective guardianship: ibid 166, 172. On the origins of the equitable jurisdiction, see further J Chambers, *A Practical Treatise on the Jurisdiction of the High Court of Chancery Over the Persons and Property of Infants* (Saunders & Benning 1842) 1–12.

[10] There are sadly always exceptions. See S Cretney, *Family Law in the Twentieth Century: A History* (OUP 2005) Ch 16, esp 583–88 (citing the use by parents of guardianship as a means to control and discipline children). A good example is the abusive conservatorship of pop star Britney Spears, which finally came to an end in Nov 2021: 'Britney Spears Settles Legal Dispute with Estranged Father over Conservatorship' *Guardian*, 24 April, 2024.

[11] See eg *K v Minister for Youth and Community Services* [1982] 1 NSWLR 311 (statutory guardian under the Child Welfare Act 1939 (NSW) ordered to consent to an abortion sought by a fifteen-year-old girl, where this was in the latter's best interests, but consent was being withheld).

[12] The shift toward tribunals in Australia started in Tasmania in the Mental Health Act 1963 (Tas) and has been followed in all other States and Territories except the Northern Territory. For a succinct review, see N O'Neill and C Peisah, 'The Development of Modern Guardianship and Administration' [2011] Sydney University Press Law Book 7 in N O'Neill and C Peisah (eds), *Capacity and the Law* (Sydney University Press 2011) (updated 28 July 2021).

[13] AH Simpson, *A Treatise on the Law and Practice Relating to Infants* (3rd edn, Steven & Haynes 1909) 183. See also Chambers (n 9) 54–74.

[14] Law Commission WP No 91 *Family Law Review of Child Law: Guardianship* (HMSO 1985) [2.23].

[15] The Guardianship and Administration Act 2000 (Qld) (GAA) s 33(2) uses this term to refer to an adult's private trustee. Where the administrator is the State, the term 'Public Trustee' is used: Public Trustee Act 1978 (Qld) (PTA).

to those granted custodianship of their property and finances. I will use that terminology from this point on.

In either case, the guardian or 'trustee', whilst not necessarily acquiring the primary rights of the protected person, is accorded legal powers to change those rights, subject always to a range of important duties designed to ensure that the powers are not misused.[16] The protected person is subject to legal disabilities during the period of incapacity, which are for the most part the darkroom negatives of the positive powers obtained by the guardian or trustee, in her stead[17] but not always. She may hence retain some of her powers, despite the incapacity. The power of an adult incapax to appoint an advocate to represent her wishes in court is a particularly important example,[18] since she may well disagree with a guardian's assessment of her best interests and need her views to be represented in proceedings. Other, especially sensitive personal powers, such as a person's right to marry, vote, or adopt a child, whilst being stripped from her during incapacity, are not subject to the decision of her guardian, but are placed in the hands of a court or tribunal instead.[19]

The powers collectively exercisable by guardians and trustees are very extensive and include the power to make custody, employment, or healthcare arrangements for a person, to enter contracts or execute wills for him or her, and to invest, or dispose of his or her private property. They also, importantly for current purposes, include the power to handle a person's legal affairs and to initiate or defend legal proceedings for him or her as a 'litigation guardian', where they are appointed to do so by a court.[20] Guardians and trustees therefore typically have both primary legal powers in respect of a vulnerable person's rights and interests, and associated

[16] There is no universal rule as to what happens to the primary rights of the incapax. In some instances, it is clear that the rights remain with her—as for example, where the right in question relates to her body, or in the case of a child whose 'estate' is subject to guardianship (see Law Comm WP No 91 (n 14) [2.23]). In other instances, however, as, for example, where the public trustee manages the property of an adult incapax, legal title to the incapax's property vests in the trustee, as in a normal trust. To the extent that there are cases in which guardians have powers in respect of an incapax's property, but are *not* vested with property rights held on the incapax's behalf, the term 'trustee' is somewhat misleading. I am grateful to Rachel Leow for this helpful point. As to the duties of a guardian see eg GAA (Qld) ss 11B, 11C, 34.

[17] cf R Leow, 'A Principal's Mental Incapacity and "Termination" of the Agent's Authority' (2024) 140 LQR 250, esp 259–64 (suggesting that the legal powers of the incapax are retained, but cannot be exercised during the period of incapacity).

[18] See eg GAA (Qld) ss 124–25. Currently, the leave of a tribunal is still required for the right to be exercised in QLD, despite the contrary recommendation of the Queensland Law Reform Commission: QLRC Rep 67 *A Review of Queensland's Guardianship Laws* (2010) Rec 21-7.

[19] GAA (Qld) s 14(3); Sch 2, s 3. Tribunals also typically reserve the power to deal with special health decisions such as electroconvulsive therapy, sterilization, or the performance of an abortion: s 33, s 68(1), s 74.

[20] This is a distinct requirement—see eg UCCPR (Qld) R 93, R 94. In Australia, the term 'next friend' was once used to refer to persons representing an incapax as a plaintiff, and 'guardian ad litem' when defending proceedings against them, but in most jurisdictions the term 'litigation guardian' is now used to refer to persons representing the incapax in either capacity: QLRC Rep 67 (n 18) [28.15] fn 1372.

rights of action that empower them to initiate and defend lawsuits bearing upon those rights. Relevantly for our purposes, a significant proportion of these rights are private law rights relating to an individual's person,[21] property, contracts, and finances.

A. Personal Guardians

The State clearly plays a central role in designing the personal guardianship system and—through courts and tribunals—in appointing appropriate persons to act in guardianship and trustee roles. It less often itself acts in an executive capacity as a personal guardian, or trustee. Most guardians of a person's personal affairs are private individuals—typically family members, who know their charge well—and the State's intervention in such cases is generally both inappropriate and inefficient in so far as the information needed to make proper judgments about an incapax's best interests in such matters usually lies in the hands of those closest to him. Family members are also usually better motivated to act on an incapax's behalf, their interests being more closely aligned with those of the incapax than those of a remote, bureaucratic agent, however benevolently disposed.[22] A public guardian ('advocate' in some jurisdictions) can nonetheless be appointed to protect an incapable adult as a measure of last resort where no appropriate private person is available,[23] the appropriateness of any potential private appointment being determined by reference to a range of considerations, including the competence of the individual concerned, their ethics, and likely fidelity to the role, as well as the prospect of any serious conflict between his or her private interests and those of the incapax.[24] The State therefore protects and enforces a person's rights in respect of his or her personal affairs where no private individual wants the job, where there are good reasons to suspect that the standard of protection offered privately will be deficient, or where there is a serious risk of capture created by conflicts between the interests of the vulnerable party and those of a family member seeking to act on their behalf. These scenarios are not unrealistic.[25]

[21] In Australia, children are most frequently represented in civil courts in personal injury matters: ALRC Rep No 84 *Seen and Not Heard: Priority for Children in the Legal Process* (2010) [13.7].

[22] *Adult Guardian v Hunt* [2003] QSC 297 [30] (Chesterman J).

[23] In respect of guardians in QLD see GAA (Qld) s 12, 14(2); Public Guardian Act 2014 (Qld), s 12(1)(f). On public guardian arrangements in the US, see generally P Teaster Jr, M Mendiondo, and E Wood, *Public Guardianship: In the Best Interests of Incapacitated People?* (Bloomsbury USA 2010).

[24] GAA (Qld) s 15.

[25] For a clear illustration see *SBG* [2015] QCAT 287 (ninety-three-year-old lady at risk of elder abuse from her son).

B. Financial 'Trustees'

By contrast, when it comes to 'trusteeship' of an adult's property and financial rights, the State currently plays a more significant protection and enforcement role, at least in my own part of the world. In 2010, the Queensland Law Reform Commission (QLRC) hence reported that the Public Trustee (a public corporation sole) is appointed to manage the financial affairs of incapable adults in some 80 per cent of cases,[26] with the consequence that in 2020 it was actively managing the assets of over 10,000 people.[27] This creates a significant administrative burden for the Trustee, which in Queensland is self-funded, and the Commission consequently recommended that the same 'last resort' norm of deferral to private appointment that currently exists in personal guardianship cases should also apply in respect of an incapable adult's financial matters.[28] It also proposed reforms (since implemented) to allow the Public Trustee to delegate its financial and property management powers to its staff or (for day-to-day decisions) to other appropriately qualified private persons.[29]

The burden on the Trustee is still significant, not least because it is simultaneously responsible for managing the property and assets of prisoners from whom capacity has been stripped during the currency of their prison terms,[30] and for administering the private estates of deceased intestates.[31] These additional cases in which the State assumes the *parens patriae* role can also be regarded as involving 'incapable persons', the former being temporarily denuded of their legal powers for reasons of public policy, the latter being dead. Like their private equivalents, public trustees (and guardians) can be appointed by courts to act as litigation guardians in relevant proceedings to protect the interests of their charges. Indeed, they can be appointed to represent a vulnerable person even when they are not already acting as that person's trustee or guardian. They are then primarily liable, as are all litigation guardians, for the costs of proceedings initiated on behalf of the incapax, including the costs of engaging legal representation, although these costs may be reimbursed from the latter's estate where (and this is often in practice the catch) it carries sufficient funds.[32]

There are serious worries about both the private cost and the quality of public trusteeship, and about the costs to the public purse of the State acting as litigation

[26] QLRC Rep 67 (n 18) [25.7]. The power of the public trustee to administer the affairs of incapable persons in QLD is contained in s 27 of the PTA.

[27] The Public Advocate, *Preserving the Financial Futures of Vulnerable Queenslanders: A Review of Public Trustee Fees, Charges and Practices* (January 2021) (ix).

[28] QLRC Rep 67 (n 18) [25.6], Rec 14–13. This reform was not implemented, probably because it is still up to the Public Trustee to decide whether or not to accept an appointment to the role: PTA s 27(3).

[29] ibid [25.29]–[25.39], Rec 25-3; GAA (Qld) s 250(A).

[30] PTA Part 7 (persons sentenced to three years or more).

[31] PTA s 29(1)(a).

[32] *Rhodes v Swithenbank* (1889) 22 QBD 577; *Stephenson v Geiss* [1998] 1 Qld R 542, 558 (Lee J). By contrast, they are not liable for costs in defending a proceeding.

guardian for incapable persons in civil proceedings. As regards the role of public trusteeship itself, the level of charges made by the trustee for administering private assets has proven scandalous, clients sometimes being charged twice for a service, charged for no service at all, or the charges being so high as to threaten entirely to consume the assets administered.[33] The quality of the decisions regarding both investment and use of the client's funds has also been highly questionable in some instances. It should not be necessary, for example, for an incapacitated adult to obtain three separate quotations before being permitted to purchase a kettle.[34] Some of the charges to the funds of the incapax have also been used to cross-subsidise the Public Trustee's other community service functions, in clear breach of fiduciary principles.[35] These irregularities are again symptoms of modern public protection systems coming under strain, with the system struggling to make good deficits in its operating budgets by clawing at the assets of the clients that it is supposed to be protecting. Whilst these problems stem mostly from error and/or escalating fiscal pressure, not the type of avarice that earlier motivated ancient kings, the manipulation of the system for public profit still leaves a bitter taste in the mouth and should place us on alert.

As regards the State's role in litigating the rights of protected persons who are unable to afford their own representative, the problems are potentially more serious still, since it has in recent years increasingly ducked its responsibility for the task, objecting to the cost in both financial and human resource terms.[36] In one case in 2009, the Public Trustee refused in principle to act in defence of an incapable client whose financial and associated legal affairs it was already administrating, even though the plaintiff in the action had undertaken to indemnify its costs.[37] As things stand in Queensland, neither the public trustee, nor the public guardian can be forced to take on the litigation role unless they wish to,[38] and the public guardian has stated openly that it 'will not act as litigation guardian for adults, children or

[33] Public Advocate *Review* (n 27) Ch 3, xv.

[34] QLRC Rep 67 (n 18) [25.43].

[35] Public Advocate *Review* (n 27) xxi. For similarly alarming stories in the US about agency self-interest, see D Hatcher, 'Purpose v Power: Parens Patraie and Agency Self-Interest' (2012) 42 New Mexico Law Review 159.

[36] See eg *Farrell v Allregal Enterprises Pty Ltd (No 2)* [2009] WASC 65 [41] (Pullin J), where neither the public trustee nor the public advocate was prepared to take on the role. In this instance, the court used its *parens patriae* jurisdiction to appoint the Public Trustee to defend the proceeding without its consent. See also *Dawson & Beasley* [2015] FCCA 480 [5] (where a public guardian that was already managing the personal and legal affairs of an incapacitated adult refused to act as her litigation guardian).

[37] *Energex Ltd v Sablatura* [2009] QSC 356. It was eventually persuaded to act.

[38] PTA s 27(3). The position in relation to the public guardian is ambiguous, there being no equivalent provision requiring the guardian's consent. In *Dawson & Beasley* (n 36) [62], [79] it was determined that under the Federal Court Rules, consent was required, but the rule was later dispensed with on appeal on a discretionary basis [2015] FamCAFC 201 since it was thought that the public guardian was sufficiently able and bound to represent her interests on the facts without the need to appoint it formally as her litigation guardian.

young people clients'.[39] This leaves the poorest and most vulnerable members of society potentially unable to act in protection of their private rights. Some cases have simply had to be suspended because the State will not act and no willing private party could be found to take up the role.[40] To act in civil proceedings, the law states that an incapax *must* have a litigation guardian[41] (an ordinary legal representative is not good enough),[42] but neither a private, nor a public representative will step in to that role if the costs exposure is too great, or if the plaintiff whose rights are being represented lacks sufficient assets from which the costs can be recouped.

The QLRC recognized the cost pressures, but (in my view rightly) insisted that courts should nonetheless have a last-ditch, residual power to force public guardians and trustees to act as litigation guardians where no private person is able or willing to do so, the proposed compromise being that their exposure to costs should be clarified and moderated.[43] Although that compromise sounds sensible enough, it did not mollify the Public Trustee, which continued to insist that it should never be compellable to act in the litigation guardian role and that the role should be pushed back to private administrators, by allowing them to act on behalf of a protected person without any litigation guardian needing to be appointed at all.[44] The Public Trustee's concern was (and remains) that if it is compellable to act, then it will, by default, become the enforcer of choice for incapable persons. Its own solution, however, is of no assistance to vulnerable persons when no private protector is prepared to act for them and there is therefore much force in the Commission's view that, when all else fails, the buck should stop with the State, which should be compellable to exercise both rights of action and defence in the best interests of an incapax, if necessary at public subsidy, as a measure of last resort.[45]

On this occasion, the public trustee's voice has proven the louder, since the proposal for last resort public compellability fell on deaf ears. If this elegiac tale of

[39] In fairness, this is because it does not have the full range of appropriate powers, or the jurisdiction fully to manage the task, and cannot insure against adverse costs orders: Office of the Public Guardian, Policy Statement: <www.publicguardian.qld.gov.au/__data/assets/pdf_file/0005/750668/policy-statement-re-requests-for-pg-to-act-as-a-litigation-guardian.pdf> accessed 25 July 2025.

[40] See eg *Fowkes v Lyons* [2005] QSC 7.

[41] UCCPR 1999 (Qld) R 93. For an exceptional dispensation in the Federal Court, see *Dawson & Beasley* (n 36).

[42] The reason is that a litigation guardian represents the best interests of the person represented, not simply his or her instructions, or wishes: A Keene, P Bartlett, and N Allen, 'Litigation Friends or Foes? Representation of 'P' before the Court of Protection' (2016) 24 Medical Law Review 333, 345. For a useful description of the Official Solicitor's understanding of his role in this regard when acting as a litigation friend in England see *RP v Nottingham City Council and the Official Solicitor (Mental Capacity of Parent)* [2008] EWCA Civ 462 [70].

[43] QLRC Rep 67 (n 18) Recs 28-2 (b), 28-4(a); 28-4(b)(2). The suggestions are (1) that it should be made clearer that no litigation guardian is liable for the costs of defending a claim in the absence of misconduct or negligence (Rec 28-4 (a)), and (2) that courts should have the power to make other parties to the litigation pay the costs of their bringing an action if the interests of justice so require (Rec 28-4(b)(2)).

[44] ibid [28.58]–[28.67], [28.85].

[45] ibid [28.96].

public recusal sounds at all familiar, you will recall from Chapter 7 a similar reluctance on the part of the British government to take any measure that would increase the current enforcement workload of the Crown Prosecution Service (CPS), despite acknowledged deficiencies in the private prosecution system. The recusal story continues in the final part of this chapter, where we shall witness the reluctance of the Australian Commonwealth to take any default role in liquidating the assets of insolvent corporations—again on fiscal grounds.

It is one thing, I suggest, to give the responsibility for administering an incapax's private assets to private persons and their advisers wherever possible, and indeed to require that the costs of administration and legal enforcement be borne by those assets, not the taxpayer, where the funds exist. It is another for the State to refuse to represent the rights and interests of the poorest and most vulnerable in civil courts on cost grounds when no private party is able or willing to act on their behalf. If the State respects the argument from private right-holder autonomy enough to devise a system for their protection *parens patriae*, then it must, I suggest, follow through by adopting the role of litigation guardian where no private person is available or willing to do so. What type of parent of the nation, is it, one might ask, that leaves their child at the doors of a court?

The issue is not easy in the current fiscal environment, of course, and is likely to get trickier still. The number and overall proportion of adults suffering some form of mental incapacity is likely to increase in line with increases in domestic population and expected lifespan, unless medical science is miraculously able to find more effective ways of keeping us capable until we die. The statistics suggest that the number of Australians aged over sixty-five will more than double by 2063, and that the number of those aged over eighty-five will triple.[46] The proportion needing either private or public representatives to administer and enforce their rights will therefore rise. At the same time, the pool of suitable private family guardians and trustees is likely to shrink as households decrease in average size.[47] So, whilst society's first choice should always be to support vulnerable persons in making their *own* decisions and representing their *own* interests wherever possible, there will always be limits on the extent that this is possible[48] and substitute decision-making will continue to play an increasingly important role. Moreover,

[46] Commonwealth of Australia, *Intergenerational Report 2023* (Commonwealth of Australia 2023) Ch 2, 6.

[47] Lone person households are currently projected to make up nearly 30 per cent of all Australian households by 2046: Australian Bureau of Statistics, *Household and Family Projections, Australia 2021–2046* (28 June 2024).

[48] On the challenges caused by our aging population, and advocating a tiered system of protection that runs from (1) informal support through (2) supported decision-making to (3) co-decision making, and only then to (4) substitute decision-making as a last resort, see E Scobie, 'Promoting Autonomy and Dignity in Later Life, A Review of Guardianship and Administration in Queensland' (2016) 10 Elder Law Review 1. An observed pressure toward the last of these options (even when it may not be required) is the fact that many aged care facilities now refuse to accept residents unless a guardian or trustee is first appointed: at 10–11.

the practical likelihood is that there will be more gaps in the protection provided by private guardians and trustees in future years than at present, not less, with the consequence that the State will face increased moral and political pressure to expand its protective role and fill the enforcement gap.

9.3 Charitable Purpose Trusts

Proceedings in respect of charitable purpose trusts cause more difficulties in terms of classification and enforcement rationale than perhaps any other set of proceedings considered in this book.[49] Such trusts are often considered alongside non-charitable purpose trusts, as a form of express trust arrangement in standard works on trusts law,[50] but courts and scholars also often refer to them as 'public trusts',[51] 'public-law–private-law hybrids',[52] or even sometimes as 'in one sense' being 'a matter of public, rather than private law'.[53] Whether one classifies them as part of private or public law depends of course on how one chooses to define the terms public and private, and the uncertainty regarding taxonomy merely reflects that fact, I think, not any real disagreement over the key legal features of such arrangements.[54]

Within the analytical framework of this book, such trusts are part of private *law*, since they entail the settlement of private property rights in accordance with the intention of a property-owner: the rights thrown into the trust 'pot' are multital private law rights that the settlor once held against other citizens. However, whilst the arrangement comprises a donation of private rights and advances the private

[49] The focus in this section is on the law in England and Wales. For coverage including Australia, New Zealand and the United States, see G Dal Pont, *The Law of Charity* (2nd edn, LexisNexis Butterworths 2017). In modern times, those wishing to implement charitable purposes often pick a different, limited-liability vehicle, such as a limited liability company, or the new form (user-friendly) charitable incorporated organization (CIO) created by the Charities Act 2011 (UK). The trust may nonetheless still offer certain advantages, including higher fidelity on the part of those in governance to settlor intentions: M Harding, 'A Fresh Look at Purpose Trusts' in S Degeling, J Hudson, and I Samet (eds), *Philosophical Foundations of the Law of Express Trusts* (OUP 2023) 201, 205–11.

[50] See eg J Hudson, B McFarlane, and C Mitchell, *Hayton, McFarlane and Mitchell: Text Cases and Materials on Equity and Trusts* (15th edn, Sweet & Maxwell 2022) Ch 9; J Penner, *The Law of Trusts* (12th edn, OUP 2022) Ch 18.

[51] *Wilkinson v Malin* (1832) 2 Cr & J 636, 655–56; 149 ER 268, 275–76; J Barratt, 'Public Trusts' (2006) 69 Modern Law Review 514; C Mitchell, 'Public Trusts 1750–1850' in D Foster and C Mitchell (eds), *Essays on the History of Equity* (Hart 2026). As Mitchell's analysis reveals, charitable trusts have only ever represented one type of public trust arrangement.

[52] K Chan, *The Public–Private Nature of Charity Law* (Hart 2016) 181 ('the adaptation of a private law institution to a variant that is more of a public law nature').

[53] P Matthews, 'From Obligation to Property, and Back Again? The Future of the Non-Charitable Purpose Trust' in D Hayton (ed), *Extending the Boundaries of Trusts and Similar Ring-Fenced Funds* (Kluwer Law International 2002) 231.

[54] For example, Matthews (ibid), in describing such trusts as public law ones means only that the trust exists for public, not private benefit, not that the trustee's obligations are owed to the State, or public as a whole.

interests of the settlor (just as making a contract or any other disposition of his property might) it is one that also advances a public interest—indeed, on the current law in most onshore jurisdictions, it is only valid to the extent that it does so.[55] Such trusts are therefore private law institutions that mediate between the private autonomy interests of settlors and collective interests of which the State happens to approve at any particular point in time,[56] coincidence between the private and public interest currently being a condition of their legal validity. They are hybrids in the sense that they are *private law* institutions that protect *both private* and approved *public interests.*

Whilst being enforceable in courts of law, charitable trusts are also now regulated in England and Wales, along with a variety of other (more popular) charitable vehicles, by the Charity Commission (a non-ministerial department of government), which has a wide range of investigatory and remedial powers, including the power to replace trustees who have acted improperly.[57] In this account, I focus exclusively on rights of action before courts of law, accepting that this leaves an important part of the public regulatory superstructure unexamined. My only (rather thin) justification for this is that it is 'rights of action' before courts that are the primary focus of the modelling in this book, not rights of complaint before public agencies, increasingly important as these now are.

A. The Rights and Duties in Charitable Trusts

As to the configuration of legal rights once trust property is settled, the settlor's private property right clearly vests in the trustee. The trustee is then subject to a range of fiduciary duties, of which loyalty to the purpose of the trust is both emblematic and pre-eminent.[58] These duties are sometimes said to be 'undirected',[59] on the basis that there are no correlative claim right-holders, there being no beneficiaries with vested equitable rights in respect of the trust fund, and the settlor himself possessing no further interest in the property, as in the case of other pure

[55] *Morice v Bishop of Durham* (1805) 10 Ves Jun 522, 32 ER 947 (Lord Eldon); *Re Endacott* [1960] Ch 232.

[56] On the tensions and challenges see Chan (n 52); M Harding, 'What is the Point of Charity Law' in K Barker and D Jensen (eds), *Private Law: Key Encounters with Public Law* (CUP 2013); *Charity Law and the Liberal State* (CUP 2014) Ch 5; A Parachin, 'Public Benefit, Discrimination and the Definition of Charity' in Barker and Jensen (eds) (ibid) Ch 6.

[57] Charities Act 2011(UK) ss 75A–85.

[58] *Children's Investment Fund (UK) v Attorney-General* [2020] UKSC 33 [20], [29], [44]–[50], [104] (Lady Arden JSC) ('a duty of single-minded loyalty'). Note that the case involved a charitable company, not a trust, but that no distinction was drawn in this regard as the nature of the fiduciary's governing duty.

[59] L Smith, *The Law of Loyalty* (OUP 2023) 294–95, 336–37; C Mitchell and J Hudson, 'Standing in Trusts Law, the Beneficiary Principle and the Juridical Nature of Trustee Duties' (2026) 142 Law Quarterly Review (forthcoming) (extending this analysis to all trusts, not just charitable purpose trusts).

purpose trusts that we canvassed in Chapter 8.[60] The trustee is also vested with discretionary legal powers to dispose of the property in accordance with the trust's purpose. To the extent that any object of that purpose stands to have his or her private rights favourably affected by the exercise of the discretionary power, he or she is subject to a private law liability—a liability in Hohfeldian terms, remember, sometimes being a good thing.[61] The legal relationship between trustees and those to whom trust funds may legally be disposed in accordance with the trust's terms is hence a correlative, multital 'power–liability' relation, the trustee's power being an ability to change the private rights of all such persons,[62] as well as to confer broader, intangible practical public benefits upon them, such as improvements in public health, or educational standards through services provided.

Important in this picture is the fact that potential charitable objects have no substantive claim rights to the trust property, or legal powers to obtain it, whether individually *or* collectively. To that extent, it is misleading to refer to the property, as Sir Samuel Romilly once did, as 'public property'.[63] It is property in which the public has an *interest* in the sense that its collective well-being stands to be enhanced through the exercise of the trustee's powers of disposition, but there is no vested public property *right*. The public interest takes the form of a *spes*, not a *ius*. Whilst objects may benefit, they are therefore not 'beneficiaries' in the legal sense[64] and the State holds no property rights on their behalf. The result is that there is no primary right-holder in respect of the trust property—either private or public—to enforce the purposes of the trust.

If this explanation seems a little pedantic, it is important for reasons to which we shall shortly come. It means that when the State is involved in enforcing charitable

[60] Note, however, that historically, settlors sometimes gave themselves, or their heirs, powers, as 'visitors' to supervise subsequent administration of the property and to take actions against the trustees in cases of maladministration: Mitchell (n 51)—a solution adopted in respect of non-charitable purpose trusts in some offshore and US jurisdictions. As to this and the question whether objects of a pure purpose trust have a correlative 'right of due consideration', see Chapter 8 Section 8.3E(i), fn 60.

[61] See Chapter 3 Section 3.2C, *Example 5*.

[62] On one view, if there is a power to dispose of assets to any particular, identified private party, the trust is not exclusively for a charitable purpose and is therefore invalid: L Smith, 'Massively Discretionary Trusts' (2017) 70 Current Legal Problems 17, 29–33; J Penner, 'Justifying (or Not) the Office of Trusteeship with Particular Reference to Massively Discretionary Trusts' (2021) 34 Canadian Journal of Law and Jurisprudence 365, 373. This does not mean, however (the point here) that the execution of charitable purposes may not enhance the property rights of private persons. If it could not, their purposes would often be defeated. The poor, for example, would get no richer.

[63] *Attorney General v Brown* (1818) 1 Swanston 265, 283; 36 ER 384, 391 (although the designation is then actually explained within the same sentence in terms of the public's interest, not its right). See also K Chan, 'The Role of the Attorney-General in Charity Proceedings in Canada and in England and Wales' (2010) 89 Canadian Bar Review 373, 400 ('rights in charitable property are public rights').

[64] P Matthews, 'The New Trust—Obligations Without Rights?' in AJ Oakley (ed), *Trends in Contemporary Trust Law* (OUP 1996) 1, 5; Smith (n 59) 21–22. There are rare cases in which charitable trusts have been regarded as trusts for the benefit of a defined and ascertainable group of individuals (see eg *The President and Scholars of the College of St Mary Magdalen, Oxford v A-G* (1857) VI HL Cases (Clark's) 189, 10 ER 1267) such that each member of the class has been vested with equitable property rights. The trust is then, in my view, no longer for a purpose, but akin to a private trust for persons.

trusts, as it often is, it does not do so as a *right-holder*[65] (save in rare instances in which the Crown's own property rights are in issue in the litigation) but rather as a party with a sufficient *interest* to be accorded a right of action, or a right of joinder, in the proceeding—a very different matter.

B. Enforcement Patterns Ancient and Modern

The modern jurisdiction of courts in respect of charitable trusts is derived historically from the King's prerogative to act as *parens patriae*, on behalf of the nation, as in the cases involving incapable persons examined in the previous section.[66] Historically, such trusts (which were overwhelmingly religious) were first enforced by 'interested' private individuals petitioning ecclesiastical courts and then, from the beginning of the fifteenth century (as delay, corruption, and the ineffectiveness of church remedies seriously put them off) by laying bills before the Chancellor.[67] There were not many of these bills, but where they were brought, the private petitioner often prayed for relief not just on his own behalf but on behalf of the wider community standing to benefit by the trust,[68] so that the claim had a wider range of interests in mind. Private bills before Chancery Courts in their turn became too slow and cumbersome to be effective—costs were too high, the value of trust property might be small, and although fiscal concessions might be made by the court where a petitioner was poor, an unsuccessful plaintiff could reportedly still be whipped for his impertinence in mounting the action,[69] which would scarcely have acted as an incentive for anyone to rush into the enforcement role.

Enforcement process improved briefly—and adopted a more public character—with the creation of the jurisdiction of the Charity Commissioners in the late sixteenth century,[70] but this early, regulatory system, which coincided with Elizabethan encouragement of more, lay charitable purposes in the wake of the Spanish War, was still driven by (and dependent upon) private complainants acting as informants about breaches of trust. Interested citizens also played an active role in the conduct of the Commissioners' inquisitorial proceedings.[71] Despite

[65] Maitland is sometimes cited for the contrary view that the public is a right holder as '*cestui que trust*', but seems in fact to have been doubtful, or at least equivocal on the point: 'I think we may say that there is no cestui que trust at all . . . . If there be any . . . it is the public': F Maitland, *Equity: A Course of Lectures* (2nd edn, CUP 1936) 51.

[66] *Attorney General v Magdalen College Oxford* (1854) 18 Beav 223, 241, 52 ER 88, 95 (Sir John Romilly MR).

[67] G Jones, *History of the Law of Charity 1532–1827* (CUP 1969) 5–9, 16–21; Dal Pont (n 49) 79–80.

[68] Jones (n 67) 8–9.

[69] ibid 20, fn 3.

[70] Charitable Uses Act 39 Elizabeth 1 c 6 (1597), re-enacted as the Charitable Uses Act 43 Elizabeth 1 c 4 (1601).

[71] Jones (n 67) 22–26, 43. 'Interested' private parties (those who might be directly or indirectly affected by a decree) could be summoned to give evidence before the commissioners and could challenge both jurors and the commissioners.

initial success, it—like the pattern of private Chancery bills before it—reportedly became so 'tedious and chargeable' that it was off-putting to petitioners and potential commissioners alike, leaving the obligations of trustees still woefully underpoliced. It had been all but abandoned by the end of the seventeenth century in favour of what may be regarded as the first enforcement action involving public rights of action before a court—the Attorney-General's action by way of information, which might be initiated either by him personally *ex officio*, or, as was almost always the case, at the relation of a private party.[72]

The relator action was the primary device for the enforcement of charitable purpose trusts from the seventeenth to the mid-nineteenth centuries.[73] It still involved a private right of action, but the right was (as in cases of public nuisance) exercisable only with Attorney-General's consent and was subject to his absolute power of termination and control in respect of any compromise. The use of the Attorney-General's name in the proceeding was a formal reflection of the modern instinct, the development of which we traced in Chapter 4, that public interests are the proper concern of the King and State,[74] but the continued use of private citizens to protect those interests nonetheless remained a practical necessity, not least because State machinery was sparse, it was still only private citizens who really knew about breaches of the terms of a trust, and the State itself could not be made liable for costs.[75]

The range of private persons granted standing to act as a relator at this time was very broad and included 'any private individual who thought a charity to have been abused'[76] whether or not they had a private interest at stake.[77] State consent for actions also seems to have been given as a matter of course.[78] But the relator's general liability for costs was a serious problem. Jones reflects soberly that, however many might in theory have sued to enforce, there were 'few altruistic enough to scatter hard-earned bread on Chancery waters',[79] and the consequence was that both Lord Romilly and Henry Brougham had, by the early 1800s, become entirely dismissive of the relator action as offering any real hope, and had begun vocally to press for alternative, statutory enforcement solutions.[80]

An important point to re-emphasize about the relator process was that although the relator used the Attorney-General's name, he was never enforcing the latter's

[72] ibid 26, 36, 52–56. See also Chan (n 52) 86–88; J Ll Edwards, *The Law Officers of the Crown* (Sweet and Maxwell 1964) 286–95.

[73] Chan (n 52) 87–88; Chan (n 63) 375–81; Dal Pont (n 49) 83.

[74] *Attorney General v Magdalen College* (n 66) 241 (Sir John Romilly MR).

[75] *Corporation of Ludlow v Greenhouse* (1827) 1 Bli NSPC 17, 48 (Lord Eldon).

[76] *Halsbury's Laws of England* (2nd edn, Butterworths 1932) Vol IV [671] (citing Shelford, *Law of Mortmain*, 424).

[77] *Attorney General v Vivian* (1826) 1 Russ 255, 38 ER 88 (Ch) 235–36 (no need for the 'least particle of private interest').

[78] Chan (n 52) 88.

[79] Jones (n 67) 162.

[80] ibid 160–64, 165–67.

own public (primary) 'right', since the State *had no* vested right in respect of the relevant trust property,[81] any more than any member of the public whose interest it purported to represent. The relator was acting in protection of the public *interest* that formed the focus of State concern in the relevant matter, in order to meet what was regarded as a *State liberty* and *duty* in respect of charitable matters.[82]

The Attorney-General's own right of action *ex officio* and the relator action are both still available today, but the introduction in 1853 of a new system allowing for any person 'interested' in a charity to either complain to the Charity Commissioners[83] (now made a permanent, central regulatory body) or, with the Commissioners' permission, to institute charity proceedings before a court,[84] put an end to the relator enforcement monopoly in courts of law. The system of complaint to the Charity Commission, updated and significantly better resourced, remains in place today in the wake of the Charities Act 2011 (UK) and is now a central plank of modern regulatory strategy, as indicated above.

Leaving aside rights of complaint to the Commission, rights of action before courts of law in respect of breaches of a charitable trust are now split three ways, between (1) the Attorney-General (or an authorized relator); (2) the Commission itself (which now shares the Attorney-General's former enforcement function and *ex officio* rights of action, by agreement);[85] and (3) private persons. Eligible private enforcers comprise trustees of the charity, anyone 'interested in' it, and any two or more inhabitants of a local area that it serves, the rights being conditional in each case on first obtaining the permission of either the Commission, or (if it refuses) the High Court.[86] The range of persons considered by courts as having an 'interest' has proven extensive,[87] and can include anyone with 'a good reason' to seek the trust's proper administration,[88] although the term has sometimes also been interpreted more conservatively, so as to require the reason to be 'materially greater than, or different from' the reasons that ordinary members of the public might have for wanting the trust enforced[89]—a restriction similar in formulation,

[81] *Attorney General v Magdalen College* (n 66) 241 (Sir John Romilly MR).

[82] Chan (n 63) 379–81 (noting variation in the language of right and duty).

[83] Charitable Trusts Act 16 & 17 Vict c 137 (1853), s LVII

[84] ibid s XLIII (alternatively, any trustee, or any two inhabitants of a locality in which the charity is administered).

[85] Charities Act 2011 (UK) s 114.

[86] Charities Act 2011 (UK) s 115. On the definition of a 'local charity' see s 293. Note that, because s 115(6) (a) technically leaves open the continued use by the Attorney-General of a relator, any private person can in theory still exercise a right of action at common law using the Attorney-General's name, provided permission is obtained, although this now seems a very unlikely route, given the width of the class given standing under the Act.

[87] See H Jing, 'Enforcing Charitable Trusts: A Study on the English Necessary Interest Rule' (2022) 42 Legal Studies 228.

[88] *Haslemere Estates Ltd v Baker* [1982] 1 WLR 1109, 1122 (obiter) (Sir Robert Megarry).

[89] Jing (n 87) 233–34; *Re Hampton Fuel Allotment Charity* [1989] Chs 484, 494 (Nicholls LJ); *Scott v National Trust for Places of Historic Interest or Natural Beauty* [1998] 2 All ER 705 (Ch) 714 (Robert Walker J). Another line of authority identified by Jing at 234–36 seems to have required a past or prospective private interest in the trust property akin to a beneficial interest, but has not been followed.

you might think, to the 'special damage' requirement that still attends private tort actions for public nuisance, although (in distinction to such actions) no damage as such need be suffered, just a different level of interest shown. The range can include settlors[90] and some (though not necessarily all) potential objects, depending on the facts,[91] but not those with a merely 'sentimental or altruistic interest'.[92] Whilst the pool of private enforcers is wide, the permission requirement for any action by a private person is significant, not least because the Commission is expressly precluded from giving that permission if it thinks the matter can be dealt with by its own, separate regulatory powers.[93] The need to obtain the Commission's *fiat* is again reportedly designed to protect trustees against the spectre of vexatious litigants, and trust assets against the risk of being consumed in defending proceedings against them,[94] and therefore has a similar logic to the rule that currently attends applications for judicial review. The prohibition on the Commission giving assent where cases fall within its own powers is presumably designed to avoid the inefficiencies of duplicative action.

The upshot is that where rights of action are concerned, power in respect of the enforcement of trustees' duties has shifted periodically between private persons and the State. The recognition of the State's interest in charitable arrangements is long-standing, having been instantiated early on in the deliberate relaxation of the normal rules about certainty and perpetuity that restrict other express trusts,[95] as well as in courts being accorded powers to administer failed charitable purposes cy-près. That interest also played a part in generating the view that rights of action should lie with the Attorney-General. The reality is nonetheless that private rights of action always played a crucial role in the absence of better developed State regulatory machinery and they continue to do so today. Logistical pressures on the Attorney-General are too great to allow for regular enforcement *ex officio*,[96] and whilst the official load has been lightened by sharing that enforcement power with the Charity Commission, a very wide range of private enforcers is also being drafted (subject always to the approval of the Commission, or High Court) to assist in the enforcement task. The State therefore does some of the work in filling what

[90] *Re Hampton* (n 89) 492 (Nicholls LJ)(local authority setting up trust). But potentially only where they are alive, if they are a natural person: *Bradshaw v University College of Wales* [1988] 1 WLR 190, 193 (Hoffmann J) (executors lacking sufficient interest).

[91] *Re Hampton* (n 89) 492 (Nicholls LJ); *R (Heather) v Leonard Cheshire Foundation* [2001] EWHC 429 (Admin) [93]; *Gunning v Buckfast Abbey Trustees* (1994) Times, 9 June (parents of children receiving education at school with charitable status).

[92] *Re Hampton* (n 89) 493 (Nicholls LJ)

[93] Charities Act 2011 (UK) s 115(3).

[94] Jing (n 87) 236–37 (citing *Scott* (n 89) 713 (Robert Walker J); Chan (n 52) 94–95.

[95] As to which, see generally P Matthews, C Mitchell, J Harris, and S Agnew, *Underhill and Hayton's Law of Trusts and Trustees* (20th edn, LexisNexis Butterworths 2022) Ch 3, esp Arts 10, 11, 13.

[96] Jing (n 87) 230. For the same concern about this in Canada and the US respectively, see Chan (n 63) 391–92; K McNabb, Note, 'What "Being a Watchdog" Really Means: Removing the Attorney-General from the Supervision of Charitable Trusts' (2012) 96 Minnesota Law Review 1795, 1805–18 (noting also the potential problem of political capture of Attorneys-General in the United States).

would otherwise be a wide gap in the enforcement process and is always joined to proceedings where the public interest is implicated, but regularly draws upon the initiative of citizens to initiate actions and still relies upon them to bear a high proportion of the costs.

C. Enforcement Rationale

Reasoning about the State's role in the enforcement of charitable trusts has suffered from a degree of question-begging and illogicality. For example, one explanation for its right of action that is quite often given in the cases and textbooks is the pragmatic one that there was (or is) simply no one else to enforce, there being no private right-holders in such arrangements, only donors, purposes, and potential objects.[97] This both begs the question why private settlors or objects could not step in, and is contradicted by the ancient and modern cases in which they have in fact done so.[98] The problem with the argument is not that there is no gap in primary right-holder enforcement—there clearly is—but the existence of the gap does not itself explain why it is the State's role to fill it. Indeed, one might equally well start from the position that, since a key duty of a trustee is to give effect to the purpose stated by the settlor, the settlor is at least as logical (and motivated?) a person to enforce as the State,[99] even accepting that she—like it—lacks any extant legal right to the trust property.

Another, more viable explanation for the State's role is therefore that it is the more efficient enforcer because (1) private individuals lack the money, expertise, and motivation to sue when their own vested private rights are not in issue[100] and/ or (2) if multiple interested individuals enforced, this would eat up all the trust property in defence costs, with consequent implications for its use to the public good.[101] From the latter perspective, the State's right of action channels enforcement initiative though a single point, allowing for coordination and cost saving.

There is no doubt something to these pragmatic arguments. The expense of litigating has certainly deterred private enforcement historically, and the State has a compelling motive of its own to enforce charitable trusts in the modern day, on account of the contribution that they make to the social economy and (thereby) to the relief of its own, increasingly long list of social welfare responsibilities. The

[97] See eg *Leahy v AG for New South Wales* [1959] AC 457 (PC) 479.

[98] As to the history see Jones (n 67). In the modern day, see the use of private trust-protectors to enforce non-charitable purpose trusts in the US: Chapter 8 Section 8.3E(i).

[99] Assuming of course that she is still alive, which she may not be (many dispositions being testamentary). Another potential problem is that if enforcement is left in the hands of the settlor, this could encourage settlors to abuse the trust mechanism and its privileges as an effective mechanism for tax-evasion, or money-laundering: Jing (n 87) 230.

[100] Chan (n 63) 378. See further Chapter 5 Section 5.3C.

[101] ibid.

incentive for the State to both allow and enforce charitable purpose trusts is especially strong when times are hard, social needs are great, and public finance is tight, for it is then that it will be most tempting for it to look to the private sector to cover off its modern social welfare functions. Its financial investment in such trusts through tax-breaks is another good motive for it to act. However, the pragmatic arguments are not all one way. It still lacks essential information about trustee impropriety, this being more readily available to settlors and trustees. Such informational asymmetry could contribute to a case for private rights of action (as we saw that it sometimes does in public law in cases of public fraud, or the breach of environmental regulations).[102] The private motivation of a live settlor, intended object or public-spirited individual can also be just as strong—or stronger—than that of the State. Furthermore, the concern about a multiplicity of private actions does not seem to have been a problem historically (if anything, the problem was getting any one to step up) and could in any event be averted by modern class-action procedures. Whilst there are therefore some decent pragmatic arguments for State rights of action, they are always fact-sensitive and contingent.

A final explanation for public enforcement rights that rises above this contingency is therefore the constitutional one about the State's unique claim to represent—or act as 'guardian' of—the public interest.[103] This is what is really meant, I think, when it is said that it has a right to represent the 'rights of the public' in such trusts, although I prefer to avoid the language of 'right' and 'beneficiary' for reasons already given: the interests of members of the public who may benefit as the objects of a charitable purpose are never, remember, anything more than *spes*. On this account, the State's right of action is not connected—as it is in a typical criminal law case—to any public law right it holds, but to its public *duty* (which is certainly political but may also be legal) to protect collective welfare and to look out for public *interests*.[104] This argument certainly provides a principled basis for ensuring that the State is joined to any private action in which the public interest is implicated (so that that interest can be properly represented before a court makes any decision that affects it), as well for giving it a right of action of its own, although it does not rule out rights of action for other parties with private interests in the proceeding, such as settlors, or potential objects.

Charitable trusts are private instruments for publicly approved purposes which advance both the personal autonomy of settlors and public welfare. The argument that suggests according rights of action to those with an 'interest' in the proceeding therefore ultimately cuts in favour of granting them to *both* public and private

[102] The information argument is not, however, conclusive in favour of rights of action on its own right, since suitably incentivised rights of complaint to the Commission could equally ensure that the asymmetry is corrected.

[103] See eg Chan (n 52) 181–82; Chan (n 63) 378–79; *Bradshaw v University College of Wales, Aberystwyth* [1987] 3 All ER 200, 202 (Hoffmann J); *Brown* (n 63) 291(Lord Eldon).

[104] This explanation chimes clearly with the language of Lord Eldon in *Brown* (n 63) 291.

agents. Where a private party is seeking to enforce a charitable trust in order to protect the public interest, there is some logic to the requirement that the permission of the Commission or a Court should first be obtained, in order to avoid duplication with the Commission's own potential enforcement action, but the concern about vexatious litigation is, as ever, much more contentious as a precondition of the right to access courts, as opposed to providing a basis for striking out unmeritorious claims when they get there. It is also hard to see why a settlor who is seeking to assert her private interest in seeing her own purpose in creating a trust fulfilled, should be required first to obtain the Commission's permission before she can lodge a claim to ensure that this is done. An alternative might be to allow settlors always to launch proceedings if they wish to do so, but to require them to notify the Commission in any such case, so that the Commission is able to join itself as party to the action.

9.4 Insolvency

A. An Overview of Insolvency Systems and Aims

Modern insolvency systems provide our final example of State involvement in the enforcement of private law rights. These are complex systems of public design which deal with the problems that occur when a natural or corporate legal person's private debts exceed their assets to such a degree that there is no realistic prospect of them being paid. Whilst personal insolvency ('bankruptcy') and corporate insolvency regimes developed at different times[105] and are governed by distinct regimes in Australia,[106] the predominant objective of each is to maximize, realize, and then distribute what remains of a debtor's assets amongst unsatisfied creditors. Since the debts in such cases invariably exceed the assets available for distribution, all unsecured creditors stand to lose. The insolvency system converts

[105] Personal bankruptcy law has medieval roots, but developed from 1542 onwards, the discharge of personal debts first being granted to traders (1705) and then (in 1861) to non-trading individuals. By contrast, the birth of corporations and corporate insolvency law is generally recognised as post-dating the Joint Stock Companies Acts of 1844–1849 (UK). See further K Van Zwieten (ed), *Goode on Principles of Corporate Insolvency Law* (5th edn, Sweet & Maxwell 2018) 9–12; V Finch, *Corporate Insolvency Law Perspectives and Principles* (CUP 2002) 7–16. M Murray and J Harris, *Keay's Insolvency: Personal and Corporate Insolvency Law and Practice* (11th edn, Thomson Reuters 2022) [2.10]–[2.14]. On the history more generally see L Levinthal, 'The Early History of English Bankruptcy' (1919) 67 University of Pennsylvania Law Review 1; B Carruthers and T Halliday, *Rescuing Business: The Making of Corporate Insolvency Law in England and the United States* (Clarendon 1998); J Edelman, H Meehan, and G Cheung, 'The Evolution of Bankruptcy and Insolvency Laws and the Case of the Deed of Company Arrangement' [2019] Lloyds Maritime and Commercial Law Quarterly 549.

[106] Bankruptcy Act 1966 (Cth); Corporations Act 2001(Cth). This is despite constant calls for rationalization (see eg A Keay, 'The Unity of Insolvency Legislation: Time for a Re-Think?' (1999) 7 Insolvency Law Journal 4; Parliamentary Joint Committee on Corporations and Financial Services, *Corporate Insolvency in Australia* (Cth 2023) (PJC) Ch 5, [5.75]–[5.76], Rec 5.77). The systems have been rationalised and codified in England and Wales in the Insolvency Act 1986 (UK).

their personal, private law claims—individual, interpersonal, bilateral claims of corrective justice against the debtor—into a lesser dividend payable from the remaining asset pool that is calculated to achieve a blunt measure of distributive justice between the debtor and the community of creditors. Creditors' corrective justice claims hence go into the insolvency mix, are extinguished, and re-emerge as distributive justice claims against the remaining fund. Individual bankrupts move forward as best they can, with their obligations (or most of them)[107] discharged. Corporations that are beyond rescue are wound up, deregistered, and formally cease to exist.[108]

The identified aims of the system include the rehabilitation of debtors,[109] maximization of the asset pool available for distribution to creditors through realization of an insolvent's property and the collection in of any debts owed, and the distribution of those assets to creditors in accordance with a ranking system that is clear and fair.[110] It thereby serves the private interests of debtors, shareholders, and creditors alike. It also serves broader, public interests,[111] preventing what would otherwise be a chaotic, decentralized free-for-all in which the quickest (or strongest) private creditor to the kill gets to stake their claim ahead of the rest of the pack; channelling multiple claims efficiently through a single debt-resolution process; promoting market stability and free enterprise by allowing lines to be drawn under failed economic ventures; and protecting the public as a whole against future harm, by cutting off the activities of badly managed entities. Some theories suggest that the rules of the system reflect what idealized creditors themselves would have agreed, had they thought about the insolvency problem beforehand, so that it expresses the unexpressed, hypothetical wishes of private parties regarding distributive choice.[112] My own view is that whilst private intentions provide an interesting

[107] Bankrupts usually remain liable, for example, to pay outstanding court fines and child support payments.

[108] They may sometimes rise again as a different entity through legitimate (legal) rescue or (illegal) 'phoenixing' (a practice of death and rebirth designed to evade obligations and gain competitive advantage).

[109] Rehabilitation is a relatively modern phenomenon (post-1705, with the biggest shift occurring in England and Wales in the wake of the Cork Report of 1982), personal debt having historically been regarded as both a sin and a crime for which imprisonment was common: Finch (n 105) 8, 13–14; J Cohen, 'History of Imprisonment for Debt and its Relation to the Development of Discharge in Bankruptcy' (1982) 3 Journal of Legal History 153. In practice, it is rarely achieved.

[110] Van Zwieten (ed) (n 105) 75–80. The basic system is one in which risk amongst unsecured creditors is shared equally, *pari passu*. A further objective identified by Goode is the detection and sanction of corporate mismanagement through the imposition of civil penalties and criminal sanctions. Whilst such sanctions are clearly important, they are not central to the process of insolvency itself and are a matter of public, not private law.

[111] *In re Pantmaenog Timber Co Ltd* [2004] 1 AC 158 [52] (Lord Millett). Liquidators—even private ones—consequently owe duties not just to creditors and shareholders during a corporate liquidation but also to the wider community; and for this reason must be completely independent: Murray and Harris (n 105) [10.200]. On the public interest in insolvency processes generally, see A Keay, 'Insolvency Law: A Matter of Public Interest?' (2000) 51 Northern Ireland Legal Quarterly 509; T Chan, 'The Public Interest in Judicial Management' [2013] Singapore Journal of Legal Studies 278.

[112] See eg T Jackson, 'Bankruptcy, Non-bankruptcy Entitlements, and the Creditors' Bargain' (1982) 91 Yale Law Journal 857 (arguing that the model reflects a Rawlsian ex ante bargain taken by real-world

construct against which to judge the rules that we have, they are unlikely to reflect the reasons of those who made them, because legislators are generally of a more pragmatic mindset and have public as well as private interests in mind.[113] In any event, all will accept that the schemes we now have are a major advance upon older practices according to which creditors enjoyed liberties to take debt enforcement into their own hands through summary seizure of a debtor's person or property,[114] or by having him slung into prison.[115]

Insolvency systems are regulated by State agencies that have their own, important role in investigating and sanctioning corporate mismanagement for the social good.[116] That is, again, another story. Our focus here is on the private law rights lying at the heart of the insolvency process itself, on the way in which they are managed, enforced and discharged through an insolvency, and the extent of the State's involvement in the process. The coverage here focuses on the main features of corporate insolvency proceedings in England and Wales, although reference is also sometimes made to the law in Australia for reasons that will become apparent, and we sometimes touch on cases of personal insolvency too for comparative purposes where this proves informative. In both jurisdictions, the State's involvement in corporate insolvency proceedings is secondary—private administrators, trustees, and liquidators are intended to be (and are in fact) responsible for the vast bulk of corporate administration and liquidation work. In England and Wales, the State nonetheless plays a key back-up role in cases of both personal bankruptcy and corporate insolvency whenever a private agent cannot be found to do the job. By contrast, Australia currently lacks an official government liquidator to deal with corporate failure, which leaves a gap where a private liquidator cannot be found. To tackle the complexity of arrangements, the following account proceeds first by

creditors placed in the 'original position' of ignorance). For a determined critique of Jackson and a rival contractarian account based on the hypothetical ex ante consent of all parties affected by the insolvency, assuming them to be free, equal, and reasonable (an 'authentic consent model') see R Mokal, *Corporate Insolvency Law Theory and Application* (OUP 2005) esp Chs 2, 3.

[113] Insolvency Law Review Committee, *Insolvency Law and Practice* (Cmnd 8558 1982) (Cork Report) [1734].

[114] Recovery of Debts by Statute Merchant Act 13 Edward 1, Stat 3, c 1 (1285).

[115] Imprisonment for civil debt was still common in Victorian times and, although moderated significantly by the Debtors Act 1869 (UK) s 4, only eradicated (again with minor exceptions) in England in 1970 (Administration of Justice Act 1970, ss 11, 12). The practice lasted longer in Australia and continues to raise concerns in the US, where it is used coercively to enforce debts owed to the State. On the difficult process of transition and the modern remnants, see B Kercher, 'The Transformation of Imprisonment for Debt in England 1828 to 1838' (1984) 2 Australian Journal of Law and Society 60; R Ford, 'Imprisonment for Debt' (1926) 25 Michigan Law Review 24; Note, 'State Bans on Debtors' Prisons and Criminal Justice Debt' (2016) 129 Harvard Law Review 1024; J Boyd, I Ramsay and P Ali, 'Contrary to the Spirit of the Age: Imprisonment for Debt in Colonial Victoria, 1857–90' (2019) 42 Melbourne University Law Review 737.

[116] In Australia, the main players are ASIC (corporate insolvency) and the Australian Financial Security Authority (AFSA) (an executive agency in the portfolio of the Attorney-General) (personal insolvency).

setting out the basic features of corporate insolvency systems and the role that private and public agents play in dealing with the property rights that get sucked into them. It then identifies the way that rights of action are allocated within the system and assesses the rationale of their current configuration.

B. Corporate Insolvency Regimes

Of the five different types of legal regime that Professor Goode has identified as existing to handle corporate insolvency—administrative receivership, administration, liquidation (winding-up), compromise, and corporate reorganization ('workout')[117]—it is only in respect of liquidation that the State plays any very significant administrative or enforcement role, and then only in England, as I intimated above. Administrative receivership[118] and administration[119] are both arrangements which enable a company's assets and affairs to be professionally managed for the satisfaction of its debts without the axe being completely dropped upon its operations, the main difference between them being that administrative receivers are appointed by private debenture holders and therefore represent the private interests and rights of a particular secured creditor, whereas administrators are court-appointed and act in the interests of all creditors. Administration is now the preferred model in England for managing the affairs of struggling corporations for precisely this reason, although it has not proven the success that was once hoped in saving companies from the chop.[120] 'Compromises' and 'workouts'—as the names suggest—are private arrangements between a failing company and its creditors made either within, or outside, the statutory corporate insolvency framework. They take a wide variety of different forms, but all involve some degree of voluntary accommodation of the private rights and interests of the parties involved. This could take the form of the postponement or forgiveness of part of the debtor's repayment obligations, conversion of the debts into equity, or another restructuring arrangement.[121] Courts must approve some of the statutory arrangements to ensure their propriety, but the State in its executive capacity otherwise has no interest or significant administrative or enforcement role. In all of these instances, those managing the property and financial affairs of a failing company are private actors.

[117] Van Zwieten (ed) (n 105) 37–56.

[118] ibid Ch 10; Finch (n 105) Ch 8; Murray and Harris (n 105) Ch 18.

[119] Van Zwieten (ed) (n 105) Ch 1; Finch (n 105) Ch 9; Murray and Harris (n 105) Ch 19.

[120] Van Zwieten (ed) (n 105) 38, 392–94, 463–68. The number of liquidations still vastly exceeds that of successful administrations.

[121] ibid 48–52, Ch 12; Finch (n 105) Ch 7 (informal rescue), Ch 10 (company arrangements); Murray and Harris (n 105) Ch 20, 21.

C. The Administrative Role of Public Agents

The final regime—liquidation[122] (bankruptcy in the cases of personal insolvents)—is the end of the line, reached when rescue of the debtor is no longer a realistic option. Here the State plays a more significant role. Where the liquidation of a company is voluntary, the members of the company (or the creditors)[123] appoint a private party to act as the liquidator. Where, however, a petition is made for a company to be wound up compulsorily,[124] the Official Receiver—a statutory office-holder within the Insolvency Service acting under the direction of the Secretary of State—is normally immediately appointed to act provisionally.[125] Once the winding-up order has been made, the Receiver is then automatically appointed to that role, with its associated responsibilities of identifying, collecting and securing the company's assets, until such time as a private liquidator can be appointed instead at a subsequent meeting of the insolvent's creditors.[126] The same, basic system applies in cases of personal bankruptcy.[127] The State's expectation is that it will hand over responsibility to a private agent whenever the company's assets are sufficient to make this a realistic possibility. Indeed, if the creditors make no decision to appoint a private agent where this is possible and in the creditors' interests, the receiver can ask the Secretary of State appoint one in default.[128]

The basic design of the system is therefore for the State to step in immediately, once the risk of a compulsory winding-up (or personal bankruptcy) is first detected, in order to prevent assets being improperly dissipated, but then to hand over to a private liquidator at the first opportunity to get down to the business in hand. Where, however, a company is assetless and no private liquidator wants the appointment for fear of not getting paid,[129] the State will carry the can as default protector of both the creditors' private interests and the broader public interest in the liquidation.

It is here that we encounter the contrast with Australia to which I earlier alluded. For, whilst the Australian Commonwealth in practice acts as Official Trustee of the estates of some 80 per cent of all personal bankrupts,[130] it provides no equivalent

[122] Finch (n 105) Ch 12.

[123] Both may nominate a liquidator, but if there is disagreement in a creditors' voluntary liquidation, the creditors' nomination prevails: Finch (n 105) 370.

[124] The petition is normally made by a private creditor but can also be brought by the company, directors and a variety of public agents (on which see further the text below).

[125] Insolvency Act 1986, s 135; Finch (n 105) 376; Insolvency Service (UK), *Technical Manual*, Ch 2, [2.4]–[2.5] <https://www.insolvencydirect.bis.gov.uk/freedomofinformationtechnical/technicalmanual/> accessed 5 December 2025.

[126] Insolvency Act 1986, s 136.

[127] Insolvency Act 1986, s 286(1) (interim receivership), 291A (first trusteeship of the estate).

[128] Insolvency Act 1986, s 137. See also s 296 (bankruptcy).

[129] Liquidators may get first bite at the cherry, but sometimes the cherry is little more than a pip.

[130] The figure in 2022–2023 was 76 per cent: AFSA, Annual Administration Statistics 2022–23: <https://www.afsa.gov.au/about-us/statistics/annual-administration-statistics/bankruptcies-and-temporary-debt-protections> accessed 5 December 2025.

State liquidator in cases of corporate insolvency. If no private actor therefore wants the liquidation job because a corporation lacks money to pay, the job simply does not get done. Assetless, or low-asset companies can remain unliquidated and uninvestigated, lying dormant for years until they are eventually deregistered.[131] This is problematic, since they thereby slip beyond the oversight that the insolvency system was partly designed to ensure. The lack of a State liquidator provides an incentive for unscrupulous directors to strip assets away from a corporation so as to ensure that there is then nothing left in its coffers to pay private liquidators to bring their own malpractice to light.[132] It also leaves a high proportion of low-asset corporate failures entirely unscrutinized.

Although there have been calls for the creation of a State liquidator's office in Australia to mirror that existing in England and other jurisdictions,[133] these have been resisted by successive governments on financial grounds, it being objected that the number of corporate deregistrations each year (some 50,000) greatly outnumbers the number of personal bankruptsies (where the State does accept a significant default trustee role) by a ratio of about five to one.[134] The preferred strategy since 2005 has instead been to rely on an 'assetless administration fund', from which private liquidators can be paid to take on liquidation work where there would otherwise be no incentive for them to do so. A Commonwealth Parliamentary Joint Committee, reporting in 2023, concluded that the funding of this scheme has been insufficient to meet the scale of the problem.[135]

Since the main interest that remains protectable in the liquidation of a wholly assetless company is the public one in determining the causes of the failure and detecting associated malpractice (the interests of creditors and shareholders being nugatory when there is nothing left in the bank for them to claim), the case for giving the State a default liquidation role in principle seems strong. Here, as in other cases we have examined, the challenge comes in persuading government to accept the financial responsibility for underwriting the operation of the system it has created, where the market fails to deliver the results that are required. That responsibility has been accepted in England, but is still to be conceded in Australia.

D. Enforcement Rights and their Rationale

What, then, of the private law rights and rights of action in this process? The legal powers of insolvent debtors and creditors to deal with their private law rights are suspended as soon as either an administrator or a liquidator is appointed to a

[131] PJC (n 106) Ch 9 esp [9.10]–[9.18].
[132] ibid [9.11]–[9.13]
[133] ibid [9.52]–[9.72]. Rec 9.73 calls for a comprehensive review to consider the costs and benefits.
[134] ibid [9.67].
[135] ibid [9.45], Rec 9.51.

failing company. An alternative protector and enforcer of their rights must therefore be found whilst assets are maximized for distribution as a dividend. In the case of a winding up, it falls to the liquidator to gather in and maximize the debtor's property. To this end, the liquidator has rights of action before courts of law to assert the private rights of the debtor to recover property that lies in third party hands, to avoid preferential or other improper dispositions that have been made at undervalue from the company's assets,[136] to claim restitution, rescind voidable contracts that the company has made, and so on.[137] In sum, any private law right—primary or secondary—which the debtor had at common law prior to the liquidation may in principle be asserted by the liquidator in a civil action, along with a range of particular, statutory rights of recovery that the company has to avoid illicit transactions, which are provided by the legislation. The upshot is that, in England and Wales, both private liquidators and the official receiver (in default) can end up exercising legal rights of action in protection of the private rights of the debtor in gathering and maximizing corporate assets, and they may do so without the debtor's consent.[138]

Beyond the rights of action that the official receiver may enjoy in gathering and maximizing a debtor's assets, it always has the right, like any other liquidator, to seek directions from a court as to how to distribute them. A number of State officers also enjoy the right to petition the court for a corporation to be compulsorily wound up. The official receiver may itself do this if it suspects that a voluntary liquidation is not being conducted with due regard to the interests of creditors or contributories, and needs to put a quick stop to what is going on.[139] The clerk of a magistrate's court enjoys a right of petition where a debtor owes fines to the State.[140] The Attorney-General may seek the winding up of a charitable corporation, for reasons canvassed earlier in this chapter. And the Secretary of State, acting through the Public Interest Unit, can apply to wind up a company in cases of serious corporate non-compliance, without even needing to prove its insolvency, if he or she is of the opinion that this is in the public interest.[141] Such 'public

[136] Any disposition from the company's assets following a winding up is void: Insolvency Act 1986, s 127. Other relevant avoidance provisions include s 238 (transactions at undervalue); s 239 (preferences); s 244 (extortionate credit bargains); s 245 (unregistered floating charges).

[137] See further Van Zwieten (ed) (n 105) Ch 13; Finch (n 105) Ch 12.

[138] Since litigation always carries risk and its costs can quickly consume the assets available for distribution to creditors, in many (if not most) cases it may be more appropriate for the debtors rights' to be settled or assigned, not litigated. If the official receiver wishes to exercise the right, the permission of the Secretary of State must first be obtained. In principle, however, the right of action exists. See further Murray and Harris (n 105) [10.250], [10.285]; Insolvency Service, *Technical Manual* [31.9.129]–[3.1.9.133], [3.19.142].

[139] Insolvency Act 1986 s 124(5).

[140] Insolvency Act 1986 s 124(1).

[141] Insolvency Act 1986 s 124(4) (b), s 124A; Finch (n 105) 379–80; A Keay, 'Public Interest Petitions' (1999) 20 Company Lawyer 296; G Davis, 'Investigations and Public Interest Winding-Up Petitions' in S Mortimer (ed), *Company Directors: Duties, Liabilities and Remedies* (3rd edn, OUP 2017) Ch 30.

interest petitions' are rare (increasingly so in recent years)[142] and tend to follow on from official investigations which have revealed a serious fraud that is being perpetrated upon the public. Although they feature only occasionally in the enforcement landscape, they can be useful where large numbers of creditors have been defrauded of small monetary sums, such that the incentive for any individual creditor to seek their own winding-up is small. Herein again, there is a collective action problem that is solved through the application of public initiative. Finally (although here we step into personal insolvency again for a second), the Official Petitioner has power to seek a personal bankruptcy order against a convicted offender where a criminal court has found the crime to have caused its victim serious loss or damage.[143]

Insolvency proceedings, rather like proceedings in respect of charitable trusts, are therefore designed for the protection of both private and public interests and the State is sometimes accorded rights of action in the service of both. When acting as the default liquidator of a corporation's assets (or, more typically, as trustee of a bankrupt's estate), it acts mainly in protection of the private rights and interests of debtors and creditors, who have been stripped of their own legal rights of action during the liquidation (or bankruptcy) process. The legal incapacity that is imposed upon the debtor in this time period requires a substitute protector and enforcer capable of exercising the debtor's rights against third parties, in much the same way that a child requires someone to protect its rights during infancy, an adult requires someone to administer his estate when he dies intestate or suffers mental incapacity, or a prisoner requires someone to act for him when stripped of his legal rights of action. Where, however, the State exercises independent rights to petition the compulsory wind-up of an entity, the story can be very different. It may certainly do so in order to protect the private interests of creditors, debtors and other contributories, but it may also act in protection of the broader public interest in safeguarding the community against continuing corporate malpractice, even where the corporation is still a going concern.

Technically, the Secretary's decision can be challenged through separate judicial review proceedings, but this is pointless in most instances: Keay, 'Public Interest Petitions' (n 141) 298. In Australia, which lacks a government liquidator, this power is vested in ASIC under Pt 5.4C of the Corporations Act 2001 (Cth).

[142] The annual number of companies wound up in the public interest ranged between 365 and 103 between 2009 and 2017, but has dropped to a much lower range (88–50) in more recent years to 2023: Insolvency Service (UK), *Insolvency Service Enforcement Outcomes 2023–24* (16 May 2023).

[143] Insolvency Act 1986, s 264; Powers of Criminal Courts Act 1973, s 39 (1) (criminal bankruptcy orders available where loss or damage exceeds £15,000).

9.5 Summation

There is no single thread of logic running through the exceptional cases we have examined in this chapter in which the State may be involved in the enforcement of private law, but there are nonetheless some identifiable themes.

The first and least controversial is that the State will act as a protector and enforcer of a citizen's private rights and interests where he or she lacks decisional capacity—whether that incapacity stems from immaturity, mental infirmity, death (cases of intestacy), or because he or she has been stripped of her legal power to deal with her own rights during a period of public incarceration. We might call this the logic of the 'incapable right-holder'. The aim in such instances is to protect the autonomy of a person who cannot themselves express it through choice. The practical job of protecting incapable persons is so large that the State's practical executive role in this sphere is a default one—it protects and enforces private rights only when no suitable private custodian can be found. In cases where familial community fails us in our incapacity, the State nonetheless remains our final harbour. This logic is most clearly evident in cases involving the guardianship and trusteeship of the rights of children and incapable adults, but it also explains in part the rights accorded to the State as the default liquidator or trustee of an insolvent debtor's assets, since in these cases too the debtor is stripped of the capacity to protect or enforce his, her (or its) private law rights. The aim in such cases is to protect the interests of the debtor in order also to protect the interests of others to whom he or she is obliged, so that the logic, whilst analogous, is not quite the same.

The second lesson is that where the State licenses a private law arrangement only because of the public benefits it brings and accords it privileged treatment for this reason, it has an interest in ensuring that the arrangement meets its aims and is properly administered. The State enforces charitable trusts not because it holds any public law right of its own, or (despite what has sometimes been said) simply because there is 'no other possible (right-holding) enforcer', but on account of the public interest in the private arrangement. Where there are overlaps between charitable purposes and its own public welfare responsibilities, this interest is especially strong. Were the State to sanction the creation of a wider range of private trust arrangements for *non-charitable* purposes that are of no detectable public benefit and which are accordingly granted no public subsidy (which it might do, if it wished to further extend the facilitative liberal institution of trust law), its standing to enforce such arrangements would be more contingent. There would be no reason for it to exercise supervisory control over enforcement of the trust by the settlor or other private parties, and the case for giving it a right to be joined to any enforcement proceeding in such cases would fall away. It might potentially be appointed to enforce the private arrangement in the absence of any other private enforcer (as in the exceptional cases involving non-charitable purpose trusts we examined in Chapter 8) but it would then be acting simply in the role of a default enforcer to protect the intentions of the settlor in the absence any private one, not as a protector of the public interest in its own right.

The third theme is that the State often sets up statutory schemes that protect both private and public law rights and interests. The insolvency system is one. Insolvency schemes protect both private parties and the public as a whole against the indiscriminate fall-out caused by intolerable levels of debt. They disable private debtors from dealing with their legal rights whilst their assets are gathered in and distributed to their creditors, and an agent is therefore required to stand in the debtor's stead to assert its legal rights against third parties. If no private enforcer can be found to act, the State assumes responsibility for ensuring the efficacy of the scheme in order to protect the private rights and interests standing in the insolvency. But the indiscriminate public harm that can be caused by wayward debtors continuing to trade also justifies the State (as well as private parties whose interests are threatened) having rights to petition courts to shut them down in the interests of the community as a whole.

Although different in terms of the risk against which it guards, the modern statutory system which allows ASIC to both investigate public corporate misconduct and simultaneously enforce the private law rights of consumers who have been adversely affected by it, is analogous. The State's enforcement of the consumer's private law rights in such instances serves the consumer, but it also serves the agency's regulatory brief in protecting the right of all members of the community to operate in a market that is not distorted by predatory economic practices. ASIC thereby enforces consumers' private law rights both to protect the consumer's own private interests and to benefit the public interests of the community as a whole. In this way, it is possible to draw analogies between all of the various public law regulatory systems that we examined at the end of Chapter 5, where public agencies act to protect both public and private interests, and the insolvency systems we have canvased above.

In all of these instances, there are live questions about the proper balance of enforcement responsibility between private and public actors. The State is not the only party—nor even obviously always the best one—to protect the personal and property interests of incapable right holders, to enforce purpose trusts, to execute the schemes of asset-gathering and distribution that are the focus of modern insolvency arrangements, or even, necessarily, to protect the private law rights of consumers. In practice, each of these tasks is too great for the State to manage on its own and private parties are heavily enlisted to assist in both risk management and law enforcement. But the State's political and legal obligations in respect of the rights of the vulnerable, in respect of social purposes advancing public interests, and in providing stable and just systems for the absolution and resolution of debt in modern, credit-dependent market economies means that it always has an underwriting role. If that is what is meant by the doctrine of *parens patriae*—that the State has an obligation to protect its people where protection is otherwise lacking—then the philosophy arguably runs through all of the examples we have considered in this chapter. As these protective tasks and their fiscal implications continue to grow, however, there is always a temptation for the underwriter to reduce or withdraw its cover and to leave it to others to do the job which it has identified as needing to be done. There is something of this recusal of the protective role in what we have seen in this chapter and it echoes the hesitations that we witnessed in previous chapters on the part of the State about its public capacities and responsibilities. The shift from welfarism to neo-liberalism—and from paternalism back to the market—that has characterized the last part of the twentieth century and the economic uncertainties plaguing the first decades of the twenty-first has changed the way the State thinks about its *parens patriae* role, and caused it increasingly to devolve its responsibility for executing that role to private initiative wherever possible.

10
Rationalizing Enforcement Choices

10.1 The Search for Common Reasons

The preceding chapters modelled some of the core enforcement patterns currently existing across public and private law respectively, and a series of exceptional departures from the basic paradigm. Once the exceptions were added into the picture, the relationship between public and private laws, public and private interests, and public and private enforcers turned out to be more complicated than previously imagined. It ended up looking something like Figure 10.1.

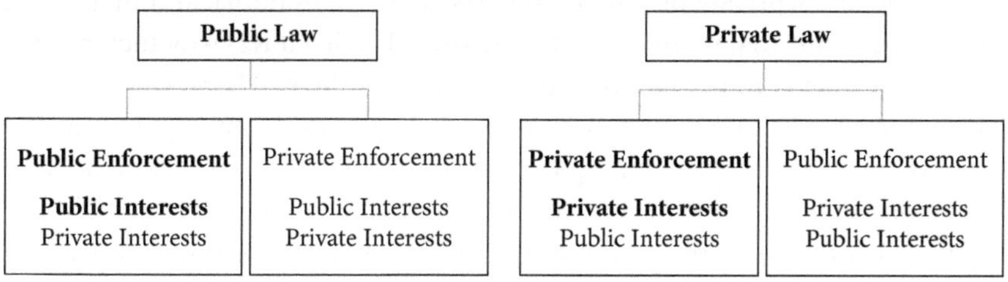

Figure 10.1 The Adjusted Enforcement Picture

In this final chapter I attempt to draw together all the material in Part III of the book, by asking whether there is anything akin to a stable logic underpinning the patterns observed—in particular, whether there is any common reason, or set of reasons, that explains and justifies the choices currently being made between public and private enforcement methods. We examined the possible justifications for particular choices in discrete legal contexts as we progressed from chapter to chapter. Here, I test their reach and limits as possible bases for making enforcement choices more generally across public and private law. This involves both some recapping, and extrapolation.

The reasons we identified for choosing one form of enforcement rather than another fall under four, broad headings—types of deontic logic, moral reasons, pragmatic arguments, and constitutional or political factors. Below, I consider each in turn, before offering some final conclusions and thoughts about future priorities and enforcement challenges.

Enforcement Rights in Public and Private Law. Kit Barker, Oxford University Press. © Kit Barker 2026.
DOI: 10.1093/9780191955006.003.0013

10.2 Deontic Logics

A. Logic 1—Rights of Action 'continue from' Primary Rights?

A key conclusion reached in Chapter 3 was that there is no necessary *analytical* connection between primary rights and rights of action. There is therefore nothing in the inherent structure of rights dictating that private law be enforceable by (or only by) individuals and corporations holding the relevant rights, or that public law be enforceable by (or only by) State agents. Everything is a choice. To revert to an earlier metaphor, it means that rights of action are baboons, not swans. They pick and choose their relationships as reason or appetite demands, rather than being bound by a single, strict fidelity.

At various points, I nonetheless suggested that there may be a degree of 'reason continuity' between primary rights and rights of action. I made this argument mainly in Chapter 8 in the private law context,[1] but the analysis extends equally to public law. The point made was that all primary rights exist for a reason (R1) (to protect either private or public interests, sometimes both), and that it is reasonable to assume that there is a further reason (I called it R2) why such rights are deliberately placed in the hands of those that hold them. There was hence most likely to be a reason, remember, why my private interest in my reputation is protected by giving *me* a primary right against you that you not defame me, even though one might equally protect that interest by giving the primary right to my mother, such that your obligation to respect me was instead owed to her. In the same vein, there is a reason why the State's interest in the loyalty of its citizens is protected by giving *it* a right that they not engage in treason, rather than giving that right to a private corporation, even though the corporation might sometimes be a more efficient enforcer. I did not say what the reasons were, in either case, for assigning the primary right to its holder (they could be moral, pragmatic or constitutional), but whatever the reasons *are* for locating primary rights in this way as between defamer and defamed (interpersonally) in private law, or between State and citizen ('state-personally') in public law, it seems likely, I suggested, that they echo forward into the configuration of the respective rights of action when a violation of the primary right takes place, or is threatened. Wherever the State holds a public law right, the reason it does so (R2) is likely also to be a *pro tanto* reason for giving it a power to enforce that right. Wherever an individual or corporation holds a primary private law right, the same is likely to be true. It is not that primary rights *themselves* 'continue into' enforcement rights—this would imply a single deontic relationship when there are two—it is that the reasons for the first

[1] Chapter 8 Section 8.4A(iii).

legal relationship between plaintiff and defendant are *pro-tanto* reasons for creating the second.

This logic suggested that the basic patterns of enforcement in the dominant paradigm—according to which public agents enforce public law and private enforcers enforce private law—makes a good deal of sense. This is because it is the State that holds most of the primary legal rights in public law and it is private parties that hold them in private law. The same logic can also explain some of the exceptions to the normal pattern, in particular those in which citizens enforce public law rights that they hold *against* the State. Examples considered in Chapter 6 were those in which a citizen sues a public official for breaching his duty not to harm her through deliberate misfeasance, or seeks to set aside a decision he has taken in violation of a statutory duty that he owed her first to give her an opportunity to be heard. It may also (a rather more difficult and doubtful case)[2] explain those in which a citizen exercises his right to seek damages for a public authority's breach of its duty to protect human rights. These are exceptions to the standard pattern according to which public law is enforced by public enforcers, but because the relevant State duty or liability is one that is owed to a citizen, they still observe the logic of giving the right of action to the holder of the relevant public law right.

The logic of continuity from primary rights nonetheless breaks down in many cases. It cannot explain any of the exceptional instances considered in this book where persons other than the primary right-holder have a power to enforce the right, such as the cases reviewed in Chapter 7 in which private parties enforce the State's public law rights in actions *qui tam* and environmental citizen suits, or the private law examples in Chapter 9 in which the State enforces the rights of incapable or insolvent persons, or consumers, or where it enforces charitable trusts. Nor does it explain any of the atypical instances examined in Chapter 8 in which the rights of one private party, A, are enforced by another private party, B.[3]

Whilst rights of action in *both* public and private law are hence often rational 'continuities from' primary rights and respect what we referred to in Chapter 8 as the basic 'right-holder rule', this is by no means always the case. Sometimes the continuity between primary right and right of action breaks down in both spheres, and persons other that the primary right-holder are empowered to enforce the right.

[2] This is a questionable example. It depends on whether the State's duty under Section 6 of the Human Rights Act 1998 (UK) is owed multilaterally to each and every individual citizen, or only to the public as a whole. This is a matter of contention (see the debate referenced in Chapter 6 Section 6.2B nn 18 and 36). The discretionary remedial regime under the Act suggests to me that the former analysis is probably the correct one, however desirable the latter might be, so that this human rights example should probably drop off this list. If a personal duty were owed directly to each and every citizen, it would be hard to justify only a discretionary damages regime. It is therefore more likely to be an example in which rights of action are granted to persons whose private interests are intended to be protected by the State's duty to the public as a whole. See Section 10B(i) and n 7 this chapter.

[3] Chapter 8 Section 8.3.

B. Logic 2—Rights of Action Align with Protected Interests of the Enforcer?

A second, formal logic potentially governing choices between public and private enforcement that has emerged at various points in the book relates not to whether the State, or a private person, holds the primary right being enforced but to the interest (or interests) that the right is designed to protect. If the purpose of the right is to protect a private interest of A, then A may enforce it. If its purpose is to protect a public interest, then the State may enforce it as a representative of the community as a whole. If the purpose of a legal right or duty is to protect *both* private *and* public interests (we saw quite a few examples of this), then we should expect enforcement rights for *both* affected private persons and State agents in a parallel public and private enforcement system.

This logic again fits current enforcement patterns pretty well—at least as well as the 'rights continuity' logic just considered and arguably better in some exceptional instances. It is able to cover much of the same ground for the simple reason that public law rights are generally designed to protect public interests and private law rights to protect private ones. This means that rights of action tend naturally to map *both* the primary right of an enforcer *and* the interests protected by the right at one and the same time. State prosecutors in cases of treason both enforce the State's own right and represent the public interest protected by that right. Subcontractors suing builders for the breach of a contract enforce their own rights, and those rights are exclusively designed to protect their own private interests. Primary rights, the interests protected by those rights and rights of action therefore line up in the great majority of cases.

(i) Interest Alignment—Protecting Enforcer Interests?

The right and interest models therefore often yield the same enforcer choice. They can nevertheless diverge for the simple reason that primary rights are sometimes designed to protect the interests of persons other than the right-holder. This is true in both public and private law.

In public law, State rights are often, we have seen, designed to protect private interests as well as public ones. This is true of the statutory norms regulating cartel activity and anticompetitive practice described in Chapter 5, the purpose of which is not just to make better markets for us all to enjoy but also to protect the economic interests of consumers and competitors. Consumers accordingly have their own rights to sue for harm suffered as a result of the breach of many of those regulatory provisions.[4] The tort of public nuisance is similarly, I suggested, a wrong against

[4] Chapter 5 Section 5.2 n 15 and text thereto. Some of the rights of competitors and consumers that are enforced are private law rights that they hold individually against the wrongdoer, but this is not always the case.

the public as a whole, but some of the interests it sets out to protect (health and property, for example) are also private ones, and individuals may consequently bring claims in protection of those interests if they can prove 'special' damage to them.[5] More broadly, many criminal laws that describe offences against the person or property protect the private interests of victims as well as community security. This not only explains why courts may order criminals to compensate their victims as part of the sentencing process, but furnishes a logical reason to give victims their own rights of action, which supplements the normal public interest justifications for their right to mount a private prosecution.[6] The same may be true, I suggested, of some duties of natural justice, which aim not just to produce better government but to protect the dignity, private expectations, and liberty of individuals affected by public decisions, and of the State's duty to protect human rights.[7] All of this means that, whilst possession of one's own public law right can certainly give one standing to sue in public law, the possession of an *interest* which the relevant public right was intended to protect will also suffice.

In private law, it is rarer for primary rights to protect interests other than those of the right-holder, but there are nonetheless clear examples in the law of property, contract, and trusts, which stem from the facilitative purposes of those institutions. The rights of trustees and fiduciaries to the property that they administer provides the most obvious case, such rights being designed to protect *only* the interests of beneficiaries. The logic of interest protection can explain why the latter therefore have rights to enforce the trustee's rights against third parties, if the trustees themselves refuse to act. The same logic may explain why the State can enforce charitable purpose trusts, such trusts existing in part to protect approved public interests, as well as a settlor's private intentions. In Chapter 8, we encountered cases in which contractual rights are constructed so as to protect third party interests, the classic case being where A contracts with B for B to pay an annuity to C.[8] The logic of 'protected interest' enforcement here again suggests that C might have a right of action to bring B before a court of law to declare the amount that B must pay, even if C is not the beneficiary of a trust of the promise and has not himself been accorded a primary right to contractual performance. There was a case close this in the *Hobart*

[5] Chapter 7 Section 7.1A(ii).

[6] On the normal public interest justification for private criminal prosecutions (safeguarding the rule of law) see Chapter 7 Section 7.3C. As things stand, private prosecution rights are not limited by the private interest logic (since anyone can prosecute, not just victims). A victim's private interest in a case of assault could nonetheless be an additional reason for according to him or her the right to commence an action.

[7] Chapter 6 Section 6.4B and 6.2B respectively. This is a more likely construction of the State's duty under s 6 of the Human Rights Act 1998 (UK) which is probably owed to the public as a whole but partly designed to protect citizens' private interests: see n 2 above and Chapter 6 Section 6.2 n 18. The same might arguably also be true of public officers' duty not to commit misfeasance in public office (the law is again very unclear) but the fact that remedies are available *as of right* in the latter instance suggests to me that that citizens themselves hold correlative rights against individual officers in that instance.

[8] *Beswick v Beswick* [1968] AC 58 (HL).

decision,[9] in which a third party, the protection of whose economic interests was an objective of the arrangement in question and whose participation was required by the contract, was granted standing to determine the meaning and effect of the relevant payment terms.

(ii) Interest Asymmetry—Protecting the Interests of Others

A model that aligns enforcement rights with protected interests therefore potentially fits more of our rights of action in *both* public *and* private law than one that is restricted by the narrower logic of continuity from the location of primary rights themselves. There are nonetheless still some cases that it, in turn, cannot explain—those in which enforcers possess *neither* a primary legal right, *nor* an interest that the primary right was designed to protect. This is because enforcers are sometimes given rights to protect the interests of *others* for moral or pragmatic reasons. This is again true in both public and private law.

For the public law examples, simply turn again to the cases in Chapter 7 in which we saw citizens acting as 'private Attorneys-General' in protecting public interests. In statutory claims under the Environmental Protection Act 1990, environmental citizen suits and actions *qui tam*, we saw, the design of the relevant laws is not to protect any private interest of the enforcer but rather to enable the latter to enforce both the rights and the interests of the public. Although enforcers have a (contingent) private *stake* in the proceeding in *qui tam* actions, this is only in the sense that they are given a financial incentive to take on the prosecutorial role. Anyone can bring the claim. The public interest is also a core feature of most private criminal prosecutions, private actions for judicial review, and *all* private relator actions in cases of public nuisance (or to enforce a charitable trust). It is true that in some of these actions courts ask whether a particular private enforcer has a 'sufficient interest', is 'aggrieved', or (in the United States) has sustained an 'injury in fact' in determining their standing to bring a claim. But the inquiry, we have seen, is conducted either as a screening operation to filter out unsuitable enforcers, to cut down upon the potential amount of litigation for public resource reasons, or to tiptoe around sensitive constitutional norms governing the respective law enforcement roles of citizens, courts, and the executive. The protection of a private interest of the enforcer is not the purpose of the right being enforced. Private enforcers are instead enlisted in a *social* cause.

The same interest asymmetry also surfaces in private law enforcement. Private agents standardly have rights of action that they use to protect the interests of their principals. The market could otherwise not function. Private and State litigation guardians act in protection of the interests of the incapable. State and private trustees and liquidators act in the private interests of creditors and debtors in

[9] *Hobart International Airport Pty Ltd v Clarence City Council* [2022] HCA 5; Chapter 8 Section 8.3D.

personal bankruptcy and corporate insolvency proceedings, as well as in the interests of the broader public. Public regulators sometimes act, we saw, in protection of the interests of consumers by enforcing their private law rights for them as part of the State's modern welfare role. And so on.

In both public and private law domains, enforcers therefore sometimes hold powers to protect the interests of others for reasons of commercial facility and personal or social welfare. Although the logic of granting enforcement rights to persons whose interests a primary right was intended to protect therefore has significant purchase and potentially more explanatory power in respect of some of the exceptions we have examined than the 'primary right-holder' model, it also still struggles to account for all of the choices made between public and private enforcement in either the public or private law domains.

10.3 Two Moral Arguments—Personal Choice and Autonomy

The above arguments have been formal and structural, tracking potential logical or deontological links between rights of action and either primary rights or the interests intended to be protected by those rights. They bear some fruit and map the contours of the current enforcement landscape quite well, but neither, I have suggested, provides a completely reliable guide. They are also rather unsatisfying to our spirit of critical inquiry in the sense that, whilst each expresses a credible logic, it does not itself express the normative driver of that logic. Rights of action roughly map onto primary rights. They also (more closely) map onto the interests designed to be protected by those rights. So what? Why should they do so in either case? And what motivates the cases we have mentioned above that simply do not fit, where enforcers protect the rights and interests of others? Here I consider whether there is any substantive reason for choosing a particular type of enforcer to enforce a particular type of law that might give either of these logics a *moral* life.

In Chapter 8, I examined two such justifications for the structure of enforcement rights in private law: the value of personal choice (sometimes called 'sovereignty' or 'control'), and autonomy. The 'choice' argument[10] concerned the moral value to a person of having 'control' over his or her primary rights, rooted in the Kantian ideal that what is ours is ours and is not to be subjected unilaterally to the purposes of others. It provided a good reason to give rights of action to individual right-holders, and a reason *not* to give them to anyone else without the right-holder's consent, the concern being that right-holders must have full dominion over the enforcement of their rights if they are to be truly free human agents. Rights of action

[10] Chapter 8 Section 8.4A(i).

and primary rights were on this view a morally consistent set, or 'package' underpinned by the same fundamental ideal.

We saw that this tracked rights of action in private law pretty well, and it breathes moral life into the 'right continuity' logic examined above. If sovereign choice is what makes rights important, then it makes sense that right-holders (and only right-holders) get to choose whether and when to enforce them. It struggled, however, to explain cases in which third parties can enforce a person's private law rights without first obtaining his or her consent—for example, those in which beneficiaries compulsorily exercise the rights of trustees that the latter are obstructively refusing to enforce, where public or private guardians enforce the rights of an incapax, or where class action representatives begin opt-*out* proceedings on behalf of other private litigants at their own motion. The *Hobart* decision was another awkward instance, the third party in that case never having obtained the permission of the contracting parties to seek a declaration of their obligations,[11] and we saw further examples in the last chapter in which State trustees and liquidators compulsorily enforce debtor rights during bankruptcy or corporate insolvency proceedings, where the debtor's consent is totally irrelevant.[12] In such cases, right-holder choice is ignored, or is overridden either in the best interests of the right-holder himself, or in the interests of other persons.

Some such cases appeared to be potentially explicable by the second moral value—personal autonomy.[13] This value was also able to explain why it is important to a right-holder to be able to enforce his own rights, but it had the added benefit of being able to justify why others can sometimes act in his best interests where he lacks decisional capacity, or is subject to some other form of legal disability. If rights exist to protect our welfare in this way then it makes sense that others can sometimes wield them in our best interests, provided sufficient safeguards are put in place. It could even potentially justify sometimes allowing a third party to enforce a person's rights in protection of *their own* interests without always obtaining the right-holder's prior consent. The allocation of rights of action became a carefully balanced decision between the interests of the right-holder, on the one hand, and the interests of other possible enforcers, on the other. The former's choice and interests generally prevailed where she had decisional capacity, but the latter could sometimes act in protection of their own interests where the right-holder owed them a duty to act in protection of those interests (the trust example), where the right was designed to protect those interests (*Hobart*), or where those interests were consistent with the right-holder's own and it was only through the collective advancement of all of them that any was likely to be realized (opt-out class action proceedings). The autonomy argument went this far, but no further as

[11] *Hobart* (n 9).
[12] Chapter 9 Section 9.4D n 138.
[13] Chapter 8 Section 8.4A(ii).

an explanation, as far we can tell from the examples reviewed. It still did not allow my mother to sue a person for defaming me just because she has a strong emotional interest in my welfare, nor did it allow third parties to sue upon my contract just because they stand to profit by its proper performance. Such cases presented too great a risk of a third party's interests clashing with the interests of the right-holder, rather than aligning with them. The autonomy argument, you will notice, tends to track the 'protected interest' logic set out in the previous section—enforcement rights generally being permitted to persons where the protection of their interests (and therefore the advancement of their autonomy) was a purpose of the relevant primary right.

At first blush, neither moral argument appears relevant to the allocation of rights of action in public law because they concern the importance of such rights to human agency and flourishing, and the State is not a human being exercising moral choice or personal autonomy of its own. The values of personal morality therefore have no bearing on the reasons why the State has rights to enforce its public law rights.[14] There are nonetheless some cases in which they are clearly just as relevant in public law as in private law. The clearest is where a citizen holds a public law right *against* the State, not the other way around, as in the examples from Chapter 6 mentioned above. A citizen's right to sue for injury to her liberty, property, or economic interests caused by an official's abuse of office is morally important both to her sovereignty as a right-holder and to her ability to live an autonomous and dignified life. The same is true of the prisoner's right to seek judicial review of the decision to discipline him in violation of a duty first to give him a proper hearing. Other examples are citizens' rights to enforce the State's duty to make social security payments, or its special liability to refund an overpayment of tax that they have made.[15] More broadly, the autonomy argument could support the right for a private person to enforce even public law rights belonging to the *State*, where these are designed wholly or partly for the protection of his or her own private interests. Where, for example, a consumer is harmed by an anticompetitive practice, her choices in life are positively implicated by being able to sue for compensation in public, as well as in private law, even though she was not the person to whom the relevant public law duty was owed. The same is true of a citizen's right to sue for harm caused by the State's breach of its duty under the Human Rights Act to protect her right to privacy, even if it is the case (as I have suggested it may be)[16]

[14] There are clearly parallel arguments in public law about the importance of the State being 'in control' of law enforcement and the need for its consent in relator actions that are premised on its status as a 'sovereign' right-holder and its role in representing the autonomy interests of society as a whole, but these arguments are, it seems to me, constitutional in nature, describing as they do the proper relationship between the State, its citizens, and their interests in respect of the law enforcement task. I therefore consider them in Section 10.5 of this chapter.

[15] Such duties may be statutory, or, in some jurisdictions, exist at common law: *Woolwich Equitable Building Society v Inland Revenue Commissioners* [1993] AC 70 (HL).

[16] See n 7 above.

that the duty to protect her human rights is owed to the whole community, rather than to her individually. It would also be true, if private persons were ever to be given rights to claim compensation for harm they have been caused by particular, illegal public decisions about them in applications for judicial review.

The values of personal choice and autonomy therefore potentially have considerable normative force and explanatory power in respect of rights of action in private law, each one respectively providing moral substance to one or other of the two logics examined in the previous section. They make ethical sense of the basic patterns in that field and describe sensible criteria according to which to allocate private rights of action in that legal domain. But they also have implications in public law, where individual enforcers hold primary rights against the State, or where State rights are designed, as they often are, for the protection of particular private interests of the enforcer.

10.4 Pragmatic Arguments

The previous chapters disclosed a number of further, pragmatic arguments. Many of these are context-specific, so that caution must be exercised in extrapolating from one field of application to another. There are nonetheless some general themes which are likely to be influential in enforcement system design, which span the divide between public and private law.

A. 'Default' Enforcement—Filling Gaps

One pragmatic basis for enforcer choice is what I referred to in Chapter 8 as the 'default' argument.[17] This suggests that private enforcement features where public enforcement is impossible, and vice versa. If there is no State agency to enforce a law then a private party will enforce it instead. If no private individual exists to protect a person's private rights, then the State will step in.

Assuming that some form of enforcement is preferable to none (that is, that using the default mode does not produce worse consequences overall than simply leaving the law in question completely unenforced), this argument is basically good. It also has considerable explanatory purchase from a historical point of view. In the early years, when no or few 'public' enforcers existed, there was, we saw in Chapter 4, no option other than to use private individuals to enforce what we would now classify as criminal laws. However inefficient or morally risky this might have been (and it often was) not enforcing such laws at all would have been worse. In the

[17] Chapter 8 Section 8.4B n 125 and text thereto.

modern day, the argument is more commonly expressed in the terms that private enforcement 'fills gaps' in public enforcement capacity[18] and vice versa, or that the two systems form a responsive, complementary *set* that safeguards the rule of law by ensuring that 'somehow' a law will get enforced. Gap-filling arguments are a consistent feature of many of the exceptions to standard enforcement patterns. At various points in the book, we have hence encountered views in public law that:

(i) private actions for breaches of the Human Rights Act 1998 (UK) compensate for the current weakness of independent human rights commissions;[19]
(ii) private misfeasance actions regulate and deter illegal behaviours missed by the crime of public misconduct and other mechanisms of public accountability;[20]
(iii) private actions for public nuisance catch forms of socially harmful conduct that otherwise slip the grip of public regulation;[21]
(iv) private citizen suits, *qui tam* actions and antitrust competition law proceedings fill regulatory holes left by understaffed, underfunded or politically compromised public agencies;
(v) recent private prosecutions in England respond to deficits in public capacity, and ensure that crimes do not go unpunished;[22] and even that
(vi) private law claims for exemplary damages provide deterrent incentives and expressions of public condemnation that are left incomplete by the criminal law.[23]

By the same token, in private law, there was a view that one reason the Attorney-General historically had the power to enforce charitable trusts was that there were no private right-holders to do the job.[24] Public guardians and trustees generally step in to enforce the rights of incapable persons, we found, where no suitable private entity will act.[25] It is sometimes said that third party beneficiary rights to enforce contracts are needed to fill a gap in enforcement incentives and ensure that a promisor's promise is not reneged upon.[26] The Official Receiver in England, we saw, fills the gap when a debtor's rights are removed and no private entity will take on the liquidation of a low-asset or assetless corporation.[27]

[18] See eg Z Clopton, 'Redundant Public–Private Enforcement' (2016) 69 Vanderbilt Law Review 285, 290 (a combination of different enforcers of the same law can 'cure existing under-enforcement and deter future under-enforcement by allowing a second agent to fill the remedial gap').
[19] Chapter 6 Section 6.2D.
[20] Chapter 6 Section 6.3B, D.
[21] Chapter 7 Section 7.1C.
[22] Chapter 7 Section 7.3.
[23] Chapter 8 Section 8.5.
[24] Chapter 9 Section 9.3C n 97 and text thereto. I doubted this view for reasons given in the text.
[25] Chapter 9 Sections 9.2A, B.
[26] Chapter 8 Section 8.3 D, n 34.
[27] Chapter 9 Section 9.4C, D.

Although the default argument is good in the form it is stated, it is nonetheless limited, for two reasons. First, it is rare these days for either public or private enforcement to be *impossible.* Most enforcement gaps can be plugged given the requisite political will, careful system design and sufficient resources. We could, for example, close most of the recent gaps in criminal law enforcement in England simply by increasing Crown Prosecution Service (CPS) funding, without defaulting to private enforcers; we could enforce purpose trusts by giving interested private parties rights to sue—a point evident from the fact that many jurisdictions have now done so; and we could solve the gap in private liquidations of low-asset companies by giving private liquidators proper financial incentives to get involved. And so on.

The second problem is that gap-filling arguments do not tell one *who* should fill a gap, only that *someone* should. They are entirely neutral as between public and private enforcement techniques and therefore provide no sense of direction to our ultimate choice. Defaulting to the 'only available enforcer' provides a short-term, tactical solution, but this is of little help to those interested in thinking strategically, as one should, about system design. The fact that private enforcement can plug gaps in public enforcement when public resources are scarce does not mean that it is either very effective in this role, or *best.*[28] The identification of 'gaps' in public enforcement should therefore be the beginning of a democratic conversation about how best to finance and configure enforcement rights, not a reason *automatically* to default to the private enforcement mode. Nonetheless, in practice there will be some occasions when the prospects of such a conversation taking place and a strategic public or private enforcement solution being worked out are so remote as to be nugatory, and the need for enforcement is urgent. Or there may be cases where an enforcement job is so vast that public enforcement could never fully accomplish the task, even with all the political will and resource in the world. In such cases, perfection cannot be allowed to be the enemy of the good,[29] and the default private option may be all that is left open and may need to be adopted to advance the general welfare and maintain the rule of law.

B. Efficiency

We considered efficiency arguments in public law in Chapter 5 and in private law in Chapter 8. It is hard to know exactly how much influence they have had

[28] S Burbank, S Farhang and H Kritzer, 'Private Enforcement' (2013) 17 Lewis and Clark Law Review 637, 714: '[j]ust because ... budgetary considerations suggest that private enforcement will remain an attractive regulatory strategy does not mean ... that the private enforcement regimes of the future will be efficacious'.

[29] J Glover 'The Structural Role of Private Enforcement Mechanisms in Public Law' (2012) 53 William and Mary Law Review 1137, 1203–04.

on enforcement system design. Although they logically apply to both private and public law, they are more apparent in the latter than the former. Of the areas we have reviewed, they are perhaps most often referenced in the competition law context, especially in the United States, where much work has been done in analysing the relative efficiency of public prosecutions and private follow-on class action proceedings in achieving deterrence.[30] By contrast, economic analysis is often denied valence in the private law context, where the predominant goal is not generally to minimize social harm but to resolve personal disputes about conflicting private interests. Here, maximizing efficiency is a secondary consideration to doing interpersonal justice. There is nonetheless no reason, I suggested, to exclude efficiency arguments from thinking about rights of action in private law alongside other systemic and moral arguments, in order make interpersonal justice more cost-effective, and they tend to point in broadly the same direction in a good many cases.

(i) General Considerations

The general conclusion I reached is that it is normally efficient for private law *mostly* to be enforced privately and for public law *mostly* to be enforced publicly, along the lines of the dominant model. Some of the key factors affecting the efficiency of enforcer choice relate to:

(i) the relative *incentives* for public and private agents to pursue an action (which must be neither too small to make the action worthwhile, nor too large, nor in conflict with the interests that are at stake in the proceeding);
(ii) the relative *information costs* to an enforcer of detecting legal infractions in either case (the costs of accessing the relevant information, both legal and factual, that is necessary to act on them);[31]
(iii) the extent to which the enforcer is able and incentivized to reduce its *enforcement costs* (for example, does the enforcer have a sufficient share of enforcement activity to be able to achieve economies of scale; how well is it resourced; does it have its own expertise; and is it exposed to competition from other enforcers?);
(iv) the extent to which enforcement by one enforcer type or another is more or less likely to *deter future infractions and associated harm* (where this is one of the objectives of the law being enforced), which is largely a function of the

[30] See the literature cited in Chapter 5 Section 5.3D n 49.

[31] Glover (n 29) 1179–81 (public enforcers are better where a larger data set is needed and the relevant information is not easily understood by non-experts, for example in the complex area of consumer credit law; private enforcers are better where geographically closer to the relevant harm, or the ones themselves to suffer it); P Bucy, 'Private Justice' (2002) 76 California Law Review 1, 8 (information asymmetries in a complex, computerized world in which wrongdoing is harder to detect mean that private enforcers with insider information will be an essential ingredient of any system of public law enforcement).

remedies and sanctions available to the enforcer and therefore contingent on the remedial framework attaching to the relevant law; and

(v) the extent to which choosing one type of enforcer rather than another may result in *freeriding* by those who interests are also advanced by the action, and who are thereby relieved of any enforcement responsibility.

Painting with a broad brush, private laws protecting private interests are better enforced by private persons affected by the infraction. This is because the latter will have a personal incentive to act in their own interests (provided, of course the personal or financial costs of legal action are not so high to put them off) and they will have best access to information about it and its consequences for those interests, so as to be able to furnish that information easily to a court, or make settlements that realistically capture the harm caused by a wrong. Public agents, by contrast, are remoter and less well motivated to act carefully in a person's interest unless there is also some public interest at stake, and they are frequently handicapped by monitoring and information deficits. How would the State know, for example, whether a contract has been breached, or the terms of a trust violated? Efficiency arguments also suggest that it makes presumptive sense *only* to give rights of action and termination to private right-holders (even where others have full access to relevant information) to prevent a wasteful multiplicity of actions and to make the negotiation of out-of-court settlements easier.[32]

By contrast, since public laws predominantly enforce public interests and the harms caused by the breach of those laws often have shared effects upon whole communities, individuals and corporations have no incentive to enforce them unless they have themselves been harmed (or stand to be), or unless significant sweeteners are offered, the latter of which may (if over-egged) encourage others to try their hand even when this is not socially beneficial. Public agencies may have better detection tools giving them access to information about regulatory infractions and data about their social effects, they are able to address those effects through a more coordinated system informed by the repeat scenarios in which they are caused, they have their own expertise, and there is less risk of conflict between their own interests and the public interests that they are seeking to protect, avoiding distorted enforcement incentives. There are also no free riders, since the community benefitting from enforcement activity is also the community paying for it through taxation, which should also mean (in theory at least) that the ballot box yields some (loose) correspondence between the level at which enforcement activity is financed and the (perceived) social benefits it brings.

There is, however, always some contingency in the above arguments. Changes in one or more of the factors caused by even the smallest contextual shift can yield

[32] J Gardner, *From Personal Life to Private Law* (OUP 2018) 209; T Liau, *Standing in Private Law* (OUP 2023) 261.

a case for an exception to the basic paradigm, or for dual (parallel) or hybrid public and private enforcement arrangements. In private law, public enforcers still make sense where the persons whose private interests are being protected lack capacity and there are insufficient incentives for unconflicted relatives or friends to intervene. It also makes sense for the State to have enforcement rights where private laws protect public interests as well as private ones (charitable trusts and corporate insolvency regimes), or where there are such serious risks of reprisal to a private enforcer (by an employer, for example) that the incentive for him or her to enforce is removed. In public law, State enforcers should not generally be granted a monopoly in enforcing laws against the State itself where there is any risk of a conflict of interest (or capture) that might distort their normal incentives to enforce. Giving private persons rights of action may also be rational where State detection of a public wrong is hard because offences are embedded in cultures of secrecy (cartel offences, for example) and private persons have ready access to inside information,[33] or where State resources have been so hamstrung by economic downturn, by political intervention or industry capture that there is no incentive for public interest cases to be properly prosecuted.

(ii) Hybrid Systems

Efficiency also clearly supports the creation of hybrid enforcement arrangements in some cases. A hybrid enforcement system, as I have defined it here,[34] is one in which a single enforcer (either public or private) protects both public and private interests within the same enforcement process, avoiding the need for duplicate, or near-duplicate legal actions by separate public and private enforcers. Diverting two enforcement trains onto a single procedural track and giving them a single driver can save costs and can work well, provided the respective interests are sufficiently closely aligned not to antagonize one another, and provided information relevant to the protection of them all can be brought together at the same time and place. By substituting one process for two, a hybrid system may also avoid some of the procedural conflicts and collective-action problems that often blight the coordination of separate, parallel (usually sequential) public and private enforcement actions,[35]

[33] An alternative here, however, is to rely on incentivized information rights, which carry less risk.

[34] See Chapter 1 Section 1.2B. The term 'hybrid' enforcement is sometimes used differently to refer to instances in which a single law can be enforced (on parallel tracks) by both public and private enforcers: see eg, S Burbank, S Farhang and H Kritzer, 'Private Enforcement' (2013) 17 Lewis and Clark Law Review 637, 661; S Bornstein, 'Public–Private Co-enforcement Litigation' (2019) 104 Minnesota Law Review 811, 811, 819–22. Confusingly, perhaps, I have myself previously used the term in this way: K Barker, 'Modelling Public and Private Enforcement: The Rationality of Hybridity' (2018) 37 University of Queensland Law Journal 9.

[35] Bornstein (n 34) 825–26. Collective action problems associated with parallel claims are said to include potential 'shirking' and 'cue-taking', although they do not always arise: Clopton (n 18) 311–31. Procedural conflicts as between public and private litigation can relate to discovery, evidential rules and standards, and amnesty/leniency rules. For discussion in the competition law context, see D Baker, 'Private and Public Enforcement: Complements, Substitutes and Conflicts—a Global Perspective' Ch 10 in A Ezrachi (ed), *Research Handbook on International Competition Law* (Edward Elgar 2012) esp

and it may avoid some of the inefficient 'overenforcement' that can flow from multiple deterrent sanctions being brought to bear on the same wrongdoer by multiple different legal actors.[36] Where a hybrid system combines punitive aims with the compensation of a great many, small, private harms, it can also be efficient in collectivizing the pursuit of claims in respect of which there would otherwise be too little private incentive to sue.

Hybrid enforcement arrangements are more prevalent in public than private law. The examples considered at the end of Chapter 5 concerned the powers of public prosecutors to seek compensation orders on behalf of the victims of a crime at the same time as seeking other punitive sentencing options, and the powers of some regulators to seek or order compensation for consumers on top of civil penalties, or to prescribe broader redress. They also include the power of private applicants for judicial review to add private law claims for damages or restitution to their review applications,[37] and the power of private persons to add private law claims for damages to their claims against public bodies for human rights violations in those jurisdictions (like Australia) where the violation does not itself give a victim any distinct secondary public law right to compensation.[38] There is, however, also an example in private law in the widely recognized right of private law claimants to add claims for exemplary or punitive damages to their tort claims. Another is a private plaintiff's right to claim an account of profits from a defaulting fiduciary for reasons of prophylaxis or deterrence, even where he or she has suffered no harm as a result of the relevant breach.[39]

There are good constitutional reasons, to which we shall come, why hybrid enforcement systems feature more often in public than in private law, but an obvious, efficiency-based explanation is that private law claimants generally lack the information required to assess the harm a wrong has caused to public interests, whereas there are at least some cases in which it is easy for the State (or a private enforcer of a public law)[40] to assess the impact a public wrong has had upon a victim, or

246–64; L Guttuso, 'Leniency and the Two Faces of Janus: where Public and Private Enforcement Merge and Converge' in C Beaton-Wells and C Tan (eds), *Anti-Cartel Enforcement in a Contemporary Age: The Leniency Religion* (Hart 2015), Ch 5. Note that basic conflicts and tensions between the protection of public and private interests (for example, between deterrent and compensatory ends) cannot be resolved simply by using a single procedure and must still be reconciled within it.

[36] Bornstein (n 34) 828, 830 (pointing to this as a potential weakness of parallel systems). Bornstein's own solution to the problems of parallel claims is greater use of agreed 'co-enforcement' by public and private enforcers acting in 'equal partnership': ibid 836. This is a different model to the hybrid approaches listed here (which are driven by a single enforcer). One of the main challenges for the model (acknowledged by the author at 868–71) lies in clashes between the cultures and interests of private and public actors that may make co-operative action difficult. For a robust defence of parallel systems of public and private enforcement as nonetheless avoiding underenforcement by filling gaps in resource and information and compensating for error, see Clopton (n 18).

[37] Senior Courts Act 1981 (UK) s 31(4); CPR 54.3 (2).

[38] See eg Human Rights Act (Qld) s 59.

[39] *Boardman v Phipps* [1967] 2 AC 46 (HL).

[40] As where a person adversely affected by a licensing decision seeks its judicial review.

victims. The importance of information costs is clear even within the hybrid public systems we have listed, in the foreshortened way in which courts and regulators ascertain victim losses. Criminal compensation orders are only used in simple cases in which full information about a victim's injury is available at the time of a sentencing hearing,[41] and public consumer redress systems normally only give consumers refunds, or their property back, excluding assessments of consequential losses,[42] or they deploy broader schemes of recompense in which credible approximations of sector losses (sometimes provided by offenders themselves) are used as the basis for wide distributive arrangements.

The reality is therefore that even these cleverly constructed hybrid systems are restricted in the extent to which they can protect private interests at the same time as protecting public ones. They pick off the lower-hanging fruit to facilitate recourse for private persons when the harm suffered is modest and easily assessable within the timeframes and other constraints of the public action but leave the compensation of losses about which information is harder to obtain to separate (usually subsequent) private litigation. Whilst further hybrid enforcement models are hence to be encouraged for pragmatic reasons, they will always be subject to practical limitations of this type.

10.5 Constitutional and Political Factors

The final set of factors encountered in this study is constitutional, or political. By constitutional factors, I mean to refer to norms concerning the relationship between private citizens and organs of the State (legislative, executive, and judicial) and the distribution of power between them as regards public and private interests. They centre on the idea of the State's role as a parent of the people; the doctrine of separation of powers; the equal subjection of State actors and citizens to the rule of law (and the associated principle of State accountability), and the importance in modern democracies of citizens' participation in their own government. By political factors, I mean shorter-term considerations of public policy that from time to time affect legislative and judicial choices about the distribution of enforcement rights.

Although we came across constitutional and political arguments mainly in the public law context, they cannot be confined to that domain. We saw in Chapter 8, for example, that civil recourse theorists present a good case for there being a *constitutional duty* on the part of the State to provide all citizens suffering private wrongs with rights of action as a precondition of its political authority over them.[43]

[41] Chapter 5 Section 5.5A, n 118 and text thereto.
[42] Chapter 5 Section 5.5B nn 129, 141–143 and text thereto.
[43] Chapter 8 Section 8.4A(iv).

There is a sense, then, in which private law rights of action are an obvious product of the State's duty as sovereign governor. It is also very unlikely that the judges and legislators who are responsible for creating private law rights of action are unaffected by background constitutional values. Indeed, a probable reason why private enforcers in private law are not more often directly involved in the protection of public interests as well as their own through 'hybrid' private enforcement systems, is that this would not only be inefficient (see above) but would violate constitutional norms about the respective role of citizens, courts and the executive, when it comes to protecting the public good. It is not generally their 'constitutional business' to protect such interests.

A. Constitutional Values

(i) The State as Parent of the People

Historically, we saw in Chapters 4 and 5, the protection of public interests in cases of serious crime came in England to be regarded as part of the personal prerogative of the Monarch and then the State as guardian of the people. This was an old view, well-known the Romans, formally lost and rediscovered. It gave rise to the modern view that it is presumptively the Attorney-General (only) and his or her delegates that have the power to enforce public law rights.

The idea that the State has not just a *sovereign power* but a constitutional *duty* to protect its citizens has also come to be seen to underpin the ancient prerogative of the King and his courts to protect the private law rights and interests of wards, the insane and other incapable persons *parens patriae*, as well as of the Attorney-General's right to enforce private charitable trusts. This was the basis of many of the cases we reviewed in Chapter 9. Although we considered only English and Australian examples of the *parens patriae* jurisdiction, the idea has been given a more expansive role in the United States, where it is said to provide the doctrinal basis for the powers of the State Attorneys-General to litigate and settle claims on citizens' behalf in cases like the tobacco litigation, in which the State itself also has a quasi-sovereign interest.[44]

The trope of the State as parent of its people is a projection from our private world to the public. Like all metaphors, it obscures as well as illuminates. In modern democracies, the State is as much a child of its people as it is their guardian and disciplinarian, and it clearly has the power to abuse as well as protect. The constitutional conception of the State as a protector of both the public and private interests of its citizens is nevertheless resilient and provides a powerful constitutional basis

[44] Chapter 2 Section 2.1 n 10. On the conflict that this can cause with citizen's own claims through the doctrine of preclusion, see G Hanna, 'The Helicopter State: Misuse of Parens Patriae Unconstitutionally Precludes Individual and Class Claims' (2022) 97 Washington Law Review 872.

for many of the rights of action that exist across both public and (sometimes) private law. It explains both the standard instances in which the State enforces public laws and many of the non-standard ones in which it intervenes to protect private law rights. The ancient ideal has become more potent with the growth of the welfare State, although it has also been challenged by the swing from welfarism to neoliberalism in the latter part of the twentieth century.

(ii) The Separation of Powers

Another factor materially affecting the distribution of rights of action across both public and private law is the doctrine of the separation of powers, according to which law enforcement in modern democracies is separated from legislation and adjudication and placed in the hands of the executive. In the United States, the unique design of the relationship between the legislator (Congress), the executive (the President), and the administrative bureaucracy[45] has impacted, we saw, upon the way in which federal laws are currently enforced. Sean Farhang's hugely important work has demonstrated beyond reasonable doubt that the swathe of private enforcement provisions in federal legislation over the past thirty years is not simply the product of right-wing or left-wing politics but a function of the antagonistic constitutional relationship between legislative and executive power and of the complex set of vetoes, checks, and balances that attend the process of getting modern regulatory provisions put into force.[46] Congress has tended to choose private enforcement as a way of securing a legislative agenda against executive obstruction and as a compromise between Congressional interests that are vigorously opposed on the desirability of public regulation. The point is that, even if one takes out the other cultural and economic factors that may be feeding the appetite for private litigation in the United States—the historic distrust of government, strong individualist ideology, intense rights-consciousness, powerful influence of interest groups, and so on—institutional factors are playing a significant role.[47] Constitutional limitations upon Federal Court jurisdiction and (potentially) the executive appointments clause[48] also bear restrictively, as we saw in Chapter 7,

[45] On which, see P Cane, *Controlling Administrative Power* (CUP 2016) Ch 3, esp 64–105, Ch 13.

[46] Chapter 7 Section 7.2D text to nn 155, 156. The fact that things go beyond politics is evident from the fact that at one time or another private enforcement has been supported by both Democrats and Republicans. On the recent Republican swing, see S Burbank and S Farhang, 'A New (Republican) Litigation State?' (2021) 11 UC Irvine Law Review 657.

[47] ibid; S Farhang, *The Litigation State: Public Regulation and Private Lawsuits in the US* (Princeton University Press 2010) 14–16. For further discussion of the factors giving rise private litigation in the US, also addressing the influence of fragmented constitutional power, see R Kagan, *Adversarial Legalism: The American Way of Law* 2nd edn (HUP 2019) Ch 3.

[48] US Const Art 2, s 2, cl 2. For a recent amicus brief suggesting that citizen suits violate the appointments clause (which seems to have failed) see *United States v DTE Energy* et al, case No. 2:10-cv-13101-BAF-RSW (ED Mich). The general supposition is that the clause does not prevent congressional authorization of private enforcement: J Miller and B Dorner, 'The Constitutionality of Citizen Suit Provisions in Federal Environmental Statutes' (2012) 27 Journal of Environmental Law and Litigation 401, 433–36.

upon the standing of citizens to launch public interest claims even where they have been expressly authorized by Congress to do so, which is not a serious factor in either the English or the Australian constitutional set-ups.

(iii) State Accountability and the Rule of Law

The principle of equality before the law requires the State to be accountable to its citizens before courts in respect of the duties and liabilities that it has.[49] That principle, I suggested in Chapter 6, has had a direct impact upon citizens' rights of action in public law. Where the State owes a particular citizen a duty, the logic of right-holding, personal sovereignty, and personal autonomy of course already suggest that she should have a right of action against it. But even where she has *no* such individual right of her own against the State, there is a strong case for granting her a power to enforce the State's duty to the community as a representative of that community. All citizens have a direct interest in the State's observance of the rule of law.

The accountability principle is most clearly instantiated in the law of judicial review, where any sufficient interest (which need not be a private one) gives a person a right of action, and executive permission to sue is quite rightly irrelevant. Were it not for courts' concerns about administration costs, standing rules would (and should, I suggested) be open. It is also, on many contemporary accounts, part of the logic of the independent, private right of action for misfeasance in public office and of private claims against public authorities for breaches of their human rights examined in Chapter 6, although in both of these cases the power of suit is currently restricted by additional conditions (the suffering of special private damage, or victim status) that inhibit its full effectiveness. I suggested that the special constitutional importance of public accountability provides a powerful case for widening the rights of action in these instances beyond their current ambit, whilst also observing the improbability of States themselves legislating such wider rights and the need, therefore, for standing decisions in these contexts to be left to judges wherever possible. This is certainly not to say that all mechanisms of accountability should lie in the private domain. Independent commissions, public ombudsmen, and even (in extreme cases of misconduct) public criminal prosecutors all have important key roles to play in holding the State and its agents to account. But private rights of action form a vital part of the constitutional accountability framework, acting as safeguards against the failure or capture of other systems controlling public power. They provide an essential level of redundancy in the enforcement system.

The principle of State accountability before the law also features in some private law cases. Indeed, if there is one instance in which the right of an individual

[49] AV Dicey, *Introduction to the Study of the Law of the Constitution* 7th edn (Macmillan 1908) 189–91, 198–99. This does not mean the State's liabilities and duties are the same as those of citizens: P Cane, 'Damages in Public Law' (1999) 5 Otago Law Review 489, 490–91.

to seek exemplary damages in a private law claim is clearly visible and generally undisputed, it is in cases involving the malicious behaviour of State actors. A significant advantage of the private law accountability mechanism in this context is that since the plaintiff's own private law rights are also always in issue in the hybrid action, his right to ventilate the issues and hold the State publicly to account for its conduct is not subject to *either* executive control *or* prior judicial permission. He may do so as of right. The unconstrained liberty of action provided by private law process in this instance proves an especially powerful tool for addressing State misbehaviour.

(iv) Citizen Participation

A final, important constitutional principle in modern democracies is that the citizen be allowed to play an active participatory role in her own governance. Typically, the principle is instantiated in our right to vote, in mechanisms of parliamentary representation and in the liberty of freedom of speech on governmental and political matters, but it can also be extended to the design of law enforcement arrangements.[50] Arguments that private enforcement rights facilitate direct citizen inclusion in public governance were mentioned in Chapter 5 as a counterpoint to normal assumptions about executive enforcement prerogative,[51] and came to light again in Chapter 7 when we were discussing public interest actions by 'private Attorneys-General' in the United States.[52] They also find resonance in modern debates about the value of regulatory outsourcing[53] and private rights to seek judicial review.[54] In this way of thinking, private suits are not simply gap-fillers shoring up the rule of law, but core components of a different, decentralized constitutional model in which citizens are authorized by the State to participate directly in the implementation of its chosen public ends. Whilst it might be tempting to think of such a constitutional model as a 'weak state' model, it has rightly been pointed out that it is not so much that the State is weak, but that it

[50] A Lahav, *In Praise of Litigation* (OUP 2017); 'The Roles of Litigation in American Democracy' (2016) 65 Emory Law Journal 1657; M Mekki, 'Litigating Climate Liability: An Example of Democracy in Litigation' (2024) 16 Journal of Civil Law Studies 123; A Alemmo, 'Beyond EU Law Heroes: Unleashing Strategic Litigation as a Form of Participation in the Union's Democratic Life' (2024) 25 German Law Journal 822; B Burbank & S Subrin, 'Litigation and Democracy: Restoring a Realistic Prospect of Trial' (2011) 46 Harvard Civil Rights–Civil Liberties Law Review 399, 414. For an excellent critical analysis, which unpicks what is meant by the claim to 'democratic' participation and suggesting that litigation tends to lead at best to a 'depoliticised' form of democratic participation which (amongst other things) conflicts with democracy's traditional commitment to popular sovereignty, see M Shapiro, 'Democracy, Civil Litigation, and the Nature of Non-Representative Institutions' (2024) 109 Cornell Law Review 112.

[51] Chapter 5 Section 5.3A.

[52] Chapter 7 Section 7.2.

[53] P Westerman, *Outsourcing the Law: A Philosophical Perspective on Regulation* (Edward Elgar 2018) Ch 5.

[54] RB Stewart & CR Sunstein, 'Public Programs and Private Rights' (1981–1982) 95 Harvard Law Review 1193, 1279–83.

chooses (democratically) to structure and express its power differently—*through* its citizens ('infrastructurally') rather than 'over' them ('despotically').[55]

On some views, private rights of action reflect this ideal of democratic self-government even when the dispute is a purely private law one relating to a person's own interests, such as a dispute about an insurance contract she has signed. This is because the exercise of a right of action results in a public judgment that creates common law rules that then 'govern' others.[56] Such rights also contribute, it is said, to the sort of transparency that is essential to meaningful public choice by bringing important information to light,[57] and they create the conditions necessary for a citizen to participate meaningfully in public discussion on (formally) equal terms.[58]

It is again hard to gauge exactly how influential these ideas have been in the construction of rights of action. Their purchase in respect of such rights in private law is likely to be very limited, since the sort of judicial law-creation that results from private litigation is cautious, interstitial, and largely apolitical, at least outside the American context. Information can also get buried in confidential settlements, and litigating parties are rarely equal in *substantive* terms when it comes to discussion in open court, whatever the formal position. Some private law cases clearly can and do have an important impact on public debate and serve a valuable role in forcing information into the public spotlight even when they fail.[59] They can nudge politicians out of their complacency and spur public agents to more diligent enforcement action. Sometimes they uncover uncomfortable truths that would otherwise never see the light of day. But, whilst these effects are excellent reasons to celebrate the private right to litigate, this does not necessarily make them the *reason* for its existence.

Even in public law, the argument about the importance of private suits to self-governance probably provides only a limited explanation of the enforcement rights we have, since most public laws are still enforced publicly. In the United States, there is doubt, we saw in Chapter 7,[60] as to how far Congress can go in

[55] Farhang (n 47) 9. See also Kagan (n 47) Ch 1, esp 10–11 (adversarial legalism constitutes a formal mode of participation in public decision-making, to be contrasted with hierarchical/bureaucratic legalism); Lahav, *In Praise of Litigation* (n 50) Ch 3.

[56] Lahav, *In Praise of Litigation* (n 50) 6, 84, 86–88.

[57] ibid 8–9, Ch 2.

[58] ibid 7, Ch 4. For a full discussion of litigation's role and limits as a mechanism of political participation, see S Lawrence, 'Justice, Democracy, Litigation, and Political Participation' (1991) 72 Social Science Quarterly 464.

[59] A good, recent example in the climate-change context in Australia was a much-publicised case in which representatives of Australian children sought a declaration that government owed them a duty of care in deciding whether to approve extensions to coal mining operations, given their potential impacts upon global warming and its potential impacts on their health and property. A duty was found at first instance and, although the decision was reversed on appeal, it provided a platform for courts publicly to affirm the data proving anthropogenic global warming: *Minister for Environment v Sharma* [2022] FCAFC 35.

[60] Chapter 7 Sections 7.2B(iii), 7.2C(ii).

delegating public enforcement to individual citizens without violating the executive appointments clause, or constitutional limitations on court jurisdiction. The devolutions of enforcement rights to citizens that we see in public law could also signal something less dramatic than a wholesale shift in the basic constitutional norms of democratic participation. It is true, as Farhang points out, that their use is now very common in federal regulatory statutes in the United States, but any rush to the conclusion that this embodies a *constitutional* movement may be too quick, given the other, institutional explanations for the popularity of such provisions that we considered above, and the pressures of short-term politics and public resource, which also seem likely to be drivers. It is to these that we now turn.

B. Politics and Public Resource

I have put politics and resource under the same heading, on the basis that the two are so often closely associated in practice. The resourcing of law enforcement *is* essentially a matter of political will, as well of private wealth and market economics. We have seen the State backing away from the resourcing of legal rights of action in many contexts in this book. It does not generally finance private rights of action in private law, other than by funding the basic system of adjudication and providing some assistance to the disadvantaged in particular cases. Much has been devolved to claims markets, mediation, and private arbitration. There are also significant deficits in government resourcing of public enforcement in both public *and* private law, such that public enforcers are now increasingly looking for ways to devolve (or share) their enforcement responsibilities to (or with) private organizations and individuals. Competition authorities in the United Kingdom are actively looking to coordinate their enforcement activity with that of private actors to achieve optimal use of their time and energy;[61] CPS criminal prosecutors rely in the United Kingdom upon private organizations to enforce laws that fall beyond their means and immediate priorities. Shortages in the resources of human rights commissions mean that most legal challenges to State human right violations are left to victims. State agents are now reluctant, we saw in Chapter 9, to take on the responsibility of acting as either litigation guardians for incapable persons or as default liquidators of corporations when private enforcers are unwilling to do the job. Sometimes, State trustees have impermissibly dipped into the pockets of the very persons they are charged to protect, in order to subsidize their own regulatory activity. Private enforcers are sporadically incentivized to prosecute public wrongs to boost the

[61] Panel remarks of Sarah Cardell, CEO of the Competition and Markets Authority,Competition Appeal Tribunal 20th Anniversary Conference (4 May 2023): <www.gov.uk/government/speeches/private-actions-and-public-enforcement> accessed 6 December 2025.

flow of civil penalties to the public treasury.[62] On at least one account, the level of funding that is provided to public agencies in the United States is now calculated in a way that *assumes* the activity of independent private enforcers:[63] private capacity is thereby 'built in' to the resource architecture of public law enforcement.

The causes of public enforcement deficit in both public and private law are various. Sometimes the problem lies in short-term economic downturn, but it can also (and this is the more probable long-term explanation in public law) be a consequence of the exponential growth in the scope and complication of the regulatory task. It may also be the result of political interference—a desire on the part of a government to neuter regulatory activity of which it disapproves (or which implicates its own freedom of action), when for one reason or another it cannot (or it would be too politically risky to try) to get the provision off the statute books. Occasionally (as, for example, in the case of the Texas Abortion Law)[64] governments avoid the use of public enforcement to sidestep constitutional constraints and human rights obligations that would otherwise inhibit their capacity to pursue a controversial regulatory goal. More broadly, fiscal conservatism, the retreat from welfarism, experiments in privatization, and belief in the power of decentralized markets have all left their mark on the resourcing of public enforcement agencies. Whatever the particular cause—be it economic or political—the effect in each case is that there are increasing pressures and temptations for the State to devolve responsibility for enforcing public laws to private citizens and entities, or at least to enlist their resources in a form of parallel, public-private partnership. This eases pressures on the public purse (pleasing fiscal conservatives) without government being seen to back away from its more politically popular public commitments.

The take-home message here is that, as long as regulatory appetite exceeds public enforcement capacity, the *supplemental* use of private enforcers to protect both public and private interests is inevitable, unless we are prepared to stomach the gap, or thrust our hands much deeper into our pockets. How often we need to revert to them then depends on the strength of society's commitment to welfarism, on the one hand, or its readiness to subscribe to the politics of deregulation, individualism and market devolution, on the other. If significant deregulation occurs, there will obviously be less law to enforce, which will also reduce the required number of public enforcers and (in theory at least) reduce the pressure on

[62] Chapter 7 Section 7.2B(ii) (actions under the False Claims Act 1863). See also provisions which allow private parties to seek civil penalties (as under the proposed French system discussed in Chapter 8 Section 8.5 n 149); and those which allow for splitting of punitive damages awards with the State in the United States (Chapter 8 Section 8.5B n 160).

[63] M Gilles and G Friedman, 'After Class: Aggregate Litigation in the Wake of AT&T Mobility v Concepcion' (2012) 79 University of Chicago Law Review 623, 626 (noting that '[p]rivate involvement in public civil law enforcement is [so] deeply embedded in our politics and culture' that many agencies 'are funded and organized on the clear, if largely unspoken, understanding that a vigorous and well-stocked private bar sits ready to deploy its ample resources to redress frauds and other harms perpetrated upon the general public').

[64] Chapter 7 Section 7.2B(i).

those that remain. But deregulation is far from being easy to achieve, as we said in Chapter 5, and even if it does occur, it will be patchy across different economic and social sectors. Some commitments—such as the most basic guarantees of our criminal laws—cannot realistically be withdrawn without a government signing its own resignation, even if its commitment to others (some areas of economic regulation, for example) weaken under the pressure of powerful industry lobbying. In practice, the regulatory and welfare challenges our societies face are now so large that they will probably only be soluble through the combined initiative of public and private enforcers. The exact ratio and relationship of the respective enforcement arrangements will depend always on context and on the pragmatic and constitutional factors I have mentioned above, but it also depends on the political choices that citizens make when deciding how to vote. In this respect, future choices between public and private enforcement models will always be our own, whether or not we realize it at the time.

10.6 Rationality and Reinvention

It is not surprising, given the breadth of the material considered in this book, that no single thread of logic runs through all of the contemporary enforcement choices it describes. The law is no purer in its reasons than we are ourselves and we should perhaps expect no more singular measure of commitment in its life than we find in our own. It is influenced by its history, politics, and constitutional values as much as it is by moral reasons and practical constraints. Moral arguments about the value of enforcement rights for our personal choice and autonomy clearly have greater valence in private law than public law, since they apply only where the grant of a right of action will promote the choice or welfare of a human enforcer, or group of such enforcers. They are relatively stable, as are enforcement rights themselves in private law. Pragmatic, constitutional, and political arguments tend to have a stronger visible influence on enforcement architecture in public law than private law, where rights of action tend to service public utility and welfare. Their impact on this architecture tends to be more variable and context dependent, and enforcement rights are in turn also more varied and unstable in their configuration across the various public law fields. It is indeed in public law that we see the greatest variety, fluidity, and innovation in the configuration of rights of action. Crucially, however, no argument that I have considered above is capable, in the end, of being siloed entirely within either the public law or the private law categories as I have constructed them.

Although no single pattern of reasoning runs through all contemporary enforcement choices, in combination they are clearly capable of providing significant support both to the dominant paradigm according to which private law is enforced privately and public law enforced publicly, and a remarkable number of the exceptions we have identified to that paradigm. We may therefore conclude with some confidence not just that the basic pattern makes sense from a number of different perspectives but also that the exceptional cases we have reviewed are not just historical anomalies, or evolutionary oddities awaiting extinction as our law works its way toward a purer ideal. They themselves give expression to a deeper rationality, responding to complex moral and pragmatic challenges of the day, as well as prevailing social, political, and constitutional conditions. Recognizing that the practices are rational in this sense (because they respond to reasons of one sort or another) does not, of course, mean that they are ideal, free from contention, or cannot be improved upon.

As the challenges of modern law enforcement increase with constraints on public resourcing, a spirit of critical reinvention is likely to be necessary in enforcement system design. We may need to think about new enforcement patterns in which more than one type of enforcer is available to enforce a public or private law, each safeguarding the other against incapacity and thereby guaranteeing the legal system as a whole against failure. In such instances, we shall need to think further about how to coordinate parallel public and private enforcement proceedings so as to conserve resource and avoid duplication and clash, and we should probably consider further whether there are additional cases in which the protection of both public and private interests is sensibly achievable in a singular hybrid proceeding without causing conflict and without overreaching informational constraints, or contradicting key constitutional norms. Where private enforcers are harnessed to the implementation of public ends by being allowed (as they currently are) to recover penalties and awards of exemplary or punitive damages against fellow citizens, we should, I have suggested, think more creatively about how to return the proceeds to the public weal, whilst preserving the private incentive for them to act on our behalf. There is an important place for private enforcers in our public as well as our private law, but the incentives must not be so great—nor the regulatory architecture governing their behaviour so weak—as to undermine its ethical integrity. Sometimes, where good public enforcement machinery exists, but is handicapped by purely informational deficit, there will be less risk and more advantage in granting private parties incentives to provide relevant information to public agencies and prosecutors, than in handing over to them the power to prosecute their fellow citizens. As governments seek to evade scrutiny and challenge in controversial political times, we must also shore up the private rights of action that ensure their accountability before the law by preserving the widest possible standing rules for citizens. This is especially important when executive respect for the limits of public power is threatened in times of turbulent instability. Prior restraints on the exercise of rights of action must generally be regarded with suspicion, the power that such rights represent instead being moderated by appropriate post-initiation checks and balances. And public enforcement powers must, I have suggested, always be subject to private scrutiny, just as private ones must be subject always to some level of State oversight to prevent them being abused in ways that harm both private and public interests.

Few of these challenges are really new. They existed in early legal systems too, and those systems offered their own precedents and solutions. Some clues as to how to exercise our spirit of critical reinvention may lie in some of those past practices, which embraced more hybridity and used more private initiative in the enforcement of public laws at times when public capacity was weak. The societies in which we now live are nonetheless very different, and the legal, social, and constitutional norms that govern the answers to these questions in the modern day are complicated and intricate in ways that our predecessors could never have foreseen.

Index

For the benefit of digital users, indexed terms that span two pages (e.g., 52–53) may, on occasion, appear on only one of those pages.